Matthew Peterson, one of the world's most innovative minds, infuses *Interactive QuickTime* with applicable insight and helpful humor. This book goes well beyond the basics, far into the best practices, with plenty of supporting scripts and sample projects. Covering a wide spectrum of topics, *Interactive QuickTime: Authoring Wired Media* addresses the building of UIs, repurposing already existing media, using physics for richer motion, and that's just getting started. The appendices along with the exploration of XML in QuickTime are indispensable resources for the active producer of QuickTime media. I am excited to have this resource available for QuickTime authors!

—Michael Shaff
founder of *Small Hands*

This book belongs on the shelf of anyone who takes multimedia development seriously. For the aspiring QuickTime media developer, it addresses the most critical authoring issues—and the techniques described are clever and applicable to multimedia development of any ilk.

—Ken Loge
Oregon Research Institute

You are holding a book written by one the smartest people I have ever met—and it has been my pleasure to know some VERY smart people—a book about one of the most exciting technologies on the planet. The writing is clear and enjoyable. It starts with material suitable for beginners and proceeds steadily through intermediate, advanced, and into previously uncharted territory . . . . It's a trip, my friend. And one worth taking . . . . Be warned: this is not an ordinary book. It can literally change your life.

—from the foreword by Steven Gulie
author of *QuickTime for the Web*

Interactive QuickTime

Authoring Wired Media

Matthew Peterson

MORGAN KAUFMANN PUBLISHERS

AN IMPRINT OF ELSEVIER

AMSTERDAM BOSTON LONDON NEW YORK
OXFORD PARIS SAN DIEGO SAN FRANCISCO
SINGAPORE SYDNEY TOKYO

Senior Editor	Tim Cox
Director of Production and Manufacturing	Simon Crump
Editorial Coordinators	Stacie Pierce, Richard Camp
Associate Project Manager	Brandy Palacios
Project Management	Elisabeth Beller
Cover Design	Laurie Anderson
Cover Image	Jake Martin/Getty Images
Text Design	Rebecca Evans and Associates
Illustration	Dartmouth Publishing, Inc.
Composition	Nancy Logan
Copyeditor	Ken DellaPenta
Proofreader	Jennifer McClain
Indexer	Steve Rath
Printer	The Maple-Vail Book Manufacturing Group

Morgan Kaufmann Publishers
An imprint of Elsevier
500 Sansome Street, Suite 400
San Francisco, CA 94111
www.mkp.com

ISBN: 1-55860-746-3

This book is printed on acid-free paper.

Contents

Foreword

Steven Gulie

Be warned: this is not an ordinary book. It can literally change your life.

I met Matthew Peterson at a QuickTime conference in the late twentieth century. I was trying to learn about QuickTime. I already knew that QuickTime could play movies and audio files over the Internet or from a CD-ROM. I even knew that QuickTime could display and synchronize other media types, such as text and VR. Matthew showed me that I had barely scratched the surface of QuickTime. I knew nothing.

There were a few other presenters at that conference: Janie Alexander showed me that you could mix virtual reality, music, and still video images in a single movie (wow); Michael Schaff showed me that you could add interactive buttons and game-like controls (cool). But Matthew...

Matthew showed me things that amaze me to this day. For example: a scientific calculator only 13 KB in size—smaller, faster, and cleaner than any C or Java program I've seen that did anything similar, yet it worked on both Windows and Macintosh computers, locally or over the Internet. And it could be dropped into a web page or a Word document like any other movie. I'd never seen anything like it.

He showed me that a QuickTime movie could actually act as a lightweight graphical application program, one that runs cross-platform and over the Internet. It completely transformed my understanding of QuickTime.

Then he showed me a QuickTime movie that allowed the viewer to create interactive drawings (a simple paint program), transferred the paintings to a server over the Internet, and received back PDF files that could be sent by email and viewed in Acrobat. I was stunned. I had no idea that a QuickTime movie could exchange data with remote file servers.

Each presentation Matthew has done since then has had the same electrifying effect. And it's always followed by a question-and-answer period, featuring the same questions: "How did you do *that*? And that? And THAT??!!"

The question-and-answer session is always too short. I've been waiting for this book a long time. And I'm here to say, it was worth the wait. This book will show you, step by step, how to do things you never suspected were even possible. This is the master wizard's recipe book.

Don't blame me if you spend the rest of your life writing books about QuickTime, as I have, or creating QuickTime movies for the Internet, as some others have. You've been warned.

Want to know something really scary? Back when Matthew first created his calculator movie, QuickTime's scriptable actions included only basic math operators—nothing more advanced than multiplication and division; no square root, no sine or cosine. Matthew derived these complex functions, using basic math and geometry, inside a 13 KB QuickTime movie.

You are holding a book written by one the smartest people I have ever met—and it has been my pleasure to work with some very smart people—a book about one of the most exciting technologies on the planet. The writing is clear and enjoyable. It starts with material suitable for beginners, and proceeds steadily through intermediate, advanced, and into previously uncharted territory. It will show you how to take multimedia to the cutting edge. And make it work there.

Along the way, you'll witness the birth of QuickTime, the untimely death of the first video game machine, and the proper way to animate an inchworm. It's a trip, my friend. And one worth taking.

But don't say I didn't warn you. You may never be the same.

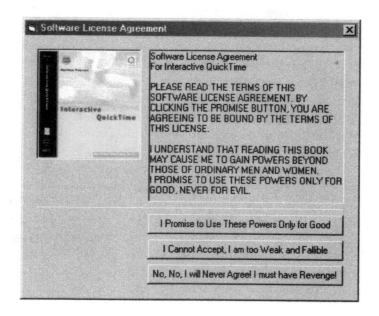

Conditions of use: Only those who accept the license agreement may read beyond Chapter 5; author not responsible for lifestyle changes due to acquisition of super powers; side-effects may include excitement, sleeplessness, euphoria, and sudden career change; do not read while driving or controlling heavy machinery; be nice.

Preface

QuickTime is a powerful technology that enables Windows and Macintosh computers to present a wide range of multimedia content, whether it's embedded in a Web page, on a CD-ROM, or integrated into a stand-alone application. This book shows you how to use QuickTime to transform your existing multimedia content (images, video, music, Flash animation, 3D, stylized text, virtual reality, and more) into interactive experiences that can respond to the user, perform calculations, evolve over time, and essentially take on lives of their own. Interactive QuickTime can also be use to build custom playback environments for audio and video.

These days, audiences expect a lot more from media than just good looks and hi-fi sound. DVDs and game consoles are replacing VCRs. Interactive television (iTV) systems are saying "move over" to broadcast and cable television. Dynamic and interactive modern Web, CD-ROM, and application developers can no longer get away with static images and text. Multimedia is expected to be active and responsive to the user. Websites and CD-ROMs limited to static images and text tend to be boring and usually don't engage the viewer. Many developers are using DHTML, Java applets, or Flash to better engage their audiences and express ideas with dynamic and interactive content. Many of these developers don't realize that QuickTime, a popular way to put high-quality sound and video on the Web, is also able to deliver rich and sophisticated interactivity. With QuickTime, you can produce good-looking *and* interactive content!

What This Book Is and Is Not

This book is a developer's guide to building interactive media using Quick-Time. Although it is centered on QuickTime, many of the concepts explored here are applicable to interactive media in general. The discussions assume little programming background on the part of the reader, but do assume at least a basic knowledge of audio, video, and how to manipulate media files. The book *QuickTime for the Web* is a good reference for those wanting to learn more about QuickTime in general.

In our explorations, we will focus mostly on the interactive aspects of QuickTime. This book is a practical guide, and thus we will be building lots of actual interactive QuickTime content. Although we will be using authoring tools such as LiveStage Pro, Macromedia Flash, Tekadence Magik, and QuickTime Pro, this book should not be seen as a user's guide for these tools. That being said, if you aren't familiar with these tools, I provide enough information to follow along so that you can build the projects presented in this book.

▶ How to Read This Book

Whenever I embark on learning a new technology, nothing propels me farther than a good example. To me, figuring out the workings of a well-implemented example is like visiting a new country instead of just reading about it. With example in hand, I let my curiosity guide me by making small modifications to the project and seeing what results. It's amazing when you say to yourself, "I wonder what would happen if I change this line to this . . . ," and then you try it and it works! I often learn a great deal from exploring such examples, but I'm usually left with only a partial understanding of how the technology works. To dig in deeper, I resort to reading. I skim the manuals, read any available white paper, and often pick up a third-party book on the technology. In the end, I never know how much of it I've really absorbed until I try to implement a real-world project. This usually reveals huge gaps in my understanding, which I inevitably fill in through extensive trial and error. Mastering a new technology can be a lot of work, but it's also fun and rewarding.

In this book, I tried to create a learning environment that would be most effective for me if I were approaching Interactive QuickTime for the first time. I present a ton of examples that cover a wide range of what is possible with Interactive QuickTime. Along with each example, I give explanations of the ideas and philosophy behind the code. Discussions of alternative implementations, common pitfalls, and useful tips and tricks are presented throughout the book to help minimize the frustrating aspects of the learning process. Whenever appropriate, I also provide a historical setting for each topic. To me, this not only makes it more enjoyable to digest and remember, it's also comforting to know about all of the intellectual energy that has been applied to these topics over the years. Finally, at the end of each chapter, I provide several suggestions of neat things to explore and try out.

The book is organized into six parts. Each part contains many short chapters that can easily be absorbed and digested in one sitting. A typical chapter will focus around one or two example projects. Most projects are created in LiveStage Pro (LSP). This is a sofware product created by a Canadian company, Totally Hip. It enables anyone to create interactive QuickTime experiences without having to learn C++ or Java. A trial version of LSP is included on the the CD-ROM that comes with this book.

LSP is a useful tool for creating QuickTime content, but it is not required in order to do sophisticated work in QuickTime. The scripting language of LSP is a shorthand for the low-level Interactive QuickTime API you would use when programming QuickTime movies with C++ or Java. An example of how to use Java to program wired movies is given in Appendix P. All of the scripting examples and techniques discussed in the book are directly applicable to programming with the QuickTime API. Furthermore, concepts such as modeling physics and interactivity in general are the same in other media such as Flash.

Note The software runs on Macintosh computers running OS 9 or OS X as well as Windows machines with OS versions 98, ME, NT, 2000, or XP.

A couple of the projects make use of other software packages such as Tekadence Magik, Metacard (or Revolution), Macromedia Flash, or a Java compiler.

Note A trial version of Tekadence Magik is also on the CD. It will run on any machine with a Java 1.3 virtual machine or better. This includes Mac OS X and Windows 98, ME, NT, 2000, and XP.

All of the projects can be found in the Projects directory on the CD, organized by chapter (see Figure P.1). A project presented in Chapter 12 can be found in the Projects/Chapter12/ directory of the CD. If you like reading computer technology books away from your computer (I often do), then you should be fine. I present the important pieces of code in the text

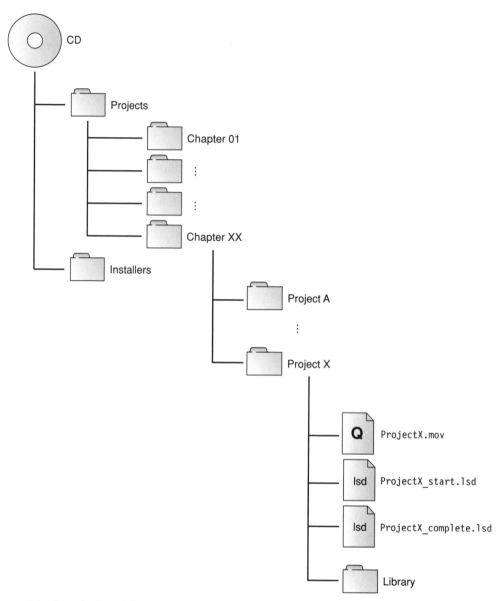

Figure P.1 Organization of the CD.

itself, so you can read through to see how things work and then go back later and try it out on the computer.

The LiveStage projects on the CD consist of a directory of media files, which by convention is named Library, and a project file with an .lsd extension. There are lots of jokes about that file extension, but it simply stands for "LiveStage document." I usually supply two versions of each .lsd file. One ends with _start.lsd and serves as a starting point for the project, with pertinent portions left for the reader to implement. The other version ends with _complete.lsd and contains the completed project. The completed project is there so that if you get stuck, or are in a hurry, or can't get the _start project working correctly, you can always refer to the _complete version. Every once in a while, I'll also include projects that are for demonstration purposes only, without anything for the reader to fill in. Those are indicated with a _demo.lsd ending. Many chapters also include example creations from third-party developers that don't typically include LiveStage Pro source files.

LiveStage Pro is capable of both creating .lsd project files and exporting them as a QuickTime document. For historical reasons, QuickTime documents are called movies and end with a .mov file extension. Along with the projects on the CD, I also include a built version of the .mov files so that you can experience them without having LiveStage Pro installed.

At the end of each chapter (starting with this preface), I present a series of exercises and suggest things to try out. I call them "explorations." I have attempted to make these explorations useful both to the individual reader and in a classroom setting.

▶ Explorations

1. Even if you're not in the mood for exploring, it's a good idea to at least glance through the explorations since they'll often include tips that aren't in the main text (like this one).

2. One of the first things that I do when I pick up a new book is skim the very beginning and the very end. What I look for is a good table of contents and some useful tail-end resources, such as a well-done index, maybe a glossary, and some interesting appendices. How does this book fare in these regards?

Acknowledgments

This is my favorite part of the book, where I get to thank the people that helped make this book happen.

I have to start by expressing my gratitude to everyone at Morgan Kaufmann, the team that not only published this book but also supplied the much needed encouragement, enthusiasm, and support over the entire journey. I am especially grateful to Tim Cox, Stacie Pierce, Elisabeth Beller, and Richard Camp. I'm proud to be an MKP author!

An ocean of gratitude to my close friend Michael Shaff, who walked with me along many a leg of this long journey. He introduced me to interactive QuickTime, as he has done with so many other people. It can be argued that he even introduced interactive QuickTime to interactive QuickTime itself, and continues to do so on a daily basis.

I'm also extremely grateful to the author of *QuickTime for the Web*, Steven Gulie. Whenever I got stuck or depressed, I could instantly get back on my feet by recalling what Steve told me after he first read a sample of my rough draft.

Elsa, I love you. Thank you for accepting the answer, "Not yet" to the question, "Is your book finished?" for so long.

I'm deeply indebted to Sean Allen and Peter Hoddie for their central roles in fathering wired QuickTime.

I owe thanks to a large number of people at Apple, including everyone in the QuickTime engineering group and the great guys in the technical publications group. Special thanks to Michael Hinkson for spearheading Apple's support for this book and to Bill Wright who went out of his way to provide me with answers and solutions to my wired needs.

And then there's the awesome team at Totally Hip Software who created THE software to build sophisticated wired movies with speed and ease and without loosing too much hair. Special thanks to Steve Israelson, David Dicaire, Selwyn Wan, Guillaume Iacino, and Chris Large.

Many improvements to this book were made possible as a result of insightful reviews and comments by John Sklavos, Brad Smith, Brennan Young, Ken Loge, Frank Lowney, Michael Shaff, Steven Gulie, Mike Matson, Bill Wright, Tom Maremaa, and Brad Ford.

Sample content for the CD was contributed by ADInstruments, Anders Jirås, Bill Meikle, Brad Smith, Brennan Young, Carl Adler, Clifford VanMeter, David Connolly, David Egbert, David Urbanic, Dion Crannitch, Elsa Peterson, Eric Blanpied, Erik Fohlin, Ffahs Leahcim, Francis Gorge, Frank

Lowney, Hans Rijnen, Ian Mantripp, Johannes Herrmann, John Sklavos, Ken Loge, Luke Sheridan, Mario Piepenbrink, Michael Shaff, Michael Vogt, Mike Matson, Ralph Bitter, Ricardo Nemirovsky, Ryan Francesconi, Thorsten Schmiedel, Todd Blume, and Trevor DeVore.

The following images printed in the book were supplied by wonderful people: Rotating Wheel Illusion image supplied by Pierre Bayerl; Hardrock Café skinned movie screen shot supplied by Michael Shaff and Fitzgerald and Robert West; Gertie frame image supplied by Dr. David L. Nathan; Pigeon Point panorama supplied by David Arrigoni; The In Light of Reverence skin screen shot supplied by Michael Shaff, Christopher McLeod and the Earth Island Institute; and the HipBot and other LiveStage-related images by the folks at Totally Hip.

Additional software on the CD was provided by Bill Meikle and Tekadence Inc.

Thank you, the reader, for reading these acknowledgments. I hope you enjoy the book. Feel free to email your comments and suggestions to me at

matthew@matthewpeterson.net.

Hi Mom, Dad, and Melissa!

Part  I

Background Information

This first part of the book briefly presents background information to help clarify some common misconceptions about what interactive movies are and how they are different from audio and video. We'll also discuss the basic structure of QuickTime movies, including aspects of the file format. Most of the book doesn't require knowledge of the file format, but it's helpful to be familiar with certain concepts and terms related to the low-level workings of interactive QuickTime.

What Is Interactive QuickTime?

Most computer-savvy people have heard of QuickTime, and in their minds, QuickTime usually means a certain format of audio and video. What is often overlooked is the vast range of capabilities bundled within the name "QuickTime." The QuickTime media engine not only plays back an enormous variety of standard audio, video, and image formats, but is also capable of presenting Flash, styled text, QuickTime VR (virtual reality), animated 3D, sprite animation, MIDI, and much more (see Figure 1.1).

A single QuickTime movie can be a composite of many different types of media, each playing in its own track. If you're not familiar with the concept of a track, just think of it as data along a timeline to be played by different media handlers. As an analogy, consider the musical score for the song "Old McDonald Had a Farm" in Figure 1.2. At the top is a set of notes

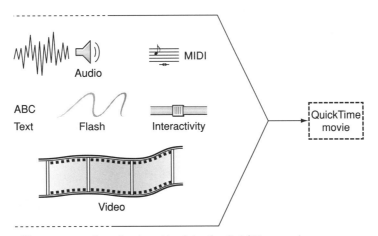

Figure 1.1 Different types of media played back by the QuickTime engine.

Figure 1.2 Musical score for "Old McDonald Had a Farm."

to be played ("handled") by a piano. Underneath that are some lyrics to be handled by a person's voice. The notes and the lyrics can be thought of as two separate tracks. The data are in two different formats, but they are synchronized along the same timeline. These are two examples of audio tracks since the media handlers will take in the note and lyric data and output sound waves.

QuickTime has many different tracks, but the majority of tracks are visual. Video, text, and VR tracks are good examples. The media handlers for video tracks, for instance, will read in video data and present it as images on the screen that change over time. Some tracks, such as Flash, have both auditory and visual information, and others have neither. An example is an HREF track that launches Web pages at different points along the track's timeline. It doesn't draw anything to the screen, and it doesn't make any sounds.

When tracks are combined, they can be arranged relative to each other in both space and time. For example, you can build a media presentation (called a "movie" in QuickTime) that starts out with a Flash track animation for the introduction, then transitions to some video and audio with a closed-captioning track spatially positioned below the video, and ends with a scrolling text track of credits. If you are near a computer, you can experience such a movie by launching the QuickTime file on the CD located at Projects/Chapter01/BehindTheScenes/TheTools.mov.

Note If you don't have QuickTime 6 installed on your computer yet, you might as well do it now. It's easy. There's a QuickTime installer on the CD.

As shown in Figure 1.3, this movie is composed of five different tracks. You might be wondering why you couldn't just have two tracks: an audio

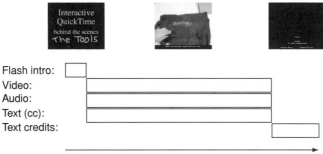

Flash intro:
Video:
Audio:
Text (cc):
Text credits:

Time

Figure 1.3 Tracks example.

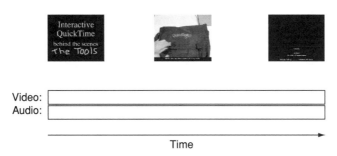

Video:
Audio:

Time

Figure 1.4 Rasterized version of the tracks example.

track and a video track. Well, you could. In fact, I've included such a version of the movie on the CD as well. It's located at `Projects/Chapter01/BehindTheScenes/TheTools_AV.mov`. In this version (see Figure 1.4) the Flash animation, closed captioning, and scrolling credits have all been converted to video (rasterized). This simplifies the movie a bit, but at a price. For example the file size of the two-track version is almost four times as big as the five-track version. This is because we've essentially converted Flash and text data into pixel information, which isn't as file-size efficient.

Besides memory and performance issues, the five-track version is much more flexible and easy to maintain. For instance, you can turn the closed captioning on and off by enabling and disabling the closed-captioning text track.

Note If you have QuickTime Pro installed, you can enable and disable tracks by selecting Enable Tracks . . . from the Edit menu.

And say you forgot to add someone to the scrolling credits. As video, it would be difficult to change, but as a text track, you can simply edit it just like you would a document in a word processor. Furthermore, Flash and text tracks can both be interactive, an aspect that can't be simulated with video.

The track is the dominant building block for QuickTime creations. But you shouldn't let the timeline aspect of a track fool you. Many track types can contain nonlinear media (as opposed to linear timeline media). Linear media are something like what you would watch on your VCR. You stick a tape in, press play, watch a little, see something interesting, press pause, then rewind and watch the interesting part again. The location on the tape that the playhead reads defines what you see on the TV screen and hear out of the speakers. Nonlinear media, on the other hand, aren't completely slaved by a timeline. A nonlinear movie doesn't have to look the same three minutes into it every time you watch it.

A video game is a good example of nonlinear media. When you insert a quarter into an arcade game, chances are you aren't going to experience exactly the same sequence of events as the last time you played the game. Maybe you turn left instead of right this time, and end by running out of fuel instead of crashing into a wall. QuickTime VR is another example of nonlinear media. In QuickTime VR, you can change what angle you view a scene, so when you play the media, you can look in a different direction each time. Both of these examples not only are nonlinear but also are interactive. Both the video game and the VR scene let the user have some impact on what happens. What gets presented is in part dependent upon what the user does, and so user interaction influences the media. Not all nonlinear media are interactive though. For instance, you could have a movie of a fish bowl where a fish swims around randomly. Every time you watch it, you would see the fish swim along a different path, but you couldn't do anything to influence the path.

Note Random movies might not be interactive, but they can be fun to watch. I placed a couple of examples on the CD at `Projects/Chapter01/RandomMovies`.

Hollywood and the rest of the movie industry have raked in trillions of dollars by catering to the public's desire to experience things that they can't experience in their everyday life. Movies about aliens and superheroes seem to do really well. Movie producers have learned that the audience is most entertained when these nonreal things seem real. Because a satisfied audience means more money, moviemakers are willing to invest heavily into things such as improved special effects, photo-realism, high-fidelity 3D sound, and so on. If you go to the movie theaters today, the aliens and superheroes look a lot more real than they did a few years ago. It's getting better every year, but there's a fundamental limit to how real they can get without making the movie interactive. An audience is never going to feel like there is a real alien standing in front of them unless they can hit it on the back of the head with a Milk Dud to make it turn around.

The interesting thing is that even small amounts of interactivity can go a long way. Remember Furbys and those Tamagotchi toys? They grossed more than many movies. I think that the Tamagotchi thing had a black-and-white display with only something like 12 × 12 pixels. Not anywhere close to photo-realism, but kids were convinced they were real. I remember reading that there were even Tamagotchi baby-sitters. Why were they so entertaining? Because they were interactive! You were able to feed the Tamagotchi and it would eat. If you overfed it, it would become unhealthy, and if you underfed it, it would cry. They interacted in a very primitive way, but it made people feel they were alive. We live in an exciting time where technologies such as QuickTime can enable the average person to mix high-quality audiovisual effects with sophisticated interactivity to produce all sorts of engaging experiences yet to be imagined. And it's not just for fun. Interactive QuickTime can be useful too, as we will see.

Using QuickTime, sprite tracks, flash tracks, text tracks, and VR tracks can all be interactive. And there are several other third-party interactive tracks as well, such as Pulse 3D and Zoomify. With the aid of these tracks, even standard audio and video can be made interactive as well. In this book, we'll be focusing mainly on the sprite track.

Sprites are a very versatile medium that can be used to build user interfaces such as buttons, sliders, and menus, as well as animations, business presentations, video games, and all sorts of interactive multimedia experiences. What came to be known as the sprite track really grew out of the work on Hypercard 3.0. Hypercard was a great way to make custom applications, but the early versions lacked rich media support. When Apple developed Hypercard 3.0, they made it so that it had access to all of the media capabilities of QuickTime. They were also moving toward getting rid of the Hypercard "player" and making it so that Hypercard stacks would be able to play inside of a QuickTime movie in order to add logic and control the media experience. They had a prototype with a nice authoring tool and everything, which they demoed at the 1996 World Wide Developers Conference. Needless to say, the QuickTime and Hypercard fans were very excited. Unfortunately, this was developed around the same time that Apple was pushing to make QuickTime cross-platform. At the time, QuickTime only worked on Macintosh computers, and Apple

Figure 1.5 Penguins movie. *Courtesy of Apple.*

wanted it to run on the Windows platforms as well. Because of this, and other reasons, Hypercard 3.0 was never released, and only a scaled-down version of the sprite engine made it into QuickTime. It was called simply a sprite track and was one of the more obscure QuickTime features. There were no tools for creating sprite tracks and only a few examples of penguins waddling across the screen (see Figure 1.5). It took a while for people to appreciate the potential power of these interactive tracks.

Today, interactive QuickTime (often called "wired" QuickTime because of its ability to contain software circuits, or scripts) has grown in popularity, and Apple has continuously developed and expanded its capabilities. In many ways, it has surpassed the capabilities of the original Hypercard 3.0 incarnation. The popular movie trailers published on Apple's website really showcase the power of interactive QuickTime and how it can add a rich dimension to traditional linear media. Interactive QuickTime is used for business and educational presentations, Web-based advertisements, and product demos and has even made its way into sci-tech applications for data visualization (for example, data collection software from ADInstruments has the ability to export wired movies; see Figure 1.6 and `Projects/Chapter01/DataVisualization/` for some samples) and simulating systems.

Explorations

1. In an attempt to find a way to measure interactivity, I devised what I call the Interactivity Quotient (IQ). You simply add up the scores from the following six questions:

   a. Active. On a scale from 0 to 2, how active is the medium? If it doesn't do anything, that's a 0. If it does lots of things, that's a 2.

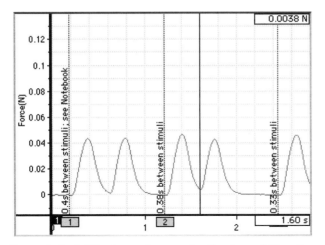

Figure 1.6 Screenshot of ADInstruments example. *Courtesy of Dion Crannitch* <dion@adi.co.nz> *and ADInstruments.*

b. Reactive. On a scale from 0 to 4, how reactive is the medium? If it doesn't respond to user gestures in any way, that's a 0. If it responds to lots of different user input, then that's a 3 or a 4.

c. Motivating. On a scale from 0 to 3, how much does the medium motivate you to interact with it? If it's not clear that it does anything, or what it ends up doing doesn't make you want to play or interact with it anymore, that's probably a 0 or a 1. If it asks you questions or somehow draws you in to try out new things, then that's a 2 or a 3.

d. Limitless. On a scale from 0 to 3, how vast is the range of things that the medium can do? If it just does a few things and the limits are obvious, like a coin that you can toss to be either heads or tails, then the limits of what it can do are obvious, and that's a 0. If it appears to have limitless outcomes, seems intelligent, or can continue to learn to do new things, then that's a 3.

e. Understandable. On a scale from 0 to 2, do the things that the medium does make sense? If it seems completely chaotic, then that's a 0. If it makes sense, even if it's not completely predictable, then that's a 1 or a 2.

f. Nondeterministic. On a scale from 0 to 2, how much does the medium make you feel that it has free will or can do things that aren't completely predictable? If it always does exactly what you predict, then that's a 0. Something that has a random outcome, like a pair of dice, would be a 1. Something that seems to have a mind of its own would be a 2.

This metric has possible values between 0 and 16, and technically shouldn't be called a quotient. A 0 value means it's not interactive at all, and 16 is a score that you might give to a real live tail-wagging puppy dog. Engaging interactive content should have a score of at least 6.

For fun, what IQ would you give to the picture in Figure 1.7 (yes, an interactive picture)? Try staring at the center dot and while doing so, slowing move the book closer and then farther away. You should see that the picture reacts to this user gesture in an interesting way! (The image file is also on the CD.)

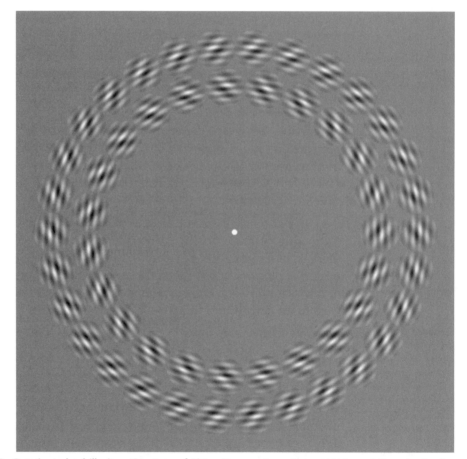

Figure 1.7 Rotating wheel illusion. *Courtesy of Pierre Bayer* <pierre@neuro.informatik.uni-ulm.de>. *For more information see: Pinna, B., & Brelstaff, G. (2000). A new visual illusion of relative motion,* Vision Research, 40, 2091–2096.

How Do You Play an Interactive Movie?

I remember a couple years ago my mom asked me what I was up to, and I told her that I was making interactive QuickTime movies. She said, "Oh, that sounds interesting, how do you play an interactive movie?" I told her that you don't really play them, you play *with* them, and that one of the cool things about interactive QuickTime is that they can run almost everywhere. She then said, "Neat. Can you send me a tape so I can watch one?"

OK, they don't play on your VCR, but one of the compelling reasons to author in QuickTime is the diversity of playback environments that are able to display QuickTime content. First of all, QuickTime plays equally well on Macintosh and Windows. Even Linux and other flavors of UNIX can experience QuickTime content via a $25 piece of software called Crossover (http://www.codeweavers.com/products/crossover/). QuickTime will pretty much work on all desktop machines out there. QuickTime comes preinstalled on all Apple machines, and several big-name PC brands as well, such as the popular Sony Vaio. And once it's installed, it's available as a resource to all applications running on the machine. It's not like other video players, where each application needs to have its own file parser and rendering engine. It takes less than a page of C++ or Java code to build a functional QuickTime movie player. It's really amazing.

Figure 2.1 shows the QuickTime framework. The default playback environment for QuickTime content is the QuickTime Player application. It's a free download from Apple.com (http://www.apple.com/quicktime/products/qt/) and gets installed with the standard QuickTime installation. After installing QuickTime, double-clicking a .mov file should launch the player. Many cross-platform CD-ROM titles simply utilize QuickTime Player as the runtime environment. Sample QuickTime content from the

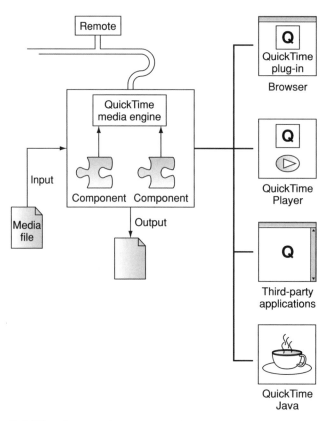

Figure 2.1 QuickTime framework.

enhanced CD of the guitarist Johannes Herrmann (interactive content by Michael Vogt) is provided in the `Projects/Chapter02/EnhancedCD/` directory.

Note An enhanced CD is interactive computer content combined with standard audio tracks on a single compact disk.

Take a look (see Figure 2.2). By distributing interactive content as a QuickTime movie, you don't have to provide (and maintain) separate executables for the different platforms. Apple has done all the work in providing robust playback environments so the developer can concentrate on the content.

Note You can also upgrade to QuickTime Pro for the bargain price of $30. This turns the player into a well-featured movie editor and a powerful media converter.

Figure 2.2 Screenshot of an enhanced CD. *Courtesy of Johannes Herrmann and Michael Vogt.*

Figure 2.3 Screenshot from the Barsark site. *Courtesy of Erik Fohlin* <erik@barsark.com>.

Perhaps the most widely utilized part of the standard QuickTime playback environment is the QuickTime plug-in, which enables movies to play in all the popular Web browsers. Entire websites can be built with QuickTime. For a good example, see Erik Fohlin's "Barsark fun site," which is included on the CD for your perusal (Projects/Chapter02/FullWebsite). Figure 2.3 shows a screenshot from this website. I love this example because it shows how multiple movies can work together to provide a rich user interface and a powerful user experience. The HTML, in this case, is there mostly as a layout framework.

Beyond the standard player and plug-in, you might be surprised at all the places where QuickTime works (see Figure 2.4). Did you know you

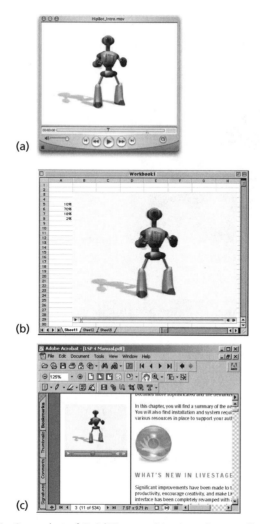

(a)

(b)

(c)

Figure 2.4 Screenshot of QuickTime working in various applications: a) media players; b) office applications, such as word processing applications, spreadsheets, and presentation software; c) portable documents, such as HTML and PDF files.

can place QuickTime movies into a PDF file and display it in Adobe Acrobat? Even word processors, such as Microsoft Word and WordPerfect, and text editors, such as SimpleText and BBEdit, let you embed QuickTime into their document formats. You can play QuickTime movies in Mathematica notebooks, Excel spreadsheets, FileMaker databases, PowerPoint presentations, and Corel Draw illustrations. Many email clients support QuickTime playback within the message itself so you don't even have to open the attachment. There are also hundreds of freeware and shareware products out there that are able to incorporate your QuickTime creations.

It's a breeze for low-level HTML, C++, and Java developers to integrate QuickTime and even easier for multimedia developers. GoLive, Director, iShell, RealBasic, Tekadence Magik, Metacard, WebGain, and Revolution are just a few examples of the many authoring environments out there capable of building QuickTime-rich applications as simple as drag and drop.

▶ Explorations

1. To get a feel for what I mean by "playing with" versus simply "playing" QuickTime, have a look at the `Projects/Chapter02/` directory on the CD (see Figure 2.5). In the `MouseToys` folder you will find some examples that visually respond to the mouse in interesting (and sometimes subtle) ways. The experiences in the `MusicToys` folder take this concept further by adding an auditory component. Integrate these ideas with more structured rules and a fun objective, and you've got yourself a video game (see the `Games` folder). And, of course, it doesn't have to be limited to fun and games. Interactive QuickTime can be made to do useful things as well. Interactive media are also a wonderful way to present information (look in the `Kiosk` folder). QuickTime can also process information and perform calculations, and in this way can function as miniature applications (check out the `Utilities` folder).

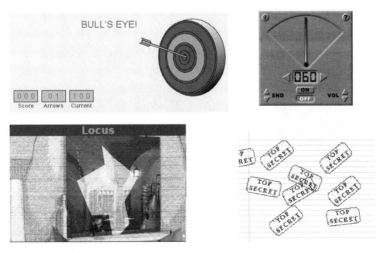

Figure 2.5 Screenshots of movies in `Chapter02`.

2. Apple's QuickTime Player, especially the pro version (affectionately called QTPro), is a surprisingly powerful application with many "hidden" features. If you wanted to explore all of its capabilities, I'd suggest Judy and Robert's book on QuickTime 6. Judy and Robert also have a useful Web resource at www.judyandrobert.com/quicktime. Steve Gulie's *QuickTime for the Web 3E* also covers many useful QTPro features.

3. When I tell people that interactive QuickTime can play in a wide range of applications that they already have on their machine, such as their word processor and their email client, a common question is "Why would you want to do that?" The first time I heard this question, I was a little puzzled because, to me, the ability to embed interactive media into documents and applications is one of QuickTime's most powerful aspects. If you haven't thought about it before, it might be a good exercise to think up several uses for embedded interactive media. You will probably want to come back to this question after making your way through a little more of the book, but I'll give you a couple of fun examples to prime your creative juices.

   In my line of work, I often find myself collaborating with my colleagues in composing text documents, including grant proposals, expense reports, journal articles, and so on. These documents often include filling in some numbers obtained through some simple calculations. One of my colleagues always seems to miscalculate and fill in the wrong numbers, causing me to have to double-check the math when I get the document back from him. At one point I got a little clever and used interactive QuickTime to create a calculator (see Figure 2.6) that I could embed in the document so that he would have all the resources to

Figure 2.6 Calculator.

do the arithmetic correctly. By the way, it worked. You can check out the calculator on the CD: `Projects/Chapter02/Utilities/QTCalc.mov`.

Another example is back when several colleagues and I had to hand-process a large quantity of graphical data. It was taking forever to do: each of us would work on it a bit, but then would quickly get tired of making marks on graphs and would stop doing it for several days, sometimes weeks. To solve the workflow problem, I used interactive QuickTime to place a simple interface on the graphical data (see Figure 2.7). This made it easy to place the necessary marks. After each mark placement, QuickTime would automatically send the data to a server. I then auto-generated several of these QuickTime files each day and emailed them to each of the people involved. We would get these interactive QuickTime movies in our email in-boxes each day, and all we had to do was make a few clicks with the mouse and then go on reading the rest of our email. This made it painless to do, and we finished the job in just a couple of weeks.

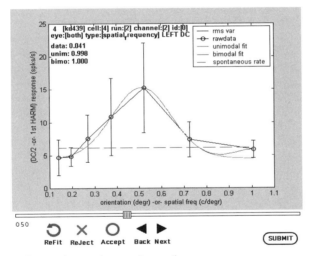

Figure 2.7 An interactive movie sent via email.

The Stuff QuickTime Is Made Of

QuickTime movies are made out of atoms. I'm not making this up. The building blocks are called QuickTime atoms, or QT atoms, and all Quick-Time movies are constructed with them.

Note Actually, there are QT atoms as well as the older "classic" atoms.

This is what makes QuickTime such an expandable and versatile medium. It's so good that the International Organization of Standards (ISO) decided to make MPEG movies in the same way (starting with MPEG-4).

▶ What Are Atoms?

Like real-world atoms (remember the periodic table?), QuickTime atoms come in different types. They can store data, and they can store other atoms (called *child atoms*). QuickTime movies usually start out with a movie atom (type moov) and movie data (type mdat).

Note You can roughly think of QuickTime atoms as a binary version of XML. They are more restrained than XML. For instance, the atom type is always four characters, and the types of atoms that can be placed into other atoms are often rigidly defined except for the generic atom container atom, which happens to be of type sean (named after Sean Allen). For a good overview of the QuickTime file format, check out the QuickTime SDK documentation.

The moov atom defines the structure of the movie, and the mdat atom holds the actual media data—audio, video, text, and so on. Parts of the media data can also come from a separate file or somewhere on the Internet. Inside the `moov` atom are one or more track atoms (type `trak`). The track atoms contain at least a header atom (type `tkhd`), which has some data in it defining different aspects of the track, such as the duration, the volume, the spatial dimensions, and so on. Track atoms also contain a media atom (type `mdia`), which really defines what type of track it is. The media atom will contain its own structure of atoms defining various aspects of the track's content. So you can think of QuickTime movies as these big tree-shaped molecules built out of different types of atoms (see Figure 3.1).

Usually, developers don't have to think about movies at that level of detail, but it helps to know they are there. For instance, it's good to know that if you want a movie on a Web page to begin playing immediately and not have to completely download first, the `moov` atom needs to be placed before the actual media data (`mdat`). Most QuickTime authoring applications do this for you automatically (it's called *Fast Start,* or *progressive download*), but a rough understanding of what's going on beneath the hood is useful. It's the same with any field. Doctors have to know about atoms and molecules, but they don't think of their patients as big bundles of atoms or molecules. They are more likely to think on the level of cells or organs. Similarly, QuickTime media developers usually think of movies as being built out of tracks. So, let's move the conversation from atoms to tracks.

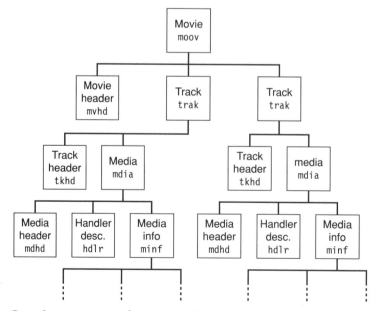

Figure 3.1 Example atom structure for a movie with two tracks.

Tracks

Some tracks are visual in nature, such as video and sprite tracks. These have visual and spatial properties that define their color, how transparent they are, where they are located, their width and height, and so on. Many visual tracks only change what you see on the screen when the "playhead" is changed. Video is a good example of this. If the video track is stopped, then all you see is a static image. Only when the playhead is changing (often called "playing") do the images on the screen actually move. Sprite, Flash, and VR tracks are examples of tracks that can change their appearance while the playhead is fixed at one position. These nonlinear media types are able to change their appearance even when the movie is stopped because they have an independent notion of time. A sprite track has an internal clock that continuously ticks. These ticks are called *idle events,* and they inform the sprite track that time has elapsed. Sprite tracks are also interactive. This means that they can respond to user events such as mouse clicks and typing on the keyboard.

Samples

You know how in kindergarten they teach you things that later turn out to be technically incorrect? Well, the stuff I said in the last paragraph about some tracks being nonlinear is wrong. Technically, by definition, all QuickTime tracks are linear. It's the stuff tracks are composed of, called *samples,* that can be linear or nonlinear (Figure 3.2).

Tracks are made up of a series of nonoverlapping media samples along a timeline. Typically, in the case of video, a sample corresponds to a change in the image that gets drawn to the screen. In this case, a sample equals a video frame. But this isn't always the case. Samples don't have to be evenly spaced nor do they have to be contiguous. And for nonlinear media, the image can change while the playhead remains stationary in one sample.

Sprite Track Samples

Sprite track samples are the epitome of nonlinear media. Sprite samples have a pool of images (see Figure 3.3) that can be displayed and manipulated (moved, rotated, scaled, hidden, revealed, and so on) in the track's visual space (see Figure 3.4). Not only can the images displayed by a sprite

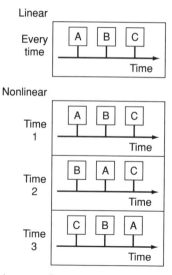

Figure 3.2 Linear media appears the same every time it is played. Nonlinear media can change each time it is played.

sample be manipulated independently of the playhead, but with Quick-Time 6, new images can be added to the image pool dynamically from the local file system or across the network. The sprite sample can be a very dynamic chunk of media. Even though the sprite sample is nonlinear, the sprite track is still linear because which sample is loaded at any one time is completely determined by the location of the playhead.

▶ Sprites

Sprites are the objects capable of displaying images in a sprite sample. We'll explore the inner workings of sprites in the next section, but for now, you can think of sprites as little slide projectors projecting images onto the surface of the sprite track (see Figure 3.5). A sample can have multiple slide projectors, but each is loaded with the same carousel of images. Each slide projector can be turned on and off, moved around, rotated, and oriented in different directions to produce different projections of its current slide image. This is essentially the way a sprite sample works except instead of a person controlling and manipulating the slide projectors, imagine the slide projectors are robots following a set of instructions. We'll call a set of instructions a *script*.

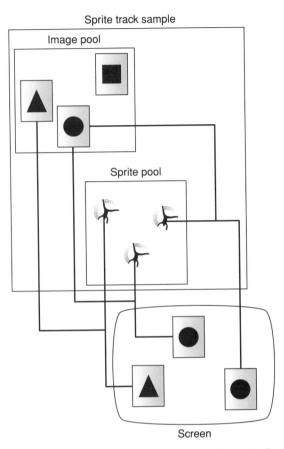

Figure 3.3 Sprite samples contain a pool of images and a pool of sprites.

▶ Scripts

The aspect that makes sprite samples so dynamic and interactive is that they can be programmed. Sprites in a sprite sample can have scripts that tell the sprite what to do when specified events happen. For instance, you can attach a script to a sprite that tells it to move forward three paces, turn left 20 degrees, then display the next image (see Figure 3.6).

You can set it up so that it executes those three instructions every time a user clicks in the area that the sprite is displaying an image. You can have it execute a separate set of instructions every time a certain amount of time elapses. By attaching scripts in this way, you can design sprites with intricate behavior.

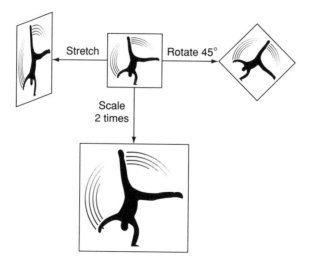

Figure 3.4 Sprite manipulations.

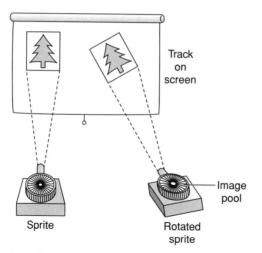

Figure 3.5 The slide projector analogy.

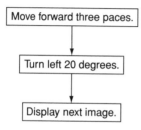

Figure 3.6 A script.

Sprites aren't the only things that can have scripts attached to them. For example, pieces of text in a text track have scripts too. It's similar to links in an HTML page except that the instructions can be much more sophisticated than simply loading a new Web page. Additionally, hotspots in a QuickTime VR panorama and buttons in a Flash movie can also have attached scripts (see Figure 3.7).

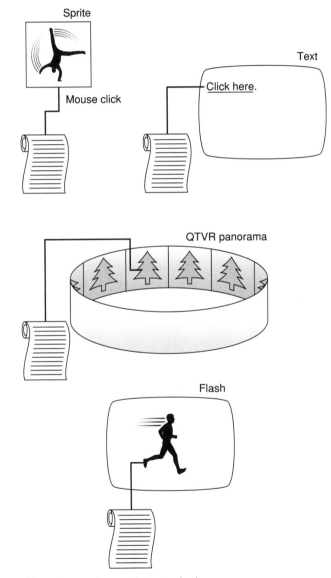

Figure 3.7 Things that can have scripts attached.

How to Make Interactive Sprite Tracks

We know that QuickTime movies are made up of tracks that have samples. Interactive sprite track samples have images and sprites, and sprites have properties and events that have code. When you get down far enough it's all made out of atoms. Knowing what something is made of doesn't necessarily let you make it. Making video and audio tracks is pretty straightforward: you get a video camera, a microphone, and you know the rest. But what about interactive sprite tracks?

When sprite tracks were first introduced in 1997, there were no tools and little documentation on how to build them. In 1998, a few tools started to emerge on the scene (see Figure 3.8). One of the first was a freeware product called Spritz from David McGravin.

Note You can apparently still download Spritz from `http://home.earthlink.net/~dmcgravin /spritz/`.

With Spritz you could make only the most basic sprite creations such as buttons and simple image sequences. More sophisticated tools came out

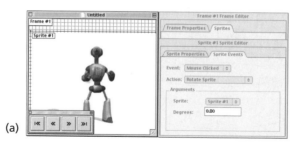
(a)

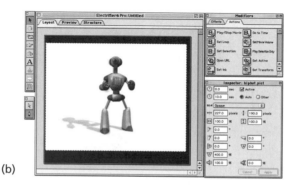
(b)

Figure 3.8 The early applications: a) Spritz; b) Electrifier Pro.

around the same time, such as Electrifier Pro, WiredZone, and LiveStage. LiveStage was the only one of these initial tools to make it to version 2.0 (LiveStage Pro). Electrifier Pro had a lot of support, but they switched to Real Media without releasing their promised second version. They left a lot of users upset, but many found a nice home in the LiveStage community.

LiveStage from Totally Hip was the brainchild of Steve Israelson who was also the lead developer on several other Mac products such as Promotion, which brought interactive animation to Hypercard. Version 1.0 of LiveStage sported a cover with a red demonic muscle man controlling a jester puppet (see Figure 3.9). It was pretty scary looking, but nevertheless they gained quite a few users. The software's tag line was "Improvisational theater for the web," a pretty forward-thinking concept. LiveStage Pro is currently at version 4.1 and is the most powerful way to create sophisticated interactive content for QuickTime. Some of the other tools for creating interactive QuickTime include VRHotwires, Adobe GoLive, Microsoft PowerPoint (Mac version only), and LiveSlideShow (also by Totally Hip).

Besides tools, Apple has libraries that let you build all aspects of Quick-Time using C/C++ or Java (good books on this topic are *Discovering Quick-Time* and *QuickTime for Java*). The latest version of QTJava has particularly good support for sprite tracks. Apple's developer site has a plethora of C/C++ and Java sample code for building QuickTime movies, including interactive ones. *Inside QuickTime: Interactive Movies,* a book from Apple is another valuable resource (available as a PDF from http://developer.apple.com/quicktime/). You can also refer to Appendix P, which provides an example of how to work on the "atomic" level to build an interactive QuickTime movie.

This was a brief overview of what interactive QuickTime is made of, both in terms of the low-level file structures and the high-level tools and constructs. In the next chapter, we'll start putting some of this knowledge

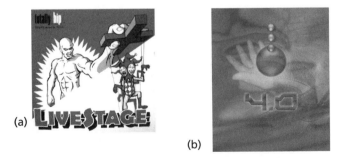

Figure 3.9 LiveStage CD cover: a) LiveStage 1.0; b) LiveStage 4.0.

to work with LiveStage Pro, the dominant tool for creating interactive QuickTime experiences.

▶ Explorations

1. The pro version of QuickTime Player provides quite a bit of information about the contents of a QuickTime movie. For example, open a movie in the player and choose Get Movie Properties from the Movie menu (only available when you upgrade to the pro version). A window will pop up for browsing and editing various properties of the movie and the tracks within (see Figure 3.10). Try it out.

2. Apple has a free utility, called Dumpster, that lets you view a movie's atomic structure. It's available for Mac and Windows (`http://developer.apple.com/quicktime/quicktimeintro/tools/`). Download it and get a submolecular view of any .mov file.

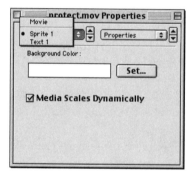

Figure 3.10 QuickTime Pro movie edit window.

Part

Wiring Existing Movies

This part of the book shows you how to add simple interactivity to your existing movies. We'll learn how to wrap up video into a custom player and add DVD features. We'll also explore important movie properties by seeing what interactive QuickTime has to offer for DRM (digital rights management). The tool we'll use to do all of this is called LiveStage Pro 4.1. A demo version is available from TotallyHip.com, and one is also included on the CD (in the Installers folder) for Mac and Windows. Let's start off by getting acquainted with LiveStage Pro.

Getting Familiar with the Tools

Today, the most powerful tool for creating interactive QuickTime movies is LiveStage Pro (LSP). It's a professional product, well-written and quite stable. We could ease into the process of creating interactive movies by first learning simpler tools such as Adobe GoLive, or by piecing some movies together using Apple's pro version of QuickTime Player, but we will run into major limitations on what we can do rather quickly. The best thing is to dive in and start learning LSP from the beginning.

A demo version of LSP version 4.01 is included on the CD (in the Installers folder). LSP is available for both Windows and Macintosh. Take a moment to install LSP on your computer so you can follow along and begin building some fun interactive content (see Figure 4.1).

The demo version of LSP is fully functional but will expire 42 days after it is first installed. This is much longer than the seven-day trial version downloadable from the Totally Hip website. LSP utilizes an anti-piracy "License Management System" called PACE InterLok. When installing LSP, you will be asked if this license management system needs to be installed. Click the "yes" button to install it. Without this component, LSP 4.01

(a)   (b)   (c)

Figure 4.1 Installer icons for the different platforms: a) LiveStage Pro installer for Windows (LSPro401DemoQT.EXE); b) LiveStage Pro installer for Macintosh OS 9 (LSPro4 Demo Installer); c) LiveStage Pro installer for Macintosh OS X (LSPro4 Demo Installer).

won't run. The installation process should be straightforward, but if problems arise, or you would like to learn more about this component, there is a FAQ available: http://stagedoor.totallyhip.com/faq/LSP_demo_pace.html. After LSP is installed, it is important to restart the computer. When you run LSP for the first time, you will be guided through an online registration process which simply involves filling in some information and clicking a confirmation button on the web page that LSP will launch for you automatically. Consumers, myself included, tend not to like anti-piracy components, but they are designed to keep the price of software down and keep small innovative software companies from going out of business. Long live Totally Hip and LiveStage Pro.

Note If you own an older version of LSP, you might consider upgrading or using the LSP 4 demo. The projects on the CD are LSP 4 projects that aren't compatible with older versions of LSP. Newer versions of LSP should be backwards compatible with LSP 4 projects.

Ever since Brian Kernighan and Dennis Ritchie wrote *The C Programming Language* in 1978, it has been a tradition to begin learning a new environment or language by first building a simple project that displays the words "Hello World" (see Figure 4.2). Since we don't want to break this long-standing tradition, let's begin learning LSP by building a Hello World movie.

As with all projects in this book, there is an associated folder on the CD. The Hello World folder is located at Projects/Chapter04/Hello World/. I suggest first copying this folder to your local hard drive so that LSP will have a place to output the movie we are about to build. Figure 4.3 shows what you should see inside the Hello World folder.

The Hello_World_start.lsd file called is a LiveStage document. You can think of an .lsd file as the recipe, and the Library folder as the bag of ingredients for building an interactive QuickTime movie. The Library folder is the standard directory that you will encounter for all LSP

> Hello World_

Figure 4.2 Hello World!

ChapterO4
   Hello World
      HelloWorld.mov
      Hello_World_complete.lsd
      Hello_World_start.lsd
      Library

Figure 4.3 Files and directories in the Hello World folder.

projects. This is where the external media used in the project are typically stored.

We can open this project in LiveStage Pro by double-clicking the Hello_World_start.lsd file. If this doesn't work, try launching LSP first to associate .lsd files with the application. In this case, when launching LSP it will ask you if you want to open an existing project or make a new project. Choose to open an existing project, and select the Hello_World_start.lsd project. After opening the project, your computer screen should look more or less like Figure 4.4.

Note As you can see from Figure 4.4, the Mac and Windows versions of LiveStage Pro have the same interface. Throughout the book, I take screenshots from a variety of platforms (Mac OS 9 and OS X and Windows 98, 2000, and XP), but you probably won't notice. LiveStage and QuickTime work essentially the same in the various environments. I'll point out the important differences when necessary. I'd like to mention that the development that went into creating this book was done on multiple flavors of Mac OS and Windows, so I can testify to QuickTime's cross-platform nature.

What we have here is a movie with a single sprite track in it. How the sprite track works will be discussed in great detail in Part III of this book, but basically it is QuickTime's main interactive track. The big empty area is called the stage (as in Live "stage"), and it provides a spatial view of the project. Now, let's get acquainted with that library we were talking about earlier. If you don't see the Library window, you can open it by choosing Show Library Window from the Window menu. The library is divided into three tabs. There is a Global tab that houses all of the media available in the Library folder located in the same directory as the LSP application (usually media are placed here for use in multiple projects). The global library comes stocked with sample media. Then there's the Local tab. This contains all of the files in the Library folder local to the project. The last

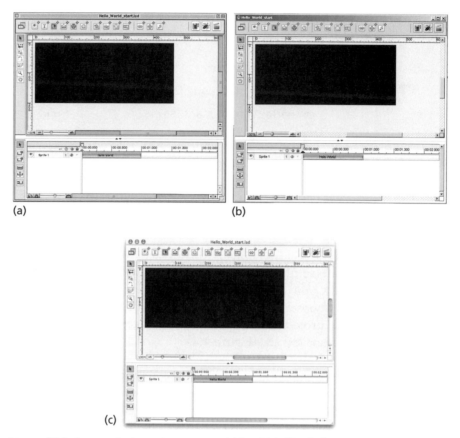

Figure 4.4 Mac and Windows project opening screens: a) Mac OS 9; b) Windows 2000; c) Mac OS X.

tab is the Scripts tab, which contains some reusable behaviors that can allow you to add interactivity with a simple drag and drop. For now, we will concentrate on the Local tab.

In the Local tab of the Library, you should see two images called "Hello.Pict" and "World.Pict" (see Figure 4.5). Adding these images to our project is easy—simply drag them from the library onto the stage. Once they are on the stage, you can position them and do other spatial manipulations. To do so, you first need to set the sprite track into edit mode by clicking the ▆ button. This will place a thick striped border around the sprite track to indicate that it is in spatial editing mode.

You can now move the Hello and World images around. By selecting the resizing tool ▣ you can resize, reposition, and rotate the images.

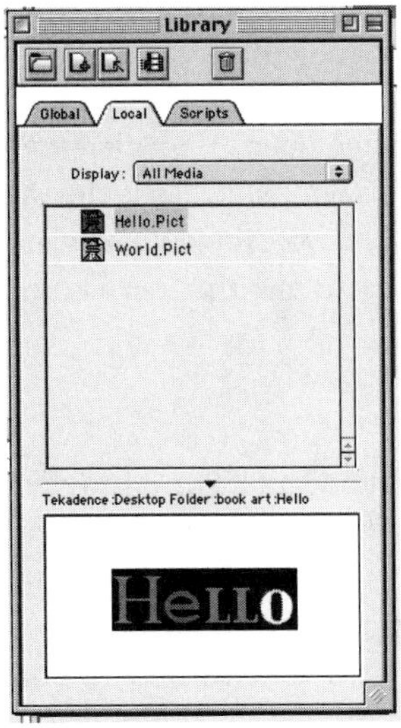

Figure 4.5 The Local tab of the Library window.

Once you have the Hello and World images positioned how you like them, you can preview the movie by clicking the ▣ button.

There you go, your first interactive QuickTime movie! Well, it's not really very interactive, but it's a good starting place. An easy way to add interactivity is through *behaviors*. Behaviors are collections of scripts. The third file in the Local library is a behavior. It's called Draggable.lsb (behaviors usually, but don't always, end in the .lsb extension).

Note Draggable.lsb and many other prebuilt behaviors can also be found in the Scripts part of the Library. Click the Scripts tab in the Library window. Expand the Behaviors folder.

This behavior makes a sprite draggable. To add it to the World sprite, drag that behavior out and drop it onto the World image, which should be sitting on your stage.

Now when you preview the project, you should be able to drag the World image around the screen. Voila, some simple interactivity. If you want, you can now export this movie by choosing Export > QuickTime Movie... from the File menu.

Note You can export even with the demo version.

You can email that movie to a friend or place it on your website, just as you can with any other QuickTime movie.

Note Previewing and exporting are essentially the same thing. The difference is that clicking on the preview button writes the movie out to a temporary file in the same directory as the `.1sd` file, and then launches the movie in a player window automatically. Choosing Export from the File menu lets you choose where to save the `.mov` file and doesn't automatically launch the movie.

What did we just do exactly?

Technically, we just built an interactive QuickTime movie that contains a sprite track with a single sprite sample. The sprite sample has two images and two sprites. One sprite is set up to display the Hello image while the other displays the World image. We also added a "draggable" behavior to the World sprite. Now, what if we wanted to change things a bit? What if we wanted to remove the "draggable" behavior and make the World sprite also display the Hello image? How would we do that? To make changes like this, we need to dig a little deeper into how LSP works.

So far, we've been hanging out in the Library window and the stage. Another important place on LSP's user interface is the track timeline (see Figure 4.6). By default, it appears just below the stage.

The track timeline pictorially displays the tracks that compose the project. All QuickTime movies are made up of tracks. They can have as little as one or as many as several hundred tracks. Our Hello World movie has a single sprite track. This sprite track has a single sample in it that is represented as a horizontal beveled bar. Our sprite track sample starts at time zero and has a duration of 1 second, as indicated by the time scale that runs along the top of the tracks. The time is displayed in a timecode, which in this case is minutes:seconds.600ths. In this format, 00:01.000 means 00 minutes, 01 seconds and 000 600ths of a second. If you have

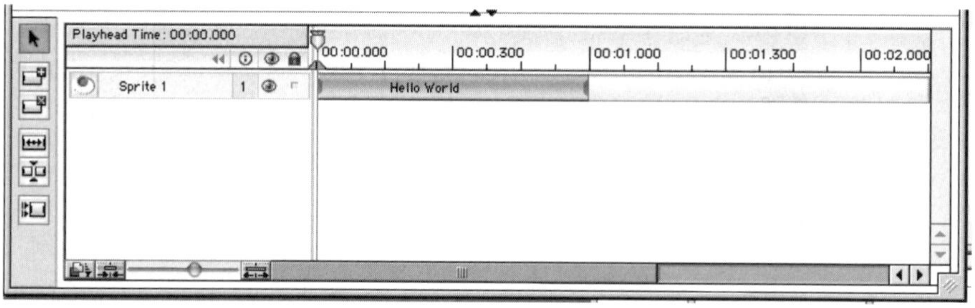

Figure 4.6 The track timeline.

ever worked with digital video editing software or audio recording software, then you are probably very familiar with timecodes, but you may be more familiar with the SMPTE (Society of Motion Picture and Television Engineers) timecode, which has the format hours:minutes:seconds:frames, and 30 frames per second (see Figure 4.7).

Double-clicking a sprite sample should bring up an editor that will allow you to modify properties of the images and the sprites contained within the sample. Double-click the "Hello World" sample and you should get a window that looks like Figure 4.8.

By default, the Images tab is showing. You probably have two images—one named Hello and one named World. On the Images tab, you can add new images, reorder them, change their names, and modify various other

LSP

00 : 00 . 000
Minutes Seconds Ticks
                  600ths of a second

SMPTE

00 : 00 : 00 : 00 . 00
Hours Minutes Seconds Frames Fraction of frame

Figure 4.7 The LSP and SMPTE timecodes.

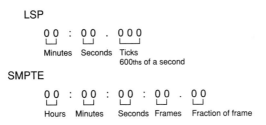

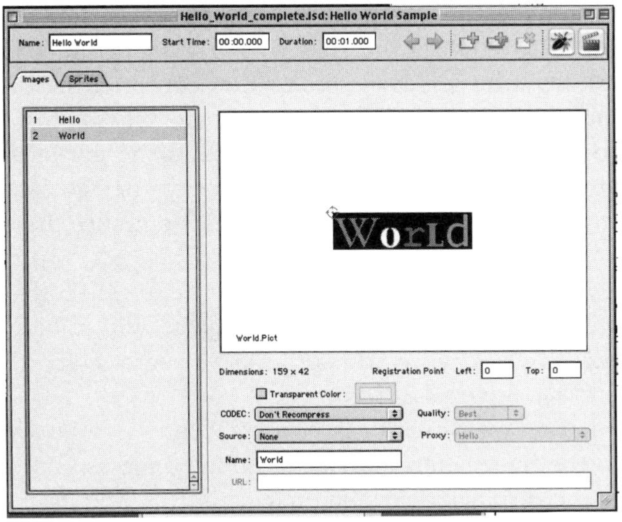

Figure 4.8 The sprite sample editor.

properties. One important image property is the CODEC property. This allows you to specify how the image should be compressed and encoded.

Note CODEC stands for code/decode. Different codecs compress images in different ways. If you already compressed your image before bringing it into LSP, then choose the Don't Recompress option to maintain your compression settings. Otherwise JPEG does a pretty good job for photographs, and Animation and PNG are both good choices for line graphics, or for images with alpha channels. These are some good rules of thumb, but choosing the optimal codec is really an art. For instance, when compressing a picture of someone's head, then you might want to try the H263 codec since it was designed and optimized for videoconferencing. The Graphics codec is one of the fastest at decompiling and has a low CPU overhead, whereas Sorenson has great image quality but a high CPU overhead. See Appendix H for more information on codecs.

Along with choosing a codec, you can also specify a Quality setting. The choices are Low, Medium, High, and Best. The default is Best quality, but at times you may want to choose a lower setting to decrease the memory requirements of the sprite sample.

That's enough with the images for now. Let's move to the Sprites tab. Sprites are the objects that display images, and we'll be doing some amazing things with them throughout the book. For now, you should just get a sense of their different properties and settings.

To place a sprite at a specific location, you can set the Left and Top properties (see Figure 4.9). You can specify the distance of the sprite from the left and top edges of the track with these properties. Try setting the Left and Top fields to 0,0 for the Hello sprite. Preview the project and the Hello sprite should now appear at the top left corner of the track.

You can make a sprite that isn't visible by unchecking the Visible property. Unchecking the Clickable property makes the sprite ignore mouse clicks. If we unchecked the Clickable property for the World sprite, it would no longer be draggable because the user's mouse dragging activity would go unnoticed (try that).

The Angle property is a useful one. It determines the number of degrees, in the clockwise manner, that the sprite will initially be rotated. Try setting the Angle of the World sprite to 45 degrees, and then previewing the project (see Figure 4.10).

One very important property is Image. This determines which image (chosen from the images tab) the sprite initially shows. Try changing the World sprite so it displays the Hello image.

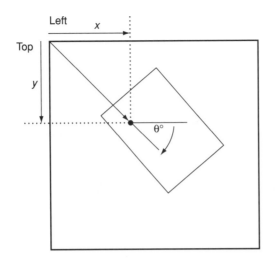

Figure 4.9 Sprite coordinate system.

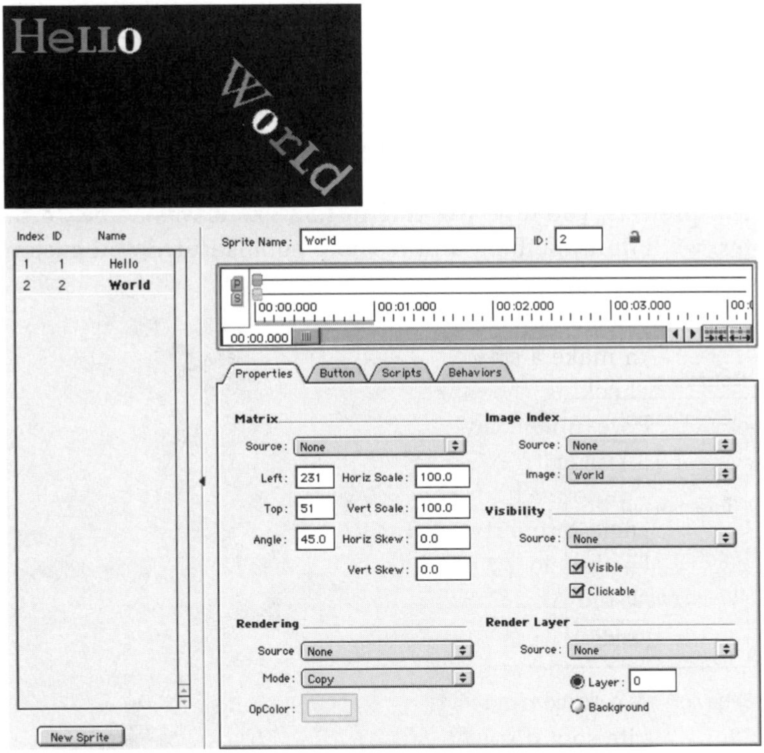

Figure 4.10 The World sprite rotated 45 degrees.

All of the properties in the Sprites tab should be considered initial settings. Most of them can be altered at runtime through scripts. The exceptions include Clickable and all of the ones labeled "Source."

We saw how adding a behavior to a sprite can change the way it acts (and interacts). You can see the list of behaviors attached to a given sprite by looking in the Behaviors tab. For example, select the World sprite from the sprite list on the left and then click the Behaviors tab. It should contain the Draggable behavior we added earlier. New behaviors can be added to a sprite by dragging them onto this tab panel. You can also remove behaviors by selecting them and hitting the Delete key.

In the last chapter, when we talked about what interactive QuickTime is made of, we didn't mention behaviors. That's because a behavior is essentially a script (or collection of scripts) stored in an external file (see Figure 4.11). Scripts can also be typed directly into a sprite's Scripts tab. As you progress through this book, you'll be spending a lot of time in the Scripts tab. The scripting language in LiveStage Pro is easy to learn, especially if you take advantage of the QScript Reference window (choose Show QScript Reference from the Window menu; see Figure 4.12). Script sniplets that you find in the QScript Reference window can be dragged out and dropped directly into a script window. We'll start scripting things in the next chapter.

Welcome to LiveStage Pro. Have a look around and get yourself acquainted. Don't worry if parts of the interface look complicated. After a few projects, you'll be working in LSP like it was home. In the next chapter, we'll do something a little more sophisticated and customize the presentation of video.

Figure 4.11 Behaviors are collections of scripts.

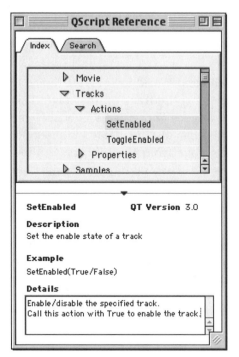

Figure 4.12 The QScript Reference window.

▶ Explorations

1. Try changing the CODEC of the Hello image to Fire (see Figure 4.13), then preview the project (make sure at least one of the sprites is displaying the Hello image first).

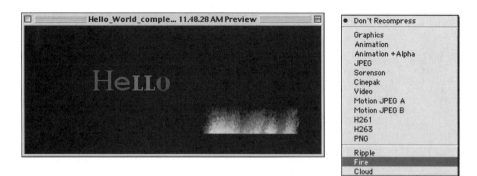

Figure 4.13 The Fire CODEC.

2. Notice that when you change the position (Top and Left fields) of a sprite in the Properties tab, you can see the effects in the stage. You can also move sprites around on the Stage and see how the spatial properties are affected.

3. When we added the Hello and World images, we did so by dragging the images onto the area of the sprite track on the stage. This actually does two things. It adds the images and creates new sprites to display the images. Images and sprites can also be created independently from each other. Try dragging an image from the Library window's Global tab directly into the Images tab. Then go into the Sprites tab and click the New Sprite button, located at the bottom-left corner. This will create a new sprite named Untitled. See if you can modify the name, image, and other properties of this new sprite.

4. Ignoring the Source fields for now, see if you can figure out what the properties labeled Rendering at the bottom of the Properties tab do. What do Mode and OpColor control? What about Layer and Background?

5

Customizing the Presentation of an Existing Movie

One of the big advantages of using QuickTime, over, say, Real or Windows Media, is that the author can enjoy a great deal of control over how the content is presented. QuickTime enables you to completely customize the look and feel of your movie's playback environment. Although the Quick-Time player is nice and slick, you aren't stuck with it for all projects. If you want, you can break out of the player's skin and make a window of just about any shape imaginable. You can also make your own controls that duplicate (even go beyond) the player's standard functionality. Figure 5.1 shows just a couple examples of what people are creating. All of this is made possible because of QuickTime's rich interactive capabilities.

Let's learn how to put a custom interface on an existing movie. Open the project Custom_Interface_start.lsd. This is located on the CD at Projects/Chapter05/Custom Interfaces. As always, it's best to bring a copy of this directory to your local hard disk so that LSP has a place to save

Figure 5.1 Examples of some cool skinned movies.

temporary files. The project `Custom_Interface_start.lsd` should start up empty. We're going to build the whole project from scratch.

Let's begin by dragging in a video clip. You'll find it under the Local tab of the Library under the `Video` directory. Drag the file `QTVideo.mov` into the track timeline. This should add two tracks to your project—a video and an audio track (see Figure 5.2).

Preview the movie and have a look at the video we will be customizing. This is the sample movie that Apple included on the QuickTime CD about the same time that the first interesting interactive movies were being developed.

Instead of playing in a standard rectangular window, say we wanted this video to play in a window the shape of the QuickTime logo. We can do this by adding a special track called a Window Shape track (also called a skin track). We do this by choosing Create Track > Window Shape from the Movie menu (see Figure 5.3). Create one and a track named "skin 1" (or something close to that) will appear in the timeline (see Figure 5.4). Double-click the skin track's sample (the long red beveled bar), and you'll be presented with an editor window that lets you specify both the shape of the window and the area of the window that constitutes the title bar or the drag region (see Figure 5.5). We specify these regions by dragging in black-and-white images, where the black areas denote the window shape.

Note   Gray pixels will be turned to black ones to make a 1-bit mask except on OS X, where different levels of gray indicate different degrees of transparency.

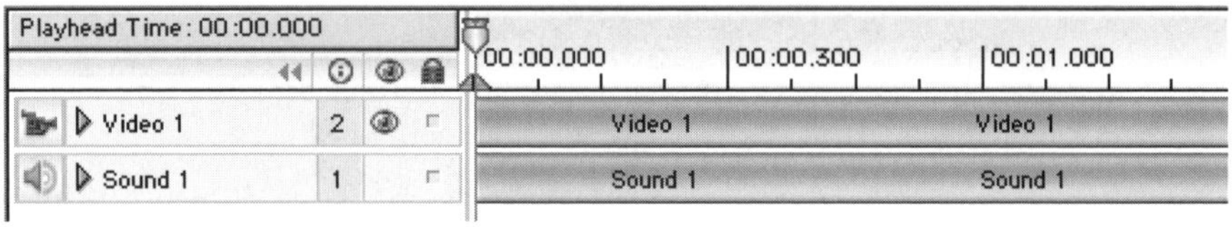

Figure 5.2   Video and audio tracks.

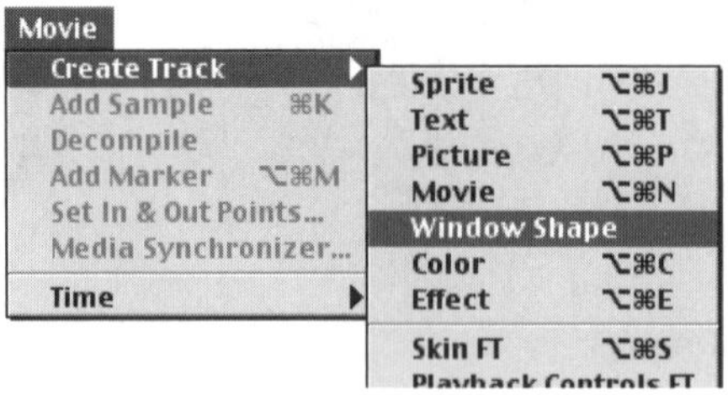

Figure 5.3   The Movie menu.

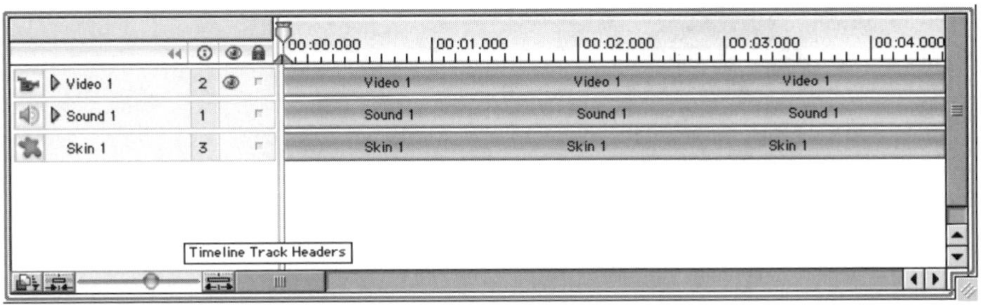

Figure 5.4 Track timeline 1.

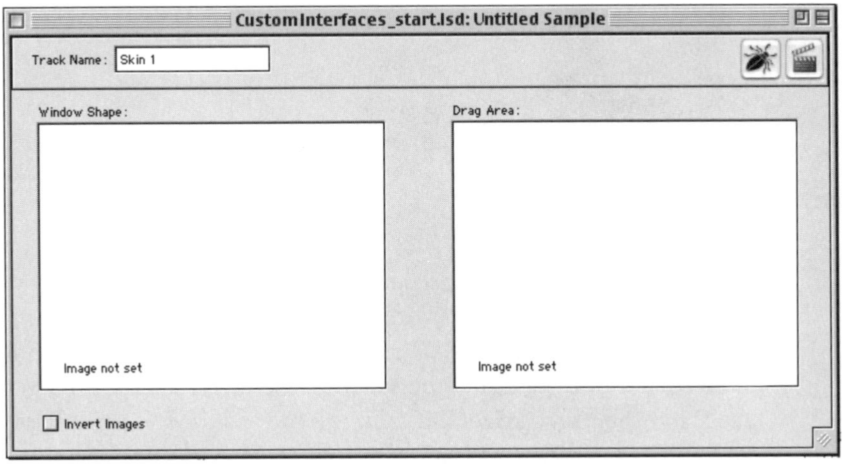

Figure 5.5 Window shape editor.

The Window Shape and Drag Area images should have the same dimensions. For our QuickTime logo window we will use the images in Figure 5.6.

The window will have the shape of a Q, with only the very top part draggable. Drag the `WindowShapeQ.Pict` and `DragAreaQ.Pict` images from the Library into the corresponding regions of the skin editor. Close the editor window and notice that the gray region of the stage now has the shape of a Q. Center the video inside the Q and then preview the movie (see Figure 5.7).

The movie should now play in a window the shape of a Q. This is great! But there are a few problems.

First of all, the background is gray, and it would look much better black. A more important issue, however, is that there don't appear to be

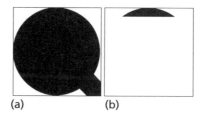

Figure 5.6 Window shape images: a) window shape; b) drag area.

Figure 5.7 Window shape previewed.

any controls to play the movie or to even close the window! Well, we actually can play the movie by double-clicking, and we can close the window through the Command-w (Ctrl-w on Windows) keyboard shortcut. Nevertheless, it would be much better to present the user with a graphical interface that they recognize. Let's fix the more serious issues first.

Let's add a simple Play/Pause button to our skinned movie. To do this, drag out the file called `PlayButton.mov` from the Local tab of the Library. Drag it onto the stage, and position it so it's just below the video but still within the window shape.

Let's also add a Close button so the user can close the window. Drag out the file called `CloseButton.mov`, and position it so it is just above the top-left corner of our video. Make sure it is within the bounds of the window shape. You can turn Enable Object Guides off from the Layout menu to make it easier to position the track where you want it. It should now look like Figure 5.8.

We just added two new tracks to our movie: PlayButton and CloseButton. Both of these are sprite tracks that I made on a previous occasion (the source projects for the buttons are included on the CD). One of the great things about QuickTime is reusability. I made the Play and Close buttons for a different project, and now I don't have to make them anymore. I can simply drag them into a project whenever I need their functionality.

Figure 5.8 The Close button positioned in Q.

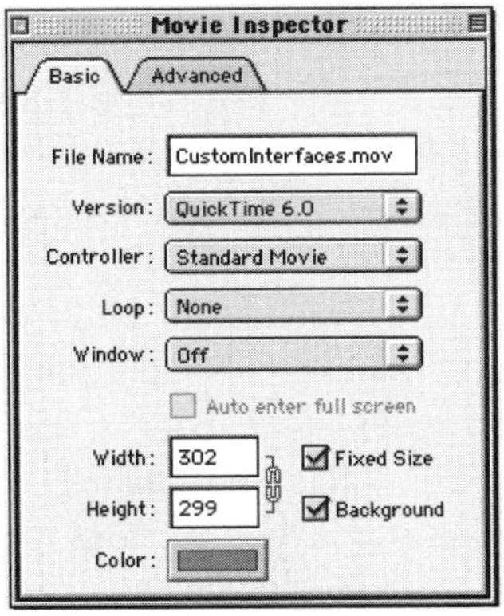

Figure 5.9 The Movie Inspector window.

As a final step, let's make the background black. Open the Movie Inspector window by choosing Show Inspector from the Window menu. The inspector shows commonly used properties for whatever object is currently selected (see Figure 5.9). If we click on the background of the stage, we should get the Movie Inspector. This is where we can change the background color of the movie from gray to black.

Note The background color isn't a QuickTime concept. It's an invention by LiveStage. When the movie gets built, a color track will be added to the movie to form the background. You can turn this feature off by deselecting the Fixed Size and Background checkboxes in the Movie Inspector.

There we go, wasn't that easy? Now preview the movie and see if our changes work as expected. Check to see if the Close button works. If it doesn't, then make sure the button isn't in the window's drag area.

The drag region can be shown on the stage by choosing Show Skin Drag Area from the View menu. This will indicate the very top of the Q with a red outline corresponding to the window's drag area. If the Close button is in the drag region, it can't receive mouse events.

Note   In general, holes can be placed in the drag region image to make clickable spots for buttons.

Being able to see the drag region while authoring is helpful, but we should probably do something to graphically indicate the drag area to the user as well. Often what people do is indicate the drag region with some texture so it's obvious to the user where to click in order to move the window. To do this, I've made an image that has horizontal grip lines the same shape as the very top of the Q (see Figure 5.10). The image is called QGrip.Pict. Drag it from the Library onto the stage and position it at the top of the movie.

Let's test it out. Much better with the grip lines, right? Now click the Play button. It starts playing, but oops, where did the grip lines go? The drag grip image we placed at the top disappears after a second into the movie because the picture's sample only has a 1-second duration. We didn't have this problem with the Play and Close buttons because I had prebuilt them to have the right duration. But it's easy to change the duration of a sample.

Let's make the grip sample (in the picture track, probably named "Picture 1") the same duration as all of the other tracks. To do this, click on the track manipulation tool  . This will turn all of the track samples a translucent silver color, and you should see handles at the ends to allow you to stretch them in time. Stretch the picture track so it is the same length as all of the other tracks. It might help to zoom out a bit by clicking on the Zoom button (see Figure 5.11). When you elongate the grip track,

Figure 5.10   Drag grip.

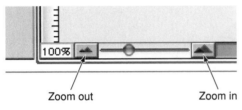

Zoom out   Zoom in

Figure 5.11   Zoom icon.

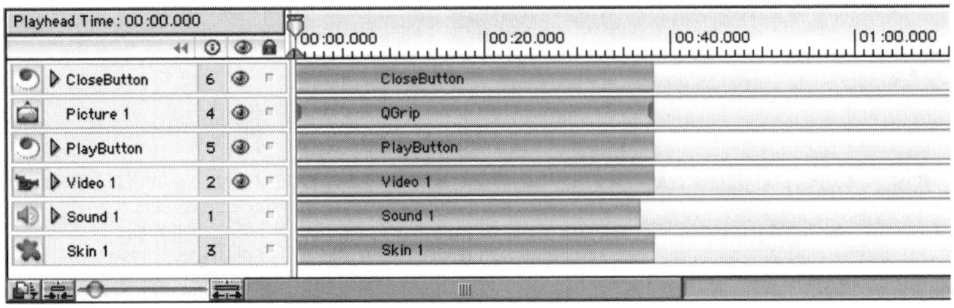

Figure 5.12   Samples are now the same duration (except for the sound).

notice how LSP aids in the temporal alignment by snapping into place when you've dragged the end close to the end of another track (see Figure 5.12). Now the drag grip image should stay visible for the duration of the movie.

There we go. We just built a fully functional custom movie player wrapped around a piece of video. To export it as a QuickTime movie, just choose Export > QuickTime Movie... from the File menu. Your creative work can now run within an equally creative playback environment (see Figure 5.13). In the next chapter we'll see how to protect this creative content so you can maintain control over not only how it gets presented, but when and where it gets presented.

▶ Explorations

1. Design your own window shape and drag region. Experiment with the ways that a custom playback environment enhances the user experience.

2. Sometimes you will want your movie to take over the entire screen. If you have the pro version of QuickTime Player installed, you can make any movie go full screen. LiveStage projects have a setting that makes a movie automatically go full screen when loaded. If you don't know how

Figure 5.13   Final results for the Q movie.

to do this already, see if you can figure out how to make changes to this setting.

3. In this chapter we used a reusable PlayButton track. LiveStage has expanded on the notion of reusable tracks in a clever way. They are called Fast Tracks (FT). For example, you can easily add movie controls by choosing Create Track > Playback Controls FT from the Movie menu. Try deleting the current PlayButton track and adding play controls through this Fast Track feature. One didactic feature of Fast Tracks is their ability to be "decompiled." Once decompiled, you can see how they are created and make changes to the scripts and other settings.

6

Digital Rights Management

Protecting intellectual property is a major issue, especially since Napster and other online media exchanging systems emerged on the scene. Although digital media on the Web are just as protected by international copyright law as any other form of media, both the content creators and the publishers are concerned (with good reason) that the Web makes it too easy to pirate and distribute media. They argue that enforcing the law is almost an impossible task. So instead of protecting intellectual property through litigation, technology has been developed to make it very difficult to infringe on the copyright in the first place. This technology falls under the category of digital rights management (DRM).

Most DRM products on the market today require sophisticated and expensive server-side technology, such as ContentGuard and InterTrust. Other DRM solutions, such as EMediator and Vyou.com, require each client to download yet another plug-in in order to view the protected content. Wouldn't it be nice if the media could protect itself? With QuickTime, this isn't a fantasy.

Note No DRM solution is 100% secure. It seems that determined individuals can always find a way to gain access to the content. Given this, it's important to find a balance that provides reasonable copy protection but doesn't make enjoying the content difficult for the legitimate customer (not to mention infringe on their fair-use rights).

QuickTime's interactive abilities allow movies to be smart. They can determine if they are playing outside of their intended environment and simply refuse to work. In this chapter we'll explore a few ways to build DRM into your movies. In doing so, we'll also learn about some important movie-level properties and how to analyze movies in QuickTime Player.

DRM is also a motivating example of the versatility of interactive Quick-Time beyond the standard multimedia and user interface applications.

Pretend you are Sean Allen, the father of interactive QuickTime. You are an avid rock climber and have produced some artistic footage of your-self climbing up the side of a cliff. Say that there a few rogue rock climb-ing sites that are known to pirate video from other climbers and place it on their site as if it were one of their own guys making it up a 12c preci-pice. If you want to protect yourself, what do you do?

Open the project `Protected_Movie_start.lsd`. It starts out empty. Let's add Sean's climbing video as one of the tracks. The video should be located in the Local tab of the Library. It's called `ClimbingVideo.mov`. Pre-view the movie and make sure the video loads correctly. It should look like Figure 6.1.

The first step in protecting your movie is to copyright it. It used to be the case that you had to do things such as register and place a copyright notice on each piece of work. In 1989, these requirements were elimi-nated. Today, you don't have to do anything to copyright your original con-tent. It's protected by U.S. copyright laws as soon as you create it.

Note If you are interested to learn more about copyright laws, visit the Library of Congress: http://www.loc.gov/copyright/.

That being said, there are still good reasons to place a copyright notice on your movies. If nothing more, it will let people know who created the con-tent and when. Adding copyright notices and other annotations to a movie is simple.

Figure 6.1 Image from `ClimbingVideo.mov`. *Courtesy of Sean Allen.*

To add a copyright annotation to our current project, go into the document settings panel by choosing Document Settings from the Edit menu. You should see a tab for annotations (see Figure 6.2).

There are a couple dozen standard annotation fields. The one we'll fill out now is the Copyright field. The standard copyright format consists of the year and the name of the owner:

© 1997 Sean Allen

I usually like to fill out the Full Name, Description, and Author annotation fields as well. The Description is useful, especially since QuickTime tracks can be removed, altered, and distorted. The Full Name field is what will be displayed as the name of the movie when presented in QuickTime Player. As for the Author field, it's a good place to put your email address so that people know how to contact you.

If you export the movie and view it with QuickTime Player, you can view the copyright and description information by opening the movie's info panel (choose Show Movie Info from the Window menu). Notice how it is nicely displayed in a prominent fashion (see Figure 6.3).

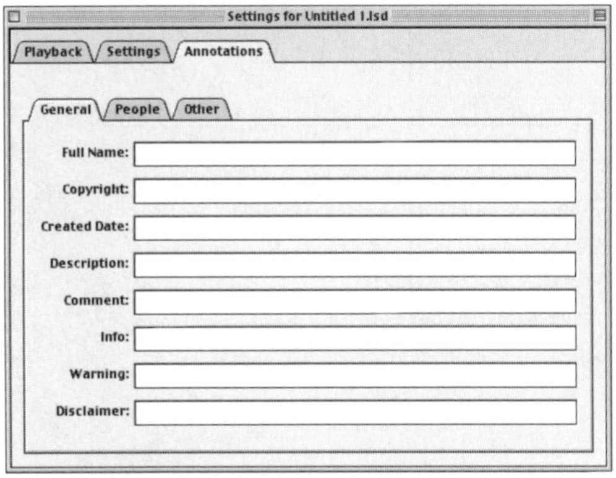

Figure 6.2 The Annotations tab.

Figure 6.3 The QuickTime Player info panel.

Now, this isn't going to stop anyone from ripping off your movie, but at least if someone gets their hands on it they'll know to whom the movie really belongs. That is, unless someone changes the movie's annotations! In the pro version of QuickTime Player, annotations can be added, edited, and deleted with ease. You simply open the movie's Properties window (choose Get Movie Properties from the Movie menu) and annotate away (see Figure 6.4). Luckily, there's a way to prevent people from editing your movie.

The second step in protecting your movie is to turn Copy Protect on (see Figure 6.5). It doesn't really prevent copying; it simply prevents the user from being able to edit and save the movie from the player or the plug-in. If someone tries to edit a copy-protected movie, it won't work and they'll get an error dialog like Figure 6.6.

You turn copy protection on in LSP's Document Settings panel. There's a checkbox under the Settings tab. With copy protection on, it'll be more

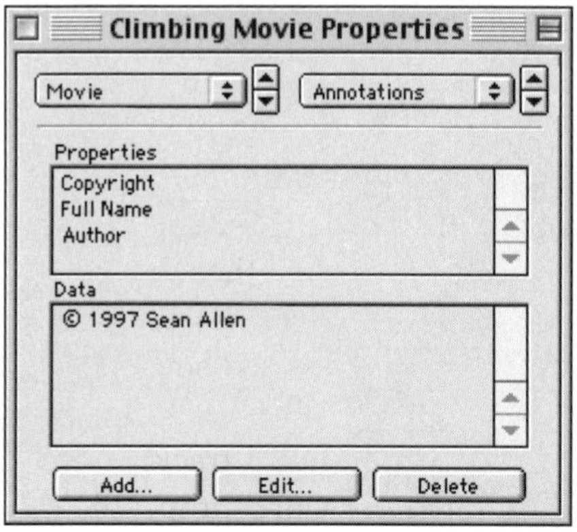

Figure 6.4 The QuickTime Pro Get Movie Properties window.

Figure 6.5 Turning Copy Protect on.

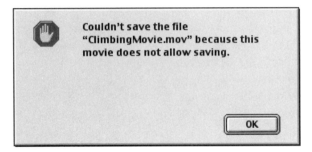

Figure 6.6 Error dialog.

likely that your copyright annotations will remain intact, but it isn't going to prevent other people from placing your content on their website. This is where QuickTime interactivity comes into play.

The third step that Sean must undergo to prevent his rivals from serving up his movie without permission involves adding an interactive sprite track. Sprite tracks are able to access information about their environment. One property that they have access to is the URL of the movie. What I've done is build a sprite track that checks to see if its URL is what it is supposed to be. If the URL isn't right, then the sprite track will disable all tracks and display a message saying the user doesn't have access privileges. I call this type of sprite track a DRM track. After reading a few more chapters in this book, you'll be able to author your own DRM tracks to behave in a custom manner, but you are free to use the one that I included on the CD (source project too). Let's see how to use it.

Drag in the movie DRM.mov from the local library. It should just cover the video on the stage. You should stretch the DRM track sample so it has the same duration as the video. In order to work properly, the DRM track needs to be the first track in the movie so it's the first track to be loaded by QuickTime. Right now the DRM track is number 2. You can determine this by looking at the index number just to the right of the track's name (under the ⊙ icon).

In order to reindex the tracks, we have to first tell LiveStage to arrange the tracks by index. To do that, click on the Track Order button at the bottom-left corner of the timeline and choose Load Order from the pop-up menu (see Figure 6.7). LiveStage will then sort the tracks by index. Now, if you drag the DRM track so it's the first track in the list, its index will change to 1 (see Figure 6.8). Now, when you preview the movie, it should look like Figure 6.9.

You can no longer view the video content in the movie since it is not playing from the correct URL. But what is the correct URL? Well, that's

Click here

Figure 6.7 The Track Order pop-up menu.

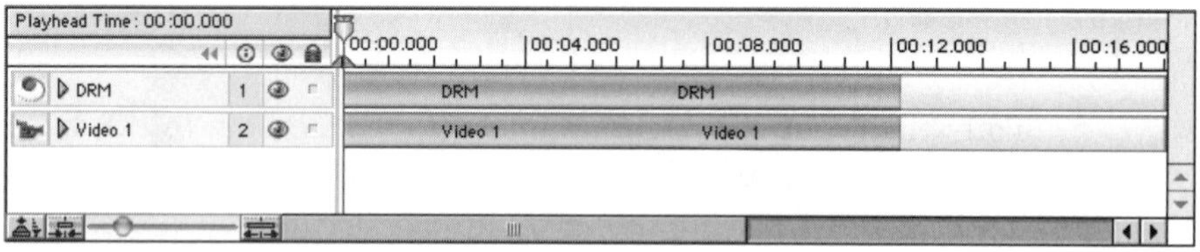

Figure 6.8 The timeline.

Figure 6.9 The DRM track movie.

something that you have to configure. Every time this movie is played the DRM track outputs the URL that it is currently playing from to the debugging window. You can open the debugging window by clicking on the button. When I run the movie, my debugging window looks like

`file:///PowerBook/Projects/Chapter08/ProtectedMovie.lsd_3.04.44_PM`

Yours will undoubtedly display something different. This is the URL of a temporary file that LSP generates when it previews a movie. To allow a URL to be acceptable to the DRM track, we need to place either a full URL or the start of the URL into the Host Computer annotation field for the movie. (The annotations can be set in the Document Settings panel). The DRM track looks at the Host Computer annotation to determine from where it is supposed to be hosted. If I wanted the movie to work from anywhere under my PowerBook hard drive, I can set the Host Computer annotation to

```
file:///PowerBook/
```

Try setting the Host Computer annotation to the equivalent for your computer and preview the movie. You should be able to view the video just fine now. This DRM track will work with movies composed of any type of QuickTime media, be it audio, VR, Flash, you name it. It's pretty robust too. Even if you know your way around the inner workings of QuickTime quite well, you'll still have a hard time viewing the content from a URL it doesn't accept. The full source project for this DRM track is included on the CD.

Sean now has a nice way to protect his video from pirate rock climbing sites. As a fourth measure, there are several server-side things he can do to prevent people from referencing the content on his site directly, but that's the topic of a different book.

▶ Explorations

1. If you are developing on the Mac and are making lots of movies, it is worth the time learning AppleScript. LiveStage and QuickTime Player are both AppleScriptable. With a simple script you can fill in a movie's annotations automatically. An example of such a script and more information about AppleScript and scripting LiveStage and QuickTime Player can be found at

   `http://www.totallyhip.com/lsdn/resources/applescripts/as_index.html`

2. Copyright law is continuously changing. Recently there was an amendment called the Digital Millennium Copyright Act (DMCA). It has interesting ramifications that some say infringe on fair-use rights. For more information see `http://www.eff.org/IP/DMCA/`.

3. What's all the commotion about Microsoft's Palladium? It's a proposed DRM solution to be integrated into the Windows OS, and many people don't like the consequences it might bring.

Adding DVD Features

The first consumer DVD players came out in 1996, and today they are so popular that several of the video rental stores around where I live only rent but a few VHS tapes anymore. Once you try DVD, linear cassette tapes are no longer acceptable. This is partially because DVDs have higher-quality picture and sound, but another important reason for their popularity is that they are interactive. My sister likes DVDs because certain releases will let you set it so you can hear the director's comments as you watch the movie. My wife likes them because you can turn subtitles on. Most DVDs that I've seen also let you change the language and access all sorts of other options. In essence, the user has a say in how the movie is presented.

With everyone watching DVDs, people are naturally going to expect more out of QuickTime movies. Most QuickTime movies on the Web today are still just audio and video tracks—the digital equivalent of VHS tapes. This is surprising because you can do much more with a QuickTime movie, in terms of interactivity, than you can with DVD. In this chapter we'll see how simple it is to add basic DVD features to any video.

Since I don't have the rights to use any actual DVD video, let's use a clip that Michael Shaff shot of a capybara at the zoo. Open the project DVDFeatures_start.lsd and drag in the video called Capybara.mov (see Figure 7.1).

Note Michael is *the* interactive QuickTime guru. A very clever and talented guy. If you have been working with wired media for any period of time, you have probably run across him either in person or online. His feedback and suggestions aided in the development of this book immensely. Check out his website at www.smallhands.com.

Figure 7.1 A screenshot from `Capybara.mov`.

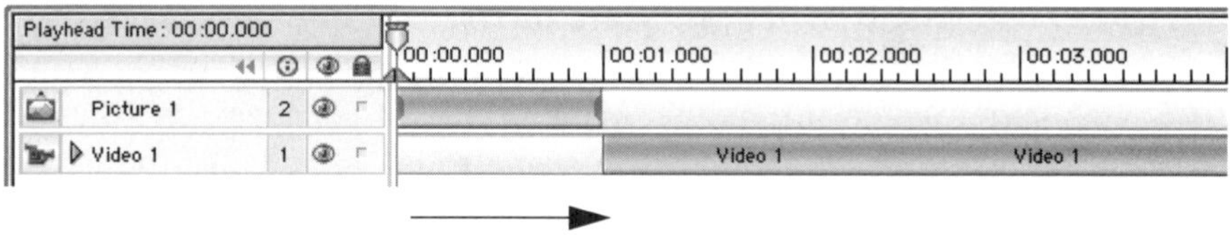

Figure 7.2 Video sample shifted in time.

The standard DVD format is to start the user off with a title page and a menu. To do this, drag the `TitlePicture.pict` file into the timeline (if you drag it onto the stage, you'll have to adjust its position, but if you drag it into the timeline, it'll be located at 0,0, which is where we want it). This will create a new picture track. We want that picture track to occur before the video starts. Right now it overlaps with the first second of the video. To fix this, we can simply shift the video forward in time a little bit using the track manipulation tool, ▐▊▊ (see Figure 7.2). Just drag the video sample to the right so the beginning lines up with the end of the picture sample. It should snap into place when it's approximately lined up.

To build a simple menu, we are going to add a text track to our movie. To do this, choose Create Track > Text from the Movie menu. This will place an empty white 1-second text track at the start of our movie. This is perfect because it is the same duration as our title page. We just need to make it visually a little smaller and line it up along the right side of the movie. We do this with the Resizing tool ⊞ . It should look like Figure 7.3.

Now let's enter the menu items. Double-click the text sample to open the text sample editor. The sample starts off named "Untitled." Let's change the name to "Menu." We'll talk more about the usefulness of sample names in a bit. In the big text area at the center of the editor, type in the following text:

```
Set Language
View Credits
Play Movie
```

These will be our DVD menu choices. There are two carriage returns between the lines. After it's all typed in, we can apply some text formatting. First let's make the font size a little bigger. Select all of the text, then set the size to 14 from the Font menu. Also set the color of the font to white.

Now that the font is white like the background, you obviously can't see the text anymore. But that's OK because we are going to set the background color to black. The background color of the text track is specified in the Layout tab. It's the color field at the bottom left, where it says Background Box (see Figure 7.4).

Now that we have the text looking the way we want it (see Figure 7.5), let's make it interactive. QuickTime allows you to make portions of text in a text track function like hyperlinks in html. LiveStage calls these links *hotspots.* Let's make the last menu item, Play Movie, into a hotspot. To do this, switch to the Text tab, choose Play Movie, then click the New HotSpot button. This will put a white box around that portion of text.

Figure 7.3 The positioned text track.

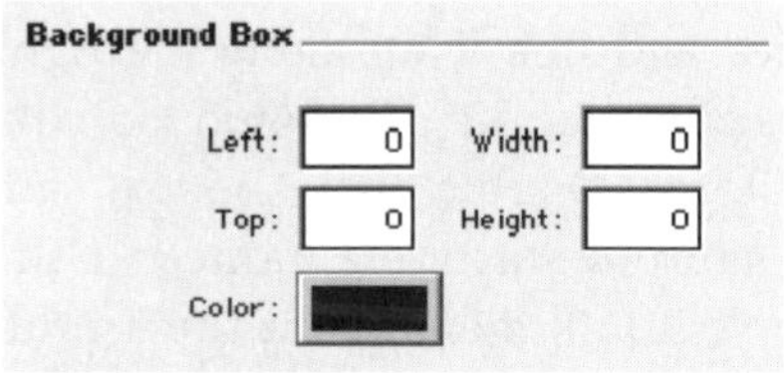

Figure 7.4 The Background Box with black color setting.

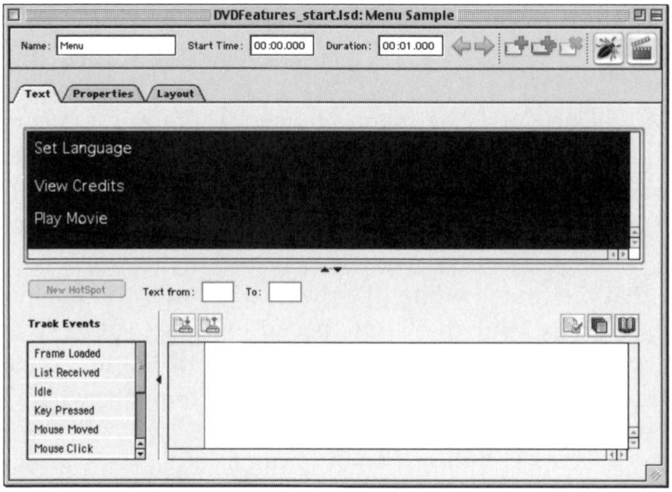

Figure 7.5 The background is now black for text.

Once the hotspot is defined, we specify what the hotspot does by attaching a script. This is going to be our first script of the book. Are you excited? Click inside of the Play Movie hotspot to select it. You'll know it's selected because the New HotSpot button will turn into a Delete HotSpot button and Track Events will turn into HotSpot Events (see Figure 7.6). One of the hotspot events is called Mouse Click. Choose the Mouse Click event and enter the following script into the script panel (see Figure 7.7):

```
[Mouse Click]
StartPlaying
```

Yes, it's that easy. This script tells the movie to start playing when you click the Play Movie hotspot. Preview the movie and try it out!

You might notice that after you click the hotspot, it starts playing immediately but it takes a second to reach the video content. This is because

Figure 7.6 Just after making a hotspot.

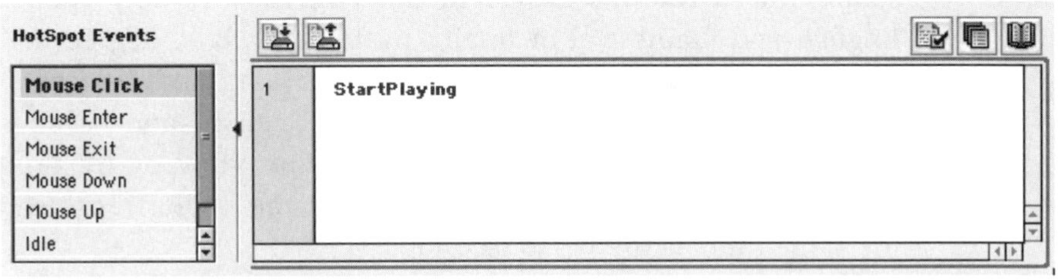

Figure 7.7 Attaching a script to a hotspot.

earlier we shifted the video track over by 1 second. We can easily add one more line to the script so that it jumps 1 second into the movie before it starts playing. Here's the new script:

```
[Mouse Click]
GoToTime(00:01.000)
StartPlaying
```

This will make the movie feel more responsive, an aspect very important for interactivity.

We hook up the View Credits menu item in a similar way. But before we do that, let's first add the credits media. From the library, drag Credits.mov into the timeline and shift it so it starts right when the video ends.

`Credits.mov` contains a sprite track that I built for this movie. It sports scrolling credits and a Menu button that takes you to the beginning of the movie.

Now we can turn View Credits into a hotspot that takes us to our Credits sample. Open the Menu text sample editor by double-clicking the text sample. Choose the text View Credits and click the New HotSpot button. For this hotspot, we'll add the following script to the Mouse Click event:

```
[Mouse Click]
GoToTime(SampleNamed("Credits").StartTime)
```

This looks like a complicated line of script, but it's actually very straightforward. It simply tells the movie to go to the start of the Credits sample. We could have entered in the timecode for the start of the Credits sample (00:07.100), but the above script is easier to read and much easier to maintain if we happen to change the duration of the video or shift the Credits sample for some reason.

The last DVD menu item to hook up is Set Language. Currently our movie doesn't have any sound at all. In the library, I've recorded two sound tracks for this movie in the two most widely spoken languages, English and Chinese. I'm finally putting my B.A. degree in Chinese language and literature to use! Drag `English.aiff` and `Chinese.aiff` into our movie's timeline and name the tracks "English" and "Chinese." You can change the names directly in the timeline view or by bringing up the Inspector window. Once renamed, offset the audio tracks so they start at the same time as the video (see Figure 7.8).

If we were to play the movie now, we would hear both audio tracks play at the same time. Having to listen to one is challenging enough. Let's have the movie default to English. To do this, simply disable the Chinese track. You can change the enabled state of any track by using the Inspector window (see Figure 7.9). Now we need a way for the user to specify

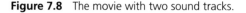

Figure 7.8   The movie with two sound tracks.

Figure 7.9 The External Track Inspector window.

which language's sound track they want enabled. We'll let the user choose the language by adding another menu.

For the language menu, let's create a new text track called "Language" and shift its sample to the very end of the movie. Using the track inspector, set the width and height of the Language track so it's the same dimensions as the rest of the movie: 317 × 237.

Open the text sample editor. Set the sample name to "Language" as well. In the text editor, add the following menu items (see Figure 7.10):

```
Choose a language:
English
Chinese
```

Go ahead and play with the font and color so that it looks good to you. You might want to add a few return characters to the top so the menu is vertically centered. You can also center-justify the text horizontally. (The justification settings are in the Properties tab under Formatting.)

Now, we're going to make "English" and "Chinese" both hotspots. Select the word "English" in the track sample editor and click the New HotSpot button. Add the following script to the Mouse Click event:

```
[Mouse Click]
TrackNamed("English").SetEnabled(TRUE)
TrackNamed("Chinese").SetEnabled(FALSE)
GoToTime(0)
```

What this does is enable the track named "English" and disable the track named "Chinese." Afterwards, the script sends the playhead to the begin-

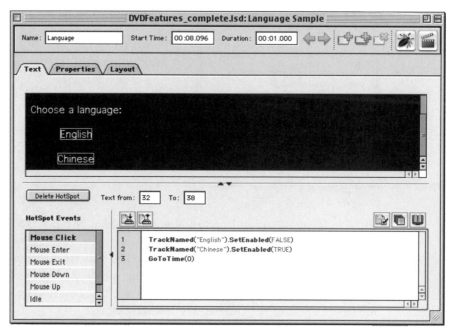

Figure 7.10 The script editor.

ning of the movie. This has the effect of switching the language from Chinese to English and then popping the user back to the main menu. Now let's implement the Chinese hotspot in the same way, but this time the Mouse Click script will be slightly different:

```
[Mouse Click]
TrackNamed("English").SetEnabled(FALSE)
TrackNamed("Chinese").SetEnabled(TRUE)
GoToTime(0)
```

We're almost done. All we need to do is go back to our main menu and set up the Choose Language menu item to link to the Language menu. You can probably guess by now what the Mouse Click script is going to look like:

```
[Mouse Click]
GoToTime(SampleNamed("Language").StartTime)
```

There you go! You've just created a sophisticated DVD-style interface for Michael Shaff's Capybara video. If you got stuck anywhere along the way,

you can always refer to the completed version of the project: DVDFeatures
_complete.lsd.

Armed with just the knowledge covered so far, you can go on to create most of the standard DVD features including subtitles, director's cuts, and even alternate endings. The cool thing is that we are just getting started. In the next part of the book, we'll dive into the world of sprite tracks and learn to create rich interactive experiences.

Explorations

1. Try adding a Full Screen item to the main menu. The script to make a movie go full screen is

   EnterFullScreen

   You can also exit full-screen mode by calling

   ExitFullScreen

2. Many DVDs have hidden features, often referred to as *Easter eggs*. Doing a search on Google with the words "DVD" and "Easter egg" should bring up many sites that list discovered Easter eggs. On the CD, I've included an image of Michael Shaff. Try adding the image as a picture track to the DVD-style movie we created in this chapter. Have it start off disabled only to become enabled when you do something special (such as a link in the menu).

Part **III**

Sprite Worlds

"Sprite" is an interesting word. It shares the same Latin origin as "spirit," and until recent years the word conjured up images of small magical creatures featured in Shakespearean plays and often associated with water (for example, rain sprites).

In the computer world, a sprite has come to mean an image that moves around a computer screen independently from other images. A sprite world is a software framework that keeps track of the properties of a population of sprites and usually provides support for the detection of events such as button presses and collisions.

The idea of a sprite world was born when Nolan Bushnell (who founded Atari in 1972) set off to build computerized versions of popular arcade games such as pinball and ping-pong. PONG, built around 1970, was his first success at this new type of game machine (historical note: Willy Higinbotham built a similar game on an oscilloscope in 1958, and Ralph Baer patented an electronic ball and paddle game in 1968). Like ping-pong, PONG featured a ball that you bounced around with two paddles, the major difference being that in ping-pong you bounced around an actual plastic ball, where in PONG you bounced around a sprite on a video display using sprite paddles.

PONG was called a "video game." Even though its graphics were far more primitive than other "video" content at the time, people were fascinated with it because it was interactive. The first coin-operated PONG machine was literally played to death and stuffed to the brim with quarters.

The original PONG was hardwired with computer chips. That meant you couldn't use the PONG sprite world to do anything else besides PONG. However, it didn't take long for a generic sprite world to be created to handle a wide range of interactive experiences. This way, new games could be developed without having to rebuild all of the circuitry for moving images around, detecting collisions, keeping score, and so on. Over the years, many such sprite worlds were developed, mostly as game machines and scripted animation environments, but they served other purposes as well. I should note that graphical user interfaces, as showcased by Apple's revolutionary Macintosh computer, are basically specialized sprite worlds.

In 1996 Apple did for QuickTime what Atari did for video. They made QuickTime interactive by creating an interactive sprite track. Compared to gaming engines, the QuickTime sprite track is a relatively basic sprite world. It doesn't come with built-in support for collision detection, motion primitives, and various features found in other engines. But this is partially by design. It is meant to be more general purpose and is sophisticated enough that these advanced features can be added by the developer. In this part we are going to enhance QuickTime's sprite world with standard video game features and techniques so that we can build rich, full-featured sprite worlds. As you will discover, these enhancements are not just for making games but are useful for a host of other applications.

A Simple World

We will start off by building a simple world of a ball bouncing around a room. As a tribute to PONG, we'll use a white square for the ball and a green background. And hey, why not throw in a rectangular paddle for fun. But before we start building, let's briefly examine how events work in a sprite track.

The sprite track is an event-based system. When notable things happen, an event gets triggered. Examples of notable things are "the mouse was clicked," "the mouse moved," and "a key was pressed." The sprite track allows you to attach instructions to an event in the form of a script. The script will be executed whenever that event occurs.

To simulate a ball moving across the screen we will utilize a very useful event called an *idle event* ("idle" ironically comes from the German word for "useless"). An idle event is traditionally an event that gets sent when the computer doesn't have anything else to do (hence the name "idle"), but in the sprite track, you can specify the maximum rate that you want these events to be sent (see Figure 8.1).

You set the rate of idle events by specifying the period of time to wait in between ticks (a tick is a 60th of a second), called the *idle delay.*

Note In the QuickTime literature, this value is often called the "idle frequency" even though it is technically a period of time (the inverse of frequency). In version 4 of LSP, they changed the name to "idle delay."

Setting a sprite track's idle delay to 60 ticks means an idle event will get triggered a maximum of one time per second. Setting the idle delay to 0 indicates QuickTime should trigger an idle event for the track as often as possible. You can also turn idle events off completely by setting the idle

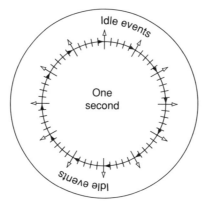

Figure 8.1 Specifying the idle rate delay.

delay to –1. I should warn you that the idle delay is an approximate value. Just because you specify an idle delay of *n* ticks doesn't mean that the next idle event will occur exactly *n* ticks after the previous one. Idle events can only be sent when the sprite track isn't busy, and thus accurate timing using the idle event is not always possible.

Have a look at the PONG_start.1sd document (Projects/Chapter08/PONG). This project has a single sprite track. Open the track inspector and determine what the idle delay is set to (see Figure 8.2). It should be set to 2, meaning idle events will be sent a maximum of 30 times a second.

Open the sprite sample editor by double-clicking the sample. You should find it has three images and three sprites. The first sprite functions as the background, the second functions as the ball, and the third, the paddle. Nothing has been scripted yet, so if you preview the movie, you'll only experience a couple of static white rectangles on the PONG background (see Figure 8.3). To make the ball move, we can simply change its position on each idle event.

In the last chapter, we learned how to add scripts to the events of text hotspots. Attaching scripts to sprite events is just as easy. Go to the Scripts tab under the Sprites panel (see Figure 8.4). The text field on the right is where we edit the scripts. Just to the left of that is a list of events, and to the very left of that is a list of sprites. Select the ball sprite, then select the Idle event, and then type in the following script:

```
[Idle]
MoveBy(10, 5)
```

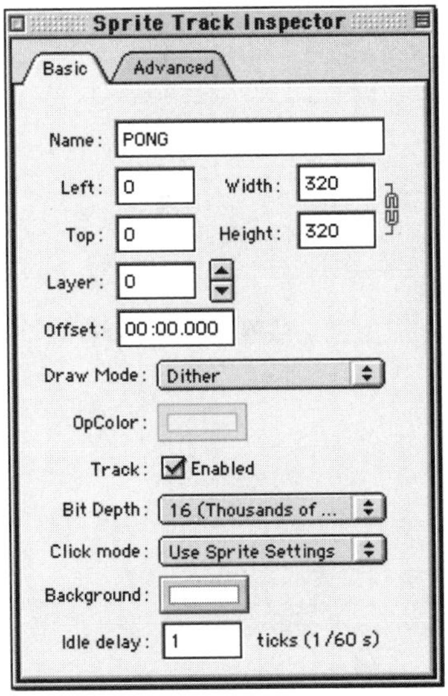

Figure 8.2 The Sprite Track Inspector window.

Figure 8.3 The start of PONG.

The MoveBy action moves the sprite by a specified amount in the x and y directions. In this case the ball will move by 10 pixels to the right and 5 pixels down the screen each idle event. Preview the movie and you'll see what I mean.

You should see the ball start at the top left and then roll off the bottom-right corner of the track. The 10 and the 5 in this case can be thought of as the velocity in the x and y directions: 10 pixels per idle to the right and 5 pixels per idle downwards. In order to change the velocity of the ball during runtime, we need to abstract these values into a sprite variable.

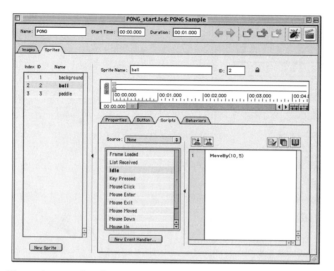

Figure 8.4 The sprite sample editor.

Note The way LiveStage's QScript uses QuickTime variables is similar to the way variables work in other scripting languages. In QScript, variables must be declared before they can be used. If they are used in more than one script, then they need to be declared in each script. Unlike C or Java, you don't have to declare a variable's type, but you do need to define its scope.

LiveStage has four different scopes in which variables can be defined. Variables in a script's local scope are only accessible from within the script. Variables in a sprite's scope can be accessed by all scripts on that sprite, but not by scripts on other sprites. The global scope is accessible by all scripts in the sprite sample. And finally there's the movie scope, which is accessible to all scripts in the movie. Movie variables can also be probed and modified by other movies. We'll discuss subtle characteristics of QScript variables as we run into them.

Variables need to be declared before they can be used in a script. Variables in the sprite's scope are declared with the SpriteVars keyword followed by a list of variable names. Let's use two variables named velocityX and velocityY instead of the constant values 10 and 5. Here's the new script:

```
[Idle]
SpriteVars velocityX, velocityY

MoveBy(velocityX, velocityY)
```

If you were to preview the movie at this stage, the ball wouldn't budge a bit. The reason is that QuickTime variables start off with a value equal to zero. Thus we need to initialize the variables to some value. The most common way to initialize variables is to set their value in the Frame Loaded event.

The Frame Loaded event gets triggered right after the sprite sample is loaded (see Figure 8.5). It's the first event to be sent to a sprite sample, which makes it a convenient location to initialize variables. Let's go ahead and script the Frame Loaded event of the ball sprite:

```
[Frame Loaded]
SpriteVars velocityX, velocityY

velocityX = 10
velocityY = 5
```

This should get our ball moving again. Functionally this produces a movie equivalent to the first, but the velocity is now a variable. Since it is a variable, we can change the direction and speed of the sprite while the movie is running, which is exactly what we want to do to simulate balls bouncing off walls.

From the geometry of physics we know that when a ball bounces off a vertical wall it reverses its horizontal velocity. Bounces off horizontal surfaces cause a reversal in the vertical velocity (see Figure 8.6). The component of velocity parallel to a surface remains unchanged. To restate this in the context of our sprite world, when the ball hits a vertical wall, we multiply the velocityX variable by –1, and when it hits a horizontal wall, we multiply velocityY by –1.

But how do we detect when the ball hits a vertical or horizontal wall? We do this by simply checking if the bounding edges of the sprite have touched or passed over any of the edges of the track. A good place to check

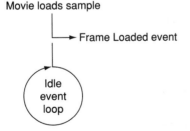

Figure 8.5 Sequence of events when a movie loads.

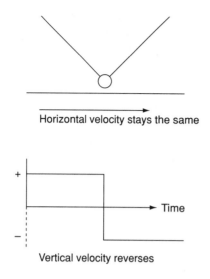

Horizontal velocity stays the same

Vertical velocity reverses

Figure 8.6 The geometry of a bouncing ball.

for this is right after we move the ball (meaning right after we perform the MoveBy() action). Here's the script:

```
[Idle]
SpriteVars velocityX, velocityY

MoveBy(velocityX, velocityY)

IF( BoundsLeft <= 0)
    velocityX = -velocityX
ELSEIF( BoundsRight >= TrackWidth)
    velocityX = -velocityX
ENDIF

IF( BoundsTop <= 0)
    velocityY = -velocityY
ELSEIF( BoundsBottom >= TrackHeight)
    velocityY = -velocityY
ENDIF
```

Place the above code in the sprite's idle event script and see if it works. The ball should now bounce off the edges of the track.

Since seeing a new scripting language can be confusing at first, let me translate the previous code into plain English:

"Start off by moving the sprite to the right velocityX pixels and down velocityY pixels. If the left edge of the sprite's bounds is less than or equal to 0, reverse velocityX. Otherwise if the right edge of the sprite's bounds is greater than or equal to the width of the track, you should also reverse velocityX. Next consider the top and bottom of the sprite. If the bottom edge is less than or equal to 0, reverse the velocityY variable. Otherwise if the bottom edge is touching or past the bottom of the track, you should also reverse velocityY."

For the rest of the book, I'll assume a basic understanding of the QScript language.

Note Refer to the QScript Reference and the LiveStage manual if you need more help understanding QScript.

We've created a sprite world of a ball bouncing in a room. It's an approximation of what a real physical ball might do (without gravity). However, I see one simple enhancement that would make it more physically accurate. Since we are moving the ball by several pixels at a time, it is very likely that we won't detect the collision with the wall until after the ball has already passed the edge of the track. Since real balls move continuously and don't normally pass through walls, we need to move the ball to where it would have been had we been able to detect the collision when the ball first touched the edge. This position correction is sometimes called a *nudge* (see Figure 8.7).

To accomplish the appropriate nudge, we need to measure the distance of the ball from the edge of the track and then move the ball so that it's the same distance away but on the opposite side of the edge. As shown in

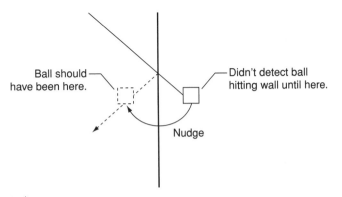

Figure 8.7 Nudge.

Figure 8.7, this is equivalent to moving the ball by twice the distance from the edge of the ball to the edge of the track. Here's our script with the nudge code in place:

```
[Idle]
SpriteVars velocityX, velocityY
LocalVars distanceToEdge

MoveBy(velocityX, velocityY)

IF( BoundsLeft <= 0)
    velocityX = -velocityX
    distanceToEdge = -BoundsLeft
    MoveBy(2*distanceToEdge, 0)
ELSEIF( BoundsRight >= TrackWidth)
    velocityX = -velocityX
    distanceToEdge = TrackWidth - BoundsRight
    MoveBy(2*distanceToEdge, 0)
ENDIF

IF( BoundsTop <= 0)
    velocityY = -velocityY
    distanceToEdge = -BoundsTop
    MoveBy(0, 2*distanceToEdge)
ELSEIF( BoundsBottom >= TrackHeight)
    velocityY = -velocityY
    distanceToEdge = TrackHeight - BoundsBottom
    MoveBy(0, 2*distanceToEdge)
ENDIF
```

Run it and see how it works!

Notice that the background image has red "walls" on all of its edges except the bottom. This was done intentionally so we could evolve it into a one-person PONG game. Let's activate that paddle sitting down there at the bottom. We need to change our collision detection to test for collisions with the paddle instead of with the bottom edge of the track.

We'll use a very simple and straightforward method to move the paddle to the horizontal location of the mouse cursor. The idea is to align the paddle with the horizontal position of the mouse. We'll do this by using a MoveTo(x, y) action, which moves the origin of the sprite to the specified x, y location.

To make it easier to deal with, I've placed the origin of the paddle at its bottom and halfway between its left and right edge. This simplifies aligning it along the bottom of the track and horizontally centered with the mouse.

Note The origin of a sprite depends on the registration point of its image. The registration point of the paddle image is shown in Figure 8.8.

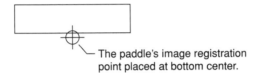

The paddle's image registration
point placed at bottom center.

Figure 8.8 The paddle origin.

Taking advantage of our strategically located origin, we can position the paddle with the following script:

`[Idle]`

MoveTo(MouseHorizontal, TrackHeight)

Add this script to the paddle's idle event and try it out.

It's getting close. The paddle doesn't interact with the ball yet, but at least we can control it. To get it to hit the ball, we just need to change the collision detection script to check for the top of the paddle rather than the bottom of the track.

The idle script on the ball sprite can access BoundsTop (see Figure 8.9) of the paddle sprite by targeting the paddle by name:

SpriteNamed("paddle").BoundsTop

Just because the vertical position of the ball overlaps the BoundsTop of the paddle, this doesn't necessarily imply the ball is touching the paddle. We need to take into account the horizontal position of the ball relative to the paddle as well. For instance, if the horizontal distance between the ball and the center of the paddle is less than half a paddle away, then we know the two objects are touching (see Figure 8.10).

How do we measure the horizontal distance from the center of the ball to the center of the paddle? We can start by determining the middle location of each sprite. The following formula will return the center position for a given sprite (see Appendix F for useful sprite geometry routines):

```
CenterOfSprite = (BoundsLeft + BoundsRight)/2
```

Therefore, the horizontal distance between the ball and paddle is

```
centerOfBall = (SpriteNamed("ball").BoundsLeft + \
  SpriteNamed("ball").BoundsRight)/2
centerOfPaddle = (SpriteNamed("paddle").BoundsLeft + \
  SpriteNamed("paddle").BoundsRight)/2
distanceBetween = centerOfBall - centerOfPaddle
```

Note In this book, some lines of script will be wrapped to fit on the page. When this happens, the wrap will be indicated with a "\" character.

This calculation will work fine, but we can simplify it in a couple of ways. The first way is to assume the center of the paddle is located at MouseHorizontal. That's where the paddle is supposed to be, but it only actually moves there when it gets an idle event. By assuming the paddle is always centered at MouseHorizontal, we can effectively allow the user to

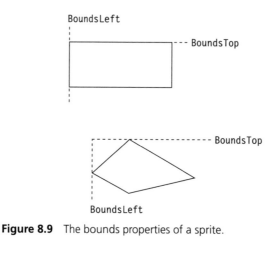

Figure 8.9 The bounds properties of a sprite.

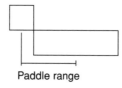

Figure 8.10 Just touching.

position the paddle in between idle events. This is because the MouseHorizontal value is updated very quickly, whereas idle events are sent relatively slowly. Therefore, assuming the paddle is located at MouseHorizontal will boost the performance of our controls. Don't forget, video game players hate nothing more than sluggish and inaccurate controls.

Another simplification is to realize that the script is attached to the ball sprite, so we don't need to use the SpriteNamed("ball") target. The sprite the script is attached to is the default target (except for Frame Loaded events where all targets need to be explicit!).

With these simplifications, we end up with the following script:

```
centerOfBall = (BoundsLeft + BoundsRight)/2
distanceToPaddle = centerOfBall - MouseHorizontal
```

When distanceToPaddle is within a certain range, it means the ball is horizontally overlapping the paddle. As shown in Figure 8.10, that range is half the width of the paddle plus half the width of the ball. We'll call this value the paddleRange. Since the ball and paddle don't change size, we only need to calculate it once. Let's add that calculation to the Frame Loaded event of the ball:

```
[Frame Loaded]
SpriteVars velocityX, velocityY, paddleRange
LocalVars ballWidth, paddleWidth

velocityX = 10
velocityY = 5

ballWidth = SpriteNamed("ball").BoundsRight - \
    SpriteNamed("ball").BoundsLeft
paddleWidth = SpriteNamed("paddle").BoundsRight - \
    SpriteNamed("paddle").BoundsLeft

paddleRange = ballWidth/2 + paddleWidth/2
```

Here's what we've been waiting for, the ball's idle script with paddle detection:

```
[Idle]
SpriteVars velocityX, velocityY, paddleRange
LocalVars distanceToEdge, centerOfBall, distanceToPaddle

MoveBy(velocityX, velocityY)
```

```
IF( BoundsLeft <= 0)
    velocityX = -velocityX
    distanceToEdge = BoundsLeft
    MoveBy(2*distanceToEdge, 0)
ELSEIF( BoundsRight >= TrackWidth)
    velocityX = -velocityX
    distanceToEdge = TrackWidth - BoundsRight
    MoveBy(2*distanceToEdge, 0)
ENDIF

IF( BoundsTop <= 0)
    velocityY = -velocityY
    distanceToEdge = BoundsTop
    MoveBy(0, 2*distanceToEdge)
ELSEIF( BoundsBottom >=  SpriteNamed("paddle").BoundsTop)
    velocityY = -velocityY
    centerOfBall = (BoundsLeft + BoundsRight)/2
    distanceToPaddle = centerOfBall - MouseHorizontal
    IF( ABS(distanceToPaddle) < paddleRange)
        distanceToEdge = SpriteNamed("paddle").BoundsTop - BoundsTop
        MoveBy(0, 2*distanceFromEdge)
    ELSE
        SetIdleDelay(-1) //Game Over
    ENDIF
ENDIF
```

Note Here I used SetIdleDelay(-1) to stop the game. At the beginning of the chapter we said that an idle delay of −1 means to not send idle events. The is a way of stopping time in a sprite world.

Note The ABS function returns the absolute magnitude of a value. In other words, it drops negative signs from numbers.

Note The double slash in *"//Game Over"* designates a comment.

What are you waiting for? Preview the movie and try it out.

It works well. The ball bounces off the paddle when it hits. When it misses, time freezes and the game is over. Besides having to close and reload the movie to restart the game, do you see anything else that makes this not such a fun game?

Here's one. There's no way to make the ball go in any direction except for 10 pixels per idle in the *y* direction and 5 pixels per idle in the *x* direction! Makes the game pretty boring. The original PONG gave the user control over the ball's direction. When the ball hit the right side of the paddle it bounced to the right. When it hit the left side, it bounced to the left. When it hit directly in the center it bounced directly up. We can implement a similar scheme by making velocityX a percentage of distanceToPaddle—40% works pretty well. We just need to add a line to our IF statement:

```
...
IF( ABS(distanceToPaddle) < paddleRange)
    distanceToEdge = SpriteNamed("paddle").BoundsTop - BoundsTop
    MoveBy(0, 2*distanceFromEdge)
    velocityX = 0.40 * distanceToPaddle
ELSE
...
```

When you preview the movie, see if you can get the ball to move in different directions. It's starting to resemble the original game.

Now that the user has more control over the ball, let's provide a way of restarting the game without having to reload the movie. An extremely simple way of doing this is to simply turn the idle event on again. For now, let's make clicking the ball do this:

```
[Mouse Click]

SetIdleDelay(2)
```

This completes our simple PONG sprite world. There is obviously a lot that can be done to make it resemble a more professional game, but the main engine is there. This PONG game touched upon many of the major concepts we will discuss in this part of the book, including collision detection, scripted motion, and modeling physics. But before we develop these concepts further, let's spend the next chapter gaining some fluency talking with sprites.

 Explorations

1. Most video games have the concept of multiple "lives," which allow the player to make a certain number of mistakes before the game ends. How would you add this concept to the PONG game? Try adding the

necessary scripts to give the player three lives before the game ends. When the game ends, you might hide the ball so the user can't click it. Some sort of graphical display that the game is over would help. You might even add graphics to indicate the number of lives left.

2. Most gamers thrive on a challenge. If a game is too easy, it isn't fun. Explore incrementing the vertical velocity (velocityY) over time so that the ball goes slightly faster with each bounce against the paddle.

3. Even though neo-vintage might be in fashion, you must admit that PONG could really use a face-lift. It's also in store for some more interesting rules and interactivity. As a thought exercise, what would it take to make PONG as interesting to a modern audience as it was back in 1970?

Talking with Sprites

In the previous chapter, we jumped right in, started manipulating sprites, writing code, and even managed to build a working PONG game! In this chapter, let's take the time to get acquainted with the locals. Say hello to the sprites.

▶ Targets

Have you ever tried to have a conversation with a teenager who didn't really want to talk, but would answer your questions? The conversation might go something like the following:

You: "Hi! What's your name?"

Billy: "Billy."

You: "Do you go to school?"

Billy: "Yea."

You: "I build interactive movies."

Billy: [silence]

You: "So, do you like school?"

Billy: "No."

. . .

It's a similar experience talking to sprites. They answer your questions, but don't really initiate conversation themselves—not unless you program them to, that is. In order to talk to a particular sprite, you need to direct your questions to that sprite.

When I was talking to Billy, Billy knew I was talking to him because I was standing right next to him. If I wanted to talk to someone farther away, I'd have to be more explicit, like "Hey Steve, how tall are you?" It's similar for sprites. If we put some code on the `Idle` event of a particular sprite, that sprite will respond without having to explicitly identify it. All other sprites need to be named or identified in some way. The QuickTime jargon for this is *targeting* (see Figure 9.1).

We can target sprites in several ways: by name, by index, by ID. We can also target the sprite that the event is on implicitly (by not using a target at all). Here are some example targets:

1. **SpriteNamed**("ball")
2. **SpriteOfIndex**(1)
3. **SpriteOfID**(5)
4. **ThisSprite**

Note Example 4 and implicit sprite targets won't work in Frame Loaded events. `SpriteNamed` can only take constant values.

Fred

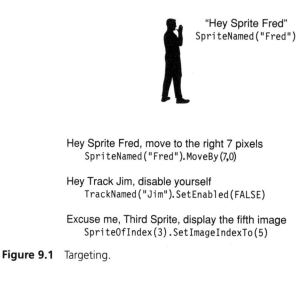

"Hey Sprite Fred"
SpriteNamed("Fred")

Hey Sprite Fred, move to the right 7 pixels
SpriteNamed("Fred").MoveBy(7,0)

Hey Track Jim, disable yourself
TrackNamed("Jim").SetEnabled(FALSE)

Excuse me, Third Sprite, display the fifth image
SpriteOfIndex(3).SetImageIndexTo(5)

Figure 9.1 Targeting.

Properties

The most common way of asking a sprite a question is by checking one of its 20 properties:

```
BoundsBottom
BoundsLeft
BoundsRight
BoundsTop
FirstCornerX
FirstCornerY
SecondCornerX
SecondCornerY
ThirdCornerX
ThirdCornerY
FourthCornerX
FourthCornerY
GetName, GetSpriteName (these are equivalent)
ID
ImageIndex
ImageRegistrationPointX
ImageRegistrationPointY
Index
IsVisible
Layer
```

The names of the properties should give you a good indication of what they refer to. Let's look at a few of them. ImageIndex is an interesting example. If I want to know what image a sprite is currently displaying, I can ask for its ImageIndex property. For example:

SpriteNamed("ball")**.ImageIndex**

If the sprite named "ball" was currently showing the third image in the sprite sample, the above code would evaluate to the number 3.

IsVisible is another property that looks pretty useful. It sounds like it should tell you if we are currently able to see the sprite on the computer screen, like asking if an actor is visible on the stage or not. But that would be something more like InView. The IsVisible property tells you if it is *able* to be viewed. If IsVisible is FALSE, then we definitely can't see the sprite because QuickTime simply won't draw its pixels to the screen. But, if IsVisible returns TRUE, there are many reasons why we might not actually be able to see it. For example, the sprite might be off the track or might be behind another sprite. Maybe the sprite's image is completely transparent, or maybe the sprite is too small to see. The words we use when coding sprites have very specific meanings that may be different from your initial expectations. That's why it's best to explore a little. Don't worry, pretty soon you'll be fluent.

The best way to practice talking with sprites is to actually write some QScript. Open the DebugStr_demo.lsd project in the Projects/Chapter09/ DebugStr/ directory on the CD. This project utilizes an output technique called *debug strings*. QuickTime has the ability to send debug strings to the application that is playing the movie. It's up to the application to decide what to do with these debug strings, and many applications simply ignore them.

Note Debug strings get their name from programmers who use them to output messages indicating what is going on in a project in order to debug it.

LiveStage Pro has a useful debugging console to display all debug strings. You can open this console from the Window menu by clicking the button.

Preview the movie and open the Debugging Console (see Figure 9.2). Click on the Test button and see what gets sent to the console. You should see the words "Hello World" appear. This appears because the Mouse Click script on the testButton sprite is sending that as a debug string:

```
[Mouse Click]
DebugStr( "Hello World" )
```

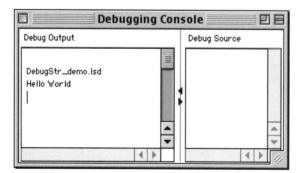

Figure 9.2 The Debugging Console.

Let's replace "Hello World" with a `GetName` property reference:

```
[Mouse Click]
DebugStr(GetName)
```

Close the old movie and preview this new movie. Click the Test button, and you should see the word "testButton" appear in the Debugging Console. This is because we are executing code attached to the sprite named "testButton." This is an example of an implicit target.

Let's try an explicit target. Replace `GetName` with `SpriteOfIndex(1)`
`.GetName`. Now when we preview the movie and click on the Test button, it should output "Arrow" to the console. That's the name of the first sprite in our sample. Try putting some other targets and properties in `DebugStr()` and get a feel for how they work.

▶ Actions

As we've all been told by our parents, communication is a two-way street. Information needs to flow in both directions (see Figure 9.3). We just learned a way to extract information from a sprite, but we need to know how to supply information as well. Telling a sprite to do something is one way of supplying information. We tell sprites to do things through actions (often called "wired actions"). In the PONG game, we used several actions, such as `MoveBy` and `MoveTo`, which both reposition a sprite visually.

Sprites understand the following 17 actions:

```
ClickOnCodec(x, y)
ExecuteEvent(eventID)
PassMouseToCodec
MoveBy(x, y)
MoveTo(x, y)
ResetMatrix
Rotate(Angle)
Scale(x, y)
Stretch(x1, y1, x2, y2, x3, y3, x4, y4)
SetGraphicsModeBy(mode, red, green, blue)
SetGraphicsModeTo(mode, red, green, blue)
SetImageIndexBy(index)
SetImageIndexTo(index)
SetLayerBy(layer)
SetLayerTo(layer)
```

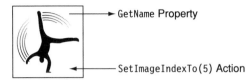

Figure 9.3 Properties versus actions: one goes in, one goes out.

```
SetVisible(boolean)
ToggleVisible
```

Most actions take parameters, but a few of them, such as `ToggleVisible`, don't take any. Let's try some of these actions. We'll use the same `DebugStr_demo.lsd` project and replace the `DebugStr` line with

```
[Mouse Click]
SpriteNamed("Arrow").ToggleVisible
```

Now when you click on the Test button, the arrow should toggle between being visible and being invisible. Let's try another action:

```
[Mouse Click]
SpriteNamed("Arrow").Rotate(15)
```

This rotates the arrow by 15 degrees each time you click on the button. Notice that the sprite rotates around the tip of the arrow. This is because I've positioned the image registration point at the tip of the arrow image (see Figure 9.4).

Note   As stated in the last chapter, the registration point is the spot on an image that defines the origin. By default it's the 0, 0 point on the image (the top-left corner). Sprites rotate and scale about their origin. You can define the image registration point of each image by going into the Image tab of the sprite sample editor and entering values for the *x*

Figure 9.4 The registration point for the arrow image.

and *y* fields. The properties `ImageRegistrationPointX` and `ImageRegistrationPointY` simply reflect the numbers that you entered for the sprite's current image. We'll talk more about image registration points in Chapter 11.

▶ Custom Actions

Notice that some actions have both a To and a By version, such as `MoveTo` and `MoveBy`. Other actions have only one version. We don't have a `RotateTo` and a `RotateBy`, just a `Rotate`. The `Rotate` action in this case is really a `RotateBy` action because it adds the value you pass in to the current rotation. How do we rotate our arrow to a particular angle without a `RotateTo` action? To do this, we need to make our own custom action, which is our next topic.

QuickTime allows us to add custom events to a sprite or, more precisely, custom event handlers (scripts that handle events). When you make a custom event handler, you associate it with an ID (a positive integer number). The event handler can then be triggered by using `Execute Event(ID)`. We can also associate a name with an event, allowing us to use the syntax `ExecuteEvent($EventName)`.

Note   The dollar sign indicates that we are referencing what programming languages call a define, or a definition. Definitions don't have anything to do with QuickTime. They are just a convenience that LiveStage provides so you can type in the name of a value instead of the value itself. When LiveStage builds the movie it replaces all of the definition names with their actual values (see Figure 9.5).

You can create a new definition by using the syntax

`#define` name = value

For example, if a script required us to convert miles to kilometers multiple times, it can be inconvenient to have to specify the conversion factor each time. A better way is to

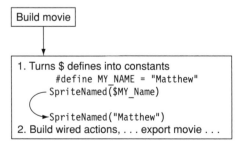

Figure 9.5   How LiveStage processes defines in a project.

create a definition called mi2km and then use that value in our script by using the name with a dollar sign in front of it:

```
#define mi2km = 1.6093

distanceAroundEarth = $mi2km * 24900
```

Definitions created in the script this way are only accessible from within the script. You can also make global definitions that are accessible from all scripts by creating definitions in the Defines window (choose Document Defines from the Edit menu).

LiveStage automatically makes a set of definitions for us. LSP makes definitions for all of the images where the define name is the name of the image, and the value is the index of the image. This allows us to make scripts more readable, such as SetImage-IndexTo($Snowman) instead of SetImageIndexTo(37). If the name of the definition contains spaces or punctuation, then quotes are needed, for example, SetImage-IndexTo($"my big picture.gif"). LiveStage makes similar definitions for the names and IDs of custom event handlers.

Another important LSP-created definition is $ThisSpriteID, which is useful for accessing the current sprite's ID when in a Frame Loaded event. Remember, Frame Loaded scripts can't use implicit targeting. Even ThisSprite doesn't work in Frame Loaded events, so the best way to access the sprite that the Frame Loaded event script is on is by using SpriteOfID($ThisSpriteID).

For an example of a custom action, open the Rotation_start.lsd project. Before we get into the code, let's first preview the movie and see what it currently does.

You should see the same red arrow as before, but now there are two Test buttons: Test and Test2. When you click the Test button, it rotates the arrow by 10 degrees each time. Clicking the Test2 button should pop the arrow back to vertical.

What I've done here is implement a ResetRotation action. I implemented it by adding a custom event named ResetRotation with an ID of 10 (this number is arbitrary). I then typed in the following script:

```
[10 ResetRotation]
LocalVars currentAngle

currentAngle = ArcTan2(SecondCornerY - FirstCornerY, \
  SecondCornerX - FirstCornerX)
currentAngle = RadiansToDegrees(currentAngle)
Rotate(-currentAngle)
```

The script for the ResetRotation action is straightforward. First we find the current rotation using a formula obtained from Appendix F. This formula returns the angle in radians. We convert it to degrees using the RadiansToDegrees function. Then we rotate the sprite by the negative of that angle to get it back to zero.

The ResetRotation custom action is called in the Mouse Click script of the test2Button sprite:

```
[Mouse Click]
SpriteNamed("arrow").ExecuteEvent($ResetRotation)
```

I'd like to reemphasize that the ExecuteEvent action takes a number. $ResetRotation is just a placeholder for the number 10. I could have used ExecuteEvent(10), but you must admit that $ResetRotation is much more informative to someone reading the code. Plus, it allows me to modify the event ID without having to change all of the scripts that refer to it.

This custom ResetRotation action acts like one of those actions that don't take any parameters. It's also possible to create custom actions that do take parameters.

Let's now make a RotateTo action that takes an angle as a parameter. We do this by first defining a new custom event handler on the arrow sprite called RotateTo. Choose "arrow" from the sprite list, then click on the New Event Handler... button. This should bring up a dialog window as shown in Figure 9.6. Enter RotateTo for the name and 11 for the ID.

We also need an angle parameter, which in the current version of Live-Stage must be implemented through variables. Let's define a global variable to act as our angle parameter. We'll call it NewAngle. Here's the script for the RotateTo event handler:

```
[11 RotateTo]
GlobalVars NewAngle

ExecuteEvent($ResetRotation)
Rotate(NewAngle)
```

Figure 9.6 Custom event dialog window.

This works by first resetting the sprite's rotation and then rotating it by the NewAngle variable. Calling this RotateTo custom action is easy. We simply set the NewAngle variable, then execute $RotateTo. It's primitive, but it works.

Let's try it by replacing the Mouse Click script on test2Button with

GlobalVars NewAngle

```
NewAngle = 180
SpriteNamed("arrow").ExecuteEvent($RotateTo)
```

Preview the movie and notice that the Test2 button will now rotate the arrow to 180 (pointing directly down).

Custom Properties

That's how custom actions are created. Custom properties can be made in a similar way using a global variable to return the property value.

Let's make a rotation property on the arrow sprite. Add a new event handler named GetRotation. The ID doesn't matter, but I like to go in order, so use 12. And here's the script:

```
[12 GetRotation]
GlobalVars TheRotation

TheRotation = ArcTan2(SecondCornerY - FirstCornerY, \
  SecondCornerX - FirstCornerX)
TheRotation = RadiansToDegrees(TheRotation)
```

This calculates the sprite's rotation angle using the same formula as the ResetRotation script. To test it, let's have the testButton sprite not only rotate the arrow by 10 degrees but also send the arrow's current rotation to the Debugging Console. Here's the Mouse Click event for the testButton sprite:

```
[Mouse Click]
GlobalVars TheRotation

SpriteNamed("arrow").ExecuteEvent($GetRotation)
DebugStr(TheRotation)
SpriteNamed("arrow").Rotate(10)
```

This time when you preview the movie, click on the Test button several times. You should expect to see 0, 10, 20, 30, and so on get sent to the

Debugging Console before each rotational jump of 10 degrees. But actually what you will see is something slightly different:

```
0
10.000
19.999
29.999
39.999
...
```

The numbers are ever so slightly off. This happens due to a phenomenon called *roundoff error.*

Note For most applications, these small errors won't make a difference, but it's crucial to know that the errors exist. For instance, you shouldn't have a script that waits for the arrow's rotation to equal exactly 30. Instead, you should allow for some roundoff errors such as

```
IF( TheRotation > 29 AND TheRotation < 31 )
  ...
ENDIF
```

To learn more about roundoff errors and how to deal with them, refer to Appendix E.

▶ Rotation Behavior

You might be asking yourself, "So, does that mean I have to type these scripts in each time I want a RotateTo action or a GetRotation property?" The answer is no. LiveStage provides a mechanism for easily adding groups of scripts to a sprite. We've used this mechanism before. It's called a behavior. A behavior is simply an external text file with all of the scripts in it.

I've included a behavior in the project with the above rotation actions. It's located in the Library folder Projects/Chapter09/Rotation/Library/Rotation.lsb. Let's briefly look at the contents of that behavior:

```
[Name]
Rotation Behavior

[Description]
Adds ResetRotation, RotateTo, and GetRotation actions.
RotateTo uses a GlobalVar named NewAngle.
GetRotation uses a GlobalVar named TheRotation.
```

```
[200060 ResetRotation]
LocalVars currentAngleMP
currentAngleMP = ArcTan2(SecondCornerY - FirstCornerY, \
   SecondCornerX - FirstCornerX)
currentAngleMP = RadiansToDegrees(currentAngleMP)
Rotate(-currentAngleMP)

[200061 RotateTo]
GlobalVars NewAngle
ExecuteEvent($ResetRotation)
Rotate(NewAngle)

[200062 GetRotation]
GlobalVars TheRotation
TheRotation =  RadiansToDegrees(ArcTan2(SecondCornerY - \
   FirstCornerY, SecondCornerX - FirstCornerX))
```

There are a couple of things I'd like you to notice about this behavior. The first thing is that I've changed the ID of each event to a much larger number. This is because numbers like 10 are very common and would increase our behavior's chances of causing a conflict. Reusable behaviors developed in this book will use IDs in the range 200000 to 200100. This range was assigned to me by Totally Hip (the creators of LiveStage Pro). No one else is supposed to use event IDs in this range. (Don't even think about it!)

Also notice that I appended an MP to the end of the currentAngle variable name. This is done for a similar reason—to prevent naming conflicts. LiveStage doesn't let you have a local variable by the same name as a global variable. So just in case someone wants to use this behavior and have a global variable named currentAngle, I usually append my initials after local variable names. Nothing special is done to global variable names because these are meant to be accessible outside of the behavior and need to be easy for people to remember and use.

There are two _complete.lsd versions of the Rotation project. They both function in the same way, but Rotation_complete2.lsd uses the Rotation behavior and the other one doesn't. The Rotation.lsb behavior was added by dragging it into the arrow's Behaviors tab from the Library.

Before I end this chapter, I'd like to talk a little about accessing custom properties on multiple objects during the same script. Say you wanted to do a calculation that used the Rotation property of two objects, for example, to calculate the time from two sprites representing hour and minute hands on a clock. Calling ExecuteEvent($GetRotation) on the first sprite will place its rotation in the GlobalVar TheRotation. Calling Execute-Event($GetRotation) on the second sprite will also place its rotation there. Does this mean we can't do calculations that require two rotation angles? No. All we need to do is save the first value of Rotation in a different variable before it gets overwritten by the second value. Saving a value like this is called *caching* (from the French word meaning "to hide something"). Here's an example script that finds the sum of two rotation properties:

```
GlobalVars TheRotation
LocalVars cachedRotation, theSum

SpriteNamed("one").ExecuteEvent($GetRotation)
cachedRotation = Rotation
SpriteNamed("two").ExecuteEvent($GetRotation)

theSum = cachedRotation + Rotation
```

▶ Explorations

1. In this chapter we learned how to add custom actions and properties to sprites. List one or two properties and actions that would be useful additions. How might you go about implementing them?

2. Custom properties don't have to deal with the geometry of a sprite. Say you had sprites in a movie that represented products in a store. How would you add a price property to these sprites?

3. Sprites aren't the only things we can talk to. Tracks and movies have properties and actions too. Different track types have unique sets of properties and actions. Take a moment to explore the QScript reference window in LiveStage Pro and see what's available. A full list of actions and properties is also available in Appendix M.

4. The following script looks like it would make a sprite rotate by 10 degrees when the movie loads:

```
[Frame Loaded]
```

```
Rotate(10)
```

But this script doesn't result in anything happening. Why? (Hint: it's in a Frame Loaded event.)

Collision Detection

As we discovered in the last chapter, custom events can be used to add actions and properties to sprites. The original purpose of events, however, was to signify that something important happened to a sprite. A Mouse Click event tells a sprite that it was the target of a mouse click. An Idle event tells a sprite that a certain amount of time has passed since the last Idle event. In this chapter we're going to add a new event that tells a sprite when it has come into contact with another sprite. This type of event is called a *collision*.

A collision in a sprite world occurs when two or more sprites partially overlap in a significant way. What is considered significant depends on the particular world you are developing. In some cases any overlap at all is significant, but often only the overlap of nontransparent regions is considered significant. No matter how it's defined, many sprite worlds couldn't function without some sort of collision detection. Before we go into actual implementations, let's first survey the four most popular 2D collision detection techniques.

1. Bounds overlap (Figure 10.1). The most basic form of collision detection is to simply determine if the bounding rectangles of two sprites are overlapping or not. This method is fast and easy to implement but has the drawback that it treats all sprites as rectangular.

2. Pixel-level detection (Figure 10.2). A very common and useful method of detecting a collision among two sprites is to see if both sprite's images draw nontransparent pixels to the same location on the screen. What is often done is to first see if the bounds of the two images overlap. If they do, the pixel data in the overlapping region of each image is treated as an array of bit values where transparent pixels are 0 and other pixels are

Figure 10.1 Bounds overlap.

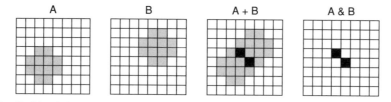

Figure 10.2 Pixel-level detection.

1. A bitwise AND operation is performed on the two arrays, and if the binary value of the resulting array is nonzero, a collision is detected. This method can work with arbitrarily shaped sprites and can achieve reasonable performance. The only problem is that it requires access to the pixel data of images, and QuickTime doesn't yet provide this access to wired sprites.

3. Radius overlap (Figure 10.3). Many sprites have a circular shape, or at least one that's more circular than rectangular. Two circles just touch when the distance between their centers is equal to the radius of the first plus the radius of the second. Thus if the distance between two circular sprites is less than or equal to the sum of their radii, we can say they are overlapping. Since distance is often measured using the Pythagorean equation of distance^2 = x^2 + y^2, a common simplification is to check if the square of the distance is less than the square of the sum of the radii (Figure 10.4). This simplification can improve the performance since it's usually faster to square than it is to take the square root, and some environments don't even have a square root function (QuickTime didn't until version 5.0). Despite being simpler in concept, this method actually requires slightly more computation than the bounds-overlap method.

4. Point testing (Figure 10.5). It is surprisingly often that a collision detection problem can be boiled down to testing one point and seeing if an object occupies that point or not. This is convenient because most sprite worlds already have a fast routine for testing if a point on the screen is

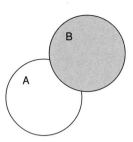

Figure 10.3 Radius overlap.

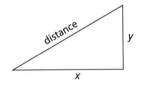

$$\text{distance}^2 = x^2 + y^2$$

Figure 10.4 Pythagorean relationship.

Figure 10.5 Point testing.

occupied by an object. It's called *hit testing* or *point testing* and is used in order to correctly handle mouse events.

As an example, consider small sprites, such as bullets or raindrops. These can usually be approximated by a single point. So to detect if they hit something, you just need to see if that something contains that point. Another example is with large movie sprites. If the sprite is moving to the right, it's often sufficient to test a point just to the right of the sprite's bounds to detect if it hits a wall or some other large object. If one point isn't sufficient, then perhaps testing a few points will do the trick.

5. Other methods. Collision detection is still an active area of research. Most of the developments deal with better algorithms for detecting the

overlap of 3D objects. Some of the tricks that are used involve breaking an object into many smaller pieces and then finding nice algorithms to hit-test those pieces. For instance all 2D and 3D surfaces can be approximated by tiling together a bunch of triangles, and fast methods for detecting the intersection of triangles have been developed and improved upon as recently as June 2001 (see http://www.acm.org/jgt/papers/Moller97/).

Bounds Overlap

Now that we've seen what's out there, let's start implementing some collision detection in QuickTime's sprite world. We'll start with the simple bounds-overlap testing.

Look at Figure 10.6 and see if you can pick out the pair of rectangles that doesn't overlap. Sure it's a trivial task for you, but we need to write a script that can determine this for the sprites. If you haven't thought about how you would write such a script, you might consider taking a moment to see if you can come up with an algorithm.

A good place to start is to realize that we can check for overlap along the x and y axes independently. There needs to be overlap along both axes to constitute a collision. So, if we check for overlap along the x axis and don't find any, then we know there's no collision. We don't have to spend any more time to check for overlap along the y axis. This type of optimization, where you exit from an algorithm because there's no point of continuing, is called *short-circuiting* (a similar technique, called *fail-fast*, is when you do a quick test to detect errors before starting a long, processor-intensive process). It's almost always a good idea to short-circuit your algorithms. Many

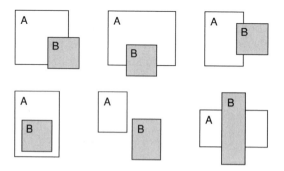

Figure 10.6 Which pair of rectangles doesn't overlap?

compiled languages (such as C++ and Java) will short-circuit a lot of code for you. For instance, consider the following code:

```
IF( x > 1 AND y > 1)
    //do something
ENDIF
```

The compiled C++ or Java program will first check if x is greater than 1. If not, then it won't even waste time comparing y with 1. LiveStage's implementation of QuickTime scripts, however, doesn't do this sort of short-circuiting. It goes ahead and checks if y is greater than 1 even if it wouldn't change the outcome. So, for optimized scripts, we have to do the short-circuiting ourselves. Here's the short-circuited version of the above code:

```
IF( x > 1 )
    IF( y > 1 )
        //do something
    ENDIF
ENDIF
```

For the bounds-overlap algorithm, we're going to want to use the same structure:

```
// calculate overlapX
IF( overlapX )
    //calculate overlapY
    IF( overlapY )
        //collision detected
    ENDIF
ENDIF
```

Now, how do we calculate overlapX and overlapY? Let's first consider overlapY (the overlap along the y axis). Figure 10.7 shows all the possible ways two rectangles can be arranged along the y axis:

1. Rectangle A can overlap the top edge of rectangle B.

2. A can overlap the bottom edge of B.

3. A can overlap both the top and bottom edges of B.

4. A can rest within the bounds of B.

5. A can be completely above B.

6. A can be completely below B.

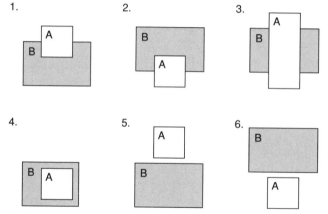

Figure 10.7 Overlap on the y axis.

All of them constitute collisions except for the last two. This means that if we can rule out the last two situations, then we know the two rectangles overlap along the y axis. Situation 5 happens whenever the bottom of A is above the top of B. We can therefore rule situation 5 out if we determine that the bottom of A is greater than or equal to the top of B. In QScript we would write

```
IF(SpriteOfID(A).BoundsBottom >= SpriteOfID(B).BoundsTop)
    //situation 5 is ruled out
ENDIF
```

Ruling out situation 5 is not enough; we have to also rule out situation 6. If we determine that there is overlap along the y axis, then we need to do a similar test along x.

Here is the resulting TestBounds function, which sets a BoundsOverlapping global variable to TRUE when sprites A and B are overlapping and FALSE otherwise:

```
[TestBounds]
GlobalVars BoundsOverlapping, A, B

BoundsOverlapping = FALSE
IF( SpriteOfID(A).BoundsBottom >= SpriteOfID(B).BoundsTop)
    IF(SpriteOfID(A).BoundsTop <= SpriteOfID(B).BoundsBottom)
        IF(SpriteOfID(A).BoundsRight >= SpriteOfID(B).BoundsLeft)
            IF(SpriteOfID(A).BoundsLeft <= SpriteOfID(B).BoundsRight)
                BoundsOverlapping = TRUE
```

```
        ENDIF
      ENDIF
    ENDIF
ENDIF
```

To call the function, we set the global variables A and B to the IDs of the two sprites we want to test and then execute the event. Let's take this function for a spin by opening the BoundsOverlap_demo.lsd project and previewing the movie (see Figure 10.8).

You'll discover that there are three sprites. Two of them are draggable (A and B) and the third is used to indicate when a collision has been detected (it's visible during a collision and invisible otherwise). A and B were made draggable through the same draggable behavior used in Chapter 4.

Let's have a look under the hood. On the Idle event of the sprite named "detector," you'll find the following code:

```
[Idle]
GlobalVars BoundsOverlapping, A, B

A = 2
B = 3
ExecuteEvent($TestBounds)
```

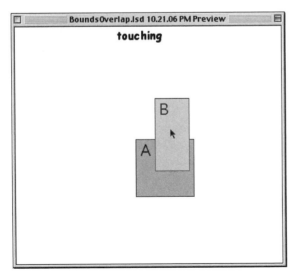

Figure 10.8 BoundsOverlap movie screenshot.

```
IF( BoundsOverlapping)
    SetVisible(TRUE)
ELSE
    SetVisible(FALSE)
ENDIF
```

This method of collision detection works best for rectangular-shaped objects. For example, the Solitaire game project (Projects/Chapter10/Solitaire/) uses this method to detect collisions among playing cards. However, if your sprites are more circular than rectangular, the next method will be much better suited.

▶ Radius Overlap

Circles have the nice feature that they extend from their centers by the same amount in all directions. The amount they extend is called the *radius*. This makes it easy for detecting collisions because we only have to see if the distance between two circles is small enough for their radii to overlap.

We can define the radius of a sprite in many ways. Here we'll just say that the radius is half the width of the sprite:

radius = (**BoundsRight** - **BoundsLeft**)/2

The distance when two circles start touching, which we'll call the *collision distance,* is the sum of the two radii (see Figure 10.9):

collisionDistance = radiusA + radiusB

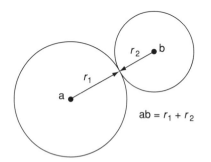

Figure 10.9 Two circles touching.

The actual distance between the centers of the two circular sprites is calculated as follows. First determine the center locations of each sprite using

```
xCenter = (BoundsRight + BoundsLeft)/2
yCenter = (BoundsTop + BoundsBottom)/2
```

Then find the distances along the x and y axes:

```
xDistance = xCenterA - xCenterB
yDistance = yCenterA - yCenterB
```

Now from good old Pythagoras we know that the two circles are going to just start touching when

$$xDistance^2 + yDistance^2 = collisionDistance^2$$

So, if we replace the equals sign with a less-than-or-equals sign, we obtain an algorithm for detecting collisions between two circles.

Note Pythagoras of Samos was a Greek philosopher, mathematician, and musician (one and the same to him) who lived during the same period as Confucius and died around 500 BC, just about 30 years before Socrates was born.

One thing to notice before we write the QScript is that every element in the final statement has a division by 2. From algebra (an Arabic word meaning "the reduction") we know that we can cancel out the division of 2 from each piece and reduce the amount of calculation that is needed.

Bringing it all together we arrive at the following function:

```
[TestRadius]
GlobalVars RadiusOverlap, A, B
LocalVars collisionDistance, xDistance, yDistance
LocalVars diameterA, diameterB, xLocationA, xLocationB
LocalVars yLocationA, yLocationB

diameterA = SpriteOfID(A).BoundsRight - SpriteOfID(A).BoundsLeft
diameterB = SpriteOfID(B).BoundsRight - SpriteOfID(B).BoundsLeft
xLocationA = SpriteOfID(A).BoundsRight + SpriteOfID(A).BoundsLeft
xLocationB = SpriteOfID(B).BoundsRight + SpriteOfID(B).BoundsLeft
yLocationA = SpriteOfID(A).BoundsTop + SpriteOfID(A).BoundsBottom
yLocationB = SpriteOfID(B).BoundsTop + SpriteOfID(B).BoundsBottom

collisionDistance = diameterA + diameterB
xDistance = locationXB - locationXA
yDistance = locationYB - locationYA
```

```
IF( (xDistance*xDistance + yDistance*yDistance) \
  <= (collisionDistance*collisionDistance) )
    RadiusOverlap = TRUE
ELSE
    RadiusOverlap = FALSE
ENDIF
```

We used a couple of standard optimization techniques here. The first was to use algebra to reduce equations to simpler forms. Another optimization was that we found a way to use only the fastest math operations. Multiplication, addition, and subtraction are faster than division and much faster than square root, which people often end up using when distance calculations are involved.

We could optimize this code a bit more by using longer expressions instead of caching temporary variables. For instance, we could make the collisionDistance calculation one long expression instead of first calculating diameterA and diameterB. But then that would be harder to read.

Note I've been emphasizing optimized code. But when developing, it is usually better to just get the code working and optimize later if needed and if there's time. I've made the mistake many times of spending hours optimizing code only to gain an almost undetectable amount of performance. See Appendix E, "Programming Techniques," for more information about optimizing QuickTime movies.

To see this function in action, take a look at the RadiusOverlap_demo.lsd project (see Figure 10.10).

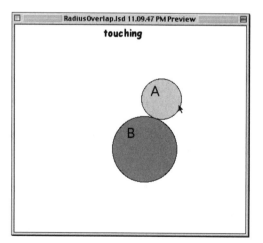

Figure 10.10 RadiusOverlap_demo.lsd project.

▶ Point Testing

The final collision detection technique we will discuss in this chapter is point testing. Point testing is where you test for the existence of a sprite by probing one or more locations on the screen. QuickTime offers a convenient function, called SpriteAtPoint(x,y), that will return the ID of the sprite found at (x,y). If no sprite exists at that point, the function will return zero (a good reason not to use zero for a sprite's ID).

Let's first examine a simple test movie as we've done with the other collision detection methods. Fire up the PointTesting_demo.lsd project. Here we have an arrow sprite and a square sprite. In this world, a collision is detected whenever the tip of the arrow is over the square. This is an ideal setting for point testing.

The idea is to find the point just above the tip of the arrow, and then use it to probe for other sprites with the SpriteAtPoint function. Here is how I've scripted the Idle event of the detector sprite:

```
[Idle]
LocalVars probeX, probeY, collisionID

probeX = (SpriteNamed("arrow").BoundsLeft + \
    SpriteNamed("arrow").BoundsRight)/2
probeY = SpriteNamed("arrow").BoundsTop - 1
collisionID = SpriteAtPoint(probeX, probeY)
IF(collisionID = SpriteNamed("rectangle").ID)
    SetVisible(TRUE)
ELSE
    SetVisible(FALSE)
ENDIF
```

The reason why I subtract 1 from the arrow's BoundsTop is to probe one pixel above the arrow (see Figure 10.11). Probing BoundsTop would detect the arrow itself.

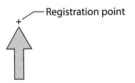

Figure 10.11 Registration point placed just above the arrow image.

As you can see by previewing the movie, point testing works great for detecting arrowhead collisions where we probe a point just outside of the arrow's bounds (see Figure 10.12). But what about situations where you want to probe points within the bounds of a sprite? For example, would it detect collisions with the center of a crosshairs image? (See Figure 10.13.) Point testing can work in these situations as well. All we have to do is make the crosshairs sprite invisible, then check the center point, and then make it visible again. This all takes place between screen updates so you don't have to worry about seeing the sprite flash or anything.

Note Drawing the sprite sample to the screen takes a lot of computational power. QuickTime only updates the pixels on the screen after something has changed visually and after all the current scripts have finished executing. Because of this, if you change the visual properties of a sprite more than once in a single script, only the final result, at the end of the script, will be drawn to the screen. By "current scripts," I mean all the scripts being executed by the same event. For instance, an idle event gets sent to each sprite in the sample one at a time in the order of the sprite index. Once the idle event is sent to the first sprite, the screen won't be updated until the last sprite in the sample finishes executing its idle event script (if it has one).

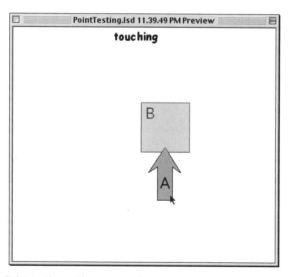

Figure 10.12   Point testing with an arrow image.

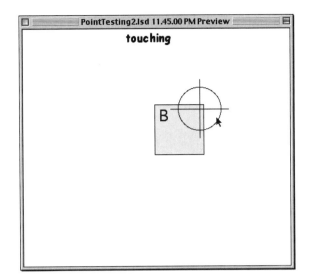

Figure 10.13 Point testing with a crosshairs image.

The project PointTesting2_demo.lsd is an example of how point testing would work with crosshairs instead of an arrow. Here's the Idle script on the detection sprite:

```
[Idle]
LocalVars probeX, probeY, collisionID

probeX = (SpriteNamed("crosshairs").BoundsLeft + \
  SpriteNamed("crosshairs").BoundsRight)/2
probeY = (SpriteNamed("crosshairs").BoundsTop + \
  SpriteNamed("crosshairs").BoundsBottom)/2
SpriteNamed("crosshairs").SetVisible(FALSE)
collisionID = SpriteAtPoint(probeX, probeY)
SpriteNamed("crosshairs").SetVisible(TRUE)
IF(collisionID > 0)
    SetVisible(TRUE)
ELSE
    SetVisible(FALSE)
ENDIF
```

Note It's important to realize that `SpriteAtPoint` doesn't detect points in exactly the same way as QuickTime's mouse hit testing. We just showed that invisible sprites aren't detected by `SpriteAtPoint`, but it might surprise you that invisible sprites *will* receive mouse events. Another difference is that mouse clicks will pass through the transparent regions of images encoded with the Animation codec or the Curve codec, but `SpriteAtPoint` doesn't take transparency into account at all.

A convenient aspect of point testing is that we can test all sprites with a single call to `SpriteAtPoint`. With the other collision detection methods, we would have to loop through and do a bounds or radius test on each sprite we're interested in. But since `SpriteAtPoint` returns the ID of the sprite at the given point, there's no need for looping.

Point testing is particularly well suited to situations where you have many targets and you want to know which one, if any, is in contact with a small object. For example, take a look at the `ShootingGame_demo.1sd` project (see Figure 10.14). This movie resembles a simple arcade game like Space Invaders, but is really the starting point for a whole universe of interesting sprite world creations. Let's see what's going on here.

We have a spaceship and some mean-looking aliens. When we click the spaceship, a bullet appears and gets fired upwards. On the way up, it probes a point just above itself. When it detects an alien, it sends a `Gotcha` action to the alien sprite, which makes the alien explode. It sounds per-

Figure 10.14 `ShootingGame_demo.1sd` project.

fectly innocent and even fun! Can you blame real aliens for not wanting to come and visit us?

One thing to notice is that we have a background picture of outer space, and the bullet needs to somehow differentiate background sprites from alien sprites. In this case I assume any sprite with a layer greater than zero is part of the background. Remember that negative layers draw on top of positive layers. The meat of the code is in the Idle event of the bullet sprite:

```
[Idle]
SpriteVars isMoving, velocity, locationX
LocalVars collisionID

IF(isMoving)
    MoveBy( 0, velocity)
    collisionID = SpriteAtPoint(myLocationX, BoundsTop - 2)
    IF( SpriteOfID(collisionID).Layer < 0 )
        SpriteOfID(collisionID).ExecuteEvent($Gotcha)
        ExecuteEvent($stopBullet)
    ENDIF
ENDIF
```

We're using SpriteVars here, which are variables that can only be accessed by scripts on the same sprite. We chose SpriteVars instead of GlobalVars so that later we can have multiple bullet sprites that operate independently from each other.

We just showed that with point testing we can determine which sprite is at a given point without having to supply any specific sprites to test. But what if we wanted to see if a particular sprite is located at a given point? Just because SpriteAtPoint returns a different ID, it doesn't mean that the sprite you are looking for isn't also there. Maybe it is just underneath another sprite. Well, you shouldn't let a little bump like this throw you. All you need to do is bring the sprite in question to the front, make sure it's visible, call the SpriteAtPoint function, and then return the sprite to its original state. The frontmost layer a sprite can have is the most negative value of a 16-bit integer, which in QScript is called MIN_SHORT (short, because it's a short integer compared to the longer 32-bit version). Here's a sniplet of code to do this:

```
SpriteVars probeX, probeY
LocalVars cachedLayer, collisionID, A
cachedLayer = SpriteOfID(A).Layer
```

```
SpriteOfID(A).SetLayerTo(MIN_SHORT)
collisionID = SpriteAtPoint(probeX, probeY)
SpriteOfID(A).SetLayerTo(cachedLayer)
IF(collisionID = A)
    //the sprite is there
ELSE
    //Nope, sprite isn't there
ENDIF
```

Point testing is particularly well suited for sprites that are moving to detect if they've run into something. This is because it's often OK to just check one or more spots at the location the sprite is about to move. Figure 10.15 shows where you would want to probe for some shapes found in the popular game of Tetris. Here we see that we can use point testing for odd shapes that are neither rectangular nor circular. Figure 10.16 shows where you might want to hit-test a sprite that can potentially run into things protruding from the ground or the ceiling. With clever placement you can often get away with a small number of points. And don't forget to short-circuit your code since once you detect a collision at one of the points, there's no need to check the other points!

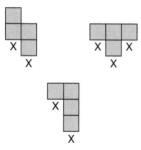

Figure 10.15   Point-testing locations (x) for a few Tetris shapes.

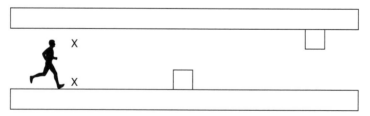

Figure 10.16   Point-testing locations near the ground and ceiling.

▶ Explorations

1. The opposite of collision is separation, which happens when two objects start off in contact and then separate. How would you go about turning our collision detection techniques into separation detection techniques?

2. In the sprite geometry section of Appendix F, there is a function for determining the distance between a point and a line. Design a function to test the collision between a circular sprite and a line. Can you think of an interesting application of this function?

3. In the second exploration of Chapter 38, I point out an example of collision detection at the movie level. Have a look. Can you think of any interesting uses of this capability?

4. For those of you who like to develop collision detection algorithms: (a) In this chapter we showed how to detect collisions between two rectangles and between two circles, but what about between a circle and a rectangle? Your solution would need to work successfully for the four tricky situations shown in Figure 10.17. (b) We showed how to detect collisions among rectangles, but what if the rectangles are rotated at arbitrary angles?

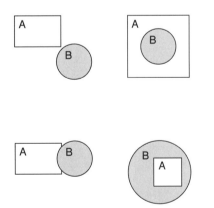

Figure 10.17 Detecting collisions between a circle and a rectangle.

Cel-Based Animation

In the introduction to this part of the book we discussed the history of interactive sprite worlds starting in the late 1960s. However, the concept of a sprite (an object that can be animated independently from the background) predates this by more than half a century. Before 1914, great animators such as Emile Cohl and Winsor McCay had to draw each frame of an animated sequence by hand. This meant that animating a character walking across a background required you to redraw both the character and the background for each frame.

Note The Frenchman Emile Cohl was one of the great vanguards of animation who some consider the first true animator. Despite his productivity and extraordinary talent, he lived the later part of his life in poverty, not able to afford simple things like electricity. At the same time, new American animators, such as Walt Disney, were on their way to great wealth. Emile Cohl died in 1938 as the result of an accident while getting ready to go see the Paris premiere of *Snow White.* The candle in his room caught his beard on fire, fatally injuring him.

In 1914, Earl Hud patented a revolutionary technique where you draw each object on its own sheet of transparent celluloid (called a *cel*), and then you layer these cels on a background. This allowed animators to create reusable characters that could be moved around on any background. This, by our definition, is a sprite. The technique came to be known as *cel-based animation*.

Many of the concepts of cel-based animation exist in the QuickTime sprite track. A registration point, for example, was a little cross drawn on a cel used to align it relative to other cels.

Note There were also mechanical registration systems that used pegs and holes.

Each image in a sprite track has a registration point that defines its spatial origin. Transparency is another key property of celluloid. Sprite images can also have transparency, allowing nonrectangular shapes to blend in nicely with the background. The ability to layer cels gave animators a powerful way to add depth to what was otherwise a 2D medium. QuickTime sprites can be layered in much the same way.

Note Actually, sprites can be layered in a much better way. Since celluloid isn't perfectly transparent, adding more layers limits the amount of light that can pass through. Cel animators were usually limited to less than seven layers. QuickTime sprites don't have this limitation.

In my opinion, the biggest concept missing from traditional cel-based animation is interactivity. The interactive component of sprites opens the door to a lot of fun stuff. Let's get started!

Picasso

Some people wouldn't consider this first project an example of cel-based animation because they equate cel-based animation with flipbook animation. But I think it's a great example because it showcases the big breakthrough of drawing on celluloid sheets: transparency! Take just about any object and draw parts of it on different sheets of transparent material so that you can move each sheet around independently. Pretty soon you'll be amused by the fun animations you can produce. The example of this that made the biggest impression on me growing up was a pop-up book that had a scene in a castle with paintings on the wall. When you wiggled a little strip of paper on the side of the page, the eyes of one of the paintings would move back and forth. This really brought the painting to life in a spooky way.

Here, we're going to re-create this effect with my rendition of Pablo Picasso's self-portrait. Open the Picasso_demo.lsd project and see this famous trick re-created before your eyes (see Figure 11.1). What I've done here is make a version of the painting where the eye sockets are transparent (due to an alpha channel).

Note There are four ways to make portions of an image transparent. Each has its own uses. The first way is to use a graphics codec that supports transparency to encode the image with one of the colors transparent. The easiest way to do this in LiveStage Pro is to add

Figure 11.1 `Picasso_demo.lsd` project.

an image into the sprite sample, and then choose Animation from the codec pop-up menu. Select which color you want to make transparent with the color chooser, and click the checkbox labeled "Transparent." Any sprite that uses this image will display it with the appropriate regions transparent. These regions will also be transparent to mouse events. This means that if you click on a transparent region, you'll actually be clicking on whatever is underneath the sprite.

The second way is to make an image with the QuickTime vector `.qti` format (referred to as the curve codec). Vector images have transparent backgrounds. Unfortunately the only tool I know of that can make QuickTime vector images is Totally Hip's WebPainter, and it only works on the Mac. It doesn't know how to import any of the standard vector formats so you're pretty much left to try to draw your vectors within WebPainter itself. If you have Macromedia's Fontographer software, you might be able to turn an existing vector into a font, and since WebPainter can turn fonts into QuickTime vectors, it's sometimes possible to import things this way. If anyone knows of a better way, please let me know! When you import a vector image into LiveStage, make sure you choose Don't Recompress or else it will rasterize (turn into a bitmap) your image. Transparent regions of vectors are also transparent to mouse events.

The third way is to use a graphics format that supports alpha channels, such as the PNG format. This allows you to get smooth gradients of transparency. Again, when you bring this into LiveStage, either don't recompress it, or compress it with the PNG or Animation+Alpha codecs. Each sprite that uses this image needs to have its graphics mode set to Alpha. There's a pop-up menu in the sprite's Properties tab for setting the graphics mode. Be careful because using the Alpha graphics mode for images without alpha information will cause no image to be displayed. The graphics mode can also be set from a script by using

```
SetGraphicsModeTo(graphicsModeStraightAlpha,0,0,0)
```

There are several types of alpha channel graphics modes. The LiveStage manual does a reasonable job explaining what each one does. I should note that the transparent regions of an alpha channel are not "transparent" to mouse events. This means that even though you can see though a transparent part of the image, it will still respond to mouse clicks. However, if you use the Animation+Alpha codec and choose the background color as transparent, then 0% composited regions will also be transparent to mouse clicks.

The final way to make an object transparent is to use the Transparent graphics mode and choose an opColor as the color to be transparent. This will work with any image. Each sprite can have a different graphics mode setting. Transparent regions, in this case, are not transparent to mouse events.

Behind the painting are two images of pupils that can move independently. Since this is an interactive sprite world, we can position the pupils dynamically to make it look like the painting is staring at the mouse cursor. The source code for the mouse positioning is not related to the current topic so I won't list it here, but it's all there in the project for you to look through.

▶ Interactive Door

Our next example project will use cel-based animation to place an interactive door in a 3D scene. Open RoomAndDoor_start.lsd and preview the movie (see Figure 11.2). You should see a 3D rendered scene with a closed door. If you click the door, it will flip through several images of the door at

Figure 11.2   RoomAndDoor_start.lsd project.

different stages of the opening process. The only problem is that we haven't set the image registration points, so the door opens in an abnormal manner.

Fixing the door requires setting the registration points of the door images so they are correctly aligned. The best way to do this is to pick a location on the door that is supposed to be fixed in space. Then place the registration point of each image at that same location. For our door, I'd pick a location just above the top-right hinge as shown in Figure 11.3.

In LiveStage, you can enter the registration point by typing in values in the provided text fields, or you can set the point with the mouse by option-clicking the image. Positioning registration points takes a little practice.

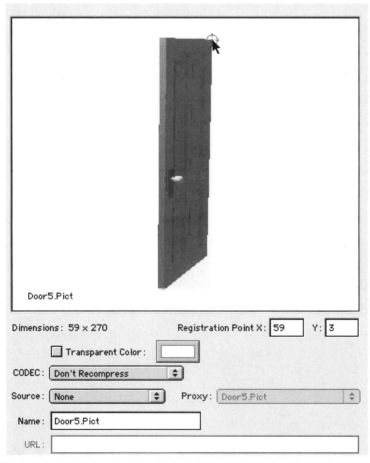

Figure 11.3 Registration point for the door. Option-click to make registration point.

Once you get them positioned correctly, you will notice that the door in our scene has shifted to reflect the new registration point.

In Chapter 4 we learned how to position sprites on the stage. Try dragging the door to its correct location. If you run into any trouble, you can do what they do on those TV cooking shows and pull the RoomAndDoor_ complete.lsd project out of the oven.

▶ Looping Images

The key to success when animating ongoing activities is to find a way to turn it into one or more series of looping images. The world is full of repetitive motion. Dogs wag their tails back and forth. Birds flap their wings up and down. It reminds me of that song about the wheels on the bus going 'round and 'round. Looping lets you use a small number of images to describe an activity that could go on indefinitely. QuickTime offers a very simple action for looping through a range of images. Here's an example (see Figure 11.4):

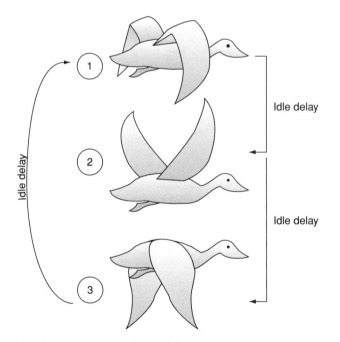

Figure 11.4 A looping sequence of a flying bird.

```
[Idle]
SetImageIndexBy(1) MIN(3) MAX(7) WRAPAROUND
```

This will increase the current image index by 1 each `Idle` event, and when it passes image 7, it will wrap around to image 3. If you leave out the `WRAPAROUND` part, then it would simply stop at image 7. This action is used a lot (we used it in the interactive door project), but it's pretty limiting. First of all, the `MIN` and `MAX` numbers (3 and 7 in this case) have to be constants. Constants aren't good for interactivity. Another problem is that this action doesn't force the image index to be in the range between 3 and 7. If the current image index is 1, calling this action will simply set it to 2. Only when the image index goes past 7 will it wrap around to 3.

The final quibble that I have with this action is that the number you place in `SetImageIndexBy` (in this case 1) has to be an integer. This means you don't have much control over the flip rate. For example, I've often wanted to use 0.5 in order to make the animation go at half the rate. For these reasons, I developed the following more sophisticated looping method (see Figure 11.5):

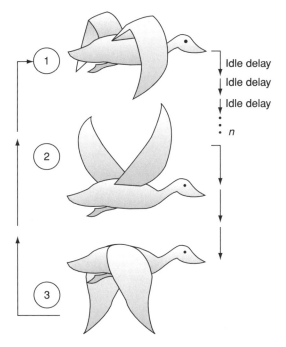

Figure 11.5 An improved looping construct.

```
[Idle]
SpriteVars flipDirection, dwellCount, running
SpriteVars idleCounter

IF(running)
    idleCounter = idleCounter + 1
    IF( idleCounter >= dwellCount)
        idleCounter = 0
        IF(flipDirection > 0)
            ExecuteEvent($NextImage)
        ELSE
            ExecuteEvent($PreviousImage)
        ENDIF
    ENDIF
ENDIF
```

This is the main script that I usually place on the Idle event. We must also implement the $NextImage and $PreviousImage events, which do the actual changing of the image index:

```
[NextImage]
SpriteVars startImage, endImage, loopImages, running
LocalVars tempIndex

tempIndex = ImageIndex + 1
IF(tempIndex > endImage)
    IF(loopImages)
        tempIndex = startImage
    ELSE
        running = FALSE
        tempIndex = endImage
    ENDIF
ENDIF
SetImageIndexTo(tempIndex)

[PreviousImage]
SpriteVars startImage, endImage, loopImages, running
LocalVars tempIndex

tempIndex = ImageIndex - 1
IF(tempIndex < startImage)
    IF(loopImages)
        tempIndex = endImage
```

```
        ELSE
            running = FALSE
            tempIndex = startImage
        ENDIF
ENDIF
SetImageIndexTo(tempIndex)
```

The sprite variables in this routine can be set at any time. The following is what each `SpriteVar` does:

- `startImage`: Index of the first image in the sequence.

- `endImage`: Index of the last image in the sequence.

- `dwellCount`: The number of idle events for which each image is to be displayed. A dwellCount of 2 means each image will be displayed for two idle events.

- `flipDirection`: Can be either 1 or −1 to flip through the images in the positive or negative direction.

- `loopImages`: A Boolean indicating whether the image sequence should be looped or not.

- `running`: A Boolean that stops the animation when false, and plays normally otherwise.

Look at the `LoopingTest_demo.lsd` project for an example of how to use this looping routine (see Figure 11.6). This project is a good example of how to add custom actions that give outside access to the properties of a sprite. As you can see, the parameters are all `SpriteVars`, which means

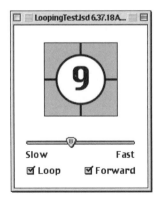

Figure 11.6 LoopingTest movie.

they are only accessible by the sprite itself. This is good because it allows multiple sprites to have the same scripts and not conflict. In order to let the rest of the world have access to these sprite parameters, we make custom actions and properties as we did in Chapter 9. The only thing different in this project is that we are calling the actions from a separate track and thus need to use MovieVars instead of GlobalVars to pass data in and out of the events. In LiveStage Pro, GlobalVars are only "global" to the local sprite track. MovieVars, on the other hand, are accessible across tracks and even across movies. We'll discuss MovieVars in Chapter 38. And don't worry about how the user interface controls work; there's a whole section on that.

▶ Inchworm Technique

A common application of cel-based animation is to loop through a series of images as a sprite moves across the screen. This is often done to make it look like a character is walking (or crawling or swimming or slithering . . .). The problem is that if you move the character by the same amount each frame, it usually makes it look like it's doing the moonwalk. To get more realistic motion, I use what I call the *inchworm technique*.

The inchworm technique is a way to capture the motion of an object in the image information. This way we don't have to write complicated scripts to move objects in the correct way.

Consider an inchworm. It basically moves in two steps. First it stretches its head out, then it scrunches its tail in. This makes it move in little spurts of an "inch" at a time. The amount the inchworm moves and when it moves needs to match the image, or else it will look like the worm is crawling on a slippery surface.

The inchworm technique uses the image registration points to position the images relative to each other. One extra image is added to the end of the sequence to specify how the last image is positioned relative to the first image when looping.

This technique is illustrated in Figure 11.7. There you see three images:

1. Stage 1 of the inchworm crawl.

2. Stage 2 of the inchworm crawl offset so that the head remains in the same place.

3. Same as stage 1 but this time the image is offset so the tail remains in the same place as it was in 2.

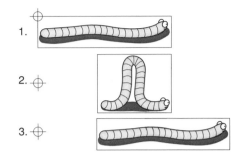

Figure 11.7 The registration point ($\oplus$) placement in the three inchworm images.

With these three images, we can make the inchworm crawl in a realistic manner by looping through the images in the following way. We start at the first image and iterate through the sequence one image at a time without moving the sprite. When we come to the last image, we cache the sprite's location, then set the sprite's image to the first image in the sequence. We then compare the new position with the cached value and correct for any differences. Here's an example script to do this:

```
SpriteVars startImage, endImage
LocalVars cachedX, cachedY

SetImageIndexBy(1)
IF(ImageIndex = endImage)
    cachedX = BoundsLeft
    cachedY = BoundsTop
    SetImageIndexTo(startImage)
    MoveBy(cachedX - BoundsLeft, cachedY - BoundsTop)
ENDIF
```

Let's try this out with some actual inchworm images. Open the inchworm_demo.lsd project and preview the movie. You'll find an inchworm crawling across the screen.

To get a feeling for some of the powerful features offered by this technique, let's rotate the sprite. Close the preview, and set the sprite's rotation angle to –15 degrees (this is done in the sprite's Properties tab by entering –15 into the Angle field). Now preview the movie (see Figure 11.8).

You'll see that the worm crawls up a 15-degree incline. We didn't have to change any of the scripting to do this. All of the motion information is encoded into the images, and when the images rotate, so does the motion. This is also true for scaling the images. If you make the sprite twice as big, it will move twice as fast.

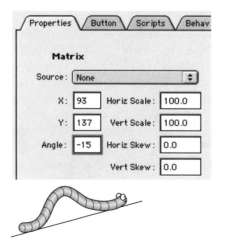

Figure 11.8 Inchworm crawling up an incline.

Another feature of the inchworm technique is that we can dynamically change the animated character by simply changing the image sequence. Different characters might move in entirely different ways. But since the motion information is stored in the images, the same script will apply.

Advanced Enhanced Inchworm Routine

We can take the concept of encoding information in the images even further. The enhanced inchworm routine lets you encode the following extra information:

1) The number of images in the sequence. This way you only have to know the start image and can forget about the end image.

2) The number of idle events for which each image should remain on the screen. This lets us define fast- and slow-moving critters.

3) Whether or not the sequence loops. Not all animated sequences are supposed to loop. It's nice to be able to use the same code for the ones that are supposed to loop and the ones that aren't.

To do this we will add an image to the beginning of the sequence that will never be displayed but simply acts as a storage of information about our sequence. We will again store information in the image registration point. For this first image, the x position of the image registration point will signify the total number of images in the sequence (including the first image). The absolute value of the y position will signify for how many idle events to display each image. A positive value for y means to loop, a negative value means not to loop. For example, a y value of 1 means to loop and display a new image on each idle event. A value of 2 means to loop and display a new image every other idle event. A value of –2 also means to display a new image on every other idle event, but being negative, it doesn't loop.

We are also going to introduce another type of image, called a *pause image*. This is an image that signifies a pause in the sequence. For instance, the animation for the shooting of an arrow might have several images for the drawing back of the bow, then a pause, and then a few images for the release of the arrow. These pause images are optional. You make a pause image by setting the *x* value of its image registration point to –999.

The choice of –999 is arbitrary, but it is good in that it's easy to remember and isn't commonly used for normal image registration points. The *y* value specifies the number of idle events to wait. You place a pause image *before* the image you want to pause.

Figure 11.9 gives a review of how this all works. Basically, you have a dummy image at the beginning of the sequence that specifies the number of images in the sequence, whether or not the sequence loops, and how long to display each image on the screen. The actual graphic that you use for this image doesn't matter because it will never be displayed. If it is a looping sequence, then there will be another dummy image at the end of the sequence that specifies how the end of the sequence is positioned relative to the start of the sequence. Again, this image will never be displayed and is only there for looping sequences. There are also optional pause images that can be placed anywhere within the sequence. They are placed before the image that is to be paused. These too are dummy images that are never actually displayed.

For the enhanced inchworm routine, we only need to know the index of the first image in the sequence. The end, the timing, and the looping is all encoded in the images. I like to give the first image a nice name, so I can use the image defines.

Look at the `triangleTricks_demo.lsd` project for a demonstration of the enhanced inchworm technique (see Figure 11.10). The triangle sports three image sequences: Roll-Right, BounceLeft, and Trick. Let's just walk through and see how each of these is set up. RollRight is a slower looping sequence with each image being displayed for 8 idle

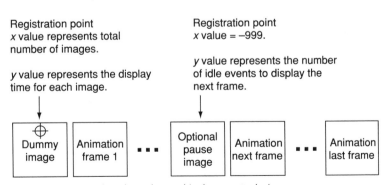

Figure 11.9 Image sequence using the enhanced inchworm technique.

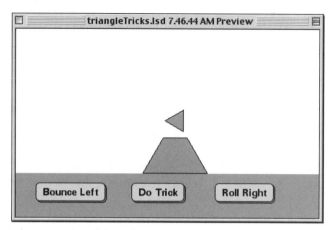

Figure 11.10 A demonstration of the enhanced inchworm technique.

events. Since it has a total of 6 images in the sequence, we set the registration point of the first image to 6, 8. The BounceLeft is a faster loop, but it has a pause image in it. It displays each image for 3 idle events and has a total of 9 images in the sequence, so the registration point is 9, 3. The pause image comes before the last image. Since it's a pause image, the x value of its registration point is –999. It pauses the last image for 30 idle events, so `ImageRegistrationPointY` is 30. The Trick sequence doesn't loop and thus the y value of the first image registration point is negative.

Onionskinning

The inchworm routine requires you to determine the correct image registration points for a sequence of images. If you've already tried making some inchworm sequences, you might have discovered that it can be tricky to determine where to place the image registration points so that motion looks right. A widespread technique to solve this problem is called *onionskinning* (see Figure 11.11).

Note The name simply comes from the transparent and layered attributes of onions.

This is where you show two cels in a sequence at the same time so that you can easily align them. Usually what is done is that the current cel is placed on top of a faded image of the previous cel. Most animation software has some form of onionskinning. Unfortunately LiveStage Pro doesn't.

But we can make a QuickTime movie function as an onionskinning tool and essentially add this feature to LiveStage ourselves.

Check out `onionskinTool_demo.lsd` for a working version of such a tool (see Figure 11.12). When you run the movie you'll be presented with an image of a hammer. You can move that hammer around the stage, and the corresponding image registration values will be displayed at the bottom of the movie. There are controls that let you go to the next image. When you do so, you will also see the previous image faded slightly. See if you can animate this hammer as if it is twirling through space. You can reuse this tool by simply replacing the images of the hammer with some other sequence of images that you'd like to animate.

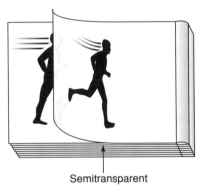

Semitransparent

Figure 11.11   The onionskinning concept.

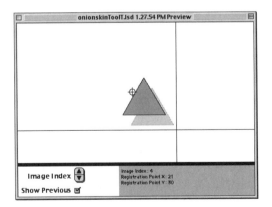

Figure 11.12   A tool for onionskinning.

This is an example of a QuickTime application. It's good to get in the habit of thinking of QuickTime not only as a platform for media, but also as a way of making useful miniapplications. We'll make more of these applications throughout the book (see the `Projects/Chapter02/Utilities/` directory on the CD for some working examples).

Coordinated Animation

So far, we've explored reusable cel-based techniques for animating individual sprites. What about animating interactions among sprites? For example, we might want to animate a sprite character that bends down, picks up another sprite, walks a few feet, and then puts it back down. This requires coordinating the individual sprite animations so it looks like they are physically interacting. If we were animating cartoons for film, it would be easy. We would position the images in each cel by eye. After all, we know what it is supposed to look like. But what if we want it more dynamic such that the sprite character can pick up any object that it comes across? For the rest of this chapter we'll explore cel-based techniques for coordinating animated sprites (which I call *co-animation*).

The basic co-animation technique is to create two synchronized sequences of images that maintain their relative positions over time. Consider the rolling triangle sequence. It consists of four images of the triangle rotated at different angles. Through the inchworm technique, we can get the triangle to roll by setting the image registration point to the same bottom-right corner in each image. Say we wanted to balance a ball on top of the triangle as it rolls across the screen. One way to do this is to create four images of the ball and then set the image registration points in each so the ball maintains contact with the top of the triangle as if being balanced. It should look like Figure 11.13. You can see it in action in the `ballAndTriangle.lsd` project. There we use a modified inchworm routine such that every time there is a `MoveBy()` done on the triangle, the same `MoveBy()` is done on the ball.

Notice that while we technically have four images of the ball, the pixel information is all coming from the same graphics file. The only thing different is the image registration point. In this way, we are capturing the motion of the ball in the image data. You might be asking yourself: "Isn't that a big waste of memory to duplicate an image just to store a couple of numbers?" I'll address that issue in the next paragraph, but first I'd like to answer another question you might also be pondering, and that is how I determined the correct image registration points to use for the ball. For

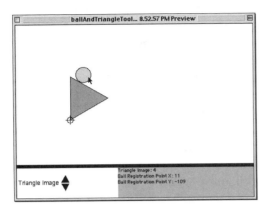

Figure 11.13 A ball balancing on a triangle.

this, I actually made another tool (see the `coanimation_demo.lsd` project). It's a modification of the onionskinning tool, this time letting you position one object relative to another object.

Now, back to the memory issue. The ball here is such a simple graphic that it's not going to add much weight (in terms of kilobytes) to the movie, especially when the movie is compressed. But if the ball image was very elaborate and did take up substantial memory, then you would be right in not wanting to duplicate it needlessly. The good thing is that since the ball images are really there just to hold positioning information, they don't have to be the exact image of the ball we want to use. Check out the `fancyBallAndTriangle_demo.lsd` project for an example of how to use the simple ball images as a guide for where to place a fancier image. The basic idea is to use two sprites for the ball, one that uses the simple image sequence that co-animates with the triangle, and another one that displays the fancy ball image over the simple ball. The simple one is made invisible, so that the fancy one is all that you see. We'll utilize a similar trick to do some more interesting things in a little bit.

Cel-Based Pushing

In grade school, many of us learned that pushing can be a very popular form of interaction. Indeed, if it wasn't for the ability of one object to push another object, then not much would get done in this physical world. Here we'll explore some ways to simulate one sprite pushing another sprite. Even in its simplest form, pushing can create a powerful illusion that sprites are real solid objects. To see this for yourself, look at the project triangleAndSquare_demo.lsd. Here we have our triangle rolling across the screen pushing anything that it comes in contact with (see Figure 11.14).

Let's look at how this is implemented. The triangle rolls across the screen using a modified inchworm routine that executes an event called $Push each time the sprite moves. In the $Push event, we perform some collision detection to see if the sprite has run into anything. If the triangle comes in contact with another sprite, then we move that sprite so that its bounds just touch the bounds of the triangle. This gives the illusion that the triangle is physically pushing the other sprite.

This works particularly well for the triangle because the point on the triangle that is doing the pushing always coincides with the edge of the sprite's bounds. For more sophisticated-looking sprites, however, this won't always be the case. Sometimes the point of contact will be inside the bounds of the sprite and might change as the sprite's image changes. The good thing is that we can incorporate the same technique used in the ball and triangle project to make a co-animated sprite that *does* have an edge at the contact point. To demonstrate this, let's use the twirling hammer sequence and make it so only the head of the hammer (and not the handle) does the pushing (see Figure 11.15).

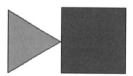

Figure 11.14   A triangle pushing a square.

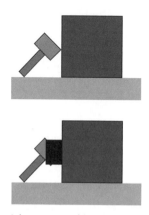

Figure 11.15   A hammer pushing a square.

The end result can be seen in the `hammerAndSquare_demo.lsd` project. Here we have a hammer with a co-animated hammer head. The hammer head sprite is invisible since it is just used to do the pushing. Go ahead and temporarily make the hammer head visible so you can see how this works. The great thing about it is that the code we wrote isn't specific for hammers and triangles. It can be reused to perform all sorts of sprite-to-sprite interactions. This is possible because we used cel-based techniques to capture physical contact and motion information inside the images themselves.

▶ Cel-Based Dragging

In this chapter, we expanded the notions of cels and sequences of cels. Usually a cel refers to a single "frame" of animation that contains image information as well as positioning information in the form of a registration point. With the inchworm techniques, we capitalized on the positioning information of a cel to represent motion information in a series of cels. With co-animation, we were able to display multiple sequences of cels in tandem, thus expanding the amount of information each animation "frame" could contain. This allowed us to create interactive objects with moveable parts. To end this chapter, I'd like to present a cel-based technique to add "virtual reality" style manipulation to objects. It's called *cel-based dragging*.

To demonstrate cel-based dragging, let's revisit the interactive 3D door project from the beginning of this chapter (see Figure 11.16). In that project we created a door that would swing open when you clicked it. Let's add a more lifelike user interface on it such that the user needs to grab onto the door knob and drag the door open. This will give them more control over the door. They'll be able to open it, close it, or position it anywhere in between.

To implement this, as you might have guessed, we're going to co-animate an invisible sprite to act as the door knob region. This sprite will receive the mouse events (invisible sprites can still receive mouse events). When the user clicks and drags the door knob sprite, it will go through its cels finding the one closest to the current mouse location and then set its image to that cel, co-animating the door with it. This is cel-based dragging, and the great thing is that the code doesn't have to know how a door works. All it's doing is finding the cel that most closely approximates the drag motion. You can now open and close the door yourself by building

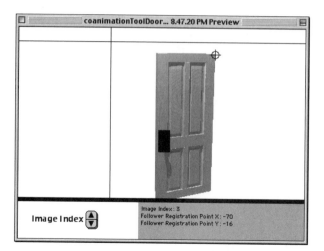

Figure 11.16 Demonstration of the concept of cel-based dragging.

the DragDoor_demo.lsd project. Fun, right? In the next chapter we'll discuss other ways to add user interfaces to sprites and movies.

▶ Explorations

1. You should see if you can get hold of a copy of one of the great pre-cel animations called *Gertie the Dinosaur* (see Figure 11.17). Every frame was drawn by hand by the great Winsor McCay. It was released in 1914, the same year that cel-based animation was invented. One of the interesting things about this film is that Winsor McCay animates himself in the film, and he would often attend showings of his film and walk up across the stage and behind the screen and be transformed into his cartoon form. He had a whole bag of tricks to make it look like he could interact with the animation. At one point, he (as his real self) would toss some food from the side of the stage and the animated Gertie would grab it and eat it. It's fun to think about what Winsor McCay would do if he had access to interactive sprites!

2. In the RoomAndDoor example, you might have noticed a nail on the room's wall. In the project I've also included an image of a picture frame. Try hanging it on the nail and placing your favorite image (or movie!) inside.

3. Both the simple and the enhanced versions of the inchworm technique only work when flipping through the images in the forward direction. How would you modify the script so it also works in reverse?

Figure 11.17 Hand-drawn frame from *Gertie the Dinosaur*. Notice the registration marks. *Courtesy of David L. Nathan, M.D.*

4. Mastering the inchwork technique takes a bit of practice. I've included a folder on the CD called `OnionSkinPractice`. Inside, you'll find a couple of sequences of images (see Figure 11.18) donated for use with this book by a talented artist from the Netherlands, Hans Rijnen. One sequence is of a walking gorilla that Hans created for a project I was working on for

Figure 11.18 A gorilla, and a mouse on a bicycle. *Courtesy of Hans Rijnen.*

Koko, the sign-language-speaking gorilla (yes, Koko uses interactive QuickTime too). There's also a sequence of a mouse on a bicycle. Use these sequences and the onionskin tool to practice the inchworm animation technique.

5. Cel-based dragging is a generic way of mapping mouse drag gestures to cel animation. The same code can let the user flip pages in a book, control a 3D joystick, and turn a crank. It's able to achieve this generality by checking all possibilities and determining the cel that best matches the drag gesture. For a small number of images, this works great, but once the number of images starts to get in the double digits, it starts getting sluggish to have to check every cel. What are some simple modifications you can make to the code so that it doesn't have to always check every cel? Think about both the general case and the case where you have a particular known sequence of cels.

User Interaction

In 1967, Douglas Engelbart filed patent number 3,541,541, and the mouse was born. The first prototype was a bulky wooden box with two metal wheels sticking out the bottom. This device, which is used by pushing it around the top of a table, narrowly beat out several of Engelbart's competing designs in a small study he did trying to find the best "pointing" device. Some of the other designs that came close to winning included a pen device, a widget that you attached to your knee and the bottom of the desk, and a stick that protruded from your forehead. Imagine if the mouse didn't win: we might all be double-clicking our forehead sticks!

The keyboard (called a Type-Writer at the time) was invented 100 years earlier, in 1867, by Christopher Lathem Sholes, patent number 79,265. It was basically the same design that we use today, with QWERTY as the first six letters on the top row. It had only uppercase letters. The first design of a keyboard that could type both upper- and lowercase letters had twice the number of keys on it! Imagine if that stuck around. Douglas Engelbart actually made his contributions to the keyboard too with the chord keyset. This was a keyboard with only five keys on it. You typed with one hand and got the full range of the alphabet by pressing multiple keys at a time, like playing chords on the piano. With this device, you could manipulate the mouse with one hand and simultaneously type with the other hand.

In this chapter, we're going to explore techniques that will allow people to interact with your movies through the mouse and keyboard. We'll start off with some simple buttons and work our way to a full UI manager. But first, get ready for a pop quiz!

▶ Pop Quiz

Take out a sheet of paper and see how well your knowledge (or intuition) matches up with the way QuickTime works (we'll learn the answers to these questions in this chapter).

1. If a sprite has its visible property set to false, it won't receive Mouse Enter and Mouse Exit events.

    a. True

    b. False

2. Typically, a Mouse Moved event will be sent to a sprite when the mouse cursor moves while over a sprite. Will a Mouse Moved also be sent if the sprite moves under a stationary cursor?

    a. Yes

    b. No

3. Which one of the following statements is true?

    a. A Mouse Exit event can be sent to a sprite without the sprite ever receiving a Mouse Enter event.

    b. A Mouse Exit event is always accompanied with a Mouse Moved event.

    c. When a movie is first launched, if a sprite happens to be under the mouse cursor, it won't receive a Mouse Enter event until the user actually moves the mouse.

4. There is no way for a sprite to differentiate a left button click from a right button click on a Windows machine.

    a. True

    b. False

5. Which statement is true for the following situation? The left button of the mouse is pressed while over a sprite, but by the time it is released, it is no longer over the sprite.

    a. Since the mouse is no longer over the sprite, a Mouse Up event will not be sent.

    b. Since the mouse is no longer over the sprite, a Mouse Click event will not be sent.

    c. Both a Mouse Up and a Mouse Click event will always be sent.

    d. A Mouse Click event will be sent as long as the mouse cursor itself hasn't moved.

6. Which statement is true for when a key on the keyboard is pressed?

    a. All sprites will receive a Key Pressed event.

    b. Only the sprite that is currently under the mouse cursor can receive a Key Pressed event.

    c. Only the sprite with focus can receive a Key Pressed event.

7. If one key is pressed, and then another key is pressed, QuickTime will send a Key Released for the first key even though the user hasn't actually released the key.

    a. True

    b. False

8. If a user presses and holds down a key, Key Pressed events will be repeatedly sent.

    a. True

    b. False

9. If two keys are pressed at exactly the same time, only one Key Pressed event will be sent.

    a. True

    b. False

10. The shift key, when pressed by itself, doesn't send a Key Pressed event.

    a. True

    b. False

The answers can be found at the end of this chapter.

▶ Mouse Event Definitions

In a sprite world, QuickTime relays mouse gestures to sprites by sending mouse events. The following events are defined.

Note   VR hotspots and text track hyperlinks can also have these events.

```
Mouse Enter        Mouse Down
Mouse Exit         Mouse Up
Mouse Moved        Mouse Click
```

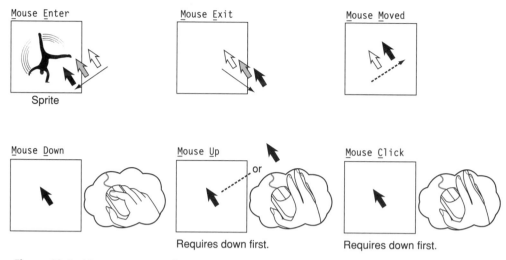

Figure 12.1 Mouse event meanings.

Figure 12.1 provides a pictorial depiction of each event.

The names aren't completely consistent, for instance, they all use the present tense form of the verb except for Mouse Moved, but if you speak English, you're used to these inconsistencies. I should note that these are the event names given by LiveStage. If you are wiring up QuickTime movies in Java or in C/C++, you will come across different names for these same events, namely:

```
kQTEventMouseEnter (Mouse Enter)
kQTEventMouseExit   (Mouse Exit)
kQTEventMouseMoved (Mouse Moved)
kQTEventMouseClick   (Mouse Down)
kQTEventMouseClickEnd   (Mouse Up)
kQTEventMouseClickEndTriggerButton   (Mouse Click)
```

Most environments define roughly equivalent events, but they are often given different names. For instance, Mouse Down is often called something more like Mouse Pressed. To make matters worse, the exact definition of these events is slightly different from environment to environment. Macromedia Flash, for instance, has an event called Roll Over, which is similar to QuickTime's Mouse Enter, but is different in that it only gets sent if the mouse button isn't pressed at the time. Also, QuickTime left out one of the most important standard mouse events, which is Mouse Dragged. Let's talk about how all of these events work and later we can create our own Mouse Dragged event.

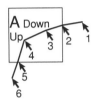

Figure 12.2 A sequence of mouse events.

Figure 12.2 shows the path of a mouse cursor moving across the screen performing a mouse click along the way. It starts out at position 1, enters sprite A at position 2, and moves to position 3, where the mouse button is pressed down. The mouse moves on to position 4, still within sprite A, where the mouse button is then released. Then the mouse exits the sprite at position 5 and continues to position 6. The following is the sequence of mouse events that will be sent to sprite A:

Position 1: no events

Position 2: Mouse Enter

Position 2: Mouse Moved

Position 3: Mouse Moved

Position 3: Mouse Down

Position 4: Mouse Moved

Position 4: Mouse Up

Position 4: Mouse Click

Position 5: Mouse Exit

Position 6: no events

Here we see that a Mouse Enter event occurs first and is always paired with a Mouse Moved. The Mouse Exit is never paired with a Mouse Moved. Mouse Moved events are only sent when the mouse is "within" the sprite. A Mouse Click event occurs right after a Mouse Up as long as the mouse is still "within" the sprite.

If you are new to mouse events, the above description might give you a headache, and you might be wondering why I'm going into all of these details. But if you are used to working with mouse events, you're probably thanking me because if you don't know how the events are defined, you can't accurately determine user interactions.

I should also point out that mouse events don't work the same way in all environments. For instance, in Java AWT, a Mouse Click would not occur

Figure 12.3 Another sequence of mouse events.

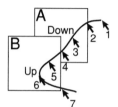

Figure 12.4 A third sequence of mouse events.

at position 4 because the mouse moved while the mouse was down. In Java, that would be considered a drag. Mouse clicks only happen when you press and release the mouse button without moving.

Let's look at another simple example. In Figure 12.3, the mouse enters sprite A at position 2, at which point the mouse button gets pressed. The mouse then exits the sprite for a while, and then re-enters the sprite at position 6, where the mouse button is finally released. The question is, will sprite A get a Mouse Up and a Mouse Click event at position 6? The answer is yes.

Let's look at Figure 12.4 for a final example. This example will produce the following sequence of events:

Position 1: no events

Position 2: Mouse Enter sent to A

Position 2: Mouse Moved sent to A

Position 3: Mouse Moved sent to A

Position 3: Mouse Down sent to A

Position 4: Mouse Moved sent to A

Position 5: Mouse Exit sent to A

Position 5: Mouse Enter sent to B

Position 5: Mouse Moved sent to B

Position 6: Mouse Moved sent to B

Position 6: Mouse Up sent to A

Position 7: Mouse Exit sent to B

At position 5, a Mouse Exit event is sent to sprite A even though it is technically within the bounds of A. This is because the mouse can only be "within" one sprite at a time, and that would be the frontmost sprite that the mouse is over. Once the mouse has exited A, Mouse Moved events are no longer sent. Note that at position 6, the Mouse Up event is sent to sprite A even though the mouse is within sprite B. This is because the Mouse Up event is always sent to the same sprite that last received a Mouse Down event. In this case the Mouse Up event is not followed by a Mouse Click event because the mouse is no longer over sprite A. What do you think would happen if the mouse were released at position 5 instead? Would this result in a Mouse Click event? The answer is yes, and that might surprise you. In my opinion this is a bug. Sprite A still gets a Mouse Click event even though the mouse has exited sprite A. The reason for this is because after Mouse Up, QuickTime simply checks to see if the sprite's bounds still contain the mouse cursor; if they do, it sends a Mouse Click event. QuickTime doesn't take into account the fact that other sprites might be in the way.

▶ Checkbox

OK. Enough of the nitty-gritty stuff. Let's build something. A checkbox will demonstrate the need for all of the mouse events except for Mouse Moved. Open the project Checkbox_start.lsd and preview the movie. You'll find a lonely checkbox that doesn't yet respond to mouse events (see Figure 12.5). To take a first stab at making it interactive, let's add the following script to the checkbox's Mouse Click event:

[Mouse Click]

```
IF( ImageIndex != $checkedUp )
    SetImageIndexTo($checkedUp)
ELSE
    SetImageIndexTo($uncheckedUp)
ENDIF
```

☐ checkbox

Figure 12.5 Checkbox_start.lsd.

Preview the movie and you'll see that you have the basics of a working checkbox. Notice that when you click down on the checkbox, exit the checkbox, and then release the mouse button, the checkbox doesn't toggle its state. This is the standard behavior of checkboxes. You have to release the mouse within the box to activate the toggle. We get this behavior because we put the script on Mouse Click. If we had placed it on Mouse Up, the checkbox would toggle no matter where we released the mouse.

Although this checkbox works, it's pretty crude. Most checkboxes give you visual feedback when you click down on them. To do this, we can add scripts to the Mouse Down and Mouse Up events as follows:

[Mouse Down]

SetImageIndexBy(1)

[Mouse Up]

SetImageIndexBy(-1)

This increases the image index by one when the mouse is pressed, and decreases the image index by one when the mouse is released. This will work because I ordered the images as follows:

uncheckedUp
uncheckedDown
checkedUp
checkedDown

Preview the movie, and I'm sure you'll agree that this is a much nicer checkbox. One subtle note is that this only works because Mouse Up happens before Mouse Click. If Mouse Up happened after, then decreasing the image index by one would do the wrong thing.

In most modern user interfaces, checkboxes also respond to Mouse Enter and Mouse Exit events, but to implement it correctly we'll need to introduce some state variables. A whole part of this book is devoted to user interfaces, so you should look at Part IV if you want to know how to make perfect checkboxes.

Let's finish up our checkbox by allowing the user to click the label as well as the box itself. Being able to click the text label is a simple nicety that users are going to expect, and unfortunately most developers (myself included) often leave it out. To do it, we're going to simply route the label's mouse events to the checkbox. We're going to use the ExecuteEvent action and pass in the names that QuickTime gives to the events (such as kQT-MouseClickEnd for the Mouse Up event). Add the following scripts to the label sprite:

```
[Mouse Click]
SpriteNamed("checkbox").ExecuteEvent(kQTEventMouseClickEndTriggerButton)
```

```
[Mouse Down]
SpriteNamed("checkbox").ExecuteEvent(kQTEventMouseClick)
```

```
[Mouse Up]
SpriteNamed("checkbox").ExecuteEvent(kQTEventMouseClickEnd)
```

Now preview your completed checkbox.

Note I should note that QuickTime provides a low-level way of delegating a sprite to handle the events of another sprite. When you build the sprite, you can specify a HandlerID (the ID of the sprite to handle events). LiveStage doesn't give users access to the HandlerID for the sprites it creates, but if you are creating the sprites through C/C++ or Java, you have this option. As we'll see in Chapter 15, you can create new sprites dynamically through a script using the MakeNewSprite action. That action takes a HandlerID as a parameter.

▶ Mouse Hit Testing

When the mouse button is pressed, sprite worlds determine what sprite should receive the Mouse Down event through a process called *hit testing*. QuickTime performs its hit testing in the following way:

1. QuickTime first checks to see if the mouse is even in the movie.

2. QuickTime then iterates through all the enabled spatial tracks in order of spatial layer starting with the frontmost layer (most negative). It finds the first spatial track that both contains the mouse position and has an opaque region at the mouse position. You can "click through" transparent regions of a track.

3. Once QuickTime finds the track, if it is a sprite track, it then proceeds to find which sprite was hit by the mouse. It does this by iterating over all the sprites, starting from the frontmost layer. It finds the first sprite

clickable that both contains the mouse position and has an *image* with an opaque region at the mouse position. Notice that I said "image." You can't "click through" transparent regions of a sprite unless these transparent regions are defined in the image itself. The Animation and Curve (vector) codecs are the only ones that I know of that can successfully define "click through" transparency (see Table 12.1).

Note The entire sprite can be made nonclickable (starting with QuickTime 6) by unchecking the Clickable property in the sprite's Properties tab. The Clickable property can't be changed through scripting.

The QuickTime hit-testing algorithm doesn't take into account the visibility property, either for tracks or for sprites. Invisible tracks and sprites can receive mouse events just like visible ones.

Mouse Enter and Mouse Exit

Mouse Enter and Mouse Exit events are always alternating. A sprite can't receive two Mouse Enter events without a Mouse Exit in between. Also, the

Table 12.1 Clickable and transparent regions.

Transparency method	Visually transparent	Mouse event transparent
CODEC: Any Graphics mode: Transparent	✓	
CODEC: PNG, Animation + Alpha Graphics mode: Copy		
CODEC: PNG, Animation + Alpha Graphics mode: Alpha	✓	
CODEC: Animation with transparent color set Graphics mode: Copy	✓	✓
CODEC: Animation + Alpha with transparent color set Graphics mode: Alpha	✓	✓
CODEC: non-Animation with transparent color set Graphics mode: Copy		

mouse can only be "inside" one sprite at a time. Let's finally define what I mean by the mouse being "inside" a sprite.

Note   A mouse position is *inside* a sprite if a mouse button press at that position would result in a Mouse Down event being sent to that sprite. The inside of a sprite is also called the sprite's *hit region*.

For a quick demo of sprite hit regions, look at the project HitRegions _demo.lsd. Preview the movie and glide your mouse over the different shapes. Whenever the mouse enters a sprite's hit region, the sprite turns black. When the mouse exits, it goes back to its original color. This was done through the following simple scripts on Mouse Enter and Mouse Exit:

[Mouse Enter]

SetImageIndexBy(1)

[Mouse Exit]

SetImageIndexBy(-1)

One thing to notice is that both the circle and the triangle have transparent regions, but the transparent regions of the triangle are still part of the sprite's hit region because the transparency was defined by setting the sprite's graphics mode to transparent. The transparent regions of the circle, on the other hand, aren't part of the hit region since the transparency was defined in the image.

Another thing to experiment with is what happens when the entire movie is pushed to the background. To try this, put your mouse over the circle so that the circle turns black, and then hit Command-Tab to bring another application to the foreground. If the new foreground image doesn't cover up the movie, you should see that the circle has turned green again. This is because a Mouse Exit event gets sent when the movie loses focus.

As you probably guessed, QuickTime has its peculiarities with regards to Mouse Enter and Mouse Exit events. For example, moving a sprite track can cause a Mouse Exit and a Mouse Enter to be sent to the sprite that contains the mouse even if the mouse remains inside the sprite the whole time. Also, during the movie loading process, especially in the browser, you can get "flickering" Mouse Enter and Mouse Exit events.

▶ Mouse Moved

The Mouse Moved event was added to QuickTime after developers (myself included) complained that there weren't low-level ways to detect mouse movement in the earlier versions. The problem is that we weren't specific enough in what we were asking for. The Mouse Moved event is useful, but not nearly as useful as a Mouse Dragged event would have been. The difference is that Mouse Moved gets sent whenever the mouse moves while inside the sprite's hit region. Mouse Dragged, on the other hand, gets sent whenever the mouse moves in between Mouse Down and Mouse Up events. Mouse Dragged gets sent if the mouse is inside the hit region or not. To see why this matters, let's wire up a draggable sprite using Mouse Moved.

Open up the project MouseMoveDrag_demo.lsd and give it a spin. Notice that if you move the mouse slowly, the sprite drags pretty well, but as soon as you move more quickly, the sprite gets left behind. This happens because the Mouse Moved event only gets sent when the mouse is over the sprite. If you move too quickly, the mouse gets outside of the sprite before Mouse Moved can be sent.

Most QuickTime developers use mouse polling to implement the drag behavior. Mouse polling is where you check the position of the mouse on the Idle event. The Draggable behavior that ships with LiveStage Pro uses polling. This is fine for small movies where there's not much going on and only a few things are draggable. The problem with this method is that it is processor intensive. Smooth drags using polling can only be achieved with a fast idle rate. On every Idle event, every sprite that is draggable has to check to see if it is being dragged or not, even if the mouse isn't moving. If I used mouse polling for the Solitaire game (Projects/Chapter10/Solitaire/; see Figure 12.6), it would be too sluggish to play even on an 800+ MHz processor. So, what's the solution? The solution is to build a drag manager.

▶ Drag Manager

In software terms, a *manager* is a component (or an "object") that keeps track of the state variables and handles the processing for a particular task or group of tasks. Usually one manager can serve multiple clients, which often makes things more efficient. Here we're going to build a manager to handle everything involved in making a sprite draggable.

Open the DragManager_start.lsd project, where you'll find two sprites, one called DragManager and the other called DragMe. Almost everything has been implemented, with only a few final touches left to be made. To

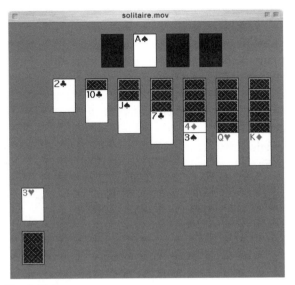

Figure 12.6 The Solitaire game.

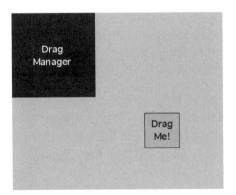

Figure 12.7 The drag manager at the start.

see how it stands now, preview the movie and try to drag the sprite (see Figure 12.7).

What happens? When you click down on the DragMe sprite, the drag manager sprite should appear. When you release the mouse button, the drag manager goes away. The DragMe sprite isn't really draggable yet. Click down on the DragMe sprite again, and this time drag it over to the drag manager. As soon as your mouse enters the drag manager, the DragMe sprite starts being dragged. This is because the drag manager is now getting the necessary Mouse Moved events. If we make the drag manager fill the entire track, then the sprite will be draggable everywhere.

To do this, add the following code to the drag manager's Frame Loaded event:

[Frame Loaded]

```
SpriteOfID($ThisSpriteID).Stretch \
  (0,0,TrackWidth,0,TrackWidth,TrackHeight,0,TrackHeight)
SpriteOfID($ThisSpriteID).ExecuteEvent($EndDrag)
```

What this does is stretch the manager so it is the same size as the track. It then calls the EndDrag event to move it off the screen. I know I've mentioned this before, but it's worth mentioning again that in the Frame Loaded event, you have to explicitly say which sprite you are targeting. Sprite-OfID($ThisSpriteID) is a convenient way of targeting the sprite that the script resides on. The reason why Frame Loaded is different from other events is because it is actually a track event and doesn't get sent to each sprite even though LiveStage makes it look that way.

Preview it now and see how it works. When you press the mouse button, the drag manager should fill the entire track. When you release the mouse button, the drag manager goes away, and you should notice that the DragMe sprite is now in a new position since it was being dragged. We just couldn't see it being dragged because the drag manager was in the way. All we have to do now is make the drag manager invisible and we're set. To do that, simply add another line of code to the drag manager's Frame Loaded script so it reads as follows:

[Frame Loaded]

```
SpriteOfID($ThisSpriteID).Stretch \
  (0,0,TrackWidth,0,TrackWidth,TrackHeight,0,TrackHeight)
SpriteOfID($ThisSpriteID).ExecuteEvent($EndDrag)
SpriteOfID($ThisSpriteID).SetVisible(FALSE)
```

Preview it and do some optimized dragging! The nice thing about having a drag manager is that you don't lose any performance when you increase the number of sprites that are draggable. You can also turn the idle events completely off (by setting the idle rate to −1) and it will still work. Let's add another draggable sprite. All we have to do is create a new sprite and add the following scripts to the Mouse Down and Mouse Up events:

[Mouse Down]
```
GlobalVars DragClientID, StartX, StartY
```

```
DragClientID = ID
StartX = GetEventMouseX
StartY = GetEventMouseY
SpriteNamed("DragManager").ExecuteEvent($StartDrag)

[Mouse Up]
SpriteNamed("DragManager").ExecuteEvent($EndDrag)
```

The Mouse Down script sets three global variables. DragClientID is the ID of the sprite that the drag manager is to move around the screen. StartX and StartY represent the position of the mouse when the Mouse Down event occurred. These were set using GetEventMouseX and GetEventMouseY, which are event properties. GetEventMouseX is similar to MouseHorizontal with the following differences (see Figure 12.8):

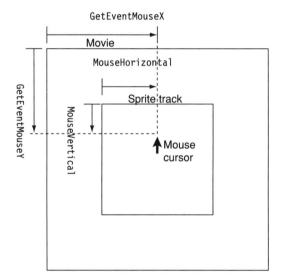

Figure 12.8 The mouse coordinate system: GetEventMouseX versus MouseHorizontal.

1. GetEventMouseX is only accessible from mouse and key events. MouseHorizontal can be accessed from any event, even custom events.

2. GetEventMouseX is constant during the execution of a mouse or key event. MouseHorizontal can change its value during the execution of an event.

3. GetEventMouseX is relative to the movie, so a value of 0 means the very left edge of the movie. MouseHorizontal is relative to the sprite track, so 0 means the left edge of the track.

The same obviously holds for GetEventMouseY and MouseVertical. The drag manager uses GetEventMouseX instead of MouseHorizontal to try to reduce drag slippage. Drag slippage happens when there is lag between the time that the Mouse Down is detected and the time that the Mouse Down script actually gets executed. During that time, the user might move the mouse. If one relies on MouseHorizontal and MouseVertical, then there is more of a chance that the values will be different from the location that the Mouse Down occurred. That isn't to say that slippage can't occur with GetEventMouseX, but it is much less likely.

When the drag manager gets the StartDrag event, it does two things. It moves to position (0,0) so that it covers the track, and it moves to layer MIN_SHORT so that it is at the frontmost layer. The line of code that sets the layer can be moved to the Frame Loaded event since it really only needs to be called once.

When the drag manager gets the EndDrag event, it simply moves to (TrackWidth,0) so that it is off the track. I should note that this assumes the image registration point for the drag manager's image is at (0,0). Moving a sprite off the track is an efficient way to hide the sprite from mouse events.

All of the work is done in the Mouse Moved event of the drag manager. Here the distance that the mouse moved is calculated, and a MoveBy() action is called on the drag client. Here's the code:

```
[Mouse Moved]
GlobalVars DragClientID, StartX, StartY
LocalVars deltaX, deltaY

deltaX = GetEventMouseX - StartX
deltaY = GetEventMouseY - StartY
StartX = GetEventMouseX
StartY = GetEventMouseY
SpriteOfID(DragClientID).MoveBy(deltaX, deltaY)
```

Since we are using MoveBy(), this drag manager could easily be modified to drag a group of sprites, in which case there would be multiple drag clients.

Double Clicks

The Mouse Click event indicates the occurrence of a single click. But what about double clicks? A double click is simple two clicks that occur within a small period of time (usually just under half a second). To detect a double click, the sprite needs to remember the time of the last click. As a quick example, open DoubleClick_start.lsd. In it you'll find a single sprite. Add the following script to its Mouse Click event:

```
[Mouse Click]
LocalVars lastClickTime

#define CLICKPERIOD = 30

IF( TickCount - lastClickTime < $CLICKPERIOD  )
    Rotate(45)
ELSE
    lastClickTime = TickCount
ENDIF
```

This rotates the sprite by 45 degrees every time it receives a double click. Here we define a double click as two clicks within half a second (30 ticks).

▶ Focus

In the drag manager, we employed a global variable, DragClientID. It referenced the sprite that was last clicked on. Internally, QuickTime maintains its own reference to the last sprite that received a Mouse Down event. Unfortunately, we don't have access to that reference through wired actions, but it's there, and it's important to know about it. It's called the *sprite with focus*.

Note The word *focus* comes from the Latin word for fireplace. It was first used in its modern sense by the German astronomer Johannes Kepler to describe the convergence of light through a lens. Kepler, as you may recall, was the one who first described the laws of planetary motion.

In the QuickTime context, when an object has focus, it receives keyboard events. Objects that don't have focus don't get keyboard events. When you fill out a form on a Web page, you only want to type into one text field at a time; in computer speak, the text field you are typing into has the "focus."

In QuickTime, sprites aren't the only things that can have focus. The sprite track itself can have focus; Flash text objects and QuickTime text tracks can have focus as well. QuickTime gives more wired action support over the focus of tracks than of sprites. You can test to see if a track can be given the focus through the CanBeFocus property. The IsFocus property will tell you if a track currently has the focus. The focus can be transferred to a particular track or sprite through the SetFocus action. Why am I going into this concept of focus? Only objects with focus can receive key events, and that is our next topic.

▶ Key Events

When you press a key on the keyboard, a Key Pressed event is sent to the object that currently has focus (if there is one). If a sprite track has the focus, a Key Pressed event is sent to the track. The current version of Live-Stage Pro (version 4) doesn't support scripting of track-level Key Pressed events. Only text track and sprite key events can be scripted.

A sprite can gain focus through a few different ways. One way is by clicking the sprite with the mouse. If the sprite track's "Can have keyboard focus" property is on (there's a checkbox for it in the sprite track's info dialog; see Figure 12.9), then focus can be also transferred to the sprite through the SetFocus action or through the Tab key.

Note The "Can have keyboard focus" property of tracks is the same as the CanBeFocus property. It can't be set at runtime. This property doesn't change the ability of tracks to gain focus through direct clicking. You can always give a text track or a sprite the focus by clicking it. What the property does do is prevent the track from gaining focus through the Tab key or through the SetFocus action. Another thing to note is that if the CanBe-Focus property is false, IsFocus will always return false even though the track might actually have the focus.

QuickTime lets the user iterate through the focusable objects by using the Tab key. Hitting the Tab key moves the focus to the next focusable object. If you don't want a track (or the objects inside of a track) to gain

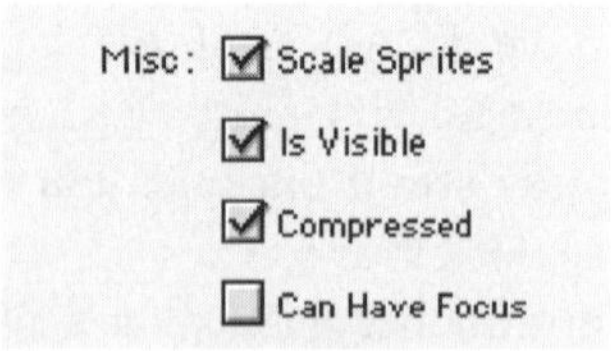

Figure 12.9 The "Can have focus" checkbox from the sprite track inspector window.

focus through the Tab key, you can set its "Can have keyboard focus" property off. Focusable objects are ordered by their index and the parent-child hierarchy. For example, the movie structure in Figure 12.10 has four focusable objects: two tracks and two sprites. If the text track starts out in focus, then repeated pressing of the Tab key will cause transfers of focus as follows:

First press of the Tab key: sprite track gains focus

Second press of the Tab key: SpriteOfIndex(1) gains focus

Third press of the Tab key: SpriteOfIndex(2) gains focus

Fourth press of the Tab key: Text track gains focus

Note It is also possible to block the Tab key from transferring focus to the next object. This is done through the EatKeyEvent action (see Chapter 19 for more information).

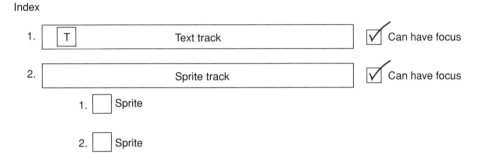

Figure 12.10 An example movie structure.

Once an object has focus, it can receive Key Pressed events. When you press and hold a key down, Key Pressed events get sent repeatedly, just like what happens in a word processor. Most environments also have a Key Released event, but this is absent from the current version of LiveStage.

Note The Key Released event was added to QuickTime in version 6, but hasn't been made accessible by LiveStage yet.

Open robot_start.lsd. In the project you'll find a single sprite with several custom events: moveForward, moveBackward, rotateLeft, rotateRight. You can call these messages to maneuver a triangular robot around the track (see Figure 12.11). What we want to do is map keys on the keyboard

Figure 12.11 A triangular robot with custom events.

to these custom events. To do this, add the following script to the robot's Key Pressed event:

```
[Key Pressed]
IF( GetEventKey = 30)
    ExecuteEvent($MoveForward)
ENDIF
```

This means that whenever we press the key with an ASCII value of 30, the MoveForward custom event will be called.

Note ASCII, which stands for American Standard Code for Information Interchange, was developed in 1963 as a replacement for Morse code. It's a way to represent letters as binary numbers. It has the advantage over Morse code in that ASCII has a fixed length of 7 bits, whereas Morse code has a variable length.

An ASCII value of 30 corresponds to the up arrow key. See the ASCII table in Appendix O for a list of values.

So, let's run it and try it out. Preview the movie and press the up arrow key, and . . . nothing happens. Why didn't it do anything? Because the robot sprite doesn't have focus yet. One way to give the robot focus is by clicking it. Try clicking the triangular-shaped robot. Now when you press the up arrow key, it should move forward.

We can now hook up the rest of the arrow keys to the other events to get a full remote-controlled robot:

```
[Key Pressed]

IF( GetEventKey = 30 )
    ExecuteEvent($MoveForward)
ELSEIF( GetEventKey = 31 )
    ExecuteEvent( $MoveReverse )
ELSEIF( GetEventKey = 28 )
```

```
       ExecuteEvent( $TurnLeft )
ELSEIF( GetEventKey = 29 )
       ExecuteEvent( $TurnRight )
ENDIF
```

Copy and paste the robot sprite so you have two robots (select the sprite in LiveStage Pro's sprite list, then copy and paste), and preview the movie. You can now choose which one has the focus by clicking one or the other. Click one sprite, and press the arrow keys to move it around, then click the other sprite to transfer focus.

Most applications that have multiple focusable objects visually show which one currently has focus. We can do this here by changing the image to one that has an outline around it. In order to do this, we need to keep track of which robot has focus ourselves since it isn't accessible through wired actions. We can do this by making a GlobalVar called FocusedRobot that holds the ID of the current sprite in focus, and then every time a robot gets clicked, it tells the "focused" robot that it lost focus, and then places its own ID into the FocusedRobot variable. In this project, I've already scripted this functionality in the GainedFocus and LostFocus custom events:

```
[10 GainedFocus]
GlobalVars FocusedRobot

IF( FocusedRobot > 0 )
    SpriteOfID( FocusedRobot ).ExecuteEvent($LostFocus)
ENDIF

SetImageIndexTo($RobotInFocus)
FocusedRobot = ID

[11 LostFocus]

SetImageIndexTo($Robot)
```

All we need to do is add a line of script to the Mouse Down events of each robot sprite:

```
[Mouse Down]

ExecuteEvent($GainedFocus)
```

Now the robots should provide correct visual feedback about their focused state (see Figure 12.12).

Figure 12.12   A robot with focus.

One limitation that you might be pondering is the fact that you have to first click a sprite to give it focus. This works for some situations, but for others we're going to want to have more programmatic control. For instance, what if we wanted to have a default robot start off in focus?

We can transfer the focus to a sprite or a track through the SetFocus action. However, in order to use the SetFocus action, you need to select the "Can have keyboard focus" checkbox in the sprite track's info panel. Once we do that, we can perform a SetFocus call on the Frame Loaded event. Append the following script to the Frame Loaded script of the first robot sprite:

```
[Frame Loaded]
```

```
SpriteOfIndex(1).SetFocus
SpriteOfIndex(1).ExecuteEvent($GainedFocus)
```

When the movie loads, the first robot will start off in focus. The only problem now is that turning "Can have keyboard focus" on also enables the Tab key to transfer focus. If you hit the Tab key, the focus will be transferred to the second robot, but visually, it looks like the first robot has the focus. We can prevent this by adding EatKeyEvent to the end of each robot's Key Pressed script. This will prevent QuickTime from processing the Tab key and transferring the focus.

With this addition, all is well with our robot movie. However, problems can arise quickly if we add sprites that aren't robots. For instance, if we add a new sprite without any scripts, clicking it will make the sprite gain focus, but the robots won't know what happened. It can be complicated to make every sprite know how to deal with focus issues. One way to solve this problem is to continuously set the focus to the FocusedSprite by calling SpriteOfID(FocusedSprite).SetFocus on an Idle event. Other solutions involve a keyboard manager.

▶ Keyboard Managers

We can gain more control over key events by using a keyboard manager. This is a similar concept to the drag manager except that instead of drag events, it captures keyboard events and then relays them to the appropriate places. There are many ways to build such a manager. I'll briefly discuss two of them. Each has its own pluses and minuses.

Click Anywhere Keyboard Manager

One type of keyboard manager I call a "click anywhere" manager. This is similar to the drag manager in that it utilizes an invisible sprite that fills the entire track. On the Frame Loaded event, we call SetFocus on this manager. After that, no matter where the user clicks, they'll click this manager sprite. This way it doesn't lose focus.

Whenever a Key Pressed event occurs, the keyboard manager stores the ASCII code in a global variable and then tells whatever sprite it wants that a key event happened. This manager should use EatKeyEvent to prevent transferring focus through the Tab key.

The downside of this manager is that it prevents other sprites from receiving mouse events. Otherwise it has great performance.

Key Polling Manager

Another way to make a keyboard manager is not to use QuickTime's Key Pressed events at all. We can use another method to detect keyboard activity, and that is by using the KeyIsDown() action. This enables us to test if a certain key is down or not, and we can test this any time from any script. The downside is that we have to check every key that we are interested in, and we need to check often enough or else we might miss keys. If you have fewer than 10 keys to check, then this type of manager might make sense.

Note   The KeyIsDown action takes the following parameters:

KeyIsDown(modifiers, key)

There are six choices for the modifiers parameters:

kNone	kShiftKey	kControlKey
kOptionKey	kCommandKey	kCapsLockKey

These constant names correspond to modifier keys on a Macintosh keyboard. On Windows platforms, kCommandKey corresponds to the "Ctrl" key, and kControlKey corresponds to the "Alt" key. The "Start" and Fn" keys can't be tested.

The key parameter is any single character string, such as "a" or "3," or one of seven constants:

kReturnKey	kDownArrowKey
kTabKey	kLeftArrowKey
kDeleteKey	kRightArrowKey
kUpArrowKey	

The action returns TRUE if the specified key is down and FALSE otherwise. So to test if the "m" key is being pressed you can script:

IF(KeyIsDown(kNone, "m"))

   //do something

ENDIF

Here we use the kNone modifier to denote that we are testing for "m" by itself with no modifiers being pressed. If we wanted to test for Option-M, then we would specify the kOptionKey modifier:

KeyIsDown(kOptionKey, "m")

If we want to test for Shift-Option-M, we use the | operator to concatenate modifiers, as in

KeyIsDown(kShiftKey | kOptionKey, "m")

We can also test if a modifier is down by itself by supplying an empty string for the key parameter. So if we want to detect when the Shift key is pressed, we write

KeyIsDown(kShiftKey, "")

▶ Explorations

1. The drag manager we made in this chapter uses relative offsets to drag the sprite. This makes it easy to adapt it for dragging groups of sprites. Try making a multisprite drag manager. How would you let the user define the group? One way is to let shift clicking add a sprite to the group. You can determine if the Shift key is down through a call to **KeyIsDown(kShiftKey, "")**. **ThisEvent.GetEventModifiers** is another way to determine what modifier keys are pressed. See Appendix N for the values that GetEventModifiers returns.

2. Explore the detection of right clicks on Windows. Modern user interface design uses right-button mouse clicks (in Windows) and control clicks (on the Mac) to get contextual pop-up menus for an object. QuickTime, being first developed on a Macintosh, doesn't provide direct information about which button on the mouse was clicked. Both the left button and the right button can produce `Mouse Click` events. However, there is a difference. The left button causes a `Mouse Down` event when it is pressed and then a `Mouse Up` and a `Mouse Click` event when it is released. The right button, on the other hand, causes all three events to be sent when it is pressed. As soon as the right mouse button is pressed, a `Mouse Down` is sent followed almost immediately by a `Mouse Up` and a `Mouse Click`. Another thing to know is that the `MouseButtonDown` property only returns true when the left button is being pressed. Thus we can detect a right-button click if we get a `Mouse Down` with the `MouseButtonDown` returning true, followed almost immediately by a `Mouse Up` event. I use the term "almost immediately" because there is a very short delay between the `Mouse Down` and the `Mouse Up` event, and this actually helps us distinguish a right-button click from a very rapid left-button click.

Check out `PopupMenu_demo.lsd` for an example of how to make a contextual pop-up menu that will work as expected both on the Mac and in Windows.

3. `GetEventKey` is the property used from within a `Key Pressed` event to determine which key was actually pressed. It returns a number representing an ASCII code. What ways can you think of to turn this number into a string value?

4. As I mentioned, QuickTime 6 supports a `Key Released` event, but LiveStage currently (version 4.0) doesn't give users scripting access to it. Even if QuickTime or LiveStage is missing a feature, you can often find a way to add the feature yourself. How would you go about implementing a `Key Released` event?

Answers to Quiz

1. False
2. No
3. b
4. False
5. b

6. c

7. False

8. True

9. False

10. True

Scripted Motion

A friend of mine from UC Berkeley wanted to make a movie to depict the visual stimulus he was using in one of his experiments. It was basically a couple of oriented black and white rectangles rapidly flashing around the screen. The way the rectangles moved could be described mathematically, so he wrote a computer program to generate an MPEG movie of his stimulus. The resulting file was over a megabyte. At the time, that was too big, especially since he wanted to embed it in his Web page. So he cut the movie shorter, changed the frame rate, and tried various types of compression. Finally, he got the movie down to 30K, but the quality wasn't very good. The rectangles were fuzzy and the frame rate was too low. Tired of working on it, he accepted that it was impossible to achieve small file sizes and good quality at the same time.

Then I came along and asked him why he didn't use wired QuickTime to make his movie. He had never heard of it. I told him that instead of linear video, he could move his rectangles around dynamically through wired actions. He was skeptical, but after a few minutes we built the movie. The edges of the rectangles were nice and crisp, and they moved around the screen according to the exact mathematical description he used in his experiments. The great thing was that the movie could play for hours and never repeat itself. He then asked, "OK, how big is the file size?" He was shocked to see that it was less than 1.3K!

My friend's original MPEG movie and the final wired version of the stimulus are both on the CD (`Projects/Chapter13/Compression/`; see Figure 13.1).

In this chapter we're going to explore various ways to animate sprites mathematically.

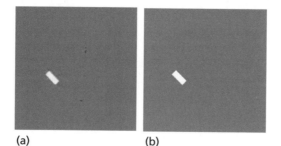

(a)   (b)

Figure 13.1   (a) MPEG; (b) wired sprite.

▶ Linear Interpolation

The "polation" part of the word *interpolation* comes from the same root as the word *polish* (to smooth). Interpolation is when you take a rough path of just a few points and turn it into a nice smooth path by finding points in between (which is why it's sometimes called *tweening*).

We'll begin with linear interpolation, which turns two points into a line. In Figure 13.2 we see two points. The start point is located at (1,3), and the end point is located at (10,8). How big of a step along the *x* and *y* directions do we need to take to get from the start point to the end point? Well, that's simple. Along *x*, we go from 1 to 10, so that's 9. And along *y* we go from 3 to 8, so that's 5. How big do the steps have to be if we want to take exactly 10 steps to get from the start to the end? We just divide the distance by 10, so 0.9 along *x* and 0.5 along *y*.

Let's make a movie where a ball moves from its current position to any new position in a specified number of steps. We'll define the new position as the location of a mouse click.

Open linearInterp_start.lsd. Have a look at the Idle event of the ball sprite, which is already implemented to move by a certain amount for a certain number of steps:

```
[Idle]
GlobalVars StepSizeX, StepSizeY, NumSteps
SpriteVars stepsLeft

IF( stepsLeft > 0 )
    MoveBy(StepSizeX, StepSizeY)
    stepsLeft = stepsLeft - 1
ENDIF
```

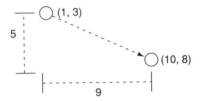

Figure 13.2 Linear interpolation.

The only thing that isn't coded is the calculation of the global variables StepSizeX and StepSizeY. We want to do this calculation every time the background sprite gets a Mouse Click event. Here's the script:

```
[Mouse Click]
GlobalVars StepSizeX, StepSizeY, NumSteps
LocalVars startX, startY, endX, endY

startX = SpriteNamed("ball").BoundsLeft + \
    SpriteNamed("ball").ImageRegistrationPointX
startY = SpriteNamed("ball").BoundsTop + \
    SpriteNamed("ball").ImageRegistrationPointY
endX = MouseHorizontal
endY = MouseVertical
StepSizeX = (endX - startX)/NumSteps
StepSizeY = (endY - startY)/NumSteps
SpriteNamed("ball").ExecuteEvent($StartMoving)
```

Once we execute the StartMoving event, the ball sprite begins making steps. After 10 steps it should arrive at its destination and stop. Run it and see if it works.

▶ Easing In and Out

The ball's movement in the last example was rather rigid. As soon as we clicked, the ball started moving at a fixed rate. Once it arrived at its destination, it abruptly stopped. This isn't how things move in the real world. Real objects usually take a little while to transition between moving and not moving. In the animation world, this is called *easing in and out*.

Movement, in general, looks more realistic if it smoothly changes speed. This means that we should not only interpolate position, but should interpolate velocity too. There are many ways to ease motion in and out,

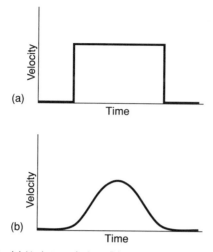

Figure 13.3 (a) No interpolation; (b) cosine interpolation.

but the one I like the best is cosine interpolation. Once you see how it works, you'll be able to design your own velocity interpolations.

Figure 13.3 displays two velocity versus time plots. The plot on the top is the way that our ball currently moves. It starts out at zero velocity, and once we click our mouse, it instantly starts moving at a fixed velocity until it reaches the final destination, where it suddenly stops. The plot on the bottom shows a cosine-interpolated velocity curve. It has a gradual transition from stopped, moving, back to stopped. Here's the equation for this curve:

```
velocityScale =  1 - cos( currentStep * stepAngle )
```

Note The cosine is a cyclic function that repeats itself every 2 * pi. So the `stepAngle` here is 2 * pi/NumSteps. I call the result of this function `velocityScale` because it tells us how much to scale each step in a linear interpolation to make it into a cosine interpolation. We can do this because I've designed the area under the cosine curve to be the same as the area under the fixed-velocity curve. The area under a velocity curve (called the *integral*) determines how far the ball will go. Having the same area means the two curves will take the ball from and to the same locations, which is what we want.

Open the project `cosineInterp_demo.lsd`. It's very similar to the `linearInterp` project, but it has a different-colored ball and, more importantly, it uses cosine interpolation instead of linear interpolation. Here's what the ball's `Idle` script looks like:

```
[Idle]
GlobalVars StepSizeX, StepSizeY, NumSteps
SpriteVars stepAngle, currentStep, isMoving
LocalVars velocityScale

IF( isMoving )
    velocityScale = 1 - COS( currentStep * stepAngle )
    MoveBy( velocityScale*StepSizeX, velocityScale*StepSizeY)
    currentStep = currentStep + 1
    IF( currentStep > NumSteps )
        isMoving = FALSE
    ENDIF
ENDIF
```

The linear interpolation is transformed into cosine interpolation by multiplying stepSizeX and stepSizeY by the velocityScale factor at each step.

Note We are performing the velocityScale multiplication inside of the MoveBy action. This is called *in-line calculation,* and it's faster than creating intermediate variables as long as doing so doesn't result in duplicate calculations (see Figure 13.4). We wouldn't want to "in-line" the calculation of velocityScale because we would have to calculate it twice.

```
In-line:    SpriteOfID(x + 3)

Separate: n = x + 3
          SpriteOfID(n)
```

Figure 13.4 In-line calculation versus separate calculations.

Preview the movie and notice how the ball's movement is much more natural than the linear interpolation version.

▶ Motion along a Mathematical Function

Parabolas are often used for describing the motion of objects where the only force acting on them is gravity. Instead of discussing the physics behind projectile motion (we'll delve into that subject in Chapter 16), I'd like to use the parabola as an example of how to move sprites along mathematical functions.

Consider the function for a generic parabola:

$$y = ax^2 + bx + c$$

By changing the a, b, and c parameters, we can get a whole family of curves. Some examples are shown in Figure 13.5.

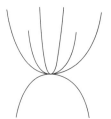

Figure 13.5 Examples of parabolas with different parameters.

But how do we pick a, b, and c parameters to get the curve to do what we want? Say we want to move a sprite in a parabolic fashion so that it jumps up a certain height and over a certain distance. What parameters do we use? The textbook way to do this is to plug in some known values for x and y and then solve the quadratic equations. You can do it that way, but there's a better way.

What I like to do is first find parameters for a given mathematical function such that the essence of the function fits snugly inside a 1-pixel by 1-pixel box. You can then easily scale that box to any size you want and not have to worry about the peculiarities of the function's parameters. This will make more sense after an example.

The idea is to fit a parabola into a 1×1 pixel box. Figure 13.6 is a blown-up picture of what that looks like. If we find the parameters to make that curve, then producing other parabolic curves is easy.

Let's quickly grind through the math to find those "magic" parameters. We know the formula for a parabola, and according to the picture, we want it such that when x is 0, y is also 0. When x is 0.5, y should be 1. And finally, when x is 1, y should be 0 again. This gives us three equations and three unknowns (a, b, and c):

$$0 = a0^2 + b0 + c$$

$$1 = a0.5^2 + b0.5 + c$$

$$0 = a1^2 + b1 + c$$

Figure 13.6 A parabola in a box.

After some scratches and scribbles on a napkin, I get the following solution:

$$a = -4$$
$$b = 4$$
$$c = 0$$

Is this what you get? Using these values, the formula of our tiny parabola-in-a-box is

$$y = -4 * x^2 + 4 * x$$

Translated directly into QScript, this becomes

```
y = -4 * x * x + 4 * x
```

And as always, it's good to do some algebraic manipulations to reduce it to its simplest form:

```
y = 4 * x * (1 - x)
```

With this form of the parabola equation, we should be able to easily control the curve to do what we want. As an example of that control, let's have a sprite jump over a wall in a parabolic fashion.

Open the project functionMotion_start.lsd. Inside you'll find a ball sprite with an EvaluateFunction custom event. This custom event gets an input value through a global variable called InputX. Its job is to set an output variable called OutputY. We can plug in any function we want. The only thing special is that the function is expected to be scaled to fit inside a 1 × 1 pixel square.

Let's implement the EvaluateFunction event with our parabola equation as follows:

```
[15 EvaluateFunction]
GlobalVars InputX, OutputY

OutputY = 4 * InputX * (1 - InputX)
```

EvaluateFunction gets called from the Idle event of the ball sprite. Let's take a quick look at how that works. Here's the script:

```
[Idle]
GlobalVars InputX, OutputY
SpriteVars numSteps, currentStep, isMoving
SpriteVars lastX, lastY, scaleX, scaleY

IF( isMoving )
    InputX = currentStep/numSteps
    ExecuteEvent($EvaluateFunction)
    MoveBy( scaleX*(InputX-lastX), scaleY*(OutputY-lastY))
    lastX = InputX
    lastY = OutputY
    currentStep = currentStep + 1
    IF( currentStep > numSteps )
        ExecuteEvent($StopMoving)
    ENDIF
ENDIF
```

Let's walk through this script and discuss what's going on. We start off by setting the input parameter (InputX) to the current step (scaled to a value between 0 and 1) and calling EvaluateFunction to obtain the OutputY value. InputX and OutputY represent a point on our micro-sized 1×1 pixel curve (in our case a parabola). Since we are using the MoveBy action, we want a change in position along the curve, not just a single point. This is achieved by caching and subtracting out the last evaluated point. The macro-sized position changes are subsequently obtained through multiplication with a scale factor (scaleX and scaleY).

You might be wondering why we are using the MoveBy action to move the ball. Why not use MoveTo and eliminate the hassle of finding the offset from the last position? There are several reasons for this. First of all, by using MoveBy, we have the ability of moving along multiple curves at once. For instance, we could have the sprite move along a parabola as it also moves up an incline or wobbles along a sine wave. The relative nature of MoveBy allows us to add motion elements together, whereas MoveTo only enables absolute positioning. Another reason for using MoveBy is that absolute position can be tricky, given that a sprite can potentially be rotated, scaled, or distorted. For scripted motion, it's usually best to work in relative rather than absolute space.

How do we choose the appropriate scaleX and scaleY? In the present example, we are attempting to coax a sprite into jumping over a brick wall

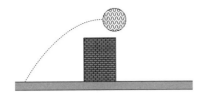

Figure 13.7 A ball jumping over a brick wall.

(see Figure 13.7). scaleY is chosen based on the height of the wall, and scaleX is the horizontal distance we would like the sprite to jump. These values are set in the StartMoving event. Let's have a look:

```
[21 StartMoving]
SpriteVars numSteps, currentStep, isMoving
SpriteVars lastX, lastY, scaleX, scaleY

scaleY = SpriteNamed("wallCover").BoundsBottom - TrackHeight
scaleX = 320
currentStep = 1
lastX = 0
lastY = 0
isMoving = TRUE
```

Is our sprite capable of leaping over a wall in a single bound? Preview the movie and find out! By moving the mouse up and down, you can change the height of the wall. Clicking locks the wall's height and executes $StartMoving on the ball. After it jumps you can click to reset and try again with a different wall height.

The only part of this example that is particular to parabolic motion is the EvaluateFunction script. The rest will generally work for any math functions scaled to fit in a 1 × 1 pixel box.

▶ Circular Motion

A couple paragraphs ago, I stated that it's usually better to use MoveBy than MoveTo. But just so you don't become anti-MoveTo, I'd like to present a situation where MoveTo is the way to go. Consider the case where you want one sprite to always be a fixed distance away from a known location. For example, say you wanted a sprite to continuously orbit about the mouse cursor in a circular manner. Using MoveBy would be needlessly complicated. Let's actually build this example.

Open and preview `CircleMotion_start.lsd`. You should be greeted by a hungry mosquito that faces left or right depending on the location of your mouse (see Figure 13.8). It presently remains at a fixed location on the screen, but knowing mosquitoes, it desperately wishes to buzz circles around the mouse. Let's grant the mosquito's wish by adding a few lines to its `Idle` event script. The `Idle` event currently contains the following script:

```
[Idle]
SpriteVars radius, currentAngle, angleStep
LocalVars positionX, positionY

ExecuteEvent($Animate)
```

Figure 13.8 A hungry mosquito.

This just executes the `Animate` event, which handles looping the image and flipping the sprite to look toward the mouse. Notice that the variables are already set up to handle moving the sprite in a circle around the mouse.

From Appendix F, we know that a point on a circle is calculated as

```
positionX = radius*cos(angle)
positionY = radius*sin(angle)
```

(See Figure 13.9.) This is for a circle centered at 0,0. We want a circle centered at the mouse cursor, so we add the mouse's location:

```
positionX = radius*cos(angle) + MouseHorizontal
positionY = radius*sin(angle) + MouseVertical
```

Now all that's needed is a simple call to `MoveTo` and the mosquito is positioned on the circle. Getting the sprite to move along a circle is achieved by simply incrementing the angle each time the script is run. Here's the resulting script:

```
[Idle]
SpriteVars radius, currentAngle, angleStep
LocalVars positionX, positionY
```

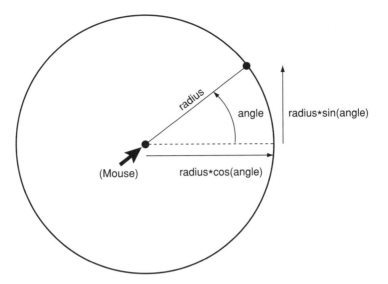

Figure 13.9 Points on a circle.

```
ExecuteEvent($Animate)
positionX = radius*cos(angle) + MouseHorizontal
positionY = radius*sin(angle) + MouseVertical
MoveTo(positionX, positionY)
currentAngle = currentAngle + angleStep
```

Preview the movie and move the cursor around. The animation is simple yet effective.

One thing you might be concerned about is that we keep adding angleStep to currentAngle each Idle event. Eventually the number is going to get so big that it will reach the maximum number QuickTime can handle. Then what happens? If it reaches the maximum number, it won't crash or anything. The max in this case is 2^{22} (4,194,303). Increasing the angle beyond that will have no effect and will simply stop the mosquito from moving in a circle. While this can happen, it probably won't. Consider the current case of 30 idle events per second and currentAngle is incremented by 1/30th of 2*PI each time. That's an increase of about half a million per day, which means it'll take over a week to reach the maximum value.

Note If you wanted to watch a circling mosquito for more than a week, there are a couple of things you can do. currentAngle will last for two weeks without any extra code by starting it off at –4,194,303 instead of 0. If you wanted it to go forever, you could add the following to the end of the Idle script:

```
    currentAngle = currentAngle + angleStep
IF( currentAngle > 2*PI )
    currentAngle = currentAngle - 2*PI
ENDIF
```

This will make `currentAngle` stay between 0 and 2*PI. Of course, this only works if `angleStep` is positive.

In other environments, a common solution would be to use some sort of `MOD` function (such as the % operator in C and Java). QScript has a `REM` function (takes the remainder), but it turns everything into an integer, which isn't good when working with radian values. If we used degrees instead of radians, `currentAngle REM 360` would do the trick. Fractions of a degree will be removed, but that won't be noticeable. Of course, if we were to use degrees, we would have to convert to radians before calling the `cos` and `sin` functions. Just multiply by PI/180. There's also a built-in function to do this called `DegreesToRadians(angle)`. See Appendix B under `REM` for more discussion.

▶ Paths

Motion defined mathematically is perfect for some applications, but often we just want to move a sprite along a path defined by a series of points (see Figure 13.10). From the outside, this sounds like an easy enough thing to do. We already know how to move a sprite to a particular point. What's stopping us from moving to a sequence of points? The only thing stopping us is where do we store that sequence of points? I guess we could just use a series of variables, such as point1, point2, point3, . . . , but hard-coding each point will make scripting tedious.

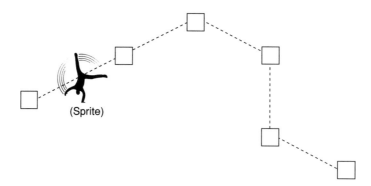

(Sprite)

Figure 13.10   A sprite moving along a path.

In QScript, there are at least three data structures that allow us to store multiple values in a single variable: arrays, strings, and QTLists. In this chapter, we'll explore arrays. (QTLists are discussed in Chapter 31. See Appendices C and D for string and QTList manipulation tips.)

The QScript used in the book so far has only defined variables to store a single value, but we can also define one to store an array of values. In the following variable definitions, simpleVar is a simple single-value variable; arrayVar is an array that can hold 10 values:

SpriteVars simpleVar arrayVar[10]

The values stored in the arrayVar variable are accessed by an index between 0 and 9 using the following syntax: arrayVar[index]. arrayVar[0] accesses the first value in the array, and arrayVar[1] accesses the second value, and so on (see Figure 13.11). The following script creates an array with four values and initializes the values to 10, 20, 30, 40:

SpriteVars array[4]

```
array[0] = 10
array[1] = 20
array[2] = 30
array[3] = 40
```

Note There are seven things we need to be aware of about how arrays work so we don't get ourselves into trouble:

1. Each element in an array functions just like a normal variable. It can hold numbers and strings, and it can be used anyplace a variable can be used.

2. If you want to use the same array in multiple scripts, you need to declare the array with the same length in each script. You can't declare myArray[4] in one place and myArray[5] in another place.

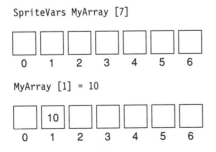

SpriteVars MyArray [7]

MyArray [1] = 10

Figure 13.11 Setting the value of an array.

3. There's no shorthand way to initialize the values of an array. The best way is to simply set each value either in a loop or in long form like the previous example.

4. There's no way to determine the length of an array at runtime. Sometimes people use the zero element of the array to hold the length of the array. That way myArray[0] is the length of the array and myArray[1] is the first actual item. Note, if you do this, you're using up one spot, so you should place the length of the array minus 1 into the zero element.

5. You should be careful not to overrun the array; that is, don't try to set the value of element 6 in an array of length 4. Doing so will probably set the value of some other variable and have undesired results. This often happens because people forget that 0 is the first index in an array.

6. LiveStage only allows 2000 LocalVars and 2000 SpriteVars per sprite track. You therefore need to be careful because two Local arrays of length 1000 each will fill up all of the LocalVar space. If you add more LocalVars, they'll start encroaching on the SpriteVar space. If you need longer arrays or more of them, you can use GlobalVars or MovieVars, which allow many times more variables. You can assign over 14,000 GlobalVars and 10,000 MovieVars. We discuss MovieVars in Chapter 38.

7. If you're coming from other programming languages, you might be tempted to do things such as set one array to another array. Arrays aren't objects; they are simply named starting points into a larger array in which all of the sprite track's variables are stored. To transfer values from one array to another, use a FOR loop.

Utilizing arrays, we're going to build a motion recorder. We'll present the user with a sprite that they can drag around the screen and trace out any path that they want. While the user moves the sprite, we'll store the *x* and *y* values of each point in a pair of arrays. We'll also provide a Play button so the user can watch the sprite move along the path that they just recorded.

Open up MotionRecorder_demo.lsd and have a look at the circle sprite's Idle event script:

```
#define MAXPOINTS = 800
SpriteVars xPoints[$MAXPOINTS], yPoints[$MAXPOINTS]
SpriteVars playing, recording, currentPoint, numPoints

IF( recording)
    IF( currentPoint >= $MAXPOINTS )
        ExecuteEvent($StopRecording)
    ELSE
        MoveTo( MouseHorizontal, MouseVertical )
```

```
            xPoints[currentPoint] = MouseHorizontal
            yPoints[currentPoint] = MouseVertical
            currentPoint = currentPoint + 1
        ENDIF
ELSEIF( playing )
    IF( currentPoint >= numPoints )
        ExecuteEvent($StopPlaying)
    ELSE
        MoveTo(xPoints[currentPoint], yPoints[currentPoint])
        currentPoint = currentPoint + 1
    ENDIF
ENDIF
```

We defined two arrays both of length MAXPOINTS = 800. Since this movie has an idle delay of 3 (20 idle events per second), 800 points is enough to record for 40 seconds.

The recording is accomplished by storing the MouseHorizontal and MouseVertical values into the currentPoint index of each array. Notice how we check to make sure currentPoint doesn't exceed MAXPOINTS. The rest of the code should be easy enough to follow.

Let's test the movie. When you first launch, you should see a red circle in the center of the stage. Drag that circle around the track along any path you choose. When you release the mouse, a Play button should appear. Clicking the Play button should trigger the circle to faithfully move along the path you just recorded.

The interactivity in this movie is very primitive, but there is something special about it. I just wasted a couple minutes playing with it. Maybe the fact that it "remembers" what you did is what's intriguing. I'm not entirely sure. This could be the topic of an interesting research project.

▶ Spline Interpolation

Since we started this chapter talking about interpolation, I thought we would end it with the same topic. Spline interpolation sounds complicated, but it's really not. Earlier we explored linear interpolation, which let us turn two points into a continuous line. Spline interpolation lets us take multiple points and approximate them with a smooth continuous curve. Splines have been around for a long time, and there are many different types. You might be familiar with Bezier splines, named after the French

Figure 13.12 Spline, a bent piece of wood.

automotive engineer who invented them. Here we're going to use Catmull-Rom splines. They were invented in the early 1970s by Edwin Catmull and Raphael Rom. Let's see how they work.

The word *spline* means a long thin strip of wood (see Figure 13.12). It's related to the word *splinter.* A strip of wood is pretty flexible. It can be bent into all sorts of shapes, but it has its limits. If you try to make a single spline go through too many bends, it's going to break. But you can increase the number of bends by piecing together multiple splines. This is exactly what we do in spline interpolation.

We want to be able to fit a curve to an arbitrary sequence of points. The problem is that the nice curves that are easy to work with mathematically can only have one or two bends in them. So with spline interpolation, you break up the sequence of points into multiple overlapping sections and fit each section with a simple curve. The most commonly used curve is a third-order polynomial, otherwise known as a *cubic polynomial.* Second-order polynomials, or *quadratics,* are also popular. For instance, Flash vectors are quadratic. The Catmull-Rom splines that we are about to use are cubic.

Note "Quad" sounds like it should be fourth order, but "quad" in this case comes from the fact that a square has four sides.

Fitting a cubic polynomial requires four points. Take, for example, the first four points of Figure 13.13 (a). These four points have been fit by a spline. Only the connection between the middle two points (2 and 3) is guaranteed to be a good fit. The curve between points 3 and 4 isn't very good at all (it doesn't even touch 4). Only by fitting another spline to the next group of points (2 through 5) will we obtain an accurate curve between points 3 and 4 (b). Continuing in this way, we can fit spline curves to each sequential group of four points (c). By considering only the good portion of the fit we wind up with a continuous closed path through all the points (d).

Spline interpolation is particularly good for sprite animation. An artist can draw a smooth curve by hand, but in a dynamic sprite world, we don't

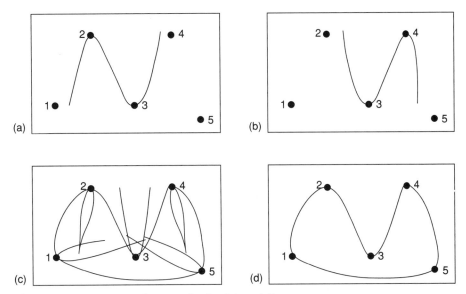

Figure 13.13 Four-part diagram of spline interpolation.

have the luxury to draw every possible curve ahead of time. Through spline fitting, smooth paths can be calculated on the fly. Let's see a demo of this.

Open `SplineInterp_demo.lsd` and run the movie. You'll see seven numbers and a ring moving smoothly along a continuous path connecting all the numbers. Try dragging some of the numbers around. As you will see, the path is recalculated on the fly.

Let's briefly discuss the meat of this project, which is the calculation of the points along a single Catmull-Rom spline segment. This is done in the NextStep event of the ring sprite. Here's the script:

```
[NextStep]
SpriteVars nSteps, step, nextX, nextY
SpriteVars x1, y2, x2, y2, x3, y3, x4, y4
LocalVars a, b, c, d, n, n2, n3

n = step/nSteps
n2 = n*n
n3 = n2*n

a = 2*n2 - n - n3
b = 2 - 5*n2 + 3*n3
c = n + 4*n2 - 3*n3
d = n3 - n2
```

```
nextX = 0.5 * ( a*x1 + b*x2 + c*x3 + d*x4 )
nextY = 0.5 * ( a*y1 + b*y2 + c*y3 + d*y4 )
```

The four points being used for the current fit are stored in the variables x1,y1 through x4,y4. The a, b, c, and d variables are standard names for the polynomial coefficients. Before those coefficients are calculated, some intermediate values are first obtained, namely, different powers of the n variable ($n2 = n^2$ and $n3 = n^3$). The variable n is a number between 0 and 1 indicating a point along the curve between x2,y2 and x3,y3. At the end of the script, we obtain the interpolated point (nextX, nextY).

We've reached the end of the chapter on scripted motion. The concepts covered here are applicable to situations beyond just sprite motion. In the next chapter, we'll expand some of these ideas further as we discuss scripted stretching of sprites.

● Explorations

1. Consider the following Idle event script:

   [Idle]

   SpriteVars deltaX

   MoveBy(deltaX, 0)

   What would you add to this script so that after the sprite exits one side of the track it will wrap around and enter the track from the other side?

2. In this chapter we made sprites move by actually changing their positions in the track. Another way to make a sprite appear to move is to drift the background in the opposite direction. One common technique is to create a background image that starts to repeat itself after a certain number of pixels, called the *period*. Usually the period is wider than the track so that duplicate parts of the image aren't shown at the same time. You then continuously scroll the image until the repeating part of the image enters the scene. At that point, you shift the image in the opposite direction by the width of the period and continue scrolling from that point.

   The scrollingBack_start.lsd project contains a scrollable image of some rolling hills. The period is 640 pixels.

   a. See if you can get the rolling hills to scroll in a seamless manner.

b. This project also has a scrollable image of telephone poles with the same period. The telephone poles can serve as a "middleground" image. Add a sprite and have it scroll the poles as you did the hills. To make it look more realistic, you will want the poles to scroll more quickly than the background hills. The difference in speed is due to a phenomenon called *parallax*. This is an effective way to add 3D depth to a 2D scene.

c. Have a look at the `scrollingBackground.mov` file for an interactive version (see Figure 13.14). The scrolling speed is tied to the position of the mouse.

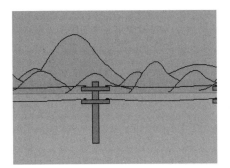

Figure 13.14 A scrolling background.

3. In this chapter we discussed easing a sprite in and out as it moves between two points. How would you adapt the technique so the sprite only eases in? Instead of easing out, it should continue moving at a steady rate.

4. When a cartoonist makes an object look like it comes to an abrupt stop, she will often have the object go past the stopping point and then snap back. This is called an *overshoot*. A related animation technique is called *anticipation*. This is where an object inches back a bit before it starts moving in a forward direction. Both of these effects make motion look more pleasing to the eye by drawing attention to starting and stopping processes. How would you implement overshoots and anticipation in a sprite world?

5. When an object moves very fast it produces motion blur. Animators sometimes use motion streaks or faded images that trail behind a moving object to make things appear like they're moving quickly. This is particularly useful for achieving apparent high-velocity motion with a

low frame rate. Similar techniques are used to overcome sampling problems when rotating an object at fast rates (rotating an object too quickly can make it look like it's rotating slowly in the opposite direction). In this case, rotational blur is applied. How can these effects be implemented with sprites?

6. When we talked about moving along mathematical functions, the example we used was a parabola. What other functions would produce interesting motion?

7. How would you change the circular motion script to produce elliptical motion?

8. In the MotionRecorder project, we simply played back the same path that the user recorded. One neat addition that makes it more interesting is to not only play back the same motion but simultaneously play back the mirrored image of the motion.

9. Spline interpolation is useful for more than just moving sprites. Splines can be used to create smooth transitions for any variable parameter. The volume of audio and the pan angle in a QTVR track are two examples. Where else would splines be useful?

Scripted Stretching

The word *stretch* has the same origins as the word *straight,* as in stretch your legs out. In the context of sprite worlds, however, stretch means to change the shape of a sprite. As we will see, this can sometimes leave a sprite in a very unstraightened state.

Many sprite worlds only allow two methods of shape modification: scaling and rotating. QuickTime sprites are much more flexible. Each of the sprite's four corners can be moved independently. This enables sprites to morph into just about any quadrilateral shape. The action used to move the corners is called Stretch. It has eight parameters representing the *x* and *y* coordinates of each corner (ordered clockwise, starting at the top left as in Figure 14.1).

Note In the low-level QuickTime calls, the Stretch action simply boils down to a matrix change.

```
Stretch( x1, y1, x2, y2, x3, y3, x4, y4 )
```

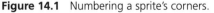

Figure 14.1 Numbering a sprite's corners.

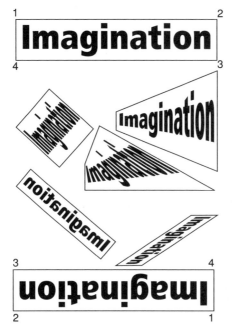

Figure 14.2 Some examples of stretch states.

The locations of the corners can also be accessed through the properties FirstCornerX, FirstCornerY, SecondCornerX, SecondCornerY, and so on. First-CornerX is the horizontal position of the top-left corner of the sprite. Well, I shouldn't say it's the top left. It's possible to stretch the sprite in such a way that the top-left corner appears at the bottom right. The first corner remains the first corner no matter how the sprite is stretched. Figure 14.2 shows some examples.

Bar Graphs

An application of stretching that I use a lot in my work is building bar graphs. A bar graph is created by simply using the length of a sprite to represent a numerical value. With the Stretch action, it's easy to elongate a sprite to any length. For example, the following script sets the height of a sprite:

```
[41 SetHeight]
GlobalVars Height
LocalVars newTop
```

```
newTop = BoundsBottom - Height
Stretch(BoundsLeft, newTop, BoundsRight, newTop, BoundsRight, \
  BoundsBottom, BoundsLeft, BoundsBottom)
```

Let's use this script to make a single-element bar graph. Open the project barGraph_start.lsd. You'll find the above script in the SetHeight custom event of the bar sprite. Run the movie and click anywhere on the scale to set the bar's height (see Figure 14.3).

One easy way to improve the look of our bar is to add a black border around it. We can do this by stretching an image behind the bar and extending it beyond the edges to form a border. Let's do this.

Add a new sprite to the sample and call it "border." Set its image to BlackSquare and set its layer to a value behind the bar sprite (10 will work). Now let's add a custom event to it, called StrechBorder, with the following script:

```
[42 StretchBorder]
GlobalVars BarID
LocalVars top, right, bottom, left

#define THICKNESS = 1

top = SpriteOfID(BarID).BoundsTop - $THICKNESS
right = SpriteOfID(BarID).BoundsRight + $THICKNESS
bottom = SpriteOfID(BarID).BoundsBottom + $THICKNESS
left = SpriteOfID(BarID).BoundsLeft - $THICKNESS

Stretch(left, top, right, top, right, bottom, left, bottom)
```

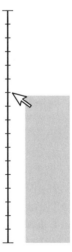

Figure 14.3 Setting the height of a bar graph element.

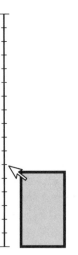

Figure 14.4 Adding a black border.

This script will make the border sprite one pixel bigger than the bar sprite on each of its edges. Now all we have to do is call this from the bar's Set-Height event (see Figure 14.4):

```
[SetHeight]
GlobalVars Height, BarID

...

BarID = ID
SpriteNamed("border").ExecuteEvent($StretchBorder)
```

Run it and you'll see how much the border improves the look of the bar. I should note that it wouldn't have worked to simply use an image with a border built in. This is because when we stretch the sprite, the image gets stretched too. This would have resulted in a border with different thicknesses on the top and bottom than on the sides (see Figure 14.5).

▶ Drawing Lines

The simple ability to draw lines greatly expands the types of things that can be built with QuickTime. Even though QuickTime doesn't explicitly expose line-drawing routines, we can accomplish everything we need

(a)

(b)

Figure 14.5 (a) A single stretched sprite, where the image contains a built-in border. (b) Two stretched sprites: the sprite in the back has a black image, and the sprite in the front has a white image.

through sprite stretching. The following script stretches a sprite into a one-pixel-thick line between two points:

```
[44 StretchLine]
GlobalVars StartX, StartY, EndX, EndY
LocalVars bigDeltaX, bigDeltaY, angle
Localvars littleDeltaX, littleDeltaY
LocalVars x1, y1, x2, y2, x3, y3, x4, y4

#define THICKNESS = 3

bigDeltaX = EndX - StartX
bigDeltaY = EndY - StartY
angle = ArcTan2( bigDeltaY, bigDeltaX ) - pi/2

littleDeltaX = ($THICKNESS + 1) * cos( angle )/2
littleDeltaY = ($THICKNESS + 1) * sin( angle )/2

x1 = StartX - littleDeltaX
y1 = StartY - littleDeltaY
x2 = StartX + littleDeltaX
y2 = StartY + littleDeltaY
x3 = EndX + littleDeltaX
y3 = EndY + littleDeltaY
x4 = EndX - littleDeltaX
y4 = EndY - littleDeltaY

Stretch(x1, y1, x2, y2, x3, y3, x4, y4)
```

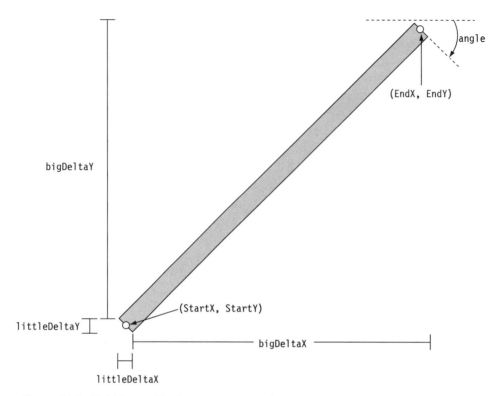

Figure 14.6 Variables used in the StretchLine script.

This script uses the ArcTan2 function to find the angle between the start and end points. We then subtract 90 degrees (π/2 radians) to determine the angle between the two corners on the same side of the line. The rest of the variables used in this script are illustrated in Figure 14.6.

To see this script in action, run the drawingLines_start.lsd project. It contains two invisible draggable sprites at each end of a red line. Try dragging the ends around to manipulate the line. I'd like you to notice one small glitch. If you drag what starts out to be the top-right end of the line, the other end is supposed to stay fixed, but it jitters slightly. We can fix this glitch through a process called *epsilon correction*. Simply add 0.0001 to the angle:

```
...
angle = ArcTan2( bigDeltaY, bigDeltaX ) - pi/2 + 0.0001
...
```

Now when you run it, both lines should remain fixed. For information on why this works, look in Appendix E.

Perspective

QuickTime sprites are inherently 2D, which can make them appear, well, deflated. Simple 3D effects can go a long way to bring sprites out of flat-land. For instance, stretching a sprite so one side is short and the other tall can create the illusion that the sprite is rotated into the computer screen. This illusion comes about because objects closer to us look bigger than objects farther away. Depicting this on a flat surface is called *perspective*. Here's a script that adds the appropriate perspective for a sprite rotated into the screen at a given angle:

```
[31 rotate3D]
SpriteVars centerX, centerY, angle3D, perspectiveFactor
SpriteVars normalWidth, normalHeight
LocalVars radians, edgeScale, deltaWidth, deltaHeight1, deltaHeight2
LocalVars x1, y1, x2, y2, x3, y3, x4, y4

#define EPSILON = 0.0001

radians = DegreesToRadians(angle3D) + $EPSILON
edgeScale = perspectiveFactor * sin(radians)
deltaHeight1 = normalHeight * ( 0.5 - edgeScale )
deltaHeight2 = normalHeight * ( 0.5 + edgeScale )
newWidth = normalWidth * cos(radians)/2

x1 = centerX - deltaWidth
y1 = centerY - deltaHeight1
x2 = centerX + deltaWidth
y2 = centerY - deltaHeight2
x3 = x2
y3 = centerY + deltaHeight2
x4 = x1
y4 = centerY + deltaHeight1

Stretch(x1, y1, x2, y2, x3, y3, x4, y4)
```

The perspectiveFactor variable is the percent increase in height when the sprite sticks directly out of the screen. This percentage will depend on how close you want the sprite to appear to the observer. I find that 10% (0.1) works well. The value will depend on the viewing geometry. The other variables used in this script are illustrated in Figure 14.7.

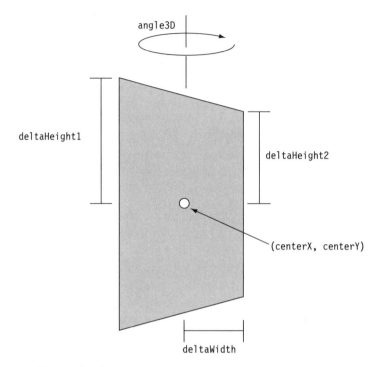

Figure 14.7 Variables used in the Rotate3D script.

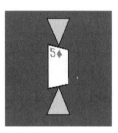

Figure 14.8 A spinning card.

Let's take this script for a spin by previewing the SpinningCard_ start.lsd project. Here we see a playing card spinning in 3D (see Figure 14.8). The perspective gives an effective illusion of depth, but there's a minor problem with the card. On one side we see the front face of the five of diamonds, but on the other side we see a mirror image of the front face. This would happen if the card were transparent, but Las Vegas would never allow transparent cards! Let's put a back on that sprite.

Have a look at the card sprite's `Idle` script. All it's doing right now is incrementing angle3D, then executing the rotate3D event. At this point we can check to see if angle3D is exposing the front or the back of the sprite and change the image accordingly. If angle3D is between 90 and 270 degrees, then the back is showing, otherwise the front. Here's the resulting `Idle` script:

```
[Idle]
SpriteVars angle3D, rotationSpeed

angle3D = (angle3D + rotationSpeed) REM 360
ExecuteEvent($rotate3D)

IF( angle3D > 90 AND angle3D < 270 )
    SetImageIndexTo($CardBack)
ELSE
    SetImageIndexTo($CardFront)
ENDIF
```

Elongating bars, spinning cards, and drawing lines are just a few applications of sprite stretching. The line drawing is something that I use a lot (I use QuickTime for scientific visualization). The example presented in this chapter only drew a single line. Of course, we could have added a few more sprites and enabled the user to draw multiple lines. But what if we wanted an unspecified number of lines (as in the movie /Projects/ Chapter02/Utilities/LineSketch.mov)? We would need a way for the sprite world to dynamically produce sprites on its own. That's the topic of the next chapter.

Explorations

1. Expanding on the concepts used to build the bar graph, how would you stretch four sprites to form a frame around the bounds of a fifth sprite?

2. The framing functionality from the previous exploration is handy for many situations. A couple of chapters ago, we explored creating a multi-sprite drag manager. One of the issues involved providing an interface for the user to select multiple sprites. How would you create an interface like the one found in most desktop operating systems and drawing programs, where clicking and dragging forms a selection box for selecting multiple sprites at once?

3. Combining scripted motion with scripted stretching can produce interesting results. Check out the examples in the `Projects/Chapter14/MoveAndStretch/` folder. Can you see how each might have been implemented? Design one of your own move-and-stretch routines.

4. What uses can you think up for line drawing in a QuickTime movie? One common situation is for interactive quizzes where the user is asked to match items on the left with items on the right. What other situations can you think of? How about in combination with audio or video? Be creative.

5. For the example of 3D perspective, we built a spinning card with two faces. Instead of having it continuously spin, make it interactive. Add the necessary scripts so that when the user clicks on the card it will turn over and display the other side.

   How would you modify the spinning card example so that the card not only spins in 3D but also rotates within the plane of the screen? Look at `spinAndRotate.mov` for an example of what I'm trying to describe.

6. At the beginning of the chapter we used sprite stretching to make a bar chart. Can we also stretch sprites to form pie charts? The stretch action itself is limited to four-sided polygons, but if we show a sprite through a circular window, we can indeed use sprites to make a pie chart. Figure 14.9 illustrates how this can be done. If we wanted to implement this

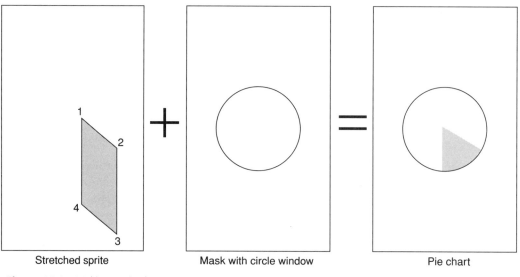

Stretched sprite   Mask with circle window   Pie chart

Figure 14.9 Making a pie chart.

idea and build a functional pie chart movie, what would be the issues? What would the script look like to stretch each piece of the pie? If you're interested and up to the challenge, try making a pie chart that will display four pieces in different colors, showing the following estimated percentages of the population that read this book:

- red: people that don't read any part of this chapter (10%)

- yellow: people that don't read this exploration (70%)

- green: people that read the exploration but don't try to make this pie chart (18%)

- blue: people that actually try to make the pie chart (2%)

7. Rotation is a form of stretching. Under what situations would the Stretch action be preferred over the Rotate action for performing a rotational stretch?

Cloning Sprites

Up until this chapter, we've been creating sprite universes with fixed populations. In this chapter we'll discuss how to make sprite populations more dynamic. QuickTime provides actions to make new sprites and delete existing ones. The actions are called MakeNewSprite and Dispose-Sprite. Let's look at MakeNewSprite first.

▶ Making New Sprites

Sprite tracks can give birth to new sprites using the MakeNewSprite action. This takes the following parameters:

```
MakeNewSprite( SpriteID, HandlerID, ImageIndex, Visible, Layer )
```

This action makes a new sprite with the specified properties. If SpriteID is already in use by another sprite, then no new sprite will be made. The HandlerID parameter determines which sprite to inherit scripts from. Pass in the ID of an existing sprite and the new sprite will share its scripts. If you don't want the sprite to inherit scripts, pass in an ID for a nonexistent sprite. I usually use 0 for this.

ImageIndex, Visible, and Layer provide initial values for these three properties. The other properties, such as spatial and graphics mode settings, are given default values. Let's see an example.

Open the document makeSprites_start.lsd and notice that it starts out with only one sprite, called "button." On the Mouse Click event of this button sprite, we have the following script:

```
[Mouse Click]
GlobalVars NextID

#define HANDLERID = 0
#define VISIBLE = TRUE
#define BACKLAYER = 10

MakeNewSprite( NextID, $HANDLERID, $Sheep, $VISIBLE, $BACKLAYER )
```

Are you ready to give birth to your first dynamically created sprite? Run the movie and click the button.

You should see a strange genetically engineered sheep appear at the top-left corner of the track (Figure 15.1). That's what the $Sheep image looks like. Well, that's sort of what the image looks like. Its background is colored black because the image has an alpha channel, but the sprite isn't in an alpha graphics mode to display it properly. The graphics mode defaults to srcCopy, but we can easily change it to an alpha mode after the sprite is made. Add the following line to the script:

```
...
SpriteOfID(NextID).SetGraphicsModeTo(graphicsModeStraightAlpha, 0, 0, 0)
```

Now when we make the sprite the $Sheep image will composite correctly with the background.

Spatial properties are also set to default values by MakeNewSprite. That means the sprite will be unrotated, unscaled, and located at the top-left corner of the screen. Let's add another line of code to move the sprite to a random location after it's made. Let's also increment NextID by 1 so we can continue making sprites with each button click:

Figure 15.1 makeSprites_start.lsd.

```
...
SpriteOfID(NextID).MoveTo(Random(0,300),Random(0,300))
NextID = NextID + 1
```

Try it out. Click the Make Sprites button as many times as you want and fill the track with randomly placed sheep.

Note How many sprites can QuickTime handle? I'm not sure what the internal limits of the QuickTime software are, but the practical limit is a few hundred. On my Powerbook, I ran a simple test movie that continuously made sprites on an idle event. At around 200, the sprite track screen refresh rate was noticeably slower, but it kept producing sprites at the same rate until around 500. Finally, at 806 it stopped and no more sprites were made. This result may vary on different platforms and configurations, but if your movie is going to be distributed, you can't control the platform. I'd advise not going much over 100 sprites.

Cloning Sprites with Behavior

So far, the sprites we've been making through the MakeNewSprite action haven't been interactive. For instance, they don't respond to mouse clicks. They still get all the normal mouse events, but they don't have any scripts associated with them. QuickTime doesn't provide ways to dynamically create new scripts, but it does provide the HandlerID parameter, which lets new sprites share the scripts of another sprite. Through this method, newly created sprites can inherit the behavior of existing sprites. We call this *cloning*.

Open the cloneSprites_start.lsd project. It's similar to the last project, but this time it starts off with a sheep sprite called "protoSheep." The button's Mouse Click script passes in the protoSheep ID for the HandlerID parameter of MakeNewSprite. This way sprites made by clicking on the button will share protoSheep's scripts. Currently, that amounts to a single script on the Mouse Click event:

```
[Mouse Click]
Rotate(10)
```

When you preview the movie, first click on protoSheep a few times to make sure it behaves correctly. It should rotate by 10 degrees each time. Then click on the button to make a new sheep. This new sheep will also rotate by 10 degrees when clicked.

So far so good. Let's give protoSheep a more sophisticated behavior. Add the following script to its `Idle` event:

```
[Idle]
SpriteVars angle
LocalVars x,y

x = TrackWidth/2 + 130 * sin(angle)
y = TrackHeight - 40 - ABS( 200 * cos(angle) )
angle = angle + pi/40
```

Before you preview the movie, what sort of motion will this script produce? Now, preview the movie. Were you right? You should see protoSheep slowly jump back and forth. Now, see what happens when you click the button and make a new sprite. Were you expecting that? There are now two sheep, but they are moving twice as fast as when there was only one sheep. Clicking on the button again will make another sheep and they'll all jump together, this time three times as fast (see Figure 15.2). What's going on?

When multiple sprites share the same script, they also share the same variables. In this case, each sheep sprite is increasing the `angle` variable by pi/40. So, when there are two sheep, `angle` is being increased twice, so the sheep move twice as fast. Does this mean that we can't accurately clone behaviors that use variables? No, we just have to be clever and account for this when we design the script.

There are many ways to clone-safe scripts with variables. One way is to use arrays instead of single variables and give each sprite access to their own item in the array. If you give new sprites sequential IDs like we do

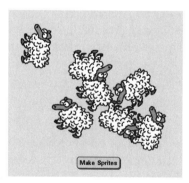

Figure 15.2 Multiple sheep sprites.

now, then we can use the sprite IDs to index the items in the array. Here's the version of the previous Idle script but with the angle variable as an array:

```
[Idle]
GlobalVars FirstVarID
SpriteVars angle[100]
LocalVars x,y, varIndex

varIndex = ID - FirstVarID
x = TrackWidth/2 + 130 * sin(angle[varIndex])
y = TrackHeight - 40 - ABS( 200 * cos(angle[varIndex]) )
angle[varIndex] = angle[varIndex] + pi/40
```

The size of the array will depend on the maximum number of sprites you wish to clone. Here we're using 100, which is usually enough (famous last words). We index the items in the array by subtracting FirstVarID from the sprite's ID. FirstVarID is a global variable that I usually set to the ID of the first prototype sprite. In this case FirstVarID is set to the protoSheep's ID on its Frame Loaded script.

Try it out. Each sheep should now jump back and forth independently without variable conflicts.

▶ Disposing of Sprites

We just learned how to make new sprites, but how do we get rid of existing sprites? There's an action called DisposeSprite. As a parameter, it takes the ID of the sprite you want to remove. Contrary to what many people think, DisposeSprite isn't just useful for removing sprites that were made dynamically. There are also situations where it's useful to dispose of normal sprites. I use the DisposeSprite action a lot to remove a sprite with an Idle event that no longer needs to be called. Since Idle events can take up precious processor time, being able to selectively remove unnecessary Idle events can often greatly increase the performance of a movie.

For an example of this, open disposeSprites_start.lsd and preview the movie. Look familiar? Yes, another jumping sheep. This time there's also text scrolling by at the bottom and two clouds, one reading "Sheep Jumper" and the other reading "Text Scroller." The scripts that make the text scroll and the sheep jump aren't on the text and sheep sprites themselves, but on the cloud sprites. The text and the sheep are just puppets being controlled by the clouds (I can't believe I'm writing this).

By setting up this puppet-controller system, we can easily turn off the activities by disposing of the controller. For instance, to turn off the jumping activity, let's add the following script to the jumper sprite's Mouse Down event:

```
[Mouse Down]
DisposeSprite(ID)
```

Now when you run the movie, try clicking on the Sheep Jumper cloud sprite. The cloud should disappear and the sheep should stop jumping (see Figure 15.3). Now that the jumper sprite is gone, QuickTime doesn't have to send idle events to it, and that saves CPU resources. We could have also set the idle delay to –1, but that would have turned off all idle events, stopping the scrolling text as well. Disposing of sprites is a more selective way of turning off activity. But what if we want to turn the activity back on?

After disposing of a sprite, it's possible to resurrect it through the Make-NewSprite action. Simply pass in the sprite's original ID for both the SpriteID and the HandlerID parameters. The sprite will be restored and continue processing idle events. The sprite will also retain its name, but other properties will be set to their default values. (The default name is " ".) I usually add a $Revive custom event handler to the controller sprite that will restore all of its properties.

Note The only property that can't be restored is the Clickable property, which isn't accessible through wired actions. The Clickable property defaults to TRUE after MakeNew-Sprite. Actually, disposing and then restoring is a good way of making a nonclickable sprite clickable.

Figure 15.3 disposeSprites_start.lsd.

Let's make clicking the sheep restore the jumper controller. Add the following script to the sheep's `Mouse Click` event:

```
[Mouse Click]
SpriteVars myControllerID

MakeNewSprite(myControllerID, myControllerID, 1, 1, 0)
SpriteOfID(myControllerID).ExecuteEvent($Revive)
```

Now you should be able to turn the jumping activity on and off. Try doing the same thing for the scrolling activity of the text.

▶ Explorations

1. Now that we know how to clone, dispose of, and restore sprites, we could go back and improve many of the techniques discussed in previous chapters. For instance, the drag manager developed in Chapter 12 was enabled and disabled by moving its position. We could improve the performance by disposing of the manager when it wasn't needed and then simply restoring it through `MakeNewSprite`. What other techniques have we discussed that can be improved with the methods introduced in this chapter?

2. I use sprite cloning when laying out a grid of sprites that all have the same behavior. This saves me from having to maintain the same script on multiple sprites (although this can also be done through a behavior). This way I'm also not tempted to waste time meticulously positioning each sprite by hand. I can simply position the sprites through a script after they are dynamically created. What would a script look like that dynamically makes nine sprites and positions them to form a grid?

3. Say you wanted to make a house furniture layout movie where the user could drag out small icons of chairs, tables, beds, and other furniture into a blueprint design for a house. You would want the user to be able to drag out as many of each furniture piece as they want. How would you design an endless "well" of draggable sprites? How would you do the drag behavior? Remember, you need to make it clone-safe.

4. In Chapter 12, we added several scripts to the label of a checkbox so it would send its mouse events to the box sprite. In this chapter we learned that when dynamically generating a sprite, we can set its `HandlerID` parameter to another sprite. How would you design a checkbox that dynamically makes its label?

5. The MakeNewSprite action has been around since QuickTime 4. But in QuickTime 6, they added the ability to generate new images dynamically as well. Dynamic images aren't discussed until Chapter 37, but it's good to start thinking about the possible applications now. For instance, we just explored how to dynamically generate a grid. This can easily evolve into a dynamic image thumbnail generator. What are some other applications?

Modeling Physics

When building sprite worlds, it's usually best to have sprites move around in a way that resembles movement in the real world. Of course we can embellish here and there, but if the core movement isn't based on physics, then the world will probably look fake. You could fill an entire book with how to apply physics principles to sprite worlds. (And someone already has! Check out *Game Physics,* by David H. Eberly; Morgan Kaufmann 2003, and *Physics for Game Developers,* by David M. Bourg; O'Reilly 2001.) Luckily we can take things a long way by understanding a few basic concepts.

Before we get started, I'd like to ease the concerns of anyone scared of physics. Many developers tell me that using physics principles for sprite animation just makes things more complicated. This is completely opposite from reality. The knowledge of physics lets us simplify things. In Chapter 13 we used a not-so-simple formula to make a sprite move along a parabola (OutputY = 4*InputX*(1-InputX)), and we used a cosine function to ease a sprite's motion in and out. By applying the basic physics principles presented in this chapter, we can achieve the same results with simple addition. I'll develop this argument further in the explorations, but first let's have a look at the principles.

▶ Forces

Arguably the most important principle to get right is Isaac Newton's second law of motion:

$$F = m\, a$$

A constant force results in a constant acceleration in the direction of the applied force. The amount of acceleration you get from a force is proportional to the mass of the object.

For simplicity, we're going to assume that sprites have unit mass so we can equate constant forces with constant accelerations. A constant acceleration simply means that the velocity changes at a constant rate. It took humankind until the end of the 17th century (when Newton published his *Principia* in 1687) to figure out that forces result in accelerations. But now that we know this, we can easily make our sprite worlds work like the real world. Let's see how.

Open the project forceDown_start.lsd and run the movie. You should see a ball drift from the bottom-left corner up and off the top of the track. Right now it moves at a constant velocity. It does this because there are no forces on it (technically no net forces on it). If there were, the ball would change its velocity over time.

Currently the ball's Idle event script is composed of a single MoveBy action:

```
[Idle]
SpriteVars velocityX, velocityY

MoveBy( velocityX, velocityY )
```

Let's add a force to the ball. We can apply it in the downward direction, which will simulate gravity. Since forces result in accelerations, which result in velocity changes, we can model a constant force by changing the velocity at a constant rate. Let's change the velocityY variable by 0.2 each Idle event:

```
[Idle]
SpriteVars velocityX, velocityY

MoveBy( velocityX, velocityY )

velocityY = velocityY + 0.2;
```

Run the movie and see what happens. The ball should start off moving as it did before, but get progressively slower in the upwards direction until it reverses and starts moving downwards. This is called *projectile motion*. It's how things move in the world when you throw them in the air.

There it is, that's how you apply forces in a sprite world.

To illustrate further, let's apply the force along a more interesting direction. Open the project forcesCenter_start.lsd, and let's change the ball sprite's Idle script to model a constant force directed toward the center of the track.

We've already discussed how to find the angle between two points in Chapter 14, when we stretched sprites into lines. We'll use a similar calculation here to find the angle between the center of the ball and the center of the track. This angle will determine how much of the force is applied horizontally and how much vertically. Here's the script:

```
[Idle]
SpriteVars velocityX, velocityY
LocalVars centerX, centerY
LocalVars acceleration, distanceX, distanceY, direction

#define FORCE = 1

MoveBy( velocityX, velocityY )

centerX = (BoundsLeft + BoundsRight)/2
centerY = (BoundsTop + BoundsBottom)/2
distanceX = TrackWidth/2 - centerX
distanceY = TrackHeight/2 - centerY
direction = ArcTan2(distanceY, distanceX)

acceleration = $FORCE

velocityX = velocityX + acceleration*cos(direction)
velocityY = velocityY + acceleration*sin(direction)
```

As you can see, the acceleration gets distributed across velocityX and velocityY according to the angle. Preview the movie and notice that the ball moves in an elliptical pattern around the center of the track (Figure 16.1). This is similar but not quite how a planet would move around a massive object like the sun. In that case, the magnitude of the force decreases with the square of the distance. Since that's easy enough to calculate, let's make that simple change. Using the Pythagorean relationship, the square of the distance is simply distanceX*distanceX + distanceY*distanceY. Since we are measuring distance in pixels, this number can go well into the thousands. To get the force back down near 1, we can divide by 10,000 or so. Let's add these changes to the line where we set the acceleration:

```
...
acceleration = 10000 * $FORCE / (distanceX*distanceX + \
  distanceY*distanceY)
...
```

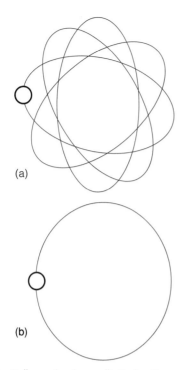

(a)

(b)

Figure 16.1 Balls moving in an elliptical pattern and in an orbit: a) constant radial force; b) radial force proportional to the distance[2].

With this modification the ball's motion should more closely resemble a planet's orbit.

 ## Friction

If you slide an object across a long floor, the object doesn't just slide forever; it slows down and eventually comes to a stop. From the previous discussion we know that if its velocity changes, it must be the result of a force. The force in this case is friction. Frictional forces always operate on an object in the direction opposite to its motion. The magnitude of the frictional force depends on the types of surfaces, and how strongly they're being pressed against each other. But these are all details for the real world to worry about. For sprite worlds, we just need to pick a friction value that looks right.

Open `friction_start.lsd` and preview the movie. You should see a box slide across the ground in a frictionless manner. We'll model a frictional

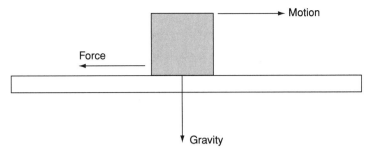

Figure 16.2 Modeling a frictional force.

force as a change in velocity as we did before, but this time the direction of the force is always opposite to the direction of movement (see Figure 16.2). There are several ways to implement this, but perhaps the most straightforward is to subtract from the velocity when it's positive and add to the velocity when it is negative. Here's our first attempt:

```
[Idle]
SpriteVars velocityX

#define FORCE = 0.2

MoveBy( velocityX, 0 )
IF( velocityX > 0 )
    velocityX = velocityX - $FORCE
ELSEIF( velocityX < 0 )
    velocityX = velocityX + $FORCE
ENDIF
```

Try it and see how it works. It probably appears to work just fine. The box slides across the floor and comes to a stop. The problem is that it doesn't really come to a stop. It's actually oscillating back and forth by very small amounts. If you scaled the movie larger you'd be able to see it. The oscillating happens because we aren't working with continuous time—we only get discrete idle events to tell us that time has passed. When the velocity gets close to 0, say, 0.1, the friction subtracts 0.2 from the velocity, making it –0.1. On the next idle event, it adds 0.2, making the velocity +0.1 again. This continues forever and the box never stops.

The friction shouldn't be causing the object to reverse directions. Let's fix this by checking if the velocity is less than the amount we are going to change it by. If it is, we can simply set it to zero. Here's the corrected script:

```
[Idle]
SpriteVars velocityX

#define FORCE = 0.2

MoveBy( velocityX, 0 )
IF( velocityX > 0 )
    IF( velocityX > $FORCE )
        velocityX = velocityX - $FORCE
    ELSE
        velocityX = 0
    ENDIF
ELSEIF( velocityX < 0 )
    IF( velocityX < $FORCE )
        velocityX = velocityX + $FORCE
    ELSE
        velocityX = 0
    ENDIF
ENDIF
```

▶ Collisions

We just completed a few examples of how to apply forces to a sprite. A steady force results in a steady change in the velocity. But there are some events in the world that result in a more sudden change in velocity. Collisions are such events. Let's examine the case of when an object collides with something much more massive than itself, such as a wall.

If the ball is perfectly elastic, bounces will change its direction, not its overall speed. If the ball is not very elastic, such as a flat tennis ball, then each bounce will reduce both the direction and the speed. The following project will let us explore bounces with different amounts of elasticity.

Open collisions_start.lsd and run the movie. Do you recognize this movie? It's basically the same PONG movie that we used to begin this part of the book. You might recall that we have already explored how to make a ball bounce with perfect elasticity. When an elastic ball bounces off a wall, it maintains the same component of velocity parallel to the wall but reverses the component of velocity perpendicular to the wall.

The current project uses the same Idle script on the ball sprite as we used in Chapter 8. Now, say we wanted to decrease the elasticity of the ball so that we get inelastic collisions. How does this change things?

An inelastic collision works similarly to an elastic one, except instead of the velocity perpendicular to the wall simply reversing, it also loses a percentage of its magnitude. We can add this notion into our script by introducing an elasticity variable. When the elasticity variable is 1, the ball is perfectly elastic, and when it's less than 1, it's partially elastic. A value of 0 means it's completely inelastic, like a clump of playdough that hits the ground with a thud when you drop it. Here's the ball's new Idle script with the elasticity factor:

```
[Idle]
SpriteVars velocityX, velocityY, elasticity
LocalVars distanceFromEdge

MoveBy(velocityX, velocityY)

IF( BoundsLeft <= 0)
    velocityX = -velocityX*elasticity
    distanceFromEdge = -BoundsLeft
    MoveBy(2*distanceFromEdge, 0)
ELSEIF( BoundsRight >= TrackWidth)
    velocityX = -velocityX*elasticity
    distanceFromEdge = TrackWidth - BoundsRight
    MoveBy(2*distanceFromEdge, 0)
ENDIF

IF( BoundsTop <= 0)
    velocityY = -velocityY*elasticity
    distanceFromEdge = -BoundsTop
    MoveBy(0, 2*distanceFromEdge)
ELSEIF( BoundsBottom >= TrackHeight)
    velocityY = -velocityY*elasticity
    distanceFromEdge = TrackHeight - BoundsBottom
    MoveBy(0, 2*distanceFromEdge)
ENDIF
```

The elasticity variable is initialized to 0.7 in the Frame Loaded script.

Run the movie and you'll see that the ball moves more and more slowly after each bounce.

As one small step for this chapter, but a final step for this part of the book, let's add gravity into the picture. This is done with one line. Just add the following line to the end of the Idle script:

```
velocityY = velocityY + 0.2
```

Congratulations! You have graduated from Part III! In the next three parts we'll apply the concepts you've mastered in this part to building user interfaces, interacting with multimedia, and communicating with the rest of the world.

▶ Explorations

1. The stance I took at the beginning of the chapter is that physics simplifies things. I hope that was demonstrated through the example projects. If you want more evidence, let's take the time to explore how to use the force principles described earlier to model a physical phenomenon that we haven't discussed yet. Let's consider the swinging motion of a hanging object, or a pendulum.

Note *Pendulum* comes from the Latin word "to hang," the same root as the words *pending* and *appendage*.

If you don't know the physics behind the motion of a pendulum, what do you do? Well, you could go to your physics textbook and look it up. But don't do that. Put your physics book away. It's just going to give you some crazy formulas with trig functions, and probably something about the period being the square root of the length over the gravity . . . forget all of that stuff for now. We're just trying to get an approximate model of swinging motion.

Think about what happens when you hold an object dangling on the end of a string. When it's at rest, it just sits there directly below where you're holding the string. If you displace the ball a little to the right and let go, it will leave your hand at a certain acceleration and start swinging back and forth. The farther you displace the ball initially, the more it accelerates when it leaves your hand.

The accelerations that we talked about in the body of the chapter were modeled by changes in velocity, which we implemented through a MoveBy action. For the pendulum, the accelerations translate into changes in rotational velocity, so we'll replace MoveBy with Rotate. By making these minor adjustments to the Idle script first presented in this chapter, we obtain

[Idle]

SpriteVars velocityR

Rotate(velocityR)

velocityR = velocityR + *???*

All we have to do is fill in the "???" part, which corresponds to the acceleration. In our thought experiment, we realized that the acceleration is bigger the farther the ball is displaced from the center. One simple way to implement that is to make the acceleration equal to the displacement. Let's try that. Here's the script:

[Idle]

SpriteVars velocityR

LocalVars deltaX

Rotate(velocityR)

deltaX = **FourthCornerX - FirstCornerX**

velocityR = velocityR + deltaX

Open the project pendulum_start.lsd to test this out. In the project, you'll find a pendulum sprite (Figure 16.3) with an initial rotation and the previous Idle script. Preview the movie and see how it looks.

Well, it works, but it's a little fast. We can slow it down by scaling the acceleration down a bit. Let's try using only 4% of deltaX:

velocityR = velocityR + deltaX * 0.04

Now that's a handsome pendulum! It swings 45 degrees to the left and 45 degrees to the right in a smooth sinusoidal fashion. You can change the swing size, say, to 70 degrees, by changing the initial angle (in the Properties tab) from 45 to 70. It works just like a real pendulum.

See how easy that was? No trig. No square roots. We didn't have to look up any fancy formulas.

a. Explore a bit. Try adding friction to the pendulum discussed above.

b. Make the pendulum interactive such that the user can, by clicking and dragging it, swing it to the left or the right and then let go.

2. So far, we've turned forces into translational and rotational movement. How about stretching? The project spring_start.lsd on the CD has a

Figure 16.3 pendulum_start.lsd.

sprite with an image of a spring. Model the spring as if it were attached to the floor and someone came along, stretched it upwards a bit, and then let go.

3. If you want more of a challenge, try modeling the following situation. There is a bookshelf standing on the ground. Something bumps into it. The bookshelf teeters a bit, but not enough to completely tip over, then it totters back and forth a few times, and eventually comes to a rest in its original position.

4. There is a whole world of physical phenomena we can represent with the ideas presented in this chapter. Name a couple of situations that would be fun (in a challenging sort of way) to model with a sprite world.

5. Carl Adler, a retired physics professor and educational multimedia developer, has a website that uses interactive QuickTime to present physics concepts. You can visit it at `http://carladler.org/QTimePhysics.html`.

6. In this chapter, we talked about elastic collisions off of planar surfaces. If you've ever played billiards, you have an intuitive understanding of how spherical objects bounce off each other. Using the circular collision detection developed in Chapter 10, how would you model the interactions of two billiard balls?

7. In Chapters 21 and 24, we'll discuss playing sound. In QuickTime, you can alter the pitch of a sound by changing the playback rate of an audio track or by modifying the controller of a MIDI instrument. Before we get into the details of sound, how might the concepts covered in this chapter apply to sound effects?

Part IV

User Interfaces

In Part III we learned all about moving sprites around in response to a variety of events, including UI events such as mouse clicks and key presses. As I mentioned before, the graphical user interface to most computer systems is really just a specialized sprite world. The sprites represent files, folders, printers, and all sorts of control widgets and graphical displays. The user can interact with them to get useful things to happen, and occasionally even get work done. In this part, we will explore building the standard user interface elements such as buttons, sliders, and text fields. Once you get the basic principles down, you can go beyond the standard elements and build your own unique graphical interfaces.

Sprite tracks let you create rich interfaces around your media, and they don't limit you to the look and feel of Apple or Microsoft. You can be creative!

Note   For creative nonstandard user interface ideas, see Erik Fohlin's Bradio player (Projects/ Extras/Bradio). For 3D controls integrated with video, see Ralf Bitter's VideoCube (Projects/Extras/VideoCube). Also have a look at the real-world interface in Anders Jiras's SnapTool movie (Projects/Extras/SnapTool).

A cost of being creative, however, is that it requires a bit of extra work to design and build your own custom UI elements. For this reason, people often prefer to use the standard OS components, which most GUI builders allow you to assemble with a single drag and drop.

Bradio.   VideoCube.

Part of what we will try to do in this section is apply the concepts of modern UI components to sprites—concepts such as managers, listeners, and accessor functions. These are powerful programming ideas that can greatly ease the task of creating and wiring interface elements.

There are many nice-looking interfaces out there, each having its own distinct look and feel. Apple's Mac OS X Aqua look and feel is particularly elegant. However, since UI elements are copyright protected, I decided to make my own look and feel. It's just a very simple design, but it makes clean-looking interfaces the way I like them. And that's the most important point. With QuickTime, you are free to design interfaces that have whatever look and feel that you want. Now that we have the look, let's start implementing the feel.

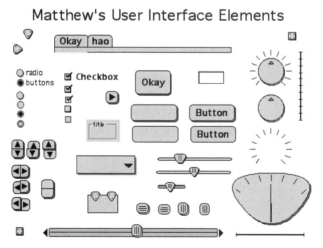

Matthew's look and feel.

Buttons

When learning how to build user interface elements, buttons are a good place to start. Simple buttons are just sprites that do something when they receive a mouse click. There are also more sophisticated types of controls, such as multistate buttons and radio button groups. We'll cover the whole range in this chapter.

Simple Buttons

Open the project SimpleButton_start.lsd. Here we have a sprite track and an instrument track. The instrument track is there to provide the button with a sound effect. It's set up to play a bird tweet sound.

The sprite sample has a couple of images and a single sprite, but no scripts have been written yet. To turn this sprite into a button, all we have to do is place a script in the Mouse Click event, and we instantly fit the definition of a button. Let's have the Mouse Click play a note on the bird tweet instrument:

```
[Mouse Click]
TrackNamed("Instrument").PlayNote(1, 0, 60, 100, 1000)
```

We'll discuss instrument tracks in Chapter 24, so don't worry about how the PlayNote action works just yet. Try out the button. When you click on it, you should hear a pleasant bird-chirping sound. But the user experience isn't very satisfying, now is it? The problem is that the button gives no visual indication that it's being clicked.

Good user interfaces will provide the user with visual feedback. The button will have a much better feel if looks like it's being pressed while the mouse is down. When the mouse is released the button should pop back in place. Up and down images have already been added to the sample, following a convention of placing the up image before the down image (see Figure 17.1). This way we can simply call SetImageIndexBy(1) and SetImageIndexBy(-1) on the press and the release events:

```
[Mouse Down]
SetImageIndexBy(1)
```

```
[Mouse Up]
SetImageIndexBy(-1)
```

Adding the above scripts should make the button feel much more interactive. Try it out.

Notice that if you click and release the button, you'll get a bird tweet, but if you press the mouse down, exit the button, and then release, you won't. As we discussed in Chapter 12, this happens because a Mouse Click event is only sent if the mouse is released while still over the sprite. This definition of the Mouse Click event is useful for UI because it gives the user a way to cancel the button click. The user might press down out of haste, but then realize that they don't really want to click the button, so before releasing the mouse, they can simply move the mouse away from the button and release without consequences.

This is the way our button currently works, but it doesn't give any visual feedback that this is going to happen. When you press the mouse down, the button goes down, but when you exit the sprite, the button stays down. Most UI systems specify that a button should return to the up state after the mouse exits. Furthermore, if while still holding the mouse down, the user enters the button again, it should go back to the down state. Let's have our button do this too:

```
[Mouse Down]
SpriteVars mouseDown

mouseDown = TRUE
SetImageIndexBy(1)
```

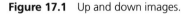

Figure 17.1 Up and down images.

```
[Mouse Up]
SpriteVars mouseDown

mouseDown = FALSE
//SetImageIndexBy(-1)

[Mouse Enter]
SpriteVars mouseDown

IF( mouseDown )
    SetImageIndexBy(1)
ENDIF

[Mouse Exit]
SpriteVars mouseDown

IF( mouseDown )
    SetImageIndexBy(-1)
ENDIF
```

Notice that I commented out the SetImageIndexBy(-1) call in the Mouse Up event.

Note   Placing // before a line means it's a comment and won't get executed.

We no longer want to decrease the image index on any Mouse Up, only when a Mouse Up is within the sprite. Let's place the SetImageIndexBy(-1) line in the Mouse Click event instead:

```
[Mouse Click]
SetImageIndexBy(-1)
TrackNamed("Instrument").PlayNote(1, 0, 60, 100, 1000)
```

We are now starting to get the feel of a professionally crafted button. We can craft it a little further by providing some visual feedback that the button is even clickable in the first place. Sometimes people highlight or underscore the button on Mouse Enter to indicate that it's active. I like to simply change the mouse cursor from an arrow to a pointing hand. This is the way the original Mac worked and it's quite effective. We do this by adding a single line of code to the Mouse Enter and Mouse Exit events:

```
[Mouse Enter]
...
SetCursor(kQTCursorPointingHand)
```

```
[Mouse Exit]
...
```
SetCursor(kQTCursorArrow)

Note   QuickTime comes with nine built-in cursors (see Figure 17.2). QuickTime also supports custom cursors, but LiveStage Pro doesn't provide access to this feature except when authoring QTVR tracks. However, a lot can be created with just the built-in ones. Have a look at Ken Loge's arrow game (`Projects/Chapter02/Games/ArrowPlay.mov`), where the open and closed hand cursors make it look like the user is grabbing onto the arrow.

If you want more cursors, have a look at the cursor track in Chapter 30.

Cursor	Constant name	Constant value
▶	kQTCursorArrow (Mac)	0
 ▷	kQTCursorArrow (Win)	0
 ✊	kQTCursorClosedHand	–19183
☝	kQTCursorPointingHand	–19182
 ✋	kQTCursorOpenHand	–19181
▶	kQTCursorRightArrow	–19180
◀	kQTCursorLeftArrow	–19179
▼	kQTCursorDownArrow	–19178
▲	kQTCursorUpArrow	–19177
 I	kQTCursorIBeam*	–19176

* LiveStagePro does not recognize `kQTCursorIBeam` by name; use the numeric value instead.

Figure 17.2   Built-in QuickTime cursors.

We just completed building a full-featured user interface component. Even though the scripts for it are short, we don't want to have to type them every time we want to make a button. This is where LiveStage behaviors come in really handy. I've gathered all of the above scripts and placed them in a reusable behavior called SimpleButton.lsb. You can examine simpleButton_complete2.lsd to see how this same project is assembled using a behavior.

Note   As with all behaviors, you can open the SimpleButton.lsb file in a text editor to see how it is implemented.

Checkboxes

Simple buttons are simple because the only thing they do is execute a script when clicked. It's easy to know when a button is clicked because a Mouse Click event is triggered. Checkboxes, on the other hand, are slightly more complicated. Checkboxes can be checked or unchecked, as opposed to just clicked. In other words, they have a state, or what is often referred to as a value.

In HTML, for example, a checked checkbox has a value equal to TRUE. Otherwise it has a value of FALSE. In order to implement a checkbox, we'll want to add a custom "value" property to the sprite using the technique discussed in Chapter 9. To do this, we will add getValue and setValue event handlers.

Open the project checkbox_start.lsd and preview the movie. You'll see it has three sprites: a checkbox, a label, and a colorful wheel (see Figure 17.3). Right now the checkbox and label don't do anything when clicked, but if you click on the wheel, it'll start turning. Click the wheel again to stop it. Let's get the checkbox working so it controls the turning of the wheel.

☐ Turning

Figure 17.3   checkbox_start.lsd.

We already built a working checkbox in Chapter 12. I've enhanced the scripts a bit and placed them into a behavior called checkboxBehavior.lsb. Add this behavior to the checkbox sprite. And while we're at it, add the MousePass.lsb behavior to the label sprite. This will pass the label's mouse events to any sprite that we specify. We, of course, want to send the events to the checkbox sprite. We do this by typing the name "checkbox" (with quotes around it) into the Sprite Name parameter of the behavior.

Note LiveStage Pro hides away behavior parameter fields. Click ▦ to show them. The parameters of the MousePass behavior should look like Figure 17.4.

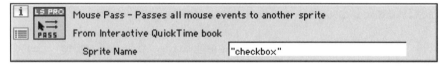

Figure 17.4 Behavior parameters.

The next step is to start and stop the turning wheel when the checkbox is checked and unchecked. Notice that I've already added an event handler called ValueChanged on the checkbox sprite. The checkbox behavior calls this event whenever the checkbox value changes. It passes in a GlobalVar called Value that reflects the checked state. Let's control the wheel by adding the following script:

```
[3 ValueChanged]
GlobalVars Value

IF( Value = TRUE )
    SpriteNamed("wheel").ExecuteEvent($StartTurning)
ELSE
    SpriteNamed("wheel").ExecuteEvent($StopTurning)
ENDIF
```

Preview the movie and try it out. We now have a checkbox-controlled wheel. But there's a glitch. It's possible to get the wheel and the checkbox out of sync. For instance, if we uncheck the checkbox to stop the wheel, we can then click the wheel to start it turning again. At that point, the checkbox will still indicate that the turning state is off. This happens because clicking the wheel bypasses the checkbox and calls $StartRotating directly.

This is a common problem when developing user interfaces. A good solution in this case is to "bottleneck" the rotation control at the checkbox. Instead of the wheel calling $StartRotating and $StopRotating directly, it should change the value of the checkbox. Let's modify the wheel's Mouse Click event:

```
[Mouse Click]
GlobalVars Value
SpriteVars turning

Value = NOT turning
SpriteNamed("checkbox").ExecuteEvent($SetValue)
```

Try it out. Preview the movie and then click the wheel. This time when it starts turning, the checkbox also becomes checked.

▶ Components

The checkbox we created follows the design guidelines for a component. Components are UI widgets that communicate through a standard set of events (see Figure 17.5). The basic components should implement the events in Table 17.1.

By keeping consistent names and IDs for these events, components can work together without naming conflicts. Let's quickly discuss each of these events:

1. The GetValue event simply places the component's local state variable into a global variable called Value. This allows any sprite in the track to access its Value property.

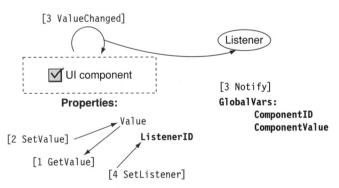

Figure 17.5 How a component works.

Table 17.1 Events implemented by basic components.

ID	Name	GlobalVars
1	GetValue	Value
2	SetValue	Value
3	ValueChanged	Value
4	SetListener	ListenerID
5	Notify	ComponentID, ComponentValue

2. The SetValue event goes the other way and sets the component's local state based on the Value global variable.

3. The ValueChanged event is triggered when the component's local state changes. The Value global variable is updated to reflect the current state.

4. A sprite can call SetListener on a component if it wants to be notified when the component's value changes. That sprite is called a "listener." You should first set the ListenerID to the ID of the listener sprite before calling SetListener.

5. The Notify event is called on the listener sprite when the value of the component changes. The global variables ComponentID and Component-Value will contain the component's ID and the component's new value.

So far, we've taken advantage of the SetValue and ValueChanged events. The uses for the GetValue event are obvious (so other sprites can query the value of the component). But what about the SetListener and Notify events?

Up until this chapter, the connections between sprites have been hard-coded through scripts. The SetListener and Notify events allow sprites and components to be connected dynamically. To see how this works and why it's useful, let's explore another type of button: the radio button.

▶ Radio Buttons

Radio buttons are similar to checkboxes except that they work in groups. When you turn one on, the rest in the group turn off. In Chapter 12 we introduced the concept of a manager. This is a nonvisual sprite that controls and helps process information for other sprites. Here we're going to create a radio group manager to keep track of which button in the group is currently selected, and then deselect the rest of them so that only one radio button is selected at a time.

Radio button managers take advantage of the listener and notification mechanism of components. This mechanism has become a standard feature of modern programming languages. The idea is to provide a way for one object to listen for events that happen on another object. In our case, the radio button manager needs to be notified when any of the radio buttons get selected. The way it does this is it sets itself as the listener of each of the buttons in the group (by calling SetListener). This way, whenever a button is selected, the manager will be informed through the Notify event.

To make it easy for the manager to know which sprites are part of the group, we use a convention where we place all of the radio button sprites immediately after the manager. This way we can simply tell the manager how many radio buttons are in the group and it'll know where they are.

What makes something a radio button? Radio buttons are similar to checkboxes. The only difference is that you can't click on a radio button to deselect it. To deselect a radio button, you have to select a different radio button in the same group. I made this change to the checkbox behavior and produced a new behavior called RadioButton.lsb.

We're now ready to build a radio button group. Open the project radioButtons_start.lsd. In it you'll find several sprites. The first is called "ColorPatch." This is the sprite that we want to control with our radio buttons. Next is the RadioManager sprite. Like many managers, it's not intended to be visible, so it has its visible and clickable properties turned off. Then there are four radio button sprites and four label sprites. The labels read "red," "yellow," "green," "blue." Let's have the radio button group control the image of the ColorPatch sprite.

Setting up our radio buttons is easy. Drag the RadioManager.lsb behavior onto the RadioManager sprite. Set the behavior's "Number of buttons:" parameter to 4 since we have four radio buttons. Now, add the RadioButton.lsb behavior to each of the button sprites. On the third button sprite ("GreenButton"), set the Initial State parameter of the RadioButton behavior to 1. This means we want the green button to start off selected (see Figure 17.6). I've already added the MousePass behaviors to the labels and pointed them to their corresponding buttons, so we're almost there.

Figure 17.6 radioButtons_start.lsd.

We haven't connected the radio buttons to the ColorPatch yet, but let's first preview the movie and verify that the radio buttons "feel" as expected. If you select one, the rest should get deselected. See how nicely that works? We just added a few behaviors and the sprites did all of the rest. The listener and notification mechanism made it possible for the radio manager to dynamically add connections with the buttons. I should note that the radio buttons don't know anything about a manager. The radio button behavior is exactly the same as the checkbox behavior except it doesn't allow a Mouse Click to turn the button off. The manager is able to control the radio buttons through the SetValue event, and the manager knows when a new radio button is selected through the notification system.

Now let's use our listener and notification machinery to connect the radio buttons to the ColorPatch (Figure 17.7). This is done by simply making the ColorPatch sprite the listener for the radio manager. Yes, the radio manager is a component too! Place the following script on the ColorPatch's Frame Loaded event:

```
[Frame Loaded]
GlobalVars ListenerID

ListenerID = $ThisSpriteID
SpriteNamed("RadioManager").ExecuteEvent($SetListener)
```

As a listener, the ColorPath will receive a Notify event whenever a new radio button is selected. So let's add the following Notify event handler to the ColorPatch:

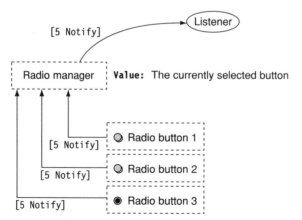

Figure 17.7 How the radio manager and the radio buttons get connected.

```
[5 Notify]
GlobalVars ComponentID, ComponentValue

SetImageIndexTo( $RedPatch + ComponentValue - 1)
```

This works because the ComponentValue of the RadioGroup is a number that represents which button is currently selected. A value of 1 means the first button is selected, a value of 2 means the second value is selected, and so on. Since the colored images for the ColorPatch are ordered in the same way as the radio buttons, converting the ComponentValue to an image index only requires offsetting by the appropriate amount.

What are you waiting for? Try it out! Our radio buttons now control the color.

There are several key benefits from using standardized components as developed in this chapter. One benefit is that components and sprites can be connected dynamically. This allows us to make things such as radio managers without having to hard-code all of the connections. Another benefit is that you can more easily separate the control from the function. In our case, we had a radio button group control the color of a ColorPatch sprite. By making the ColorPatch a listener, we were able to place all the code that actually changes the color inside of the ColorPatch itself. This way, the radio buttons don't have to know anything about the ColorPatch. If we wanted to change the type of control component from a radio group to a slider or a menu, we can easily do so. All we have to do is make the ColorPatch a listener of the new component. In fact, in the next chapter, we'll try that. We'll replace the radio group with a slider.

Explorations

1. It's often useful to enable and disable simple buttons. Clicking on a disabled button has no effect. Most user interfaces will visually mark a button as disabled, usually by fading or graying it out. One convenient way to fade out a sprite is by modifying its graphics mode. (A list of graphics modes is provided in Appendix G.) I like to use the following script to fade the sprite by 50%:

   ```
   SetGraphicsModeTo(blend, 32767, 32767, 32767)
   ```

   Explore adding a buttonEnabled property to the simple button project.

2. Product simulation on Web pages is growing more and more popular, and interactive QuickTime is the most versatile medium for that purpose. Say you wanted to simulate a product with buttons on it, such as a cell phone. What would be a good way to make the buttons look like they are actually being pressed when the user clicks on them with the mouse? To make it photo-realistic, you might want to photograph the cell phone with each button in its pressed and unpressed states. But how would you take a picture in the pressed state without getting your finger or some other object in the way?

3. In Chapter 14 we explored stretching four sprites to form a frame around another sprite. Can you think of a way to adapt this technique to make the sprite look like it's popping out of the screen? How about making it look like it's being pressed into the screen? This is a way to dynamically make any sprite image look like a button.

Sliders

Sliders have been used as user interface elements since the earliest calculators were created. They are relatively simple UI widgets. A slider consists of a small handle (often called the *thumb*) that the user can slide along a rail. While building the slider, we will see an example of how to build compound components.

Note The first educational "software" also had a slider interface. It was a machine invented by B. F. Skinner in 1954, and called the "Slider Machine."

A compound component is one that is built up from multiple sprites that operate together as if they were one unit. One way to build a slider is by using two sprites: one for the thumb and another for the rail. But here we are going to use four sprites—one for the thumb and three for the rail. The rail will be made up of a left cap, a middle section, and a right cap (see Figure 18.1). This implementation is more flexible because it allows you to scale the middle section to make the rail any length without scaling and distorting the caps.

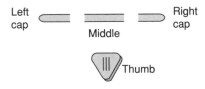

Figure 18.1 Anatomy of a slider.

Open the project slider_start.lsd. In this project we have the exact same ColorPatch sprite that was used in the last chapter's radio button project, but here I've removed the radio buttons and replaced them with the four pieces of our slider.

To get the slider working, drag out the behavior called SliderBehavior.lsb from the local library, and add it to the sprite named "slider." This sprite is really just the thumb of the slider, but it will be representing and managing the other three sprites that make up the rail.

The slider behavior uses the same component events that we developed in the last chapter (GetValue, SetValue, ValueChanged, SetListener, and Notify). If you compare this behavior to last chapter's radio button behavior, you'll notice that, for the most part, the component event scripts are the same. Where the behaviors differ are in the Mouse, Idle, and Frame Loaded scripts.

The slider gets "assembled" in the Frame Loaded script. The behavior assumes that the slider is made of four sprites in the following order:

1. Thumb

2. Left cap

3. Middle section

4. Right cap

It uses the left and right cap sprites to define the length of the slider and resizes the middle section so that it fills the space between the two caps. The slider behavior confines the draggable thumb to the space of the middle section as well.

If you decide to create your own images for the slider, just make sure that you add the necessary spacing to the images such that the min and max values of the slider correspond to when the thumb's left edge is lined up with the left edges of the left and right caps (see Figure 18.2).

For the images used here, I had to add a bit of empty space to the caps so that the thumb would line up correctly. This is another example of stor-

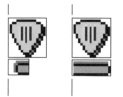

Figure 18.2 Thumb alignment with the caps.

ing information in the images (as we covered in Chapter 11). If we didn't do this, we would have to provide extra information to the behavior for it to know at what point the thumb bumps up against the ends of the rail. This can obviously be different for different-shaped thumbs and different-styled rails. Encoding this information into the images makes it easier to manage and allows us to design reusable behaviors.

When laying out the user interface, the length of the slider is specified by positioning the two caps. Try shifting the left cap to the left a little bit. Now when you run the movie, the rail should get stretched to the correct length, and the thumb should get positioned in the correct starting position.

The thumb's starting position is determined by the "Initial value" parameter of the slider behavior. Have a look at the slider behavior. It has three parameters:

- Initial value
- Min value
- Max value

The min and max values are 0 and 100 by default. For this project, we want the slider to change the image index of the ColorPatch. Since the ColorPatch has four images, let's set the min and max values to 1 and 4.

Now, we have to change the Frame Loaded script on the ColorPatch to set itself as the listener of the slider instead of the RadioManager.

```
[Frame Loaded]
GlobalVars ListenerID

ListenerID = $ThisSpriteID
SpriteNamed("Slider").ExecuteEvent($SetListener)
```

That's all there is to it. Preview the movie and try it out.

This demonstrates the modularity of the component listener-notification mechanism. By keeping the control separate from the function, we were able to easily swap a radio button control for a slider. You would think that sliders and buttons would act very differently, but since they both follow the same component guidelines, they are interchangeable.

One thing that might not be obvious from the last example is that a slider represents continuous rather than discrete values. The current range is from 1 to 4, but the slider can have a value between 1 and 4 (such as 2.3 or 3.8). To demonstrate this, let's also have the slider control the horizontal

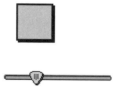

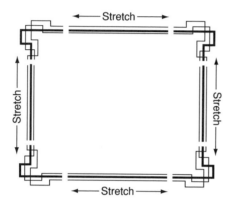

Figure 18.3 Slider project.

Figure 18.4 Border with ornate corners and stretchable sides.

position of the ColorPatch sprite. This just requires the addition of one line to the ColorPatch's Notify event:

```
[5 Notify]
GlobalVars ComponentID ComponentValue

SetImageIndexTo( $RedImage + ComponentValue - 1)
MoveTo((ComponentValue - 1) * 50, BoundsTop)
```

Changing the value of the slider will now control both the color and the horizontal position of the ColorPatch (see Figure 18.3).

As we discussed at the beginning, the slider is a good example of a compound component. Because it's built out of multiple sprites, we can easily resize it without having to redo the artwork. This general technique can be used in all sorts of other situations. For example, this would be a good technique to use if you wanted to make a frame with fancy corners that could be resized to fit around any picture. You could simply break up the frame into multiple parts. The four fancy corners would each be fixed-sized sprites, and the edges would be stretchable (see Figure 18.4). We'll use this technique in the next chapter to place a frame around a text field.

Explorations

1. The slider we built in this chapter allowed the thumb to be placed at any pixel location along the rail. However, many variables that you might want to control with a slider have a limited number of discrete values (such as the ColorPatch!). Try modifying the behavior of the slider so it will snap into place at certain values along the rail.

2. How would you modify the slider such that clicking anywhere along the middle section centers the thumb at that location?

3. See if you can create a movie with two sliders and have one drive the value of the other.

4. You can think of a knob as an angular slider. There are images for a knob component on the CD. There is also a knob component behavior. Explore hooking the knob up to the angle of the spinning card introduced in Chapter 14.

5. On the CD there's a digital calculator movie I made a while back (Projects/Chapter02/QTCalc.mov). It would be fun to make a slide rule movie, or maybe even an abacus!

Text Input

The first user interfaces for personal computers were text based. UNIX, DOS, Tandy, Commodore, and even the original Apple computers were all driven by a textual interface called the command line. But relatively quickly, text input receded from being the exclusive interface to being just another UI element appearing when appropriate and convenient.

QuickTime supported interactive text tracks from very early on, but originally the text could not be dynamically modified. You couldn't use them as an input text field. Before the dynamic text tracks were introduced with QuickTime 5, I would have to use sprites to build editable text fields. As you typed, each new letter would be a new sprite with an image of the corresponding letter. I even built an entire chat client this way called QTChat (see Figure 19.1). In the first couple of months following its release, QTChat was downloaded thousands of times and received quite a bit of online media attention. Part of it was because people didn't think that such a thing was possible with QuickTime, but more importantly, people realized that this added a new level of interactivity.

Beginning with version 5, dynamic, editable text tracks are a standard feature, but many developers still haven't latched on. This is not because there is not a need for it, but because it is a little tricky to use. In this chapter, we'll explore using text tracks as input fields. After a few examples, you'll discover that they aren't as tricky as myth has fashioned them.

Open the project EditableText_start.lsd. As you can see, it's an empty project with no tracks at all yet. To add a text track, simply choose Create Track > Text from the Movie menu. This will produce a blank 200 × 200 pixel text track. If you preview the movie and try to type into it, it won't let you. By default, QuickTime text tracks aren't editable, or in QScript-speak, they start off in the kNoEditing state.

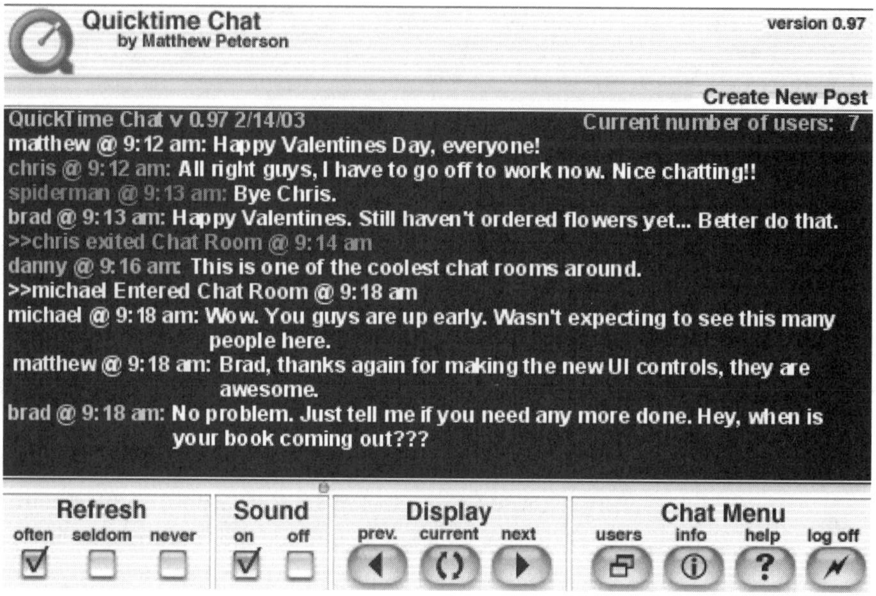

Figure 19.1 QTChat.

Text tracks have four edit states:

- kNoEditing—not editable
- kDirectEditing—editable by the user
- kScriptEditing—editable by scripts
- kDirectEditing+kScriptEditing—editable by the user and by scripts

The edit state can be changed at any time through the SetTextEditState action. Let's make our text track editable by both the user and scripts by adding the following script to the Frame Loaded event of the text track:

[Frame Loaded]

SetTextEditState(kDirectEditing+kScriptEditing)

Test it out (see Figure 19.2). You should now be able to type text in, select text with the mouse cursor, move the text caret around with the arrow keys, and perform cut/copy/paste operations by the standard keyboard shortcuts. It works just like a standard text area.

An easy improvement would be to have the text area start off in focus. Currently, you have to click in the track area to give it focus. If we add

This is an editable text track|

Figure 19.2   An editable text area.

SetFocus to the end of the Frame Loaded script, it'll start off in focus, making it feel more responsive to the user. Of course, for this to work, the track's Can Have Focus property must be checked.

Note   Calling SetFocus on a text track that has the Can Have Focus property enabled will automatically enable direct editing by the user.

Right now, if you press the Enter or Return key in the text track, you'll get a new line of text. Often for simple text entry, it is useful to limit the field to a single line of text. Single-lined text input areas are usually called *text fields.* Multilined ones are usually called *text areas,* but these naming conventions aren't very strict.

Let's make a single-lined text field. This is where most developers feel it gets tricky. Most authoring environments have a single checkbox that you can use to specify whether a text area is single-lined or multilined. In QuickTime, however, we have to do a bit more work. But in the end, the QuickTime solution is more flexible and will allow you to customize your text field in interesting and useful ways.

To make a single-lined text field, we need to place a script on the text track's Key Pressed event. Like the sprite equivalent (discussed in Chapter 12), this event is called for every key that gets typed while the text track is in focus. It's important to note that when the text track is user editable, the Key Pressed event is called after the text is modified. In other words, when you type the letter Z, a "Z" character gets added to the text track and then a Key Pressed event is called. The trick to making a single-lined text field is to delete Return characters after the user types them. Let's see how this works. Add the following script to the text track's Key Pressed event:

```
[Key Pressed]

#define RETURN = 13
#define BACKSPACE = 8

IF( ThisEvent.GetEventKey = $RETURN )
    EnterText($BACKSPACE)
ENDIF
```

Note   QuickTime has an action called EatKeyEvent. The current LiveStage manual says that you should call this to prevent a text track from processing the Key Pressed event. This

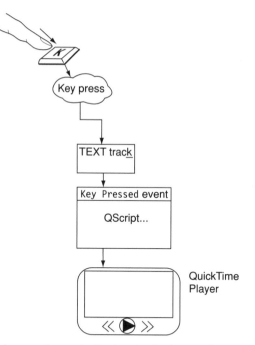

Figure 19.3 A key event goes to the text track, then to the Key Pressed event, and then to QuickTime Player.

is not an accurate description of what EatKeyEvent does. EatKeyEvent is used to prevent QuickTime Player from processing a key event. Certain keys have special meanings for QuickTime Player (see Figure 19.3). The Spacebar key starts and stops the movie, and arrow keys jog forwards and backwards. The Tab key moves the focus to the next focusable object. In the pro version of the player, the Delete key can actually delete the current movie selection! To prevent a keystroke from triggering QuickTime Player actions, you can call the EatKeyEvent action on the Key Pressed event.

Try it out. Hitting the Return key should have no effect. The script we added enters a Backspace character right after the user hits the Return key. This way, all Return characters get deleted instantly. The Backspace character is entered through the EnterText action, which takes an ASCII character as a parameter (see Appendix O for a list of ASCII characters).

Note The EnterText action will only work if the text track is in one of the script editing states.

This method of creating a single-lined text field works pretty well, but there are a couple of imperfections. First of all, we are only deleting

Return characters that the user types. It's possible for the user to enter a Return character without typing it. They can copy text from somewhere else and paste it into the text track. This can happen, but we're going to pretend it rarely happens. It's possible to prevent it by detecting a Paste key and then looping through all of the new text and removing all the Return characters, but it's usually not worth the effort.

Another imperfection is that the text field currently wraps lines that extend beyond the edge of the track. To see this for yourself, try typing in a lot of text. When it passes the right edge, it will wrap around and continue on the next line. While this is a nice behavior for multilined text, this isn't usually how single-lined text fields work.

One way to prevent text wrapping is to set the text box to a very wide value. The text box, by default, is the same size as the text track, but we can change this in the Layout tab of the text track editor (see Figure 19.4). The text box and the text track bounds are independent (see Figure 19.5). Let's make the height 25 and the width 5000. While we're at it, let's also offset the text box away from the top and left edges. Right now, the text is snug up against the top and the left. It usually looks better if there is a little breathing room. Offsetting the left and the top by 5 pixels will do.

In summary, here are the text box parameters to enter:

Left: 5   Width: 5000

Top: 5   Height: 25

![The Layout tab showing Text, Properties, Layout tabs with Text Box fields: Left: 5, Width: 5000, Top: 5, Height: 25]

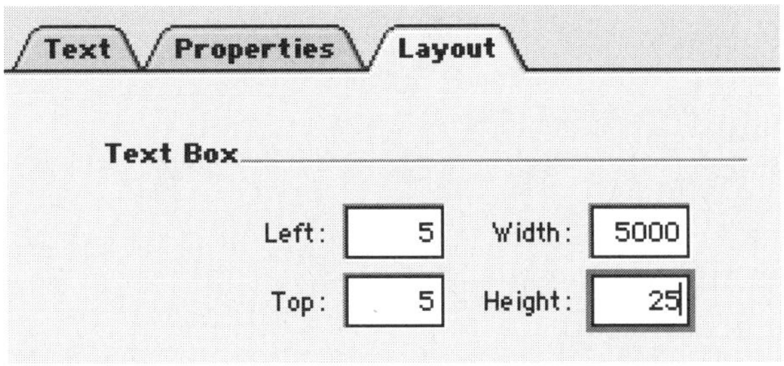

Figure 19.4   The Layout tab.

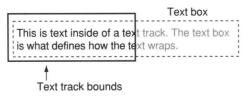

Figure 19.5   The text box versus the text track bounds.

You can, of course, tweak these values if you are using a different font or are expecting potentially really long lines of text (more than 5000 pixels worth).

To match our new text box size, set the height of the text track to 25. Try the movie with these new settings and see how the look and feel is improved.

▶ Filtering the Input

We just saw that it is possible to filter the input to a text track by deleting characters that we don't want. We did this with the Return character in order to make a single-lined text field. This is a flexible technique that can be adapted to other scenarios. For instance, we can use this technique to modify characters as they are typed. For example, say you wanted a text field that only allows uppercase characters. One way of doing this is to detect lowercase letters and then delete them and insert the uppercase equivalents. Here is an example script that does this:

[Key Pressed]

```
#define LOWERCASE_A = 97
#define LOWERCASE_Z = 122
#define UPPERCASE_OFFSET = -32
#define BACKSPACE = 8

IF( ThisEvent.GetEventKey >= $LOWERCASE_A )
    IF( ThisEvent.GetEventKey <= $LOWERCASE_Z )
        EnterText($BACKSPACE)
        EnterText( ThisEvent.GetEventKey + $UPPERCASE_OFFSET )
    ENDIF
ENDIF
```

If you look at the ASCII table in Appendix O, you'll see that the lowercase letters are 97 through 122. Here we check if the incoming character is within this range. If it is, we subtract 32 to convert from lower to upper case.

Note   In this script we used nested IF statements. We could have used just one IF statement:

```
IF( ThisEvent.GetEventKey >= 97 AND ThisEvent.GetEventKey <= 122 )
...
ENDIF
```

But the nested version executes faster and is easier to read.

You can try out an example of such a text field by previewing Upper-CaseTextField_demo.lsd.

Text Field Component with Border

As we've just shown, it is possible to create a text track all by itself. But, there are several reasons why text fields work much better in combination with sprites. First of all, a text track doesn't have a border. Most user interfaces use a border to denote and define a text field. With sprites, framing the text track with a border is easy. Another reason is that text tracks don't support custom events (at least LiveStage Pro doesn't support them). So all of our UI techniques, such as custom properties, listeners, and notification events, won't easily work with a text track alone. However, if we use a sprite to represent the text track, then that sprite can handle all of the standard component events we've developed over the last couple of chapters.

Open TextField_start.lsd. This project has a text track and a sprite track. The sprite sample contains three sprites that form a border around the text track, a label sprite, and a red arrow. The first sprite forms the middle of the text border and is called "TextField." This sprite will also function as the text track's ambassador to the sprite world. It'll handle all of the events necessary to make the text track function as a component. The TextField sprite will also manage the LeftCap and RightCap sprites, which form the two ends of the text border.

Let's build a text field component to control the rotation angle of the arrow (see Figures 19.6 and 19.7). We start by adding the TextField.lsb behavior to the TextField sprite. This behavior has a single parameter, which is the name of the associated text track. In our case it's named "AngleField," so enter that into the Text Track Name parameter (don't forget to enclose the name in quotes). This behavior is similar to the slider behavior in that it handles all of the component events and is also in charge of assembling multiple sprites together to form a compound component. In this case it assumes that the behavior is added to the middle of

Figure 19.6 Anatomy of a text field.

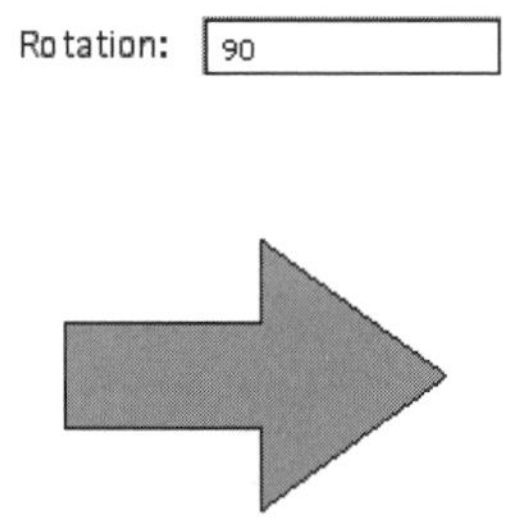

Rotation: [90   ]

Figure 19.7 TextField project.

the text border and is followed by the LeftCap and then the RightCap sprites.

The TextField behavior will set the contents of the associated text track when the $SetValue event is called. Likewise, it will get the contents when $GetValue is called. It's also set up to execute the $ValueChanged event when the text field is set by the user, but it needs to be told when this happens. This requires us to add a script on the Key Pressed event of the text track (see Figure 19.8).

Open the text sample of the AngleField track and add the following script to the Key Pressed event:

```
[Key Pressed]
#define RETURN = 13

IF( ThisEvent.GetEventKey = $RETURN )
    TrackNamed("Sprite 1").SpriteNamed("TextField").ExecuteEvent \
      ($EnterPressed)
ENDIF
```

This script informs the TextField sprite that the user has entered a value into the text field. It does this by calling the $EnterPressed custom event defined by the TextField behavior.

Now let's make the RedArrow sprite a listener to the text field component by adding the following script to its Frame Loaded event:

```
[Frame Loaded]
GlobalVars ListenerID

ListenerID = $ThisSpriteID
SpriteNamed("TextField").ExecuteEvent($SetListener)
```

This will allow RedArrow to receive $Notify events whenever a new value is entered into the text field. In this project I've already added a script to the $Notify event that rotates the sprite by the component's value. As you can see, we're using the Rotation.lsb behavior developed in Chapter 9.

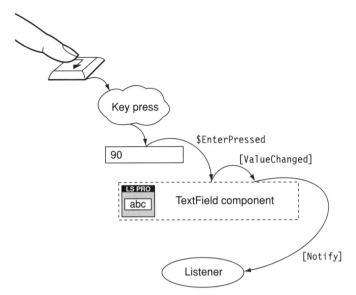

Figure 19.8 An event at the text track triggering the custom event on the sprite.

That's all there is to it. Preview the movie and try entering 180 into the text field to make the arrow point downwards.

Recursive Connections

To further showcase the benefits of using the component mechanisms, have a look at the TextAndSlider_demo.lsd project. In it you'll find a slider and a text field component connected to each other such that changing the value of one will update the value of the other. This is done by calling $SetValue on each of the $ValueChanged events. What I'd like to point out is that this doesn't cause an infinite loop. Components ignore $SetValue events that take place while the $SetValue event is being executed. This prevents the slider from setting the text field and in turn setting the slider in a recursive loop (see Figure 19.9). Try it out. By the way, you can learn more about QScript recursion in Appendix E.

Multilined Text Areas

By default, text tracks are multilined when you set their editing state to kDirectEditing. The only thing different from standard multilined text areas is the lack of a scrollbar. It's possible to create a scrollbar with wired

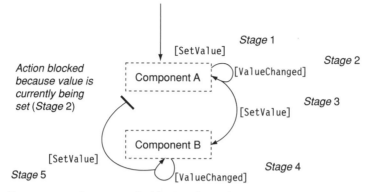

Stage 1

[SetValue]

Stage 2

Action blocked
because value is
currently being
set (*Stage 2*)

Component A

[ValueChanged]

Stage 3

[SetValue]

Component B

[SetValue]

Stage 4

Stage 5

[ValueChanged]

Figure 19.9 Two compounds connected with recursion resistance.

sprites, but it is a little intricate. If you'd like to explore how one works, look at the `ScrollingTextArea_demo.lsd` project.

▶ Password Fields

As you saw at the start of this chapter, we can filter characters as they get typed into a text track. As an example, we changed lowercase characters to upper case. You might be tempted to build a password field this way by simply turning all characters into the `"*"` symbol. It's certainly possible to get this to work, but the problem is that you have to remember what character each `"*"` symbol actually stands for. This can be quite difficult to manage perfectly, especially when the user can select multiple characters and copy and paste. Because of this, I usually don't bother trying to make my own password fields. I simply use the password fields supported by Macromedia Flash.

Let's build a password field component in a similar way to the text field component, but instead of a text track, we'll use a Flash track. Open the project `PasswordField_start.lsd`. It starts out with just a sprite track. To create the password field, drag out the file `password.swf` from the local library and place it on the stage just to the right of where it says: "Enter Password:."

Rename the Flash track from "Flash 1" to "Password." Just like with the text field, we also have an associated sprite that will handle all of the component events. The only difference is that this time the sprite doesn't need to be visual because the flash password field has the border built in.

Drag out the `Password.lsb` behavior and add it to the sprite named "password." The behavior's Flash Track Name parameter needs to be set to the name of the Flash track, in our case, "Password." And now we have to add one line of code to the Flash track to inform the sprite when a new value has been entered. To do this, double-click the Flash sample to bring up the Flash sample editor (see Figure 19.10).

In the Frame Loaded event of the first frame, add the following script:

```
[Frame Loaded]

TrackNamed("Sprite").SpriteNamed("password").ExecuteEvent \
    ($EnterPressed)
```

You are probably wondering to yourself why the Frame Loaded event is signaling an $EnterPressed event. The reason is that although Flash has keyboard events, QuickTime doesn't let you call them or add scripts to them. So, what I've done is capture the key events in the Flash movie, and when an Enter key is pressed, I execute the action on the first frame using Flash's Call() function (see Figure 19.11). If you have Macromedia's or Adobe's Flash authoring tool, you can see how I made this password field by opening the Password.fla file that is included in the project directory. If you don't have the Flash authoring tool, you can just reuse the password .swf file whenever you need a password field.

Now that we have our password component in place, let's make it do something. When the user types in a correct password, let's have the sprite

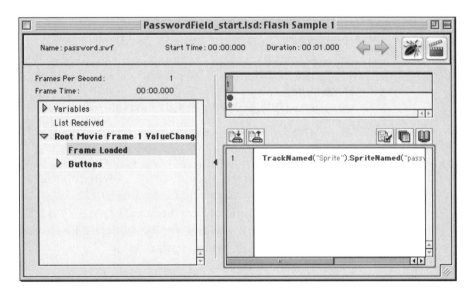

Figure 19.10 Flash sample editor.

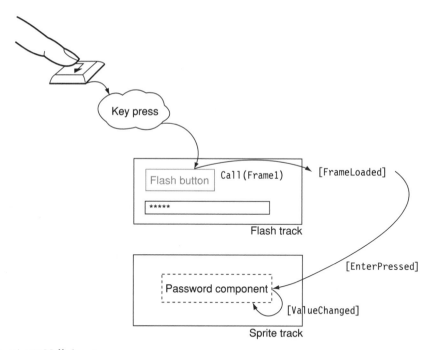

Figure 19.11 The Call() function sequence.

named "Greeting" become visible. Place the following script in the $ValueChanged event of the password sprite:

```
[3 ValueChanged]
GlobalVars Value

#define PASSWORD = "joshua"

IF( StrCompare( Value, $PASSWORD, FALSE, FALSE ) )
    SpriteNamed("Greeting").SetVisible(TRUE)
ENDIF
```

Try it out. Preview the movie and type "joshua" into the password field and hit Enter. An image should appear saying: "Greetings Dr. Falken. Would you like to play a game?" (see Figure 19.12).

This is a good example of how to incorporate an .swf file into a QuickTime movie. In the next chapter we'll investigate Flash further by using it to construct a pull-down menu component.

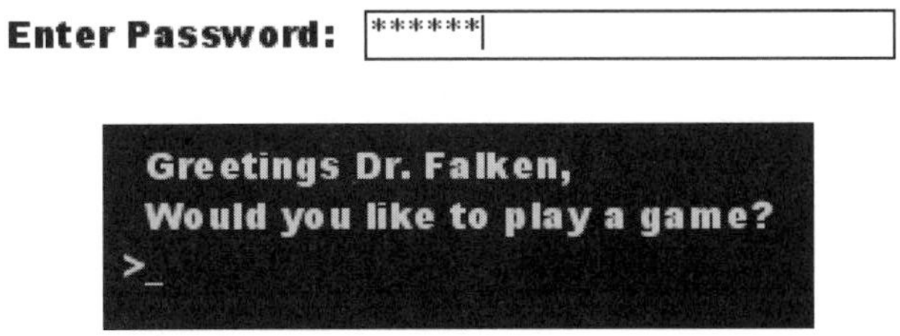

Enter Password: `******|`

```
Greetings Dr. Falken,
Would you like to play a game?
>_
```

Figure 19.12 Password Field project.

⏵ Explorations

1. A while back, I saw a nice text field enhancement on a Web page. It was a crowded page, and it had a search field. The text field started out with the word "Search" in it, but as soon as you clicked it, it cleared itself so you could start typing without having to delete the contents. It's a neat way of naming a text field on a crowded page. How would you go about doing this in QuickTime?

2. If a text track has its Can Have Focus flag set, then you can transfer focus to it through the SetFocus action. How would you set up a series of four text fields for entering an IP address? Each field should hold three digits, and when you finish typing in the three digits, it should automatically transfer the focus to the next field. This way the user can type in all the digits continuously as if it were a single text field. Hitting the Period key should also move the focus to the next field.

3. In this chapter we discussed input text, but output text is equally valuable (if not more so) to a user interface. My favorite text display components are tooltips. Those are the text labels that pop up after a while when you hold your mouse over an object. What would be a good way to implement tooltips in QuickTime?

20

Menus

I once heard someone state that, with the exception of the menu, the standard computer user interface elements are just software versions of physical controls that existed long before computers. Buttons, radio groups, dials, and sliders were common mechanical interfaces, and checkboxes and text fields were common paper form elements. But have you ever seen an interface where you make a hand gesture and a list of choices pops up, allowing you to choose one, and then the list goes away? Well, yes! Menus are probably the oldest form of user interface. Supposedly, even the ancient Egyptians had menus. You go to a restaurant and with a snap of the fingers a waiter brings you a list of choices. You point to one of the choices and the waiter promptly takes the list away and brings you what you ordered. Computers brought about a lot of new things, but menus aren't one of them. Here we'll show how to bring this ancient user interface to modern QuickTime movies.

As with the password field in the last chapter, we'll take advantage of Flash to do most of the menu work for us. Making menus in Flash is not only simple, but it enables you to produce some slick visual effects as well. A lot of people nowadays like making semitranslucent menus or ones that animate when they open and close. Flash is well suited for these sorts of effects. And since you can set a Flash track to be alpha composited over the movie, the effects will be visually integrated with the rest of QuickTime.

To get started, open the project FlashMenu_start.lsd. It starts out with a single sprite track with two sprites. The first sprite, named "Menu," will serve as the sprite representation of our Flash menu. This sprite is nonvisual, and so it has its visible and clickable properties turned off. The second sprite will display images of some of my wife's artwork (her name is

Elsa). The menu we are about to construct will provide the user a way to select which image to view.

Let's add the menu to the project. Drag in the Flash file called Flash-Menu.swf. Change the name of the track to "Menu." Before we go on, take a second to preview the movie and see how the menu works. When you click the title, a list of four menu items pops up (see Figure 20.1). When you make a selection, the list is dismissed. The list also gets dismissed without a selection after a timeout period or if the user clicks away from the list. This is standard menu behavior.

Right now, the menu covers half of the sprite track. Let's make the menu composite with the rest of the movie by changing the Draw Mode of the Flash track to Alpha Channel (use the track inspector). This way, all of the translucent parts of the menu will allow the sprite track to show through. Preview the movie and have a look. Click the menu title as before, and . . . nothing. Why didn't the menu items show up? If you move the mouse to where the menu items were supposed to appear, QuickTime will refresh that part of the screen and draw them correctly. What's happening?

This is a problem that developers often run into when integrating alpha-composited flash tracks into a movie. This happens because QuickTime is always trying to optimize playback performance. One of the best ways to improve the performance of a movie is to only update the pixels on the screen when it's necessary. This is especially important when compositing multiple tracks together. In this case, QuickTime is realizing that most of the Flash track is transparent, and so it is only updating the very top-left portion where the title resides.

This drawing bug will probably be fixed in a future version of Quick-Time (it might even be fixed as you read this), but we can fix it ourselves

Figure 20.1 FlashMenu_start.lsd.

and help QuickTime optimize playback performance at the same time. We fix it using a technique called *clip region optimization*. QuickTime provides a way to specify which region of a visual track to draw to the screen. That region is called a clip region. If you are ever involved in a project that requires high-frame-rate video and the composition of multiple spatial tracks (such as the awesome movie trailers on Apple's site), then clip region optimization is a must.

So we can see what's going on, temporarily set the Flash track's Draw Mode back to Dither. We're going to add a simple script to our Flash track. Open the Flash sample editor and add the following to the Frame Loaded script of "Root Movie Frame 1":

```
[Frame Loaded]
TrackNamed("Menu").SetClipRegionTo(#RegionFromRect(0,0,228,30))
```

There are a few important things to point out about this script. First of all, it's targeting itself. The Flash track is named "Menu." Normally, you don't have to explicitly target the track that the script is on, but Flash Frame Loaded events are an exception. Other events in Flash, such as the mouse events, don't require explicit targeting, but the Frame Loaded event does.

Note   Implicit track targets in a Frame Loaded event do work when executed through Flash's Call() action triggered from a Flash button click.

A second thing to notice is the # symbol. In QScript, a # symbol denotes a "preprocessor directive," which tells LiveStage to do something before it compiles (processes) the script (see Figure 20.2). We've seen it before with definitions (#define NAME = value). Here the statement tells LiveStage to create a clip region from a rectangle. The parameters are

```
#RegionFromRect(x,y,width,height)
```

In our case, we want to set the Flash track's clip region to the very top portion, 228 pixels wide and 30 pixels tall. Let's see what this does when we preview the movie. When the movie loads, only the very top of the Flash menu should be visible. Now, click on the menu title and the track should expand to full size. If you then select one of the menu items, the track will collapse back to its starting state and only show the top section. This isn't magic. I've already placed a script on the menu title button to expand the clip region:

```
SetClipRegionTo(#RegionFromRect(0,0,5000,5000)
```

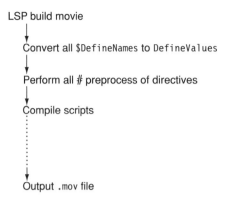

LSP build movie

↓

Convert all $DefineNames to DefineValues

↓

Perform all # preprocess of directives

↓

Compile scripts

⋮

↓

Output .mov file

Figure 20.2 Preprocessor directives within the LSP compiling stages.

You can see it for yourself by looking at the Mouse Release event for the button with ID 21. This doesn't actually set the clip region to 5000 by 5000 pixels. Setting the region larger than the size of the track simply results in revealing the entire track. We could have used the actual width and height of the track, but 5000 is easier to maintain.

Note QScript can be added to Flash buttons and frames when authoring in either Macromedia's Flash or Adobe's LiveMotion. This is done by adding an FSCommand with the following format:

```
FSCommand("QuickTimeScript(QScript)","SetClipRegionTo(#RegionFromRect \
  (0,0, 5000,5000)")
```

The SetClipRegionTo action can be replaced with any valid QScript. This FSCommand doesn't do anything on its own. When it is added to a LiveStage project, LiveStage Pro finds all the FSCommand actions with a QuickTimeScript(QScript) command, and conveniently inserts the QScript into the corresponding fields.

After selecting a menu item, the Flash track knows to go back to the 228 × 30 clip region (see Figure 20.3) because the Frame Loaded event is called after each menu selection (remember, it gets called through Flash's Call action). This is similar to how the password field worked in the last chapter, where keyboard presses triggered the Frame Loaded event.

What we've done is specify which part of the movie to draw to the screen at which time. This technique can greatly improve the playback performance of a movie. And if we set the Flash track's Draw Mode back to Alpha Channel, we'll see that we also fixed the drawing glitch with the movie items not showing up. Now that we've covered the major tricks for incorporating Flash content, we can continue building our menu component.

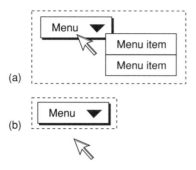

Figure 20.3 (a) When the menu button is clicked, the clip region shows the entire Flash track. (b) When the menu is no longer active, the clip region is minimized to just show the menu button.

Open the sprite sample editor, and add the `FlashMenu.lsb` behavior to the menu sprite. As with the password behavior, we need to specify the name of the associated Flash track. Set the Flash Track Name parameter to "Menu."

We also need to inform the menu sprite when a new item is selected. We do that by adding another line to the Flash sample's `Frame Loaded` script:

```
[Frame Loaded]
TrackNamed("Menu").SetClipRegionTo(#RegionFromRect(0,0,228,30))
TrackNamed("Sprite").SpriteNamed("Menu").ExecuteEvent \
  ($MenuItemChanged)
```

The $MenuItemChanged event of the menu behavior serves the same purpose as the $EnterPressed event from the last chapter. It informs the component that a new value has been entered. The component can then trigger the $ValueChanged event and notify any listeners.

In our case, we want to change the image of the art sprite to correspond to menu selection. Since the value of the selection is an integer between 1 and the number of menu items, we can easily map the value to the image index. Add the following script to the `ValueChanged` event of the menu sprite:

```
[3 ValueChanged]
GlobalVars Value

SpriteNamed("Art").SetImageIndexTo(Value + 1)
```

And that's all there is to it. When you preview the movie, you should be able to select which piece of art you want to view.

Have a look at the `FlashMenu.fla` file in the project directory. That's the Macromedia Flash project used to build the menu .swf file. I've placed comments inside of it describing how it works and how to add new menu items.

Over the last few chapters we have built all the major user interface elements. We designed all of them to conform to the specification. They all used the same variable names and implemented the same set of component events. This allowed us to connect user interfaces easily and dynamically. Many of the components were made up of multiple sprites and even other tracks, but there was always a single sprite that represented and unified the other pieces. These techniques are not specific to user interfaces. We'll use these same techniques in Parts V and VI as we interact with new types of tracks and integrate resources outside of the movie.

Explorations

1. If you aren't familiar with Flash, it is a valuable environment to explore. Download a trial version of either Macromedia Flash or Adobe LiveMotion. We'll discuss Flash tracks further in Chapter 26. One of QuickTime's strengths is its ability to handle such third-party tracks.

2. Here we focused on pull-down menus, but sometimes contextual pop-up menus provide a cleaner interface. What would be the design issues in getting pop-up menus working?

3. Menus don't have to be textual. They can be iconic or graphical in other ways. For example, have a look at David Connolly's cross between a pull-down menu and a map (Projects/Chapter20/MapMenu/; see Figure 20.4).

Figure 20.4 A cross between a pull-down menu and a map.

Part V
Multimedia

In the early 1960s, the term *multimedia* was born out of a push for improved education by supplementing textbooks with audio, video, and other ways of presenting information. Growing up, I remember being confused about what it referred to. When I was in elementary school, there was a room that had the words "multi media" on the door. It was a small storage room that housed a couple of TVs, some VCRs, a few overhead projectors, and an old film projector. In high school, the multimedia "guy" was the one that people went to when the auditorium microphone stopped working. In college, a multimedia computer was simply one that had a CD-ROM drive in it. It wasn't until I started dabbling with QuickTime that I began to appreciate that there really are many different ways of presenting information. QuickTime made it easy to understand because it has different track types for the different types of media. It has the basic audio and video tracks, but then there are also text tracks, virtual reality tracks, instrument tracks, 3D tracks, effect tracks, HREF tracks, vector graphics tracks, and so on. And then there's the track type that is able to glue all of them together and make them cooperate, and that's the sprite track. In this part of the book we are going to cover a wide assortment of track types and explore ways to control these tracks and make them work together using wired sprites. We'll even talk about third-party tracks, which are able to be incorporated into QuickTime through QuickTime's component architecture.

Audio and Video

When most people think of QuickTime, they think about audio and video. These are the most commonly used track types and are the reason Quick-Time files are called "movies." Audio and video tracks by themselves aren't very interactive, but combined with text, Flash, and sprite tracks they can come to life in interesting ways.

As we explored in Chapter 7, a DVD-style interface can greatly enhance the experience of a standard movie. And it's so easy to do. But that's obviously just the tip of the iceberg. Have a look at the interactive movie trailers at `www.apple.com/trailers` and the enhanced short films at `www.bmwfilms.com` for a look at where this technology is going.

Some DVD titles allow the viewer to watch scenes that were cut from the movie or different takes of the same scene. Why not add some level of viewing control throughout the film? Imagine movies where you can look around and see what's happening off to the side of the main camera. Maybe you can switch perspective from one character's eyes to another. This would make the viewer an active participant in the movie. Several cinema pioneers have played with the idea of allowing the audience to see multiple views of the story at the same time. The most mainstream is probably Mike Figgis's *Timecode,* where the audience is presented four simultaneous camera feeds. Such movies allow the viewer to switch their attention from one view to the other and, in this way, provide a certain degree of interactivity. But using attention as a user interface element can be tiresome and frustrating. Interactive media solve this problem by enabling media developers to provide sophisticated interfaces for the viewer to switch between perspectives. For a wonderful example of such an interface check out Cliff Vanmeter's video matrix interface on the CD (`Projects/Chapter21/VideoMatrix`).

Advertisers love the idea of interactive video. Take all of the product placement in movies and TV shows these days. What if while watching a movie you were able to click a product you see to get more information, or even order it right there and then. This technology wouldn't have to be limited to products (thank goodness). You should be able to click or "mouse over" characters too. An interactive media platform could display information about the character and maybe even something about the real-life actor as well. It would be sort of like VH1's *Pop-Up Video* show, but where you were in control of what information you got and when you got it. Movies such as *Lord of the Rings* might have a scrolled-up map that could interactively open and close to indicate where in Middle Earth the characters are at any moment.

And then there's a whole uncharted universe of artistic expression where the interactive component is as important as the images and sound. For example, to experience one aspect of what it's like to attend a Balkan music and dance festival, enjoy interacting with Ryan Francesconi's *Palios* movie (Projects/Chapter21/Palios; see Figure 21.1). For an example of an interactive music composition, try Francis Gorge's *Ziqzap* creation (Projects/Chapter21/Ziqzap; see Figure 21.2). Notice how adventurous it is to have control over the music but still enjoy it as it evolves in a composed manner.

These are just a few of the possible creations you can make with an interactive palette. What does the palette of interactive audio and video look like? QuickTime gives us full control over the rate, volume, location of the playhead, the balance/bass/treble of the audio, the clip area, the graphics mode . . . you can even move tracks around and enable/disable them to interactively switch between scenes. The bottom line is that you have a lot of control over the playback of audio and video. We could obviously spend an entire book about all the fantastic things you can create,

Figure 21.1 Palios.

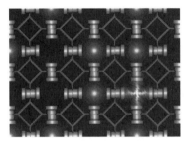

Figure 21.2 Ziqzap.

but in this chapter, we'll explore just a few of the possibilities. We'll start with audio and then do some cool stuff with video.

▶ Audio

For our audio example, we're going to interact with the balance of a looping audio track. The balance property is an integer value between –128 and +128. It specifies the relationship between the amplitude coming out of the left and right speakers: –128 means the audio is only coming from the left speaker, 0 means the amplitude is the same in both speakers, and +128 means the sound only comes out of the right speaker. Values in between represent different ratios. By changing the balance, you can make the audio sound like it is coming from different locations. It's a powerful effect.

Note To make sure your speakers are set up well for stereo, load the *AudioBalance* demo movie. When you click on the button labeled "Left," the audio should sound like it's coming from the left. Clicking on the "Center" and "Right" buttons should shift the sound to the center and the right accordingly. Some computer speakers have separate volume settings for the left and right. Get all that adjusted correctly or else the following example isn't going to sound right.

To see how this works, open the project called HeyYou_start.lsd. Inside you'll find an audio track and a sprite track. The sprite sample has two sprites in it: a bush and a little rodent (see Figure 21.3). The Idle event of the rodent is currently set up to have it follow the mouse cursor wherever it goes. We're going to make it so that the sound also follows the mouse position as well.

A simple way to accomplish this is to map the left and right edges of the track to –128 and +128 balances. This isn't always going to be completely

Figure 21.3 HeyYou_start.lsd.

accurate because the perceived audio source depends on the location of
the speakers, which might not perfectly coincide with the width and size
of your monitor. But this approximation usually produces a convincing
result. Since human sound localization is strongly influenced by visual
cues, it doesn't have to be physically accurate to sound right. Let's add the
following code to the rodent's Idle event:

```
[Idle]
LocalVars mouseX mouseY newBalance

mouseX = MouseHorizontal
mouseY = MouseVertical
MoveTo( mouseX, mouseY)

newBalance = mouseX/TrackWidth * 256 - 128
TrackNamed("sound").SetBalanceTo(newBalance)
```

Preview the movie and notice that the audio sounds like it is coming from
the location of the mouse.

Besides balance, another property of audio that changes with the spatial
location of the source is volume. When the sound is far away, the volume
decreases. The volume also goes down when the sound is blocked by an
object. You no doubt noticed that there is a bush sitting in the middle of
the track. Let's have the volume decrease when the mouse is behind the
bush. How much the sound will decrease will depend on the thickness of
the bush, but since that's up to us, we can just pick a number. Let's use a
value of 75 when behind the bush and 255 elsewhere.

Note   Volume ranges from 0 to 255.

To implement this, we'll use the bounds collision detection developed in Chapter 10:

```
[Idle]
LocalVars mouseX mouseY newBalance behindBush

mouseX = MouseHorizontal
mouseY = MouseVertical
MoveTo( mouseX, mouseY)

newBalance = mouseX/TrackWidth * 256 - 128
TrackNamed("sound").SetBalanceTo(newBalance)

behindBush = FALSE

IF( BoundsLeft > SpriteNamed("bush").BoundsLeft )
    IF( BoundsRight < SpriteNamed("bush").BoundsRight )
        IF( BoundsTop > SpriteNamed("bush").BoundsTop )
            IF( BoundsBottom < SpriteNamed("bush").BoundsBottom)
                behindBush = TRUE
            ENDIF
        ENDIF
    ENDIF
ENDIF

IF( behindBush )
    TrackNamed("Sound").SetVolumeTo( 75 )
ELSE
    TrackNamed("Sound").SetVolumeTo( 255 )
ENDIF
```

Now when you preview the movie, it should sound like a pretty thick bush. Of course, real sound occlusions can change the frequency of the sound too. A sound passing through an object might become more muffled and lose some of its high-frequency signal. QuickTime gives us some control over that too. We can alter the bass and treble like you can on most stereo systems. As with the balance property, the bass and treble have values between –128 and +128 and a default value of 0. The action to change these properties is setBassTrebleTo(bass, treble).

Getting back to our project, in addition to the bush decreasing the volume, let's also increase the bass and decrease the treble:

```
[Idle]
...
IF( behindBush )
    TrackNamed("Sound").SetVolumeTo( 75 )
    TrackNamed("Sound").SetBassTreble( 128, -128 )
ELSE
    TrackNamed("Sound").SetVolumeTo( 255 )
    TrackNamed("Sound").SetBassTreble( 0, 0 )
ENDIF
```

Another way we could have changed the frequency content of audio is to change the rate. Decreasing the rate will shift the frequencies lower, but it'll also make the sound play more slowly, which wouldn't have sounded very realistic in our case.

Note   For a demo of how well QuickTime can handle dynamic changes in playback rate, explore Brennan Young's MousePitch example (`Projects/Chapter21/MousePitch/`), which maps the playback rate of an audio tone to the horizontal mouse position.

The audio properties and actions discussed here are available for more than just pure audio tracks. Movie tracks (discussed in Chapter 28) and Flash tracks (Chapter 26), as well as multiplexed (or MUXed) tracks, such as MPEG, have the same audio properties. And as we'll see in Chapter 24, there are even more ways to interact with sound by using instrument (MIDI) tracks.

▶ Video

Now, let's talk about interactive video. Video DJs (VJs) have been interacting with video as an art form for some time now. The main idea is to dynamically splice, mix, and resample the video in real time. It's usually done along with a background beat. You can do cool things such as change what a person does or says by jumping around and altering the sequence of the video playback. You can also produce some really interesting audio-visual effects. It's all based around changing the rate of playback and the position of the video playhead. QuickTime gives full control over these parameters. Video can also be manipulated spatially, as we will explore in the next two chapters. But now, let's learn to assert some control over the time-based properties of linear video.

Our example project is KangarooCandy_start.lsd. Interesting name? Go ahead and open the project, and before we get started, have a quick preview of the movie to see what the video looks like. It's a kangaroo that sits there and then bends its head down to the grass and stops. What we are going to do is allow the user to toss a piece of candy to the kangaroo. We will then control the video so it looks like the kangaroo bends down, eats the candy, pulls its head back up, chews for a moment, and then waits for the next treat. It's all going to be nice and fluid.

The basic technique for altering the time course of video playback in an interactive way is to build what is called a *state machine*. A state machine is something that has multiple labeled states and rules that define when to switch from one state to another state. These days, it's very common to represent state machines using a visual language called UML (Unified Modeling Language). The UML state diagram that we will be implementing for our candy-eating kangaroo is shown in Figure 21.4.

What this means is that the kangaroo will wait at state 0 (see Figure 21.5) until the candy lands and the EatCandy event is executed. This will then cause the movie to play forward (state 1) until it hits the end of the movie. We then go to state 2 and play in reverse (rate = –1) until we hit the beginning of the movie. This moves us to state 3 where we play forward until we get back to the time in the movie where we wait (state 0).

We'll represent the state of the kangaroo with a SpriteVar called rooState. On each Idle event we will check to see if a state transition condition has been met; if it has, then we enter the specified state. I typically script state logic using a SWITCH statement. It lets you do different things under different conditions (or what are called *cases*). It works like an IF/ELSEIF statement, but it's a little easier to read.

Here's the script to place in the Idle event of the kangaroo sprite:

```
[Idle]
SpriteVars rooState

SWITCH rooState

    CASE 0
        //do nothing, just wait
    ENDCASE

    CASE 1
        IF( MovieTime >= GetMovieDuration )
            SetRateTo(-1)
            rooState = 2
        ENDIF
```

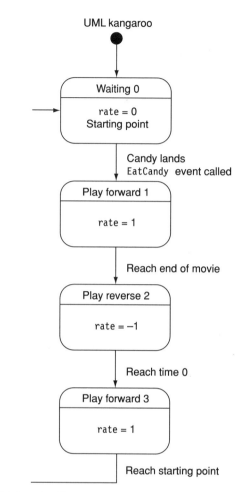

UML kangaroo

Waiting 0

rate = 0
Starting point

Candy lands
EatCandy event called

Play forward 1

rate = 1

Reach end of movie

Play reverse 2

rate = −1

Reach time 0

Play forward 3

rate = 1

Reach starting point

Figure 21.4 UML diagram.

```
ENDCASE

CASE 2
    IF( MovieTime = 0 )
        SetSelection(0,MarkerNamed("wait").StartTime)
        SetPlaySelection(TRUE)
        SetRateTo(1)
            SetLoopingFlags(kNoLoop)
        rooState = 3
    ENDIF
ENDCASE
```

Click on
the candy
to feed
it to the
kangaroo!

Figure 21.5 The kangaroo waiting for candy.

```
    CASE 3
        IF( MovieRate = 0 )
            rooState = 0
        ENDIF
    ENDCASE

ENDSWITCH
```

We've introduced a few new techniques here, so let's go over this script case by case.

When the rooState is 0, that's easy. We don't do anything, just wait.

When the state is 1, we are checking for the MovieTime to reach the end of the movie. When it does, we start playing the movie in reverse (-1) and jump to state 2.

When the state is 2, we wait for the movie to reach the beginning. We then set the selection on the timeline and start playing in the forward direction, which brings us to state 3.

When in state 3, we wait for the movie to stop playing, after which we return to state 0.

Note   The SetSelection action specifies a section of a movie's timeline. It takes the following parameters:

SetSelection(startTime, endTime)

Under the default settings, changing the movie's selection doesn't affect the movie's playback. But, if the PlaySelection property is set to true by calling SetPlaySelection(TRUE), then QuickTime will only play the selected portion of the movie. When it reaches the end of the selection it will stop (unless looping is on, then it will loop the selection). Setting the selection is a useful technique for precisely altering the playback time course of a movie. It's a good idea to first set the selection before calling SetPlaySelection(TRUE); otherwise things can go wrong on Windows platforms.

Note In CASE 2, we used the notion of a *time marker*. A time marker is a way to give a name to a time along a movie's timeline so we can reference it more easily. In this example, we have a time marker called "wait." Even though time markers are single points in time without a duration, LiveStage Pro still requires you to access the StartTime property of the marker. Right now that's the only property that markers have, but in the future you can imagine other properties being made available.

That's how the kangaroo state machine works. We just need to kickstart the machine when an EatCandy event is triggered. This event gets called when the candy hits the ground. Let's look at the script:

```
[200 EatCandy]
SpriteVars rooState

SetPlaySelection(FALSE)
SetRateTo(1)
rooState = 1
```

Here we remove the restrictions on the section being played and start playing in the forward direction. This is state 1, so we set the rooState variable to reflect that.

Try previewing the movie and do what you've always wanted but were never allowed to do at the zoo . . . feed a kangaroo candy!

We developed some new techniques in this example, but we also used several methods from previous chapters. To "throw" the candy along a parabolic path, we modeled the force of gravity as discussed in Chapter 16. Since video can't have associated scripts, we used the techniques developed for user interface components (Chapters 19 and 20) and represented the video with a sprite named "kangaroo."

Using time markers, playing selections, waiting for the movie to stop or reach a point in time, changing the rate—these are the basic techniques for controlling linear media. You can really build some fun interactive video. I showed this kangaroo movie to a couple of people, and they had such a kick that they fed the kangaroo about 10 candies and still weren't bored with it. I've found this to be the case anytime you make video interactive. Even the slightest amount of interactivity has a huge appeal.

Loading Linear Media

Before we go on to discuss other media types, we first need to talk about media loading. One of the great features of QuickTime is that you can play movies over the Web, and you can even start watching them before they've completely downloaded. This is called *fast start* or *progressive downloading.* It's perfect for watching linear video because the beginning downloads first, so you can start watching the video while the rest downloads in the background.

When working with interactive video, however, chances are the movie is going to jump around the timeline and not play strictly from the beginning to the end. If you try to jump to the end of a movie that hasn't completely downloaded yet, QuickTime will take you to the farthest point in the movie that has been downloaded so far. This has the potential of making the interaction look wrong. One solution is to wait for the entire movie to download before starting the interactivity. This is usually accompanied with a progress bar so the user can know how long to expect to wait.

QuickTime indicates how much of the movie has been downloaded through the MaxLoadedTimeInMovie property. I think it's important to look at a quick example of how to present a progress bar while the movie downloads and then start playing once it has completely loaded.

To see how this works, open the project LoadingProgress_demo.lsd. The medium we are going to use is a song by Sean Allen titled "Youth in Mind." Along with this audio track the project also has a sprite track for displaying a progress bar. All we have to do is code the Idle event on the progress bar sprite to stretch itself as the movie loads. Here's the script:

```
[Idle]
SpriteVars percentLoaded, maxWidth
LocalVars x1, y1, x2, y2, idleCount

#define MAXCOUNT = 10

IF( percentLoaded < 1 )
    percentLoaded = MaxLoadedTimeInMovie/MovieDuration
    percentLoaded = percentLoaded*idleCount/$MAXCOUNT
    IF( idleCount < $MAXCOUNT )
        idleCount = idleCount + 1
```

Figure 21.6 LoadingProgress_demo.lsd.

```
        ENDIF
        x1 = BoundsLeft
        x2 = x1 + maxWidth * percentLoaded
        y1 = BoundsTop
        y2 = BoundsBottom
        Stretch(x1,y1,x2,y1,x2,y2,x1,y2)
        IF( percentLoaded >= 1 )
            ExecuteEvent($FinishedLoading)
        ENDIF
    ENDIF
ENDIF
```

Once the movie is loaded, the MaxLoadedTimeInMovie will equal Movie-Duration. If you place this movie on a slow server, you'll see the progress bar gradually stretch across as the movie downloads (see Figure 21.6). When the movie is viewed off of a local hard drive, MaxLoadedTimeInMovie is instantly equal to MovieDuration. For this reason, this script also scales the progress bar over 10 idle events. This is done not only because it looks good, but because the first few idle events are the most shaky (irregular). Those first few events take place as the movie is still getting "situated," so it's best to hold off scripting anything you want to look smooth for at least a few idle events.

▶ Explorations

1. At the start of this chapter, I claimed that interactivity can add entertainment value to traditional film. But is this really true? Maybe movie-goers don't want to do anything when they watch a story. Maybe they just want to sit, watch, and eat popcorn. Maybe interactivity is only for video games. As an exploration into new creative possibilities, try to come up with a few "new" ways that interactivity can enhance the viewing experience of a movie but not overburden the viewer with things to "do." Are any of the ideas feasible for the theater, or is interactive film more suited for an individual viewer?

2. For our audio project, we used the balance property to add a spatial dimension to sound. When working with a QuickTime VR scene, it's also effective to increase the volume of sound sources when they are being viewed straight on, and gradually decrease the volume as you look away. There's a demo of this on the CD contributed by Ian Mantripp. It's called PanoSound. It includes a behavior that you can reuse in your own projects. Try it out.

3. When transitioning from one sound to another, a common technique is to perform a cross-fade. That's where you decrease the volume of the first sound as you increase the volume of the new sound. There's an example of this (AudioCrossFade) on the CD. An interesting twist on the cross-fade would be to use the balance as well. How would you create an effect where the new sound fades in from the right and pushes the first sound off to the left?

4. We used a simple state machine to build our interactive kangaroo video. That state machine didn't have any branching. One state led into another in a fixed way. For more intricate interactive pieces, one state might have multiple different states it can transition to depending on what happens. This is called *branching,* and it's easy to do. Instead of having just a single IF statement inside of each CASE block, you would have IF-ELSEIF statements. How would you change the UML diagram of our kangaroo movie if we allowed the user to throw two types of candy—one that the kangaroo likes and another that the kangaroo doesn't like? Make it so when the user throws the good candy, the kangaroo behaves as it currently does, but when the crummy candy is thrown, the kangaroo bends down but then pulls her head up again out of disgust.

5. In the introduction to this chapter, we mentioned being able to click objects in a video as it plays. Clickable regions in a video are called *video hotspots.* There are lots of ways to produce such hotspots. For example, you can use sprites in an invisible sprite track that move along with the items in the video. A transparent Flash track is another good solution. One company, eline Technologies Inc., has a product that makes it easy to create video hotspots. They have a free demo version at http://www.elinetech.com/.

6. A dynamic video resampler is a fun way to make video interactive. What you do is take any video, add an invisible sprite track that gets key events, and hook the keys up so they jump to different parts of the video. Some keys might also change the playback rate. You then dynamically change and remix the video by typing. Try it.

7. At the end of this chapter, we created a progress bar. The recent version of LiveStage Pro added a feature called *Fast Tracks.* These are prebuilt sprite tracks that make it easy to add common features to a project. One of the Fast Tracks is a progress bar. Remember, you can "decompile" Fast Tracks in order to examine/modify how they are built.

22

Effects

QuickTime can add standard video transitions and effects to linear video. You do so by adding an *effect track*. Effect tracks can take input from multiple tracks and combine them visually in interesting ways. For instance, instead of simply having one video track abruptly cut to a different video track, it can do so gradually with a cross-dissolve or a fade or a zoom effect. These effects are similar to what you would find in most video-editing programs, except that effect tracks are dynamically produced at runtime, whereas video-editing software permanently alters the video data.

Since effect tracks are computed on the fly, you would think that you should be able to make them highly interactive. You are correct in thinking that it *should* be possible, but QuickTime hasn't implemented wired actions for manipulating effect tracks . . . yet. Maybe in a future version. But even though you can't directly manipulate the parameters of an effect track, you can still enable and disable it as you can any track. Using this method you can set which effect is active and gain some interactivity that way. Let's see an example.

Open the project VideoTransitions_start.lsd. Here we have a sprite track, two video tracks, and two effect tracks. The video tracks are sequential and overlap for one second. The effect tracks are located at the overlap region. Currently only the first effect track, the *explosion effect,* is enabled. You can view the effect's settings by opening the effect sample editor (double-click the sample; see Figure 22.1). The explosion effect makes one spatial track transition into another spatial track through what (somewhat) resembles an explosion (see Figure 22.2). Preview the movie to see what I mean.

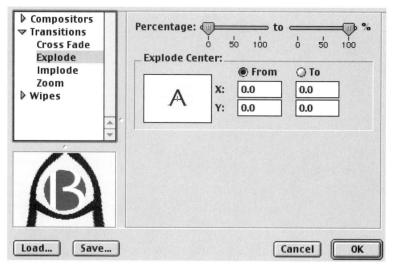

Figure 22.1 Effect sample editor.

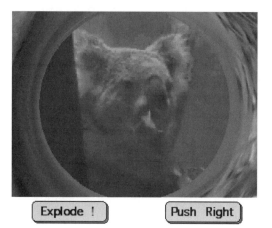

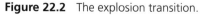

Figure 22.2 The explosion transition.

The second effect track is a *push transition* (sometimes called a *wipe*). This track is currently disabled, which is why you only see the explosion and not the push when you run the movie.

At runtime we can dynamically switch between these two effects by enabling one and disabling the other. To demonstrate this, let's add scripts to the two buttons, PushRight and Explode, which allow the user to pick which transition they want to see. For the PushRight button sprite, place the following script on the Mouse Click event:

[Mouse Click]
TrackNamed("Explode").**SetEnabled**(FALSE)
TrackNamed("PushRight").**SetEnabled**(TRUE)
GoToTime(0)
StartPlaying

A similar script should be placed on the Explode sprite to enable the Explode track and disable the PushRight track. You get the idea. This is one way to dynamically change the transition effect between two tracks. Try it out.

A different method is more appropriate for transitioning between images, such as in a slideshow. Since images don't change over time, you can have one effect track with multiple samples (see Figure 22.3). Each sample can be a different transition effect. Since each effect sample can be named, it makes it easy for a script to play a particular sample. For example, an effect sample named "PushRight" can be invoked with the following script:

[Mouse Click]
LocalVars start end

#define SAMPLENAME = "PushRight"
start = **SampleNamed**($SAMPLENAME).**StartTime**
end = **SampleNamed**($SAMPLENAME).**EndTime** - 1
SetSelection(start,end)
SetPlaySelection(TRUE)
StartPlaying

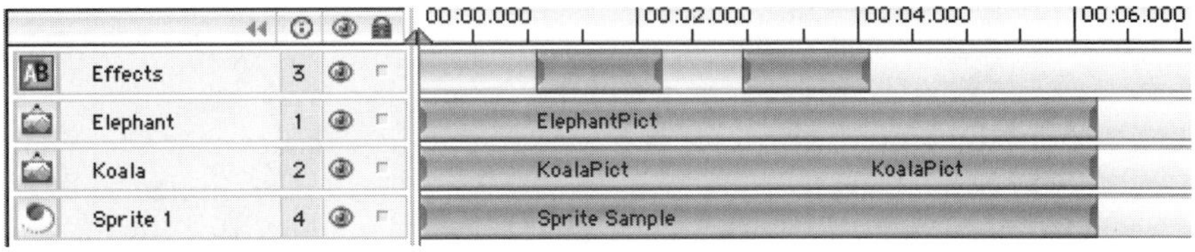

Figure 22.3 Track layout for image transitions.

This will perform the PushUp effect and then stop at the end and display the result of the transition effect. The reason for subtracting 1 from the end time is to stay within the effect. You can find an example of this in the `ImageTransitions_demo.lsd` project.

As you can see, by playing different effect samples, either by enabling/disabling them or by jumping to different time points, you can exert some control over your transitional effects. But it's a very limited amount of control. In the next chapter, we'll explore ways to make our own video transitions without the use of effect tracks. This will allow us to have full control, but we'll be limited in the types of effects we can produce. A push effect is no problem, but an explosion effect would be very difficult to emulate.

Effect tracks aren't only for transitions. You can also use them to composite two tracks together. Effects can be applied to a single track as well, allowing you to add filters such as blurring, embossing, and color adjustments. You can even add dynamic filters to a track such as lens flares and virtual film noise. Furthermore, some effects don't need any source and can generate their own images. For example, QuickTime can generate dynamic cloud and fire effects.

Codec Effects

Some of these effects not only work as tracks but can be applied to sprite images as well. These include the cloud, fire, and ripple effects. I said earlier that QuickTime doesn't yet provide any wired actions that would let sprites manipulate the properties of effects. However, the ripple effect (technically the ripple codec) is an exception. With this effect, you can actually interact with the ripples using the actions `ClickOnCodec` and `PassMouseToCodec`. For fun, let's build an interactive ripple movie.

Open the project `Ripples_start.lsd` and go into the sprite sample's Image tab. Here we have two images. The first is called "background" and is a pleasant blue water gradient. The other image starts out as a black rectangle, but we're going to encode it with the ripple effect. To do that select the image named "ripple" (see Figure 22.4) and change the codec to "Ripple" from the Codec pop-up menu. Now, any sprite that uses this image will create a translucent ripple effect on the sprites underneath. It's important to know that you can only see the ripple effect when it is drawing over another sprite's image (you can't see it over the sample background, for instance).

Figure 22.4 Ripple.

From a script, you can interact with the ripple effect, making it look like you are dropping little pebbles onto a liquid surface. This can be done by calling ClickOnCodec(x,y) and passing in the location to create the ripple. You can also call PassMouseToCodec, which makes ripples at the mouse location. The ClickOnCodec action currently only takes constants for the x and y parameters. This means that you have to hard-code ahead of time all the locations at which you want to create ripples. This is fine if you have something like a faucet that always drips in the same location, but it makes it difficult to create ripples in arbitrary locations.

To handle user mouse clicks, we're going to call the PassMouseToCodec event every time the mouse moves over the "ripple" sprite:

[Mouse Moved]

PassMouseToCodec

Once you have that in place, run the movie and let your mouse wade around for a while. It can be very relaxing. If you have an image on your Web page with a body of water, it would be fun to turn it into a movie and use this effect so you get ripples when the mouse passes over the water. People would just think it's another image and will be pleasantly surprised if their mouse happens to cross over.

This example shows that sprite images don't have to be static pictures. In the next chapter we'll see how video (or any spatial track, for that matter) can be the source of a sprite's image.

▶ Explorations

1. Here's something interesting. If you have the pro version of QuickTime installed, take a look at what tracks are in the VideoTransitions.mov file. What are all of those extra video tracks doing there? They don't have to be there, but why does LiveStage Pro make them? I haven't figured it out yet.

2. It was stated earlier that it's difficult to make ripples at any arbitrary location because the ClickOnCodec only takes constant parameters. But it's actually possible to use PassMouseToCodec to make a ripple at any location on a sprite. Simply move the sprite so the place you want the ripple to be is directly under the mouse location, then call PassMouseToCodec and move the sprite back to its original location. What would the script to do this look like? Try making a movie that produces ripples in a circle.

Image Overrides

Sprites can get their image data not only from images but from other tracks as well. This is a very powerful feature as it lets you do things that you couldn't do otherwise. Video and other visual tracks can't be moved around the movie in a smooth way. You can change the position (matrix) of a track, but it can cause the entire movie to flicker when you do it and can produce other undesired side effects. Sprites, on the other hand, can freely fly around the track. By playing track data through the image of a sprite, you gain the ability to spatially manipulate tracks like you can sprites. Routing the visual data from a track through a sprite's image is called an *image override* (see Figure 23.1). This lets you move, rotate, stretch, and apply graphics modes to tracks just like you can do with normal sprite images (see `Projects/Extras/VideoCube/` and `Projects/Chapter21 /VideoMatrix/` for some examples).

As with everything, image overriding doesn't come without a cost. Playing a video track through a sprite will cut the video performance by about half. For low- to medium-quality video, this isn't an issue, but for processor-demanding media, you're going to feel the slowdown. Another limitation is that interactive tracks won't be able to get UI events when playing through a sprite. This includes mouse and keyboard events. This means that VR, Flash buttons, and text tracks will lose most of their interactivity as image overrides. Furthermore, track alpha channels will not be rendered correctly. But even with these limitations, image overrides open a lot of interesting doors. In this chapter, we'll create our own interactive push transition effect for video.

Open the project called `ImageOverride_start.lsd`. It starts out with just a sprite track. Preview the movie and click the elephant and koala buttons. This causes a push transition between the elephant and koala pictures.

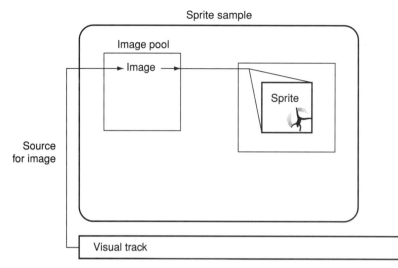

Figure 23.1 How image override works.

Right now these are simply sprite images, but we can override these images with video.

Drag out the `koala.mov` and `elephant.mov` video movies from the library and place them in the timeline. You should now have two video tracks named "Video 1" and "Video 2." Change the names to "Koala" and "Elephant" so it will be easier to figure out which is which. Now, go into the sprite sample's Image tab. There you'll find several images. The first two should be named "KoalaPict" and "ElephantPict." Let's change the source of these images to the Koala and Elephant video tracks. To do this for the KoalaPict image, select it, and then choose "Koala" from the "Source:" pop-up menu (see Figure 23.2). Similarly, set the source of the ElephantPict image to "Elephant." There we go. Now we should be able to transition between the two video tracks (see Figure 23.3). Preview the movie and see how it works.

Now that we know it works, let's examine how the sprite track is put together. If you look in the sprite sample, you'll notice that the first sprite is named "Scroller." You can think of this sprite as a manager for a push transition effect. It's a nonvisual sprite that controls the scrolling of the koala and elephant sprites. It's constructed to handle multiple images. Right now we only scroll two images, but we can easily add more.

In the `Idle` event of the scroller sprite, you'll see two defines: STARTINDEX and ENDINDEX. These define the index range of sprites that are to be scrolled. This sprite also has a custom event called StartScrolling. This

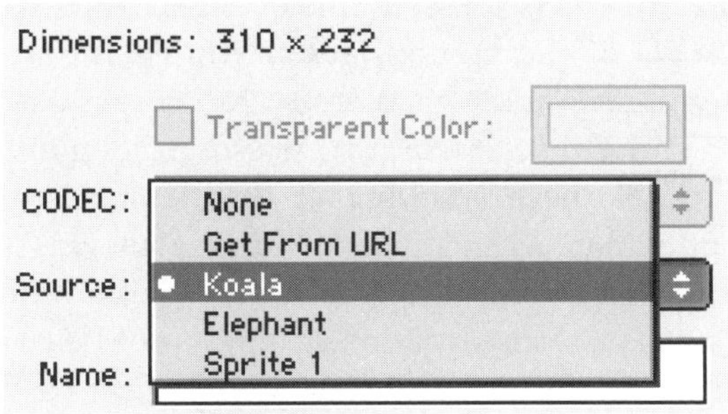

Figure 23.2 The "Source:" pop-up menu.

Figure 23.3 ImageOverride project.

event takes a GlobalVar parameter called ScrollToSprite, which is the ID of the sprite that is to be scrolled into view. I'd like to just take a moment to discuss how the StartScrolling script works. Here's the script:

```
[500 StartScrolling]
GlobalVars ScrollToSprite
SpriteVars scrollDeltaY scrollCount
LocalVars spriteTop topDistance numSteps

#define TOP = 0
#define SPEED = 10

spriteTop = SpriteOfID(ScrollToSprite).BoundsTop
topDistance = $TOP - spriteTop
numSteps = ABS( topDistance / $SPEED )

//round it off
scrollCount = numSteps DIV 1
scrollDeltaY = topDistance / scrollCount
```

When one of the buttons is pressed, this event is called with the Scroll-ToSprite set to the ID of the appropriate sprite. For instance, when you click the koala button (BtnKoala), then ScrollToSprite is set to 2, which is the ID of the koala sprite. The StartScrolling script then finds the number of steps needed to get there scrolling at the defined speed ($SPEED). I should say the approximate defined speed because we will want to modify the speed slightly so that the scroll can take place in an integer number of steps. Depending on its starting location, it might not be possible to move that exact distance in an integer number of steps unless we allow for some flexibility in the speed. What we will do is pick the closest speed that works.

To do that calculation, we first find out how far the sprite is from the top of the track (topDistance). We then determine how many steps it would take to cover that distance going $SPEED pixels at a time. In general this isn't going to be an integer. Normally to convert a number to an integer you would truncate it or round it, but QuickTime doesn't come with truncate and round functions. If you look in Appendix B, you'll find QScript expressions for a bunch of mathematical functions that aren't built into QuickTime. Truncate and round are in there. Here, as a tribute to the elephant in our video, we'll use the truncate function, which amounts to simply DIVing by 1:

```
scrollCount = numSteps DIV 1
```

Now that we know how many steps to take to approximate our target $SPEED, we can determine the exact speed we need to go to get the sprite from its current location to the top of the track in scrollCount steps:

```
ScrollDeltaY = topDistance / scrollCount
```

Once we've calculated the number of times to scroll (scrollCount) and the distance to scroll each time (scrollDeltaY), the scroller sprite's Idle event will proceed to scroll all of the "video" sprites, decreasing scrollCount until it reaches zero.

That's how the push transition works. It's a lot more flexible than using an effect track. For one, it works with an unlimited number of video tracks, while an effect track can only transition between two at a time. Our transition can take place at any time, whereas effect tracks only operate at fixed movie times.

Now that you know how to do image overrides, you'll probably find lots of uses for them. Any visual track can operate as the source of sprite images. This includes text tracks, Flash tracks, and even other sprite tracks. I use text tracks for image overrides a lot, especially if I want to have dynamic text that needs to be rotated 90 degrees to fit along the y axis of a graph.

Don't you wish you could do similar things with audio? Well, you can with instrument tracks, which is the topic of the next chapter.

▶ Explorations

1. Here we built a push transition. What other transitions are possible using image overrides?

2. In Chapter 19 we explored what it would take to make a tooltip interface. How about using image overrides with a text track? For a demo of this, examine the project ToolTip_start.lsd. In that project, the value of the tooltip is dynamically set to the name of the sprite that is under the mouse cursor (using SpriteAtPoint). Right now, the tooltip pops up as soon as the mouse is over a sprite. How would you change this so it works more like normal tooltips and only displays after the mouse is over a sprite for a certain duration?

MIDI Instruments

When sprite tracks were first becoming popular, besides the interactivity part, the thing that really amazed people was the file size. You can package a sprite movie with lots of rich animation in a 20K file. Producing the same visual effects with video would often take up many times more space, even when highly compressed. MIDI (Musical Instrument Digital Interface) does the same thing for audio.

Note This is an understatement. MIDI completely transformed the music scene in only a few years after it was introduced in 1983.

The MIDI version of Beethoven's "Moonlight Sonata" is only 12K. Compare that to 10 megs for the MP3 version. It can do this because MIDI is just a description of the musical score. This then gets fed into a synthesizer, which can be either a physical device connected to the computer or a software instrument. The sound quality that gets produced depends on the quality of the MIDI device.

QuickTime comes with a large variety of software instruments that have pretty good sound. They're many times better than the first MIDI computers that came out in the late 1980s. Besides playing back a musical score, you can build scripts that interactively play MIDI instruments. It's this aspect of MIDI that we'll discuss in this chapter.

In order to script MIDI, you have to add one or more instruments to your movie. As you probably guessed, you do this by adding an instrument track. One instrument track can contain several instrument definitions. QuickTime has a standard set of built-in instruments defined by the General MIDI specification (GM). This includes pianos, flutes, horns, stringed instruments, percussion, and sound effects.

Note See Appendix I for a listing of the instruments.

QuickTime also allows you to add new instruments from sampled sound files. Have you ever heard "Jingle Bells" played with sampled dog-barking instruments? Well, QuickTime lets you do cheesy things like that too.

We'll work with sampled sound instruments in a bit, but first let's get familiar with MIDI by using the built-in instruments. To get started, open the project Chords_start.lsd.

Here we have a sprite sample containing three sprite buttons with musical notation. The first button has an image of a single note (middle C), the second has a C chord, and the third has a C arpeggio (see Figure 24.1). We're going to hook those buttons to a piano instrument so that they play the corresponding music fragments.

We haven't yet added an instrument track to the movie. To do this, choose Create Track > Instrument from the Movie menu. This will create a new instrument track called "Instruments 1." An instrument track can have hundreds of instruments defined within. For now, we're just going to define a built-in piano instrument. Double-click the instrument sample and click the Add Built-in... button (see Figure 24.2). This should bring up a dialog like the one shown in Figure 24.3. Let's use the Default Synthesizer, and under the Piano category, choose the Acoustic Grand Piano instrument. All of these instruments that you see here are standard GM instruments. Before you click OK, you can try the instrument out on the little piano at the bottom of the dialog. Make sure when you click a note that you actually hear a sound. It's good to verify that audio and MIDI work now so you don't go crazy wondering what's wrong with your scripts. After you hear the note, click OK and you should see that a piano

Figure 24.1 Chords project.

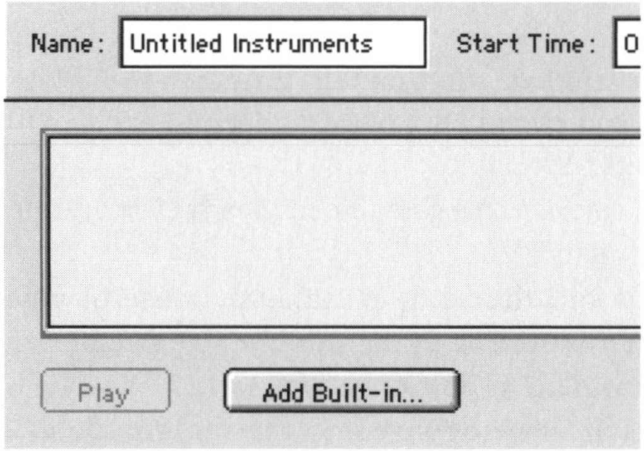

Figure 24.2 Instrument sample editor.

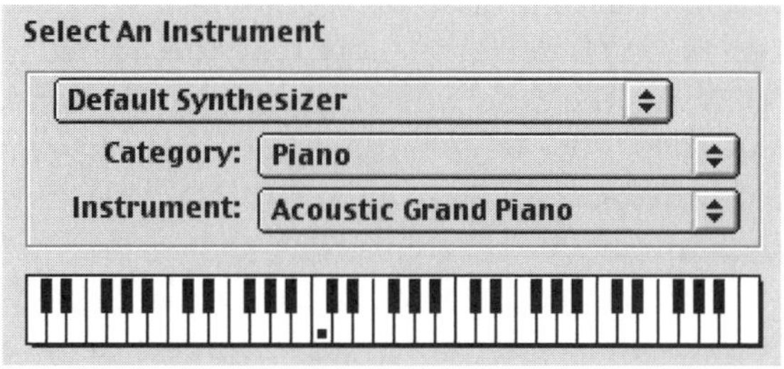

Figure 24.3 Choosing Piano in the dialog.

was added to the instruments sample with an index of 1. As we will see next, you target instruments by index.

Now that we have our instrument in place we can start waking up the neighbors. Let's first get the simple C note working. Open the sprite sample and place the following script on the note sprite's Mouse Down event:

```
[Mouse Down]
```

TrackNamed("Instruments 1").**PlayNote**(1,0,60,100,600)

Before we get into what all of the parameters do, preview the movie and verify that you get a piano sound when you click on the top sprite. Did you hear the sound? Good, you now have your very own musical instrument. At the moment, it only plays one note for a fixed duration, but the PlayNote action gives you full control over these attributes. Here are the PlayNote parameters:

```
PlayNote( InstrumentIndex, Delay, Pitch, Velocity, Duration )
```

By specifying an InstrumentIndex of 1, it means we're using the piano, which is the first and only instrument in our sample. We are using a Delay of 0. Time is measured in the movie's time base. For movies built with LiveStage, this always means that 600 is 1 second.

Note You can determine the movie's time base through the GetTimeScale property.

As we'll see in a bit, the Delay parameter is useful when you want to play a sequence of notes. The Pitch parameter specifies the note. This is an integer in the standard MIDI range of 0 to 127. A value of 60 represents middle C (which is the note depicted by the button), 59 is B, 61 is C#, and so on (see Figure 24.4). The next parameter is the Velocity, which specifies how hard the note is to be played. This basically corresponds to the volume of the note, and it takes a value between 0 and 127. The final parameter is the Duration, which determines how long the note is to be sustained. Our value of 600 means the note will be played for 1 second.

When you first clicked the Note button, you might have noticed a short pause before the note was actually played, but after that, subsequent clicks gave a more-or-less immediate response. This is because these instruments are pieces of software that need to be loaded and initialized. Since the initialization time can create a noticeable and unwanted delay, many developers preload their MIDI instruments right when the movie loads. The way to do this is to simply play a note on a Frame Loaded event. Since you probably don't want to hear the note, you can pass in zero for the velocity and it won't make a sound. Let's preload our piano instrument by placing the following script on the note sprite's Frame Loaded event:

```
[Frame Loaded]

TrackNamed("Instruments 1").PlayNote(1,0,60,0,0)
```

The way we have it now, the note will play for 1 second after you press down on the Note button, even if you release the button right away. Most pianos, however, will quiet the note when you release a key (unless you

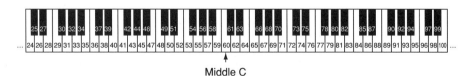

Middle C

Figure 24.4 A piano keyboard with MIDI numbers on the keys.

are stepping on the sustain pedal). We can implement this functionality for our mini piano too. To do this, let's increase the duration of the note on Mouse Down to something long like 100,000 or so:

[Mouse Down]

TrackNamed("Instruments 1").**PlayNote**(1,0,60,100,100000)

And now on the Mouse Up event, we can quiet the note by playing the same note with zero velocity and zero duration:

[Mouse Up]

TrackNamed("Instruments 1").**PlayNote**(1,0,60,0,0)

This overrides the previous MIDI command for that instrument's note and stops it immediately. Try it out.

This is how you play a single note, and it makes for a simple way to add sound to your QuickTime creations. However, if you are going to use MIDI for simple auditory feedback, why not play a chord instead of a single note? The wider frequency band of chords produces a much richer and more sophisticated sound than single notes. We'll make the second button play a chord.

The most common C chord is the simple triad where you play C, E, and G together. That corresponds to 60, 64, and 67 in MIDI. Place the following scripts in the Mouse Down and Mouse Up events of the chord sprite:

[Mouse Down]

TrackNamed("Instruments 1").**PlayNote**(1,0,60,100,100000)
TrackNamed("Instruments 1").**PlayNote**(1,0,64,100,100000)
TrackNamed("Instruments 1").**PlayNote**(1,0,67,100,100000)

[Mouse Up]

TrackNamed("Instruments 1").**PlayNote**(1,0,60,0,0)
TrackNamed("Instruments 1").**PlayNote**(1,0,64,0,0)
TrackNamed("Instruments 1").**PlayNote**(1,0,67,0,0)

This will play all three notes at the same time when the mouse is pressed and will quiet them when the mouse is released. Preview the movie and notice that the chord sounds much classier than the simple note. If you want to make the chord sound even fancier, you can play the notes with slightly different delays instead of having them all strike abruptly together. This is how chords are played on a harp, one note at a time in rapid succession. This type of chord is called a *broken chord* or an *arpeggio* (*arpa* means "harp" in German). I usually like to stagger the notes by a delay of 30 (which corresponds to 50 milliseconds), but you can adjust the delays so they sound good. Here are the Mouse Down and Mouse Up scripts for the arpeggio sprite:

[Mouse Down]

```
TrackNamed("Instruments 1").PlayNote(1,0,60,100,100000)
TrackNamed("Instruments 1").PlayNote(1,30,64,100,100000)
TrackNamed("Instruments 1").PlayNote(1,60,67,100,100000)
```

[Mouse Up]

```
TrackNamed("Instruments 1").PlayNote(1,0,60,0,0)
TrackNamed("Instruments 1").PlayNote(1,0,64,0,0)
TrackNamed("Instruments 1").PlayNote(1,0,67,0,0)
```

The Mouse Up script is exactly the same as the Mouse Up script for the chord sprite, but the Mouse Down script has different delays for the three notes. Preview the movie and see what a nice strum the Arpeggio button makes.

Besides just playing notes, you can also adjust other parameters of the instrument by changing various controller values. This allows you to control things such as pitch, blend, sustain, and reverb. You can think of the controllers as a bunch of sliders that you can move around to tweak the instrument. Each controller modifies a different aspect of the sound. For instance there is a controller called kControllerReverb, which allows you to control the amount of reverb. For a list of all of the different controllers see Appendix I. To modify a controller, use the SetController action:

```
SetController( SampleIndex, InstrumentIndex, Delay, Controller, Value )
```

The InstrumentIndex and Delay parameters are the same as with the PlayNote action. QuickTime requires that you pass in the index of the sample you want to affect (track sample, not sound sample). Since my instrument tracks usually only have one sample, I always use a value of 1 for the SampleIndex parameter. The next parameter specifies which controller you want to modify. The last parameter is the value you want to set the controller "slider" to. Acceptable numbers are between –128 and +128, and you aren't limited to integers.

As an example of using controllers, let's turn our nice piano into a twangy cowboy piano by having it modulate in a random way. Perhaps you have seen that modulation wheel found on the bottom-right corner of many electronic keyboards? We can access such a controller by using kControllerModulationWheel. Place this script on the Idle event of the note sprite:

```
[Idle]
LocalVars value

value = Random(-127,127)
TrackNamed("Instruments 1").SetController \
  (1,1,0,kControllerModulationWheel, value)
```

This will set the modulation wheel to a random value on each idle event and will affect all the notes played on the first instrument. This is just a silly example, but now that you know how it works, you can start manipulating your instruments in some really cool ways.

SoundFonts

So far we've been playing with the built-in GM instruments that come with QuickTime, but you aren't limited to that. QuickTime also supports SoundFonts and Downloadable Sound (DLS) files.

SoundFonts are just what the name implies. They are files that you install at the system level to provide more instruments than the standard GM synthesizer. Each SoundFont file can hold many megabytes worth of audio samples. You can find numerous SoundFont files on the Web (check out www.thesoundsite.net, www.hammersound.net, and www.dashsynthesis.com). The files are denoted with the .sf2 file extension. Many of the free ones are of very good quality.

SoundFonts are installed at the system level similar to text fonts. On Mac OS 9, you simply place the .sf2 files into the System/Extensions/ QuickTime Extensions directory. On Mac OS X, they go in the Library/ Audio/Sounds/Banks directory. On Windows, place the files (or aliases to the files) in the WINDOWS/System32/QuickTime directory for NT, 2000, and XP and in WINDOWS/System/QuickTime on Windows 95, 98, and ME.

Once installed, all the instruments in the SoundFont will be available when choosing an instrument from the Add Built-In... dialog. You can also tell QuickTime to use the SoundFont as the default synthesizer instead of the standard QuickTime Music Synthesizer. This is done by opening the QuickTime control panel and selecting Music from the pop-up menu. You should see a list of available synthesizers and SoundFonts to choose from (see Figure 24.5).

Figure 24.5 Synthesizer selection menu.

Let's build a simple example project using a SoundFont. We'll use a SoundFont donated to the book (for noncommercial use) by Ken Loge. It's in the SoundFonts folder and is called SontageBank.sf2. Install that into the QuickTime extensions folder on your computer (using the procedures mentioned two paragraphs ago) and then open the project SoundFonts_start.lsd.

This project already has an instrument track called "Sontage," but we haven't defined any instruments yet. Double-click the instrument sample and click the Add Built-in... button. This time, let's choose the Sontage Bank-01 SoundFont instead of the Default Synthesizer. This particular SoundFont has 21 instruments across three categories (see Figure 24.6). Let's choose the Hello There instrument under category 1. Click the mini keyboard to hear the instrument (clicking middle C, the key with the dot, will produce a note at the natural pitch).

The button in the sprite track is already set up to play note 60 with the first instrument. So preview the movie and say "Hello" to SoundFonts. Notice the rich stereo quality of the sound. SoundFonts provide a way to experiment with interactive hi-fi.

The biggest disadvantage of using SoundFonts is that they have to be installed by the user. You can't yet embed a SoundFont into a QuickTime movie. You can't install text fonts in a movie either. Maybe someday. But these issues can easily be solved by using an installer.

Downloadable Sounds (.dls files) are similar to SoundFonts. DLS is part of the MPEG-4 specification. Contrary to what the name implies, .dls files need to be installed in the same way as SoundFonts. If you want to deliver QuickTime experiences with custom instruments, but don't want the user to have to install anything, then you'll need to use sampled instruments.

Sampled Instruments

QuickTime provides a simple way—sampled instruments—to turn an audio file into a custom instrument that can be embedded into an instrument track. They aren't as high quality as SoundFonts, but they are quite flexible and can be used for more than just music. In the next example

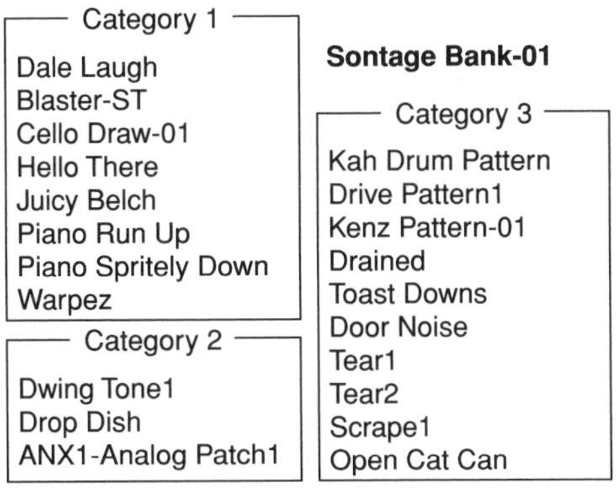

Figure 24.6 Sounds in the Sontage Bank-01 SoundFont.

project, we're going to use sampled instruments to perform some primitive speech synthesis. We'll use instruments from my voice saying the numbers 0 through 9 and then dynamically read off numbers from a text field.

Open the project SampledSound_start.lsd, which has an instrument track, a sprite track, and a text track. Double-click the instrument sample and you'll see that I've already created nine instruments from .wav files. The audio .wav files contain recordings of my voice speaking the numbers zero through eight.

Note   Audio files used as instruments are limited to 256 kilobytes. Because of this limitation, you might have to lower the bit depth or sample rate of your audio files. Since compression is not supported for MIDI instrument samples, I find it's best to use basic .wav files.

Open the instrument sample editor for the Numbers track. As you can see, I've already added all the numbers except for the Nine instrument. So let's do that now. Drag out the nine.wav file from the numSounds folder in the Local Library. Drag it into the instrument sample editor where all of the other numbers are listed (see Figure 24.7). This will add a 10th instrument called "nine." To hear what it sounds like, you can select it and click the Play button. You should hear a nerdy voice say the word "nine."

We have instruments for all of the digits now. Let's build a simple script to speak out the numbers in the editable text field that has already been added to the movie. To do this, open the sprite sample, and add the following script to the button sprite's Mouse Click event:

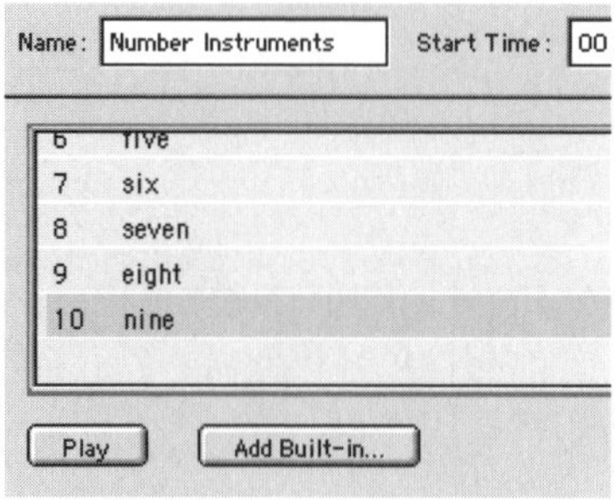

Figure 24.7 The instrument sample editor.

```
[Mouse Click]
LocalVars digit delay textLength textValue
LocalVars i

#define DURATION = 300

textLength = TrackNamed("TextField").GetTextLength
SetString(textValue, TrackNamed("TextField").GetText(0,textLength)

delay = 0
FOR i = 1 TO textLength
    digit = SubString(textValue, i - 1, 1 )
    delay = delay + $DURATION
    TrackNamed("Numbers").PlayNote(digit + 1, delay, 60, 127, \
      $DURATION)
NEXT
```

Let's walk through this script to see what it does. It first gets the length and string value of the text field and places these values in the textLength and textValue variables. The script then loops through each character in the string and plays the middle C note (60) on the corresponding instrument. It assumes the character is a number and it adds 1 to it because 0 corresponds to the first instrument. If the character isn't a number, QuickTime will treat it as a zero.

We use note 60 because this is the unaltered audio sample without any pitch changes. If you wanted me to sound more like the Terminator, you could use a lower pitch value. As we loop through the digits, we keep increasing the delay by half a second ($DURATION = 300, which is half of 600). This spaces out the playback of each digit to make it sound like speech.

Note In general, to find the duration of an instrument sample, you can open the audio file in LiveStage Pro or QuickTime Player and get the duration from the Info window. Live-Stage Pro also lets you use timecode values for the delay and duration parameters. For example, you can use 0:1.000 to specify 1 second.

You might have noticed that I have an `InitNumbers` custom event handler that loops through all of the instruments and initializes them as we did earlier for the piano instrument. This gets called on the `Frame Loaded` event.

Now we're ready to try it out. Preview the movie, type in a number, and click on the "Say Number!" button.

This is a simple starting point for a mini speech engine, but it's already quite useful. I used this very engine in my research to call out temperature values from an experiment that I was running where I needed to make sure the temperature stayed within a certain range. When the temperature started to drift out of the range, it would start calling out the temperature values to alert me. It was better than just a simple beeping alarm because it was important to know if the temperature was too low or too high and by how much. It worked out pretty well and had the added benefit that, being QuickTime, it could run from within a Web page, so I could actually monitor my experiment from anywhere in the world! But being a typical grad student, I usually remained right there in the lab room.

You might not have noticed it, but we just introduced a couple new functions in the last script. `SetString` and `SubString` are string manipulation functions. We'll explore more about string manipulation in the next chapter, which is all about text tracks.

Explorations

1. Now that you know how to interact with MIDI, try building a new type of instrument. Have a look in the `Projects/Chapter02/MusicToys/` directory for some examples of what others have done.

2. Creative Labs (`www.creative.com`), co-creators of the SoundFont format, provide a free SoundFont editor for Windows called Vienna SoundFont Studio. It lets you edit SoundFonts and design your own. Try it out.

3. We saw how instrument tracks are useful for more than just music and sound effects. They can be used to do some simple speech synthesis. What other interesting uses can you think up?

4. QuickTime also supports MIDI files (.mid or .midi). These contain a musical score for multiple instruments. Unfortunately, MIDI music tracks can't be manipulated in ways beyond what you can do with other audio tracks. However, you can use a MIDI music track to play a background beat and then dynamically play along with an instrument track. How would you go about doing this? What would be involved to get the timing of the notes right?

5. Using the Delay parameter of the PlayNote action, it's possible to line up a whole series of notes. Small melodies and "ditties" can be created this way. Have a look at some of the simple examples that Brennan Young has provided (in the Ditties folder). Try your hand at composing some of your own.

6. Instrument tracks can be a good way to generate random background sounds. How would you create the sounds that you might hear at a busy restaurant? What about canned laughter? What about the sounds coming from a nearby freeway or a small pond deep in the woods? Some sound effect companies provide CDs full of randomized background soundtracks such as these. The problem is that they often aren't suitable for Web-delivered interactive movies because they can take up megabytes to store enough so it doesn't sound looped. It would be useful if someone would produce truly dynamically generated sounds in the form of an instrument track and a sprite track that developers could easily add to their movies.

7. Since sampled MIDI instruments are relatively low quality, and Sound-Fonts require the installation of a special file, developers sometimes resort to audio tracks. If you play an audio track at different rates, can you achieve different notes? Assuming a rate of 1 is middle C, how would you play a middle D note? (Hint: Doubling the rate is the same as increasing by one octave.)

Text Tracks

We saw a glimpse of what you can do with text tracks back in Chapter 19, when we talked about text input for user interfaces. Here we'll explore their utility in more depth. Text tracks are extremely versatile. For example, check out the TextInvaders sample project on the CD (Projects/Chapter25/TextInvaders). It's a space invaders game I made out of a single text track (see Figure 25.1).

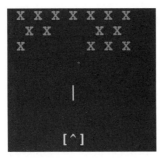

Figure 25.1 TextInvaders.

▶ Scrolling Ticker Tape

Let's start off by building a scrolling ticker tape like the ones you see running along the bottom of certain TV broadcasts. As with most things, QuickTime provides multiple ways of implementing this, but the best is to manipulate the text box. We modified the text box in Chapter 19 to prevent the text from wrapping. We'll employ that technique here as well, but we'll also shift the location of the box to make the contents scroll.

Open the project TickerTape_start.lsd. You should see a long horizontal text track displaying a string of periods (see Figure 25.2). If you double-click the text sample, you'll see that it actually contains more than just periods. It has a long string of text with some fake news in it. To make it scroll, we're going to shift the text box location to the left by calling the SetTextBox action in the text track's Idle event. Once the text box has reached a certain distance, we'll pop it back to zero again. This makes it look like the text wraps around, and the periods at the beginning and end help to provide a seamless transition. Here's the Idle event script:

```
[Idle]
#define MAXSCROLL = -1120
#define DELTA = -3

IF( GetTextBoxLeft < $MAXSCROLL )
    SetTextBox(0,GetTextBoxTop, GetTextBoxWidth, GetTextBoxHeight)
ELSE
    ScrollText( $DELTA, 0 )
ENDIF
```

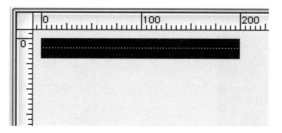

Figure 25.2 TickerTape_start.lsd.

With this script, run the movie and see how it looks. The text should scroll by smoothly. You can adjust how fast it goes either by changing the $DELTA define or by changing the idle rate. The idle rate is set in the text track inspector or header just as with sprite tracks.

The ScrollText action simply shifts the text box by the specified amount. SetTextBox, on the other hand, specifies the location and size of the box in absolute terms. We use the SetTextBox action to reset the box after it has passed the $MAXSCROLL location. Unfortunately QuickTime doesn't give us access to the actual size of the textual content, so we don't know what the real max scroll position is. This currently needs to be determined by guessing (the number of characters times an average character width is one way to get an estimate).

An alternative, less interactive way to scroll text is to select the Scroll Out checkbox in the Properties tab and choose the Horizontal Scroll and Continuous Scroll options. This will link the text scrolling with the movie's timeline so that the text scrolls as the movie plays. This second method is simpler but more limiting. It's limiting not only because it might conflict with other time-based media, but it also doesn't update the scrolling parameters when the text changes.

Note You can overcome the timeline limitations by placing the text track into a movie track (see Chapter 28).

The ScrollText and SetTextBox actions allow more control, but they're missing a key factor, which is how far to scroll to reach the end. Neither method is ideal. Maybe QuickTime will add some better scrolling support in a future release.

▶ LCD Clock

There are many other text track attributes that can be accessed through scripting, such as the font, the background text, and alignment (justification). Various display flags can also be scripted.

The most important property of a text track is the text content itself, and that can be completely manipulated through scripts. For the next example we'll create a digital clock (see Figure 25.3), which will demonstrate how to update the contents of a text track to dynamically display information.

Open the project LCDClock_start.lsd. Here we have a sprite track that contains an image resembling the face of an LCD clock accompanied by a text track with an LCD background color. The goal here is to make the text field continuously display the current time.

We're going to use a technique that I call *clear-append*. Basically you clear the text field and then append each part (hour, minute, second). To make it easy, we'll first develop ClearText and AppendText custom events that we can call to perform these functions.

Figure 25.3 LCD clock project.

To make a `ClearText` custom event, go into the sprite track and add a custom event to the clock sprite. Call it `ClearText` and give it an event ID of 800 (as a convention). Since text tracks don't have a `Clear` action, we'll have to make our own by using `ReplaceText` and replacing the entire content of the text track with an empty string. `ReplaceText` takes the following parameters:

```
ReplaceText( NewText, Start, End )
```

The `Start` and `End` parameters designate the region of the text to replace. You can think of `Start` and `End` as cursor locations where the first cursor location has an index of zero (see Figure 25.4). So if you wanted to replace just the first two characters with the text "Hello," you would script

```
ReplaceText( "Hello", 0, 2 )
```

For our `ClearText` function, we want to replace the entire text with an empty string. To do this, we first need to obtain the length of the text contents (the number of characters). And it's important to remember from Chapter 19 that we can't modify the contents of a text track until we call `SetTextEditState` with the `kScriptEditing` flag. Taking all of this into account, here's the `ClearText` script:

```
[800 ClearText]
SpriteVars textTrackID
LocalVars textLength

TrackOfID( textTrackID ).SetTextEditState( kScriptEditing )
textLength = TrackOfID( textTrackID ).GetTextLength
TrackOfID( textTrackID ).ReplaceText( "", 0, textLength )
```

Now, as you can see, I'm using a `SpriteVar` called `textTrackID` to target the text track. There are a couple reasons for this. First of all, I want this `ClearText` function to be reusable, so I don't want to hard-code the name of the track in the script. I want to be able to pass in which track I want to clear. The reason that I'm using the ID, instead of the name like we usually do, is because QuickTime doesn't yet allow `TrackNamed` to take a vari-

Text track: ABCDEFG
Text caret positions: 0 1 2 3 4 5 6 7

Figure 25.4 Text selection start and end points: "BCD" is selected as a result of `SetSelection` (1,4).

able. Both TrackNamed and SpriteNamed only take constants in QuickTime version 6.0 and earlier. This should be "fixed" in a later release, but for now, using the ID will work just fine.

Obviously, to call the above event, we first need to set the textTrackID to the text track's ID. Let's do that in the Frame Loaded script of the clock sprite:

```
[Frame Loaded]
SpriteVars textTrackID

textTrackID = TrackNamed("LCDText").GetID
```

The second function we need for our clear-append method is an Append-Text function. Make a new custom event on the same sprite and call it AppendText (ID = 801). For this function, we will also use the ReplaceText action, but instead of replacing the entire content, we'll just replace the very last cursor position of the text track. Here's the script:

```
[801 AppendText]
SpriteVars textTrackID newText
LocalVars textLength

TrackOfID( textTrackID ).SetTextEditState( kScriptEditing )
textLength = TrackOfID( textTrackID ).GetTextLength
TrackOfID( textTrackID ).ReplaceText( newText, textLength, textLength )
```

The script appends the newText variable to the end of the text track. Here we set the text edit state to kScriptEditing again. I usually place it in any text-editing function I make. It doesn't hurt to call it even if we are already in kScriptEditing mode.

Now we have all of the machinery to start displaying some textual data. As indicated by the name, in the clear-append method, you first clear the text field, and then you append all of the pieces of data to build up the display. To see how this works, let's start by just displaying the seconds. Place the following script in the Idle event of the clock sprite:

```
[Idle]
SpriteVars newText

ExecuteEvent($ClearText)

newText = LocalSeconds
ExecuteEvent($AppendText)
```

Note The "Local" in LocalSeconds means it's in the local time zone. Of course, seconds are the same in all time zones, but LocalHours will probably be different from GMTHours. That is, unless you live near the same longitude as Greenwich, or have been tricking your computer into thinking you do.

Preview the movie and you should see the current seconds displayed live in our text track. Pretty cool, right? OK, now let's build up the full time in the following format:

hours : minutes : seconds

Here's the script:

```
[Idle]
SpriteVars newText

ExecuteEvent($ClearText)

newText = LocalHours
ExecuteEvent($AppendText)

SetString( newText, " : " )
ExecuteEvent($AppendText)

newText = LocalMinutes
ExecuteEvent($AppendText)

SetString( newText, " : " )
ExecuteEvent($AppendText)

newText = LocalSeconds
ExecuteEvent($AppendText)
```

Notice that to append the " : " part, we use the SetString function. You might be tempted to do something like

```
newText = " : "
```

But the = operator only works with numbers, so the above expression would actually set newText to a numeric value of zero. When setting a variable to a string value, you always need to use the SetString function.

Run the movie and check out the LCD clock we just made. Depending on what time it is, you might notice a few things that are strange about this clock. First of all, when the minutes or seconds are less than 10, it only displays one digit. Most clocks pad a zero in front so there are always two digits showing. This is easy enough to do. Let's add another custom event called PadZero, which prepends a "0" in front of newText if necessary. Here's the script:

```
[802 PadZero]
SpriteVars newText

IF( StrLength(newText) = 1 )
    SetString( newText, StrConcat( "0", newText ) )
ENDIF
```

We just introduced two new functions in this tiny script. The StrLength function returns the number of characters in a given string. Here we are checking to see if newText has one character, and if so, we add a zero to the front of it.

We prepend the zero by using the StrConcat function. This stands for string concatenation, and it basically connects two strings together into one. And again, we use the SetString function to place the result back into the newText variable.

Note   I should point out that QuickTime also has an AppendString function, but since it only works with variables (you can't pass in constants like we did with the "0" above), I hardly ever use it. StrConcat is more flexible.

To utilize this in our code, let's modify our Idle script to read like the following:

```
[Idle]
SpriteVars newText

ExecuteEvent($ClearText)

newText = LocalHours
ExecuteEvent($AppendText)

SetString( newText, " : " )
ExecuteEvent($AppendText)

newText = LocalMinutes
ExecuteEvent($PadZero)
ExecuteEvent($AppendText)

SetString( newText, " : " )
ExecuteEvent($AppendText)
```

```
newText = LocalSeconds
ExecuteEvent($PadZero)
ExecuteEvent($AppendText)
```

As you can see, I only zero-padded the minutes and the seconds. In the United States, the hour is usually not zero-padded. Another strange thing (unless you live outside of the United States or are in the military) is that the hour is displayed in 24-hour mode. This is reasonable, but being a Californian, I am more familiar with a 12-hour clock with an AM/PM indicator. To do this, we can simply check to see if LocalHours is greater than 12; if it is, we subtract 12 from it and place a "PM" at the end. Here's the script:

```
[Idle]
SpriteVars newText
LocalVars isPM

ExecuteEvent($ClearText)

newText = LocalHours
isPM = newText > 12

IF( isPM )
    newText = newText - 12
ENDIF
ExecuteEvent($AppendText)

SetString( newText, " : " )
ExecuteEvent($AppendText)

newText = LocalMinutes
ExecuteEvent($PadZero)
ExecuteEvent($AppendText)

SetString( newText, " : " )
ExecuteEvent($AppendText)

newText = LocalSeconds
ExecuteEvent($PadZero)
ExecuteEvent($AppendText)

IF( isPM )
    SetString( newText, " PM" )
ELSE
    SetString( newText, " AM" )
ENDIF
ExecuteEvent($AppendText)
```

Have a look and see what you think. Pretty nice LCD clock, right? Well, now that I look at it, maybe I'm being a little picky, but the font could be a little bigger. QuickTime provides a way to change the font of text in a text track. What you do is select the text you want to modify with the SetSelection action, and then you call SetTextSize. This works great for changing text that is already there, but it's a little backwards when you are building up the text dynamically as we are doing. In our case it would be better to set the font size first and then add the text instead of having to go back afterwards and set a selection. To achieve this functionality, I usually make the AppendText custom function do this work for me. Here's an enhanced version of the AppendText script:

```
[800 AppendText]
SpriteVars textTrackID newText fontSize
LocalVars textLength newTextLength

TrackOfID( textTrackID ).SetTextEditState( kScriptEditing )
textLength = TrackOfID( textTrackID ).GetTextLength
TrackOfID( textTrackID ).ReplaceText( newText, textLength, \
  textLength )
IF( fontSize > 0 )
    newTextLength = TrackOfID( textTrackID ).GetTextLength
    TrackOfID( textTrackID ).SetSelection( textLength, newTextLength )
    IF( Platform = kMacintosh )
        TrackOfID( textTrackID ).SetTextSize( fontSize )
    ELSE
        TrackOfID( textTrackID ).SetTextSize( fontSize * 0.75 )
    ENDIF
ENDIF
```

If you don't specify a fontSize (fontSize = 0), then this is the same as the previous version. It just uses the default font size. But if you do specify a fontSize, then after the text gets appended, this script goes back and selects the newly added text and changes the size.

One neat thing about the above script is that the size will be set to look approximately the same on Macintosh and Windows machines. If you're a Web or multimedia developer, you are probably well aware that the Mac and Windows have different definitions of font size. In Windows, fonts of the same point size are about 1.33 times larger on the screen than they are on the Mac (see Figure 25.5). This is because Windows defines the resolution to be 96 dpi (dots per inch), but the Mac defines it to be 72 dpi. I have

12 point font on the Macintosh

9 point font on Windows

9 point font on the Macintosh

Figure 25.5 Font sizes on the Mac and in Windows.

no idea why Windows uses 96, but 72 has been a standard (more or less) for over two centuries now (the famous printer Francois Didot used 72 dots per inch back in 1770), and 72 dpi is also the definition used by PostScript printers and Adobe PDF documents. Regardless, the fact is that if you want the fonts to look the same size on both platforms, you have to multiply by a scale factor of 72/96 or 0.75.

Now that our AppendText function supports it, let's set the font of the time to be 12 points (by the Mac definition). While we're at it, let's remove the " : " between the minutes and the seconds, and just make the seconds in a slightly smaller font, like 9 point. Here's the final Idle script:

```
[Idle]
SpriteVars newText fontSize
LocalVars isPM

fontSize = 12
ExecuteEvent($ClearText)

newText = LocalHours
isPM = newText > 12

IF( isPM )
    newText = newText - 12
ENDIF
ExecuteEvent($AppendText)

SetString( newText, " : " )
ExecuteEvent($AppendText)

newText = LocalMinutes
ExecuteEvent($PadZero)
ExecuteEvent($AppendText)

SetString( newText, " " )
ExecuteEvent($AppendText)

fontSize = 9
newText = LocalSeconds
```

```
ExecuteEvent($PadZero)
ExecuteEvent($AppendText)

fontSize = 12

IF( isPM )
    SetString( newText, " PM" )
ELSE
    SetString( newText, " AM" )
ENDIF
ExecuteEvent($AppendText)
```

You could, of course, go on and make the AppendText function support other text properties such as the actual font (SetTextFont), the style (SetTextStyle), and even the color (SetTextColor). But since the color only accepts constants, you'd have to code a few common colors and assign them to integers. For example, a textColor of 3 in the following script would indicate green:

```
IF( textColor = 1 )
    TrackOfID( textTrackID ).SetTextColor( 65535, 0, 0 ) //red
ELSEIF( textColor = 2)
    TrackOfID( textTrackID ).SetTextColor( 0, 65535, 0 ) //blue
ELSEIF( textColor = 3)
    TrackOfID( textTrackID ).SetTextColor( 0, 0, 65535 ) //green
ENDIF
```

Note   QuickTime color channels take values between 0 and 65,535.

The clear-append technique is an easy way to dynamically build up the contents of a text track. With a simple modification you can make a display panel for movie properties such as MovieTime, Volume, and so on. Or you can even get "creative" like they are in Hollywood and display a bunch of random data to make it look like your movie is doing something important.

Text Links (Hotspots)

Text links are the first things that come to people's minds when talking about interactive text. As we saw earlier (Chapter 7), adding text links (hotspots) to a QuickTime text track is easy. Seeing that we already introduced them, I don't want to go too heavily into text links, but I would like to introduce a technique I call "text toggle links."

A text toggle link is like a checkbox without the box. Instead of toggling a check in a box, you toggle the label's value. Say you had a text link labeled "Turn sound off," and by clicking it you would turn the sound off, but also change it to read "Turn sound on" (see Figure 25.6). That's a toggle link. It's a fast and useful way to add multistate buttons to your movie. Let's build one.

Open the ToggleLink_start.lsd project. It contains a single text sample named SoundSwitch with the contents "Turn sound off." Nothing has been scripted yet.

Open the text sample editor and let's define a link. We're going to make the entire sample a link, so select all the text and click the New HotSpot button. In the editor, LiveStage indicates hotspot regions with a box outline.

We can now script what we want the link to do. Click anywhere in the hotspot region and the New HotSpot button should turn into a Delete HotSpot button indicating that a hotspot is selected. You can edit the location of the hotspot with the "Text from:" and "To:" fields. For the toggle link functionality, add the following script to the hotspot's Mouse Click event:

```
[Mouse Click]
#define TEXT1 = "Turn sound off"
#define TEXT2 = "Turn sound on"
#define ONVOLUME = 255

SetTextEditState(kScriptEditing)
IF( MovieVolume > 0 )
    SetVolumeTo(0)
    ReplaceText($TEXT2, 0, GetTextLength)
ELSE
    SetVolumeTo($ONVOLUME)
    ReplaceText($TEXT1, 0, GetTextLength)
ENDIF
```

Up state **Turn sound on**

Down state **Turn sound on**

Figure 25.6 A toggle link.

When we preview the movie, the text should toggle visually between the two states with each click.

As a final touch, let's add some mouse feedback to let the user know that their click is going to do something. One way of adding feedback involves changing the style of the text link on Mouse Down and Mouse Up. QuickTime provides the following two methods for changing the appearance of a text link:

```
SetTextLinkColor(linkIndex, red, green, blue)
SetTextLinkStyle(linkIndex, style)
```

We're going to utilize the second action. Since normal text is smaller than bold text, we can make it look like the text is getting pressed into the screen by starting with bold, switching to normal text on Mouse Down, and returning to bold on Mouse Up. Here are the scripts:

[Mouse Down]

SetTextLinkStyle(1, kNormalFace)

[Mouse Up]

SetTextLinkStyle(1, kBoldFace + kUnderlineFace)

And let's start the link off bold by adding this script to the Frame Loaded event (you need to click away from the hotspot to access the Frame Loaded event):

[Frame Loaded]

SetTextEditState(kScriptEditing)
SetTextLinkStyle(kBoldFace + kUnderlineFace)

In these scripts, we call the SetTextLinkStyle action and pass in the index of the link and the style flags.

Note You can find the available style flags in Appendix N.

We are using 1 for the link index because we only have one link. The links are indexed in order of occurrence in the sample.

Note QuickTime doesn't provide methods for determining the number of links, the location of links, or the current text attributes of links. QuickTime also doesn't let links move around in the sample. Once you define a hotspot between characters 5 and 10, it is always between 5 and 10 no matter how you change the text. Of course, if you change the text so that there are only 7 characters, then the link will only be between characters 5 and 7, but as soon as you add more characters, the link will be back to its full size again. At runtime, inserting text before a link doesn't move the link; it just shifts some of the characters before the link into the hotspot region.

▶ Searching Text Captions

One of the most common uses of text tracks is to create captions. Text captions that are always on are called *open captions,* or *subtitles.* Ones that can optionally be turned on and off are called *closed captions* (cc). With Quick-Time's interactive abilities, you can easily create closed captioning and provide a user interface to turn it on and off. But that's pretty boring. Even your wimpy TV can do that. We're going to do something that I always wished my TV could do and that's text searching.

Have you ever watched a movie and afterwards wanted to go back to all the points in the movie where Ace Ventura says "ALLLLL righty then"? OK, your taste in movies may be more sophisticated than mine, but you must agree that a search feature would be a handy addition to DVD players.

If you have the pro version of QuickTime Player, then you already have a movie text search feature. Open a movie with text and choose Find from the Edit menu. It works well. Two problems with this functionality is it doesn't work in the browser, and it doesn't work if you only have the standard version of the player. As a result, many QuickTime users don't have access to this useful feature. Tragic, yes, but never fear. You can add text-searching capabilities right into your movies. This way they will work anywhere QuickTime works, and you can customize the interface any way you want. Let's build an example of this to see how it's done.

Open the project TextSearch_start.lsd. The audio and video we're using in this project comes from the movie in Steve Gulie's book *Quick-Time for the Web,* in which he discusses the design of the 409-B Widget-Spanning Tube Gasket (see Figure 25.7). Synchronized to the audio and video we have a closed-caption text track. For our search field we'll use a Flash track. The reason for using Flash in this case is it enables us to make an interface with just a single track. Having a single track is better in this case because after we wire it up, we can export just the Flash track and reuse it as a "search" track that we can simply add to any movie. Using the pro version of QuickTime Player, you can copy and paste tracks from one movie to another, so someone wouldn't even need a fancy authoring tool like LiveStage to add a search field to their movie.

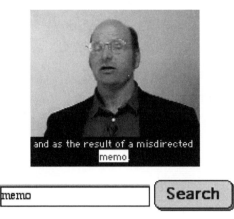

Figure 25.7   TextSearch project.

Note   For a description of how to add tracks and do other cool stuff with QuickTime Player, refer to the book *QuickTime for the Web.* Oh, and check out this chapter's explorations.

Text searching is performed using the FindText action on the text field. The FindText action has the following parameters:

FindText(searchString, red, green, blue, flags)

It takes the string to search for, a color (red, green, blue), and a flag. The specified color will be used to highlight whatever text is found. The red, green, and blue parameters take the standard QuickTime color range from 0 to 65,535.

The flags parameter determines the search options, which include

```
kSearchAgain
kSearchCurrentSample
kSearchCaseSensitive
kSearchReverse
kSearchWraparound
```

These are similar to the standard options found in most text search dialogs. As usual, you can combine multiple option flags through the " + " operator. For example, to perform a case-sensitive search in the reverse direction, you should supply kSearchCaseSensitive+kSearchReverse as the flags parameter.

Note   See Appendix N for more information.

To use QuickTime's default behavior without any option, use 0 for the flags parameter.

Advanced Each of the search options have very specific meanings that aren't exactly obvious from their names. If you want to do serious text searching, you'll need to know what each of them actually means. Briefly:

kSearchAgain: This means to start searching from the end of the current text selection. You can query and modify the text selection range through GetSelectionStart, GetSelectionEnd, and SetSelection(startIndex, endIndex).

Note You have to explicitly target the text track when using SetSelection since the movie also has a SetSelection action. If you call SetSelection without a target, it defaults to the movie target, which has the effect of selecting a range along the movie's timeline. See Chapter 21 for information about the movie's SetSelection action.

An important thing to realize is that when the sample first loads, the selection is at the end of the text. For example, if the sample has 20 characters, GetSelectStart and GetSelectionEnd will both return 20. Because of this, if you don't change the selection, and only use the kSearchAgain flag, you might miss matches in the current sample. When using the kSearchAgain flag, I usually set the selection to the beginning of the text sample by calling SetSelection(1,1) on the text track.

Note Don't call SetSelection on the Frame Loaded event. It won't work. It needs to be called after the frame has loaded.

kSearchCurrentSample: By default, QuickTime assumes you don't want to search the text sample you are currently viewing. It starts looking in the next sample (even if there isn't a next sample!). Use this flag if you want to begin searching the current sample. It doesn't mean to only search the current sample, but just to begin looking in the current sample.

If you use this in conjunction with the kSearchAgain flag, you won't be able to search the current sample unless you first set the text selection to the beginning of the sample.

kSearchCaseSensitive: By default, searching is case insensitive but diacritic sensitive. Thus searching for "cafe" will match "cafe," "Cafe," and "CAFE" but not "café." By supplying the kSearchCaseSensitive flag, "cafe" will only match "cafe." QuickTime doesn't yet support diacritic-insensitive searching.

Note A *diacritic* is a mark placed on a character to modify its phonetics, such as an accent or an umlaut.

kSearchReverse: Using this flag tells QuickTime to search in the reverse direction. Sounds simple, but it's not. If you have just loaded a movie and call FindText with just this flag, you won't find anything. This is because QuickTime starts looking in the previous sample, and there isn't a previous sample. Use kSearchCurrentSample to make it find the last match in the current sample.

Be careful using kSearchReverse in conjunction with the kSearchAgain flag. Remember, kSearchAgain actually means to continue searching from the end of the text selection. If you call FindText and find something, the text it finds gets selected. If you then call FindText again with kSearchReverse + kSearchAgain, QuickTime will simply find the thing that it has already found. To make it work in reverse the way you would expect, move the text selection just before the current selection:

LocalVars selectionStart

selectionStart = **TrackNamed**("text").**GetSelectionStart**

TrackNamed("text").**SetSelection**(selectionStart,selectionStart)

TrackNamed("text").**FindText**("alllll righty", 65535, 0, 0, \
  kSearchReverse+kSearchAgain)

kSearchWraparound: This simply tells QuickTime to treat the movie as a loop where the first sample comes after the last and the last sample comes before the first. If the playhead is in the last sample, calling FindText with kSearchWraparound as the only option will find the first occurrence of the text in the movie.

ALLLLL righty then, let's wire up our Flash search button so we can find what Steve has to say about widget-spanning tube gaskets.

Double-click the Flash sample to bring up the Flash sample editor (see Figure 25.8). We're going to place a script on the Mouse Release event of button 5 (located under Root/Buttons). It's the only button in the movie. By the way, Flash has a different event scheme than QuickTime. Mouse Release in Flash is similar to Mouse Click in QuickTime. We'll discuss Flash more in the next chapter. The Mouse Release event should already have the following script in it:

[Mouse Release]

#define SEARCHTRACK = "caption"

Let's start off hard-coding a search. We'll have QuickTime look for the first occurrence of the word "memo" in the movie. Here's the script:

[Mouse Release]
#define SEARCHTRACK = "caption"

TrackNamed($SEARCHTRACK).**FindText**("memo", 0, 65535, 65535, \
  kSearchCurrentSample)

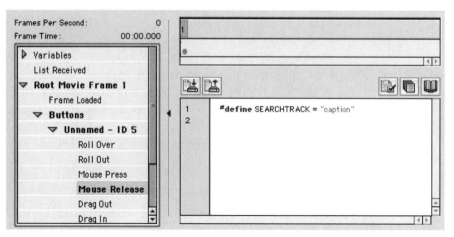

Figure 25.8 Flash sample editor.

Figure 25.9 The Variables node.

Try it out and make sure we have everything set up correctly. Clicking the Search button should move the current time of the movie to the part where Steve says, "a misdirected memo."

So far so good, but as much as I like the word "memo," a search feature isn't very useful with a hard-coded search string. What we need to do is pass the value of the Flash text field into the FindText action.

Dynamic text fields in Flash correspond to Flash variables. In this case, I named the variable Value. You can see it listed under the Variables node (see Figure 25.9). To get the value of a Flash variable, use the action

GetFlashVariable(path, variableName)

Since the text field is at the root level, the path is simply "". The variable name is "Value". Replacing the hard-coded "memo," we get

```
[Mouse Release]
#define SEARCHTRACK = "caption"

TrackNamed($SEARCHTRACK).FindText(GetFlashVariable("", "Value"), 0, \
    65535, 65535, kSearchCurrentSample)
```

Preview now, and try searching for the word "the." This should highlight the first word in the movie. Now, click the Search button again. Hmmm. It still highlights the first word in the movie. Is that the only "the" in the movie? Let's try another word. Search for the word "rubber." This should take us to the part of the movie where Steve says, "for the 5 cent rubber washer."

As you'll notice, there is a "the" in this sample. If you now change the search string back to "the," QuickTime should find this "the" rather than the first "the." But clicking the Search button again doesn't take us anywhere new. Let's add the kSearchAgain flag so that we can find more than one occurrence of a search string. The action should look like

```
TrackNamed($SEARCHTRACK).FindText(GetFlashVariable("", "Value"), 0, \
   65535, 65535, kSearchCurrentSample+kSearchAgain)
```

Preview the movie now, and search for "the" again. This time it skips past the first occurrence and only finds the second, third, fourth, and fifth occurrences. What's going on? This happens because the kSearchAgain flag tells QuickTime to start searching after the current text selection. When a sample first loads, the default selection is at the very end of the text. Even though we specify the kSearchCurrentSample, the kSearchAgain option causes us to miss the current sample. What to do?

There are several ways to work around this. For searching captioned movies, I personally like to use the following scheme:

1. First search the current sample using kSearchCurrentSample.

2. On subsequent searches for the same string, use kSearchAgain.

3. When the search string changes, go to the beginning of the movie and search the current sample.

To implement this, we need to store the search string so we can determine if the user is searching for the same thing again or has entered a new search string. This is why I have another variable in the Flash movie called LastValue. So all we have to do is compare Value with LastValue. If they are equal, then it means it's a searchAgain. If they are different, then it's a new search, and we need to start searching from the beginning of the movie.

Here's the script as described above:

```
[Mouse Release]
#define SEARCHTRACK = "caption"
```

```
IF( StrCompare( GetFlashVariable("","Value"), \
  GetFlashVariable("","LastValue"), FALSE, FALSE )
    TrackNamed($SEARCHTRACK).FindText(GetFlashVariable("", Value), \
      0, 65535, 65535, kSearchAgain)
ELSE
    GoToTime(0)
    SetFlashVariable("", "LastValue", GetFlashVariable("","Value"), \
      FALSE )
    TrackNamed($SEARCHTRACK).FindText(GetFlashVariable("", Value), \
      0, 65535, 65535, kSearchCurrentSample)
ENDIF
```

Here we've introduced a couple new actions: StrCompare and SetFlash-Variable. StrCompare is a function that determines if two strings are equal. It takes the following four parameters:

StrCompare(String1, String2, CaseSensitive, DiacriticSensitive)

String1 and String2 are the two strings to compare. CaseSensitive and Dia-criticSensitive are two Boolean parameters that specify whether or not to consider case or diacritical marks when comparing the strings.

SetFlashVariable is similar to GetFlashVariable except it takes a value as the third parameter.

We now have a useful search dialog that we can place on any movie with a text track.

You probably noticed that it's a little more difficult working with Flash variables than it is sprite track variables. LiveStage actually lets us use MovieVars in Flash scripts, just like you can in text tracks. You just can't use GlobalVars, SpriteVars, or LocalVars. However, using MovieVars always requires LiveStage to add a sprite track when it compiles the movie. It needs a sprite track to house the variables. LiveStage calls this track "Movie Variables." Since we wanted the search field to be a single track, I limited the search script to Flash variables.

Note We could have also used QTLists, which I discuss in detail in Part VI.

In the next chapter we'll dive more into how to integrate Flash in your QuickTime movies.

▶ Explorations

1. At the beginning of the chapter, we implemented a scrolling ticker tape display by shifting the text box. This method produces smooth scrolling, but we had to add ". . . . . ." to get the beginning and end to stitch correctly. Another method to produce a ticker tape is to remove some characters from the front and place them at the end. This limits how smoothly it can scroll to the width of the characters, but the end result is fine to my eye.

   See if you can implement a ticker tape in this way. You can use the following code sniplet to move one character from the beginning to the end of the text sample:

   ```
   ReplaceText(GetText(0,1),GetTextLength, GetTextLength)
   ReplaceText("", 0, 1)
   ```

2. Use the clear-append method to continuously display the date in a text track. First display it in the MM/DD/YYYY format, but for a challenge, have it formatted like

   Wednesday July 23, 2003

   To calculate the day of the week, refer to the calendar entry in Appendix B.

3. ASCII art can be both visually and intellectually appealing. I've seen some great pictures made out of text characters. There are even groups on the Internet dedicated to ASCII art as a serious form of expression. You should search around. You'll find some neat stuff.

   With QuickTime's text tracks, you can create dynamic and interactive ASCII art (ASCII movies?). On the CD, I've included two simple examples in the ASCIIArt directory. Try making your own. The only rule is that the movie can only contain a single text track. That means no MovieVars. Be creative! (Someone should make an ASCII movie website.)

4. In this chapter, we developed a function to add a zero to the front of a number. It was used to make the minutes and seconds display in a fixed time format. This is done commonly in programming and is called zero-padding. Our function only padded up to one zero. Say you wanted to make an odometer with seven digits. Design a zero-padding function that will pad up to six zeros if necessary.

5. Once you have the zero-padding function from above, you can build an interactive counter out of a single text track. What I mean is, consider a text track with the following content:

< 0000000 >

The "<" and ">" characters are both text links. Clicking the ">" link increments the number by one to produce

< 0000001 >

Similarly, clicking the "<" link decreases the number. How would you build a text track that works like this?

6. In this chapter, we produced a Flash track that can perform text searching. I've included a built version of that Flash track on the CD (`Projects/Chapter25/TextSearch/SearchTrack.mov`). If you have a registered pro version of QuickTime Player, you can easily add a searching field to any movie. Try adding search to the movie on the CD located at `Projects/Chapter01/BehindTheScenes/TheTools.mov`. To do this, open both this and the SearchTrack movies in QuickTime Player. Copy the entire duration of the SearchTrack movie by choosing Select All from the Edit menu and then choosing Copy (also from the Edit menu). Now go over to TheTools movie, Select All, and then choose Add Scaled from the Edit menu. This will paste in the search track and temporally scale it to fill the current selection.

There's only one more thing you have to do. The SearchTrack movie only searches for text in a track named "caption." The problem is that in this movie the track we want to search is called "Closed Caption." But that's OK, we can change the name of the track. To do that, open the movie properties window by choosing Get Movie Properties from the Movie menu. Go to the General properties for the track named "Closed Caption." At the bottom, you'll see a button labeled "Change Name." Click that to change the name to "caption."

If you don't like the position of the SearchText track, you can move it by clicking on the Adjust button in the track's Size property panel. Getting proficient at using QuickTime Player takes a bit of exploration. Steve Gulie's book *QuickTime for the Web* and Judy and Robert's book *QuickTime 6 for Macintosh and Windows* are both good references for learning about QuickTime Player's many features.

7. When using the `FindText` action, QuickTime will change the text selection. (This feature was added in QuickTime 6.) You can get the selection by using `GetSelectionStart` and `GetSelectionEnd`. Seeing if the selection has changed is a good way to determine if the `FindText` action actually found anything. But there are a couple of tricks.

First of all, QuickTime doesn't update the selection right away after FindText is called. You have to check on a later event, such as the next idle event, to get the new text selection. It's also possible for some new text to be found but the selection to remain the same. This happens when it finds the text in a later sample that occurs at the same character location. Therefore, you also have to check to see if the MovieTime changed. One last thing to be aware of is that you should use GetSelectionEnd to determine if the selection changed. Using GetSelectionStart is no good because, when using the kSearchAgain flag, just calling Find-Text will move the selection start to the selection end even if it doesn't find anything. Only the selection end won't move if it doesn't find anything.

Armed with this information, how would you implement a sprite track that determines how many times a certain word occurs in a text track? Think it over. What search flags would you use? Would you need to first jump to a certain time? Once you arrive at a solution, try implementing it.

8. Like HTML, the styles and formatting of a QuickTime text track can be defined in a text-based way. This makes it easy to dynamically produce styled text tracks (even multisampled ones) from a server or an application. All it needs to do is output a text file with special formatting tags and then load that text file into QuickTime. The pro version of Quick-Time Player can also export a text track to a text file with the appropriate tags. Look at Appendix K for more information.

26

Flash Tracks

Flash is a wonderfully interactive medium that works even more wonderfully when combined with QuickTime. It's such a nice combination for many reasons. Flash is great for vector animation, sound effects, and light weight media, but isn't quite up to the task if you want high-quality, high-performance audio and video. It's getting better all the time (Flash MX now supports a limited version of the Sorenson codec), but it doesn't yet come close to the wide range of audio and video options that QuickTime provides, let alone streaming video and all of the other powerful track types such as QTVR and MIDI. Flash and QuickTime can also be tightly integrated visually. Flash tracks can be alpha composited with other tracks to make them look and feel like part of the movie instead of just a separate track. Flash interactivity can also be well integrated with the rest of the application. Flash buttons and frames can trigger not only Flash Action-Scripts, but also QuickTime scripts (QScripts) (see Figure 26.1). This means that a Flash interface has access to all the things accessible to a

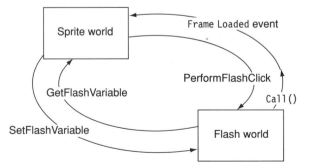

Figure 26.1 Flash communication gateway.

sprite interface. It goes the other way as well. The rest of the movie can target and control Flash tracks in many powerful ways, as we'll explore in this chapter.

Since it takes a bit of engineering work to integrate Flash, QuickTime is usually about one version behind the current Flash version. For instance, QuickTime 6 supports Flash 5, but Flash 6 is already out (called Flash MX). But this usually doesn't cause problems since Flash is backwards compatible (most features of MX movies will work in a Flash 5 player), and it also takes a while for developers to upgrade and get acquainted with new versions. So by the time developers are really up and running with MX, QuickTime will hopefully support it. In the meantime, Flash 5 is very powerful, so let's get started.

▶ Controlling QuickTime from a Flash Button

LiveStage provides two ways to place scripts on Flash buttons and Flash frames. You can type the script on the LiveStage side, or you can type the script on the Flash authoring tool side. Both ways have their strong points. In earlier chapters, we've already placed scripts on both Flash frames (Chapter 19) and buttons (Chapters 20 and 25) using the LSPro script editor. To review, you bring in your Flash movie, double-click the Flash sample, and that brings up the script editor. You can then browse the tree of Flash objects and find buttons on different frames and in different movieclips. Once you find the button you are interested in, you can then add a script to any of its mouse events (keyboard events aren't supported yet).

One confusing aspect of this is that the names and definitions of the Flash events are different from the sprite counterparts. Here's a Rosetta stone:

- Roll Over—Similar to the sprite Mouse Enter but it's not called if the mouse is down.

- Roll Out—Similar to the sprite Mouse Exit but again isn't called if the mouse is down.

- Mouse Press—Same as the sprite Mouse Down event.

- Mouse Release—Same as the sprite Mouse Click event. That is to say it is only called when the mouse is pressed on the button and then released while still over the button.

- Drag Out—Similar to the sprite Mouse Exit but is only called when the mouse is pressed on the button and then while still down exits the button.

- Drag In—Similar to the sprite Mouse Enter but is only called when the mouse is pressed on the button and then while still down exits and then enters again.

- Mouse Release Outside—Similar to the sprite Mouse Up event, but is only called if the mouse is released while outside of the button (after a Drag Out event).

- Mouse Enter Down—This event is supposed to be called when the mouse enters while down as a result of clicking on a different button. But this doesn't appear to be supported by Flash 4 or 5.

- Mouse Exit Down—This event is supposed to be called when the mouse exits while down as a result of clicking on a different button. But this doesn't appear to be supported by Flash 4 or 5.

Any script you can place on a sprite event you can also place on one of these Flash button events. The only exception is the use of variables. GlobalVars, SpriteVars, and LocalVars are not available on Flash events. As we discussed in the last chapter, MovieVars can be used, but LiveStage will add a special sprite track for you when the movie gets compiled. This is not specific to Flash though. This is true anytime MovieVars are used, even from sprite tracks. In the last chapter we built a search field that worked around using MovieVars by simply using Flash variables. But, besides variables, scripts on Flash events have access to all of the movie properties, can target other tracks, and can manipulate sprites and everything we are used to.

As a simple example, if you wanted to have a Flash button set the movie rate to half speed, you just place the following script in that button's Mouse Release event:

[Mouse Release]

SetMovieRate(0.5)

LiveStage provides a second way of adding such scripts to button events. You can add the script in the Flash authoring tool (either Macromedia's or Adobe's) by adding a special FSCommand to the button action.

Note FS stands for "Future Splash," the original name of the Flash platform created by Jonathan Gay.

The Flash `FSCommand` action takes a command name and an argument string. If the command is "`QuickTimeScript(QScript)`", LiveStage will recognize it and compile the argument as QScript. It has the same effect as typing the QScript in LSPro's Flash sample editor, but it is sometimes useful to be able to place the scripts on the Flash side, especially if you will be using the same `.swf` file many times and always want the same QScript attached.

Another good reason to add the scripts from the Flash authoring side is to make it easier to modify the `.swf` file. If you build a LiveStage project with a Flash track, and later edit the `.swf` file, it's possible that the buttons will be moved and LiveStage will no longer know which script is associated with which button. Placing the scripts in the `.swf` file itself gets around this problem.

One drawback with using the `FSCommand` approach, however, is that you don't get the QScript editor, and large multilined scripts become difficult to enter. By the way, you can either use a semicolon or "\r" to represent new lines since the `FSCommand` expects a single line for the argument. I should also note that adding scripts this way will have no effect if brought into QuickTime directly. You still need to go through LSPro to compile the scripts defined by the `FSCommands` into QuickTime wired actions.

▶ Controlling a Flash Button from QuickTime

Flash's ability to control QuickTime means that you can build vectorized interfaces for your movies. These interfaces can also be tightly integrated such that QuickTime can also control Flash. We saw earlier how Flash variables can be manipulated using the `SetFlashVariable` and `GetFlashVariable` actions. We can also execute custom Flash events by triggering button clicks. QuickTime provides a wired action to do this called `PerformFlashClick`. It has the following signature:

`PerformFlashClick( ButtonPath, ButtonID, MouseEvent )`

With this action you can simulate clicks on any button in a loaded Flash sample. Actually, it lets you simulate not only clicks but any of the Flash mouse events discussed earlier. This provides QuickTime with a way to trigger both ActionScripts and QScripts associated with buttons.

The `ButtonPath` parameter is a string locating the movieclip in which the button resides. For buttons at the top level of the movie, you can simply use "".

ButtonID is the ID that the Flash authoring tool assigns to the button. LiveStage displays the ID in the Flash sample editor.

The MouseEvent parameter is a code specifying which of the nine button events to trigger. To make the button event naming scheme even more complicated, the names of the codes are nothing like the actual event names. Like all QuickTime constants, they start with a "k." Here's a decoder ring for you:

- kIdleToOverUp—Roll Over

- kOverUpToIdle—Roll Out

- kOverUpToOverDown—Mouse Press

- kOverDownToOverUp—Mouse Release

- kOverDownToOutDown—Drag Out

- kOutDownToOverDown—Drag In

- kOutDownToIdle—Mouse Release Outside

- kIdleToOverDown—Mouse Enter Down

- kOverDownToIdle—Mouse Exit Down

Let's use PerformFlashClick in an actual project to see how this works. Open the project TriggerFlashButton_start.lsd. The .swf file used for the Flash track here has a movieclip of a swimming fish and two hidden buttons that start and stop the movieclip's playing state.

Note If you look at the source file, SwimmingFish.fla, you'll find that these two buttons are positioned just below the bottom edge of the movie, but given the way Flash resizes movies on preview, you can actually click on the buttons when testing it from the Flash authoring tool (see Figure 26.2).

If you double-click the Flash sample (see Figure 26.3), you'll find two buttons named "Swim" and "DontSwim."

Note LiveStage Pro recently added a way to name buttons in the Flash authoring tool. It uses the same FSCommand structure used to add QScript. For example, to name a button "Bob," use the following FSCommand:

```
fscommand("QuickTimeScript(QScript,ButtonName=Bob)", \
  "QScript goes here...")
```

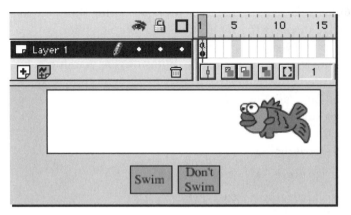

Figure 26.2 SwimmingFish.fla in the Flash authoring tool.

Name : swimmingFish.swf   Start Time : 00 :00.000   Duration : 00 :01.000

Frames Per Second :   12
Frame Time :   00 :00.000

List Received
▽ **Root Movie Frame 1**
    Frame Loaded
  ▽ **Buttons**
    ▷ **Swim – ID 46**
    ▽ **DontSwim – ID 48**
      Roll Over
      Roll Out
      Mouse Press
      Mouse Release
      Drag Out
      Drag In
      Mouse Release Outside
      Mouse Enter Down
      Mouse Exit Down
  ▷ Movie Clips

1   //Don't swim script

Figure 26.3 The LSP Flash sample editor.

The button names and comments were added using the special FSCommands described earlier. Before you close the sample editor, note that the Swim button has an ID of 2, and the DontSwim button has an ID of 4. We'll need these IDs in a moment in order to trigger them with the PerformFlashClick action.

In this project, we also have a sprite track with a checkbox sprite inside. What we are going to do is hook up the checkbox so it controls the swimming state of the Flash fish. To do that, enter the following script in the checkbox's `ValueChanged` script:

```
[3 ValueChanged]
GlobalVars Value

#define FISHTRACK = "Fish"
#define SWIMON = 2
#define SWIMOFF = 4
IF( Value = TRUE )
    TrackNamed($FISHTRACK).PerformFlashClick("",$SWIMON, \
        kOverDownToOverUp )
ELSE
    TrackNamed($FISHTRACK).PerformFlashClick("",$SWIMOFF, \
        kOverDownToOverUp )
ENDIF
```

And that's all there is to it. Preview the movie and see if you can start and stop the fish with the checkbox.

Controlling Flash Movie Properties

Besides accessing variables and performing button clicks, there are several actions that give QuickTime control over the playback properties of a Flash movie. For instance, you can jump to different frames in the Flash movie by using the `GoToFrameNamed` and `GoToFrameNumber` actions. The frame name is the optional label defined in the Flash authoring tool. The frame number is simply the frame index starting with 0.

Since scripts can also be attached to frames, jumping to a frame is another way to trigger scripts in a Flash movie. The `GoToFrame` actions have the same effect as calling the QuickTime movie `GoToTime` action with the frame's start time, but they are more convenient to use. The other standard play control actions, such as `SetRateTo` and `SetVolumeTo`, also work for Flash movie playback (as with any track).

There are also a few other specialized Flash track actions such as `SetZoom`, `SetPan`, and `SetZoomRect`. These let you zoom into different regions of a Flash movie. `SetZoom` and `SetPan` take values in percentages (such as 50 for 50%). Since Flash graphics are vectors, they scale well, so zooming will produce smooth results. Zooming and panning Flash images can be useful for maps and situations where you want to have access to different levels of detail (see the example in the explorations). Zooming and panning can also be performed on QTVR tracks, as we'll explore in the next chapter.

Explorations

1. Communicating back and forth between Flash and sprites takes some practice. When learning a new technology, it's good to build a testing environment (called a *test harness*) that enables you to quickly and easily try things out and discover what works, what doesn't, and why. I added a Flash test harness on the CD (Projects/Chapter26/FlashTest-Harness/). It contains the source file for a Flash movie and a LiveStage Pro project that includes a sprite track with a simple test button. The Flash movie (.swf file) has two variables (Foo and Bar) and a button (ID = 12). The button has some Flash ActionScript associated with it that rotates a small Flash arrow to the value of the Foo variable (see Figure 26.4). Try a few things:

   a. Make it so that the Flash button gets triggered when the sprite test button is clicked.

   b. The Foo variable starts off with a value of 45. Try changing the Foo variable to –45 and then triggering the Flash button. This should make the arrow turn 45 degrees counterclockwise.

   c. This time, try setting the Foo variable to half of the Bar variable, and then trigger the Flash button. Since Foo and Bar are also text fields, you can edit them at runtime.

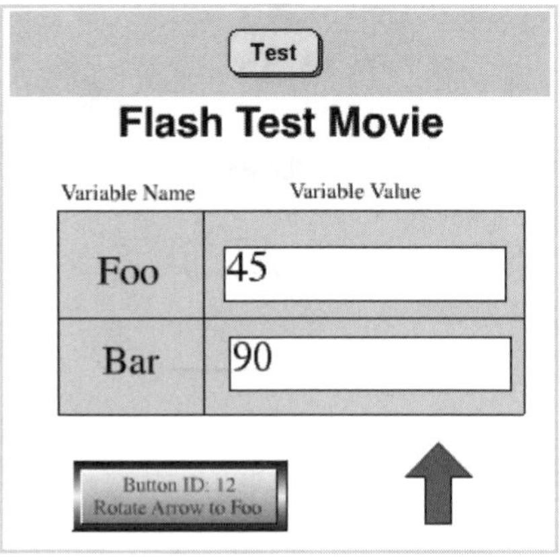

Figure 26.4 Flash test harness.

d. Now let's go the other way. Make it so that clicking on the Flash button moves the sprite button to the right 10 pixels.

e. Make it so that clicking on the Flash button moves the sprite to the right Foo pixels.

If you can get through the above five steps (a–e), then you have mastered communication between Flash and sprite tracks.

2. Now that we've discussed Flash in more depth, it might be good to go back and look at how the password field was built in Chapter 19. It uses Flash's Call action to trigger a Frame Loaded event. We used it as a notification for when the user presses the Enter button. You can also Call the frames of child movieclips.

3. Look at the project in the PanAndZoom directory. It has a Flash track of a world map (see Figure 26.5). It also has a sprite track with buttons navigating the map (panning north, south, east, and west and zooming in and out). I've already hooked up the "zoom in" and "zoom out" buttons. Try hooking up the pan buttons in a similar fashion. Note that you can't pan until you zoom in a bit.

4. Flash tracks can be used as dynamic dictionaries. If you call SetFlash-Variable for a variable that doesn't exist, a new one will be made for you. This provides an easy way for QuickTime to create key-value pairs through a script. Can you think of situations where this would be useful?

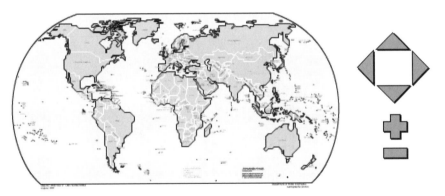

Figure 26.5 A world map with zoom and pan buttons.

27

QTVR

QuickTime has the ability to turn flat images into 3D scenes. It's called QuickTime Virtual Reality (QTVR). QTVR comes in a couple of flavors. The most common is the pano. This is a panoramic picture with a mouse interface that puts the user in control of what direction they want to gaze. Multiple panos can be associated together to form "multinode" QTVR. For example, you can make a multinode pano that lets people experience multiple rooms inside of a house. In this case, each room would be its own node. One node can connect to another node through hotspots, which are regions in the pano that do something when clicked. For instance, you might have one room node transition to an adjacent room node when the user clicks on the door between them. Traditional QTVR panos usually allow the user to get a full 360-degree view of the space, but place limits on how far the user can look upwards or downwards. In QuickTime 5, they removed that limitation with cubic VR, which allows the user to look in all directions including directly up and directly down.

Object movies are another flavor of VR. QTVR object movies let you look around the outside of an object, as opposed to panos, which let you look all around the inside of a space. Object movies are commonly used for new products; a company wants to let eager consumers spin them around and look at the products from different angles.

In my mind, the big thing missing from QTVR is time. Sure, you can look around and jump from node to node, but nothing actually happens in a QTVR scene. You can't move any of the internal objects around, and everything is pretty static. If you leave a node and then come back to it, it's exactly the same as when you left it. It's as if time has stopped. In this sense, it isn't very "real." This is where sprites come into play. For our first example, we're going to learn how to place an interactive sprite into a QTVR scene.

Open the project HockeyGuy_start.lsd. Before we do anything, first preview the movie and have a look at the pano. It's an outdoor scene with a big open snowy field and some farms in the distance. It's sort of fun to look around in the different directions, but there's nothing really dynamic going on.

To make things more interesting, let's place an interactive object on the snowy field. To do that, let's open the sprite track and add a behavior to the hockey guy sprite. The behavior to add is called VRSprite.lsb. What this does is map a sprite into a QTVR scene so that it maintains its same "virtual" location no matter how the user changes the pan, tilt, and zoom. The behavior has parameters that let you specify the location of the sprite in angle coordinates, but let's just use the default values for now.

Preview the movie and you should see a hockey guy sprite staring right at you (see Figure 27.1). Go ahead and zoom, tilt, and pan around. The hockey guy should zoom, tilt, and pan as well, as if he was part of the scene.

Since the hockey guy is a sprite, he can respond to mouse clicks and do all the things that normal sprites can do. As an example, let's add a little bit of interactivity. Have the hockey guy turn a bit each time we click on him. The sprite sample has images of him from several different angles, so we can make him turn by simply iterating through the images. Add the following script to the sprite's Mouse Click event:

[Mouse Click]

SetImageIndexBy(1) **MIN**(1) **MAX**(8) **WRAPAROUND**

Figure 27.1 Hockey guy project.

Let's preview the movie with this script in place. Now we have an interactive hockey guy! He'll turn a bit to the left with each click.

From here, the possibilities are wide open. Add a hockey puck to the scene and make an interactive QTVR game. Swap out the QTVR media with that of a hockey rink and have the guy explain the rules of the sport in an interactive way. You can now turn static panoramic images into interactive 3D worlds.

As a final example with our hockey guy, let's see how to make him move around in the scene. We obviously can't use the normal MoveBy action since that's only suitable for a 2D world. The code in the VRSprite behavior has several SpriteVars that define the sprite's VR location (see Figure 27.2):

- anglePosX = the pan angle of the sprite location
- anglePosY = the tilt angle of the sprite location
- angleWidth = the width of the sprite in terms of pan angle
- yPixelsUp = the offset of the sprite in the *y* direction
- extraScale = how much to scale the sprite at normal zoom

The angle values are all in radians. To move a VRSprite around, all you have to do is modify the values of these SpriteVars. For example, let's make our hockey guy not only spin, but also move to the right with each mouse click. We can do this by adding a small amount to anglePosX each time. Here's the script:

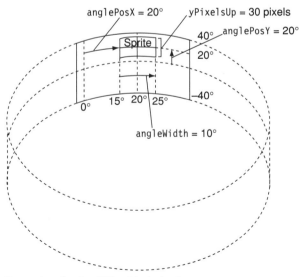

Figure 27.2 Parameters for the VRSprite behavior.

```
[Mouse Click]
SpriteVars anglePosX

anglePosX = anglePosX + DegreesToRadians(10)
SetImageIndexBy(1) MIN(1) MAX(8) WRAPAROUND
```

This will make the sprite move 10 degrees to the right with each click.

When I first made the VRSprite behavior about two years ago, Bill Meikle added it to his VRHotWires application. Right after Bill added my behavior, Anders Jirås was one of the first to try it out. He's the one that supplied me the pano and the hockey guy images for this example. (Thanks Anders!)

Note   VRHotWires is a great application for QTVR authoring. There's a demo of it on the CD along with some tutorials. You can also buy it from vrhotwires.com.

Controlling VR

Sometimes I think that QTVR developers are really orienteers at heart since a common thing that QTVR enthusiasts like to add to their panos is a compass. Compasses provide great ways for users to orient themselves when interacting with a pano. Let's take this concept a little further by building a compass that also functions as a knob. This will enable users not only to see where they are looking, but also to direct their gaze by turning the compass.

Open VRCompass_start.lsd. Here we have a VR pano of a beautiful California coastal location called Pigeon Point (see Figure 27.3). This is actually the spot where the first outline for this book was written. The sprite track on the right has a single sprite with the image of a compass needle. That's going to be our compass/knob.

Note   QuickTime VR panos have the following properties (see Figure 27.4):

- PanAngle—the current left-right direction you are looking (0 to 360).

- TiltAngle—how far up or down you are looking (–90 to +90).

- FieldOfView—how many total pan degrees are currently visible. The lower and upper limits on this depend on the aspect ratio of the pano. Usually the range is from 5 to 36 degrees.

- NodeID—the ID of the current VR node.

Figure 27.3 A pano with a compass.

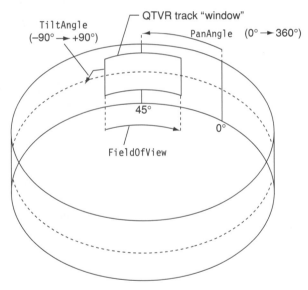

Figure 27.4 The properties of VR panos.

They also have the following actions:

- SetPanAngleBy(degree)
- SetPanAngleTo(degrees)
- SetTiltAngleBy(degrees)

- SetTiltAngleTo(degrees)

- SetFieldOfViewBy(degrees)—how many degrees to zoom in or out

- SetFieldOfViewTo(degrees)—set the number of pan degrees visible

Let's start by adding to the compass sprite the knob component behavior developed in Chapter 18 (KnobBehavior.lsb). We can make the knob function as a compass by setting its value to the pano's PanAngle property. Let's do that in the knob's Idle script:

```
[Idle]
GlobalVars Value
SpriteVars mouseDown

IF( mouseDown = FALSE )
    Value = PanAngle
    ExecuteEvent($SetValue)
ENDIF
```

Here we're only setting the value if the mouseDown SpriteVar is FALSE. If you have a look at the behavior, mouseDown is TRUE when the knob is being turned by the user. Also notice that we simply use PanAngle instead of TrackNamed("Pano").PanAngle. We can do this because QuickTime movies currently only allow a single QTVR track at a time; therefore the target is implicit.

Note   It's even implicit if the pano is in a movie track (see Chapter 28).

Preview the movie and try it out. When you pan around Pigeon Point, the compass should tell you which direction you are looking. Well, almost. When you look west (out toward the water), the compass currently points downwards. Also, when you pan to the left, the compass rotates to the right. We can easily fix these two "bugs" by making the degrees go counterclockwise instead of clockwise, and offset the compass by 90 degrees to make up correspond to north. Let's fix the offset first by setting the knob behavior's Angle Offset parameter to 90. Then, let's reverse the direction of the angle measurement by subtracting the PanAngle from 360:

```
[Idle]
GlobalVars Value
SpriteVars mouseDown
```

```
IF( mouseDown = FALSE )
    Value = 360 - PanAngle
    ExecuteEvent($SetValue)
ENDIF
```

This way when we preview the movie, the compass should be more accurate.

Currently, you can turn the compass with the mouse, but it doesn't yet update the pan angle. Since the knob behavior is a component, we can easily be notified when the knob's value changes and then update the pan angle. Let's do that by adding the following `ValueChanged` script to the compass:

```
[3 ValueChanged]
GlobalVars Value
SpriteVars mouseDown

IF( mouseDown = TRUE )
    SetPanAngleTo( 360 - Value )
ENDIF
```

Here we're only updating the pan angle when the knob is being turned by the user (`mouseDown = TRUE`). This is an optimization more than anything. You can update the pan angle whenever the value changes and that won't cause any problems, but it might slow the panning down a tad. Again, we subtract the `Value` from 360 to make the angle's directionality match the pano. Try it out!

▶ Multinodes, Hotspots, Cubics, and Maps

We can spend a whole book on QTVR, and one is in development at Morgan Kaufmann as I write. To save space, but still cover a lot of ground, let's build a project that uses several important QTVR features, including multinodes, hotspots, cubic panoramas, and maps. We'll build a virtual Moiré Ceiling Museum. This is a nonexistent museum comprised of four connected rooms, with each ceiling covered in a unique moiré pattern (see Figure 27.5).

Note   Moiré patterns are the interesting shapes that emerge when high-resolution lines or dots are digitized at a lower resolution (aliased). The name comes from a certain type of fabric made out of goat hair (mohair), and not the last name of some 18th-century French scientist like some people assume.

Figure 27.5   A moiré pattern.

We'll let the user move from room to room (node to node) by clicking the doors (hotspots) in between the rooms. The interesting stuff in each room is on the ceilings to showcase the fact that you can look straight up in cubic panos. We'll also include a map that indicates which room the user is currently in. Clicking the map will also let the user jump directly to any of the other rooms. Ready?

Open MoireMuseum_start.lsd. Inside you'll find a QTVR pano with four node samples. Each node corresponds to a colored room (red, yellow, green, and blue). On the right of the pano, you'll find a sprite track that will serve as the map for the museum (see Figure 27.6). Let's begin by hooking up the map.

Open the map sprite track and notice that there are four room sprites (RedRoom, YellowRoom, GreenRoom, and BlueRoom). Each of these sprites has associated $Enter and $Exit custom events. We will call these events when we want to enter or exit a particular room. The scripts have already been typed in except for one line at the bottom of the $Enter event. To the end of each of the $Enter event scripts, add the following line:

```
[100 Enter]
...
...
GoToNodeID(ID)
```

The GoToNodeID action allows scripts to set the current node in a multi-node pano. Each node has an ID that can be modified in the node sample editor. In this project, the ID of each node matches the ID of the corresponding room sprite. This simplifies making links between the nodes in the pano and the sprites in the map. If you preview the movie, you'll be able to move from node to node by clicking on corresponding points in the map.

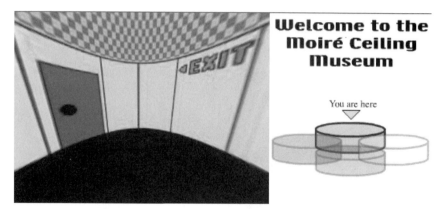

Figure 27.6 The Moiré Ceiling Museum.

Now, let's add scripts to the door hotspots in each room so that the user can also move around the museum by clicking on the doors. Since the rooms are arranged in a circular pattern, each node has two door hotspots. For example, double-click the first node sample to bring up the node editor. On the left you'll see a list of hotspots. In this case there's a BlueDoor and a YellowDoor hotspot. Select the BlueDoor hotspot and enter the following script into its Mouse Click event:

[Mouse Click]

TrackNamed("Map").**SpriteNamed**("BlueRoom").**ExecuteEvent**($Enter)

With this script in place, clicking on the blue door region of the node will execute the $Enter event of the BlueRoom sprite. Add similar scripts to each of the hotspots in each of the four nodes. Obviously, BlueDoor hotspots should execute the $Enter event on the BlueRoom sprite, RedDoor hotspots should execute the $Enter event on the RedRoom sprite, and so on. Once this is done you should be able to preview the movie and transition from room to room by clicking on the doors. Since entering a room is accomplished through the map sprites, the map is always kept up to date. Well, almost always . . . .

There's one small bug. On the QTVR controller, next to the zoom controls, QuickTime provides a back button. The back button takes the user to the last node they were in. Right now clicking on the back button works, but since the room sprites weren't informed, the map gets out of synch. This is an easy bug to solve. All we need to do is add an idle event that checks to make sure the current node matches the room indicated on the map. If there's a discrepancy, then the map should get updated. Let's add the following script to the RedRoom's Idle event:

```
[Idle]
GlobalVars currentRoomID

IF( currentRoomID != NodeID )
    SpriteOfID( NodeID ).ExecuteEvent($Enter)
ENDIF
```

The NodeID property corresponds to the node currently being viewed.

We now have a fully functional virtual Moiré Ceiling Museum sporting multiple nodes, a map, and great ceilings!

Since there's a lot more to QTVR than covered in this chapter, I'd like to end with a list of seven tips for working with QTVR.

1. What appears to be a QTVR track in LiveStage Pro is really a collection of tracks that make up a QTVR scene. A QTVR pano usually contains a QTVR track, a pano track, and a video track for storing the image data of the panoramic scene. If the pano contains hotspots, that data is stored in a separate video track. LiveStage Pro does a good job of sheltering the developer from having to deal with this bundle of tracks, but it's important to know they are there.

2. QTVR nodes are similar to samples and occur at different times in the movie. One consequence of this is that changing the location of the playhead can change the node. If you want to play linear media along with QTVR content, you'll need to be aware of this. For example, you won't be able to play a looping audio track on the same timeline as a multinode VR without unwanted switching between nodes. One way around this is to use a movie track, which is the topic of the next chapter.

3. QTVR doesn't have a SetZoom action. You change the zoom by setting the field of view (FOV) with the SetFieldOfViewTo action. Setting the FOV to a small angle is equivalent to zooming in. Most panos don't let you zoom in more than a few degrees FOV, and don't let you zoom out more than about 36 degrees. The FOV range depends on the aspect ratio of the pano.

4. As we saw in the multinode project, regions within a pano can be designated as clickable hotspot regions. Hotspots have scripts associated with them. They can also be enabled and disabled through the EnableHotSpot(ID) and DisableHotSpot(ID) actions. QTVR also has a mode where it highlights all of the hotspots with an outline so the user can see where they are. The user can toggle in and out of this mode through a button on the QTVR controller. This mode can also be set through the ShowHotSpots and HideHotSpots actions.

5. The current version of QuickTime has a limitation that a single movie can't contain two QTVR nodes active at the same time. One way around this limitation is to use two movies either embedded in a browser or running in the player. For an interesting example of this, have a look at the PanCam example by Francis Gorge and Brieuc Segalen. Launch both `pan.mov` and `cam.mov` and manipulate the video camera to change the pan angle in the other movie.

6. Object movies work similarly to panos (see the `cam.mov` movie in the PanCam example). They have `PanAngle` and `TiltAngle` properties and so on. They also have the notion of view state. For instance, the object in the Object movie can be displayed differently when it's being manipulated with the mouse (`kMouseDownViewState`). You can get and set the current view state through `GetCurrentViewState` and `SetViewState`.

7. As you already saw with the examples in this chapter, movies with QTVR content have a special movie controller called a QTVR controller (there are actually three different types of QTVR controllers). If you try to switch to a non-QTVR controller, such as the standard movie controller or the "none" controller, the QTVR content will stop functioning. It won't be able to pan or tilt either through the mouse interface or through wired actions.

Since some people think the VR controller gets in the way, several techniques have been developed to hide it. One is to use a skin that hides all controllers. If you are embedding the movie in HTML, then you can turn the controller off in the embed tag (this is different from the none controller). Another way is to load the QTVR movie into a movie track (the topic of the next chapter). Look at Luke Sheridan's AcadiaTour piece for an example that hides the controller and replaces its functionality with a custom interface.

▶ Explorations

1. Interactive panoramic photography is a beautiful and often underappreciated art form. Have a look at the ArtistsDwelling piece by Anders Jirås (see Figure 27.7). It's an outstanding example of the unique aspects of this art form.

Figure 27.7   ArtistsDwelling.

2. When a user comes across QTVR content, they are sometimes tempted to pass over it as a static image, not knowing that it's actually an interactive scene. One way to draw the user's attention is to have the QTVR start autopanning slowly when the movie first opens and then stop autopanning once the user starts to interact with it. How would you design a mechanism to detect when the user starts to interact with a pano? What if you wanted to have the pano start autopanning after the QTVR is left untouched for a certain period of time?

3. In this chapter we made a simple compass to help orient the user. The arrow interface of a compass has been around for a long time. One alternative interface is the heads-up display in David Connolly's City-Center movie (see Figure 27.8). What are some other creative ways to display the same information? Compasses usually just display the PanAngle information. How would you design an interface that also shows TiltAngle? How about FieldOfView?

4. What can QTVR panos be used for? Panos are usually used to give someone the experience that they are looking around a physical space. But QTVR's scrolling interface can just as easily be applied to graphical data. Have a look at the pano of network server load from Frank Lowney (Projects/Chapter27/DataPano/). What are some other applications of this medium?

Figure 27.8 CityCenter.

5. Tim Monroe made a scripting language for creating QuickTime VR content. It's called VRScript, and the source code has been made available (it's a great source of sample code for QuickTime authoring). You can download it from `http://developer.apple.com/samplecode/Sample_Code/ QuickTime/QuickTime_VR/vrscript.htm`. There's no official support, but Bill Meikle, the creator of VRHotwires, maintains an unofficial support page: `http://www.vrhotwires.com/VRSUPPORT.HTM`.

6. In Chapter 13 we explored scrolling motion. How is scrolling motion related to a QTVR pano? How would you place a QTVR pano interface on the scrolling background developed in Chapter 13?

MovieTracks

Movie tracks (also known as movie in a movie or MIAM) were originally created so that QuickTime could import SMIL (Synchronized Multimedia Integration Language) documents. Movie tracks allow movies to be embedded inside other movies but still maintain their own independent timeline. This means an audio file playing in a movie track can continue playing even if the parent movie is paused (see Figure 28.1). The introduction of movie tracks in QuickTime 4.1 finally gave a way for developers to break out of the traditional linear media constructs for all track types.

Another powerful feature of movie tracks is that content can be loaded dynamically from either a local source or a remote URL. This greatly excited QuickTime developers because it meant they had more control over the loading characteristics of their movies. Before, developers had to incorporate all media in the same QuickTime file to create a seamlessly integrated presentation. Consequently, users had to download large quantities of media even if they were only going to view part of the experience. Now, with movie tracks, you can download media only when it is needed. For example, consider a multinode VR movie where each node has its own theme song playing in the background. Ideally you would only want to download the new theme song if you enter a node. This is especially true for Internet users in countries such as New Zealand who have to pay their ISP per bit downloaded instead of per month like it usually works in the United States. Users are often reluctant to download things unless they are going to use them. Movie tracks allow developers to control what media gets downloaded when.

Since movie tracks are still considered new, many developers shy away from them, claiming that they are too complicated. But with a simple example you'll see that they are really pretty simple and an invaluable

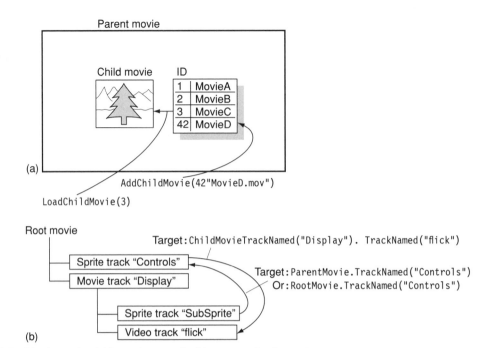

Figure 28.1 Movie tracks: (a) how they work; (b) communication gateway.

addition to your QuickTime toolkit. In this chapter we'll cover all of the basics: how to create and set up a movie track, how to dynamically load content, and how to target the tracks inside. Let's get started.

Open the project VideoZoo_start.lsd. This project starts out with a sprite sample containing three button sprites, each displaying a different animal (elephant, koala bear, and wallaby). In the project directory, there is a folder called SmartVideos that contains the animal movies that correspond to the three buttons. What we're going to do is hook the buttons up so that they load the appropriate content inside of a movie track.

To add a movie track to our project, choose Create Track > Movie from the Movie menu. This will create a 200 × 200 gray-colored movie track positioned at the top-left corner. Reposition and resize it on the stage so it fits snugly inside of the large center frame (see Figure 28.2).

Double-clicking the movie track sample will bring up an editor that lets us configure its various settings. The checkboxes at the top left define how the movie track is to be synchronized with its parent movie. Selecting the time checkbox means that you want the movie track's timeline to be synchronized to the parent such that when the parent movie plays, the child plays as well. If you also select the duration checkbox, then the child movie will be temporally scaled to the same time duration as the parent

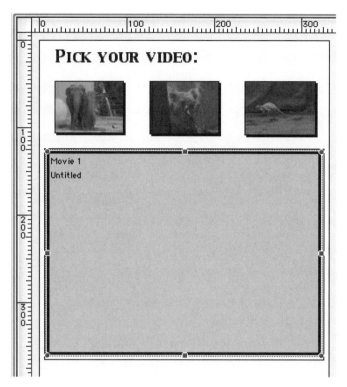

Figure 28.2 Movie track placement.

movie. The audio checkbox specifies if the volume of the parent should also control the volume of any audio in the child movie. Selecting the draw mode checkbox means that the child movie will draw with the same compositing as defined in the movie track. We don't want to select any of these options for this project.

The option menu on the right lets you specify how child movies will be placed in the movie track. The choices are the standard SMIL layout options (see Figure 28.3):

- Clip—Don't scale the movie, just clip the right and bottom edges if it is too big.
- Fill—Scale the movie to fill the track.
- Meet—Scale the movie so that it is as large as possible but still fits entirely within the track. Keep the aspect ratio the same.
- Slice—Scale the movie so that it covers the entire track, but keep the aspect ratio the same. Clip either the right or bottom edge if necessary.

In our case, we want to use the fill layout.

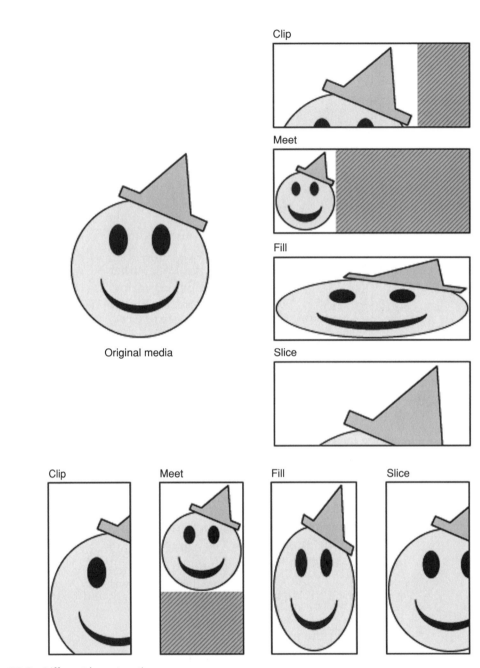

Figure 28.3 Different layout options.

In the center of the sample editor, we have playback options such as autoplay and loop settings. Let's turn autoplay on and have it loop from the beginning.

At this point, we could predefine the URLs of the movies that we want to load by clicking the Add New URL button. But I find it's more flexible to add the movies dynamically through a script. So, we're done defining our movie track sample.

Note   It's even possible to actually embed a small child movie inside of the track so it gets saved with the movie. This is only advisable if the movie is really small (less than 50K), such as a MIDI file, text track, or a lightweight image. What happens is that the entire child movie gets loaded into memory, which is a bad idea for large movie files since it defeats all of QuickTime's optimized memory management.

Let's now set up our three button sprites so they dynamically load their corresponding movie files into the movie track. Before a child movie can be loaded, it first needs to be added to the sample using the AddChildMovie action. This action takes an ID and a URL (either an absolute or a relative URL). Adding a movie simply means registering the URL with the movie track and assigning it a unique ID. In our case, we have a one-to-one mapping between the button sprites and URLs to add, so we can simply use the sprite's ID as the unique ID of the added movie.

Once a child movie is added and assigned an ID, it can be loaded into the movie track using the LoadChildMovie action. Here's the Mouse Click script to do all of this for the Elephant button:

```
[Mouse Click]

TrackNamed("Movie 1").AddChildMovie( ID, "SmartVideos/Elephant.mov" )
TrackNamed("Movie 1").LoadChildMovie( ID )
```

That's all there is to it. Clicking on the sprite will make the SmartVideos/ Elephant.mov movie load into the movie track and start playing (since the autoplay setting is on). Before we test it out, we might as well enter similar scripts for the koala and wallaby sprites. Simply replace the URL parameter with SmartVideos/Koala.mov and SmartVideos/Wallaby.mov.

Of course, there's a more modular way to write the script using string concatenation:

```
[Mouse Click]

AddChildMovie( ID, StrConcat("SmartVideos/", StrConcat( GetName, \
  ".mov" )))
TrackNamed("Movie 1").LoadChildMovie( ID )
```

This way we would be able to use the exact same `Mouse Click` script for all three sprites, just as long as we assign the sprite the same name as the movie file. Given that we only have three buttons, hard-coded URLs will work just fine.

Preview the movie and try it out. Click each of the buttons to load each of the three animal movies (see Figure 28.4).

Note In case you are wondering, the relative URLs work because when LiveStage previews the movie it's actually building a temporary movie in the project's directory. If you want to place this on your Web server or on a CD, just make sure the child movies remain in the same position relative to the parent movie as they are with the `.lsd` project file.

One thing that you probably haven't realized is that the animal movies contain more than just a video track. Each of them also has a hidden text track that contains a short blurb about the animal. We'll call these info tracks. If we add a text track in the parent movie, we can read in and display the contents of the info track after each movie loads. Let's do that.

Figure 28.4 VideoZoo project.

Choose Create Track > Text from the Movie menu and position the text track so it fills the empty space just under the movie track. Rename the text track as "Display" and set the justification property of the sample to "Center."

What we want to do is wait for each child movie to load, then get the contents of the info track and push it into the display track. We know how to get and set the contents of a text track, but how do we target tracks inside of a child movie? The same targeting scheme we've been using all along generalizes to movie tracks in an intuitive way. To target the "Info" track inside of a movie track named "Movie 1," we simply use the following construct:

```
ChildMovieTrackNamed("Movie 1").TrackNamed("Info")
```

Note There are other ways to target it as well. If we added the movie with an ID of 5, we could also target the child track using `MovieOfID(5).TrackNamed("Info")`. But this way is prone to ID conflicts if another movie happens to be loaded somewhere else with the same ID.

I should note that you can target a track inside of a movie track only after the child movie has loaded. The question is, when does it get loaded? If the movie is coming from the local drive, it'll probably load instantly, but if it's loading over the network, it might take a while. For this reason, it's best to keep checking for it to load on an Idle event. As an example, place the following script on the Idle event of the background sprite:

```
[Idle]
SpriteVars loadingInProgress
LocalVars infoLength displayLength tempString

IF( loadingInProgress = TRUE )
    infoLength = 0
    infoLength = ChildMovieTrackNamed("Movie 1") \
      .TrackNamed("Info").GetTextLength
    IF( infoLength > 0 )
        loadingInProgress = FALSE
        displayLength = TrackNamed("Display").GetTextLength
        SetString( tempString, ChildMovieTrackNamed("Movie 1") \
          .TrackNamed("Info").GetText(0, infoLength))
        TrackNamed("Display").SetTextEditState(kScriptEditing)
        TrackNamed("Display").ReplaceText(tempString, 0, displayLength)
    ENDIF
ENDIF
```

When `loadingInProgress` is TRUE, this script keeps checking the info track until it has some content (GetTextLength > 0).

Note   If the movie hasn't loaded yet, accessing the `GetTextLength` property will return nothing, meaning it won't return 0 or any other value. In the above script, `infoLength` won't be modified until at least part of the movie has loaded into memory.

Once the text track's `GetTextLength` property is greater than zero, we can assume the entire text sample has loaded. This is because each text sample loads all at once, so if any of it has loaded, then the entire text sample has loaded. Once loaded, we can set the `loadingInProgress` variable back to FALSE and then transfer the text from the child movie to the parent "Display" text track.

The only thing to do now is turn `LoadingInProgress` on by calling the `$StartLoading` custom event. This is done at the end of each `Mouse Click` script for the button sprites:

```
[Mouse Click]
...
...
SpriteNamed("Background").ExecuteEvent($LoadInfo)
```

We now have a dynamic video loader that also gathers information from the movie and displays it in a text field.

These are the basic methods for working with movie tracks. We utilize these methods in the next chapter when we discuss third-party tracks.

▶ Explorations

1. In the last chapter, we talked about how to hide the QTVR controller by loading the QTVR content into a movie track. This is extremely easy to do. We don't even need to write a single line of QScript. Just create a movie track with the same spatial dimensions as the QTVR scene, then add the URL to the QTVR movie into the movie track sample using the Add New URL... button. Explore the demo project `HideQTVRController _demo.lsd`.

2. Movie tracks are a good way to add looping background sounds to a movie. Try adding background music to the Moiré Ceiling Museum movie from the last chapter.

3. In this chapter we loaded movies from the local drive through a relative URL. However, one of the most powerful features of movie tracks is that movies can be loaded over the network. Try loading a remote piece of media into a movie track. Since QuickTime supports a wide variety of media formats, you shouldn't have any problem finding content. Flash files, text files, image files of almost any format, MP3 files, even M3U files and a wide assortment of other audio and video formats can all be loaded into a movie track.

4. We explored how to target a track within a child movie, but how do child tracks target the parent movie? QuickTime provides the `Parent-Movie` target, which allows movies playing inside of a movie track to get properties and executed actions on the parent movie. Since child movies can themselves contain child movies, there's also a `RootMovie` target, which accesses the topmost movie in the chain of a parent movie. When would it be useful for a child movie to access its parent? When would it be important to access the root movie?

5. How would you use several movie tracks to build a repurposable front page to a QuickTime newspaper? After the movie is built, you should never have to build it again. To change the contents of the newspaper, all that should be required is to replace the child media files.

6. At the beginning of the chapter, we mentioned that movie tracks were invented to support SMIL. What is SMIL? It's an XML format that describes how media are arranged in space and time. Have a look at the SMIL project on the CD (`Projects/Chapter28/SMIL`).

Third-Party Tracks

With every new version of QuickTime, Apple has made it easier and easier for third parties to create new track types. QuickTime has an extensible architecture where new pieces, called *components,* can be installed to add all sorts of new functionality. Apple has a submission and registration process for third-party components to become approved extensions to Quick-Time. This lets the component show up as an option in the QuickTime installer, and it can even be set up to dynamically install when a user runs a movie that requires the component. There are several third-party track types out there already. The ones I know of include:

- Pulse 3D—Enables rich interactive 3D animation. You can create 3D characters with behaviors and actions, such as jump, walk, run, and then you can trigger them from QScript. This is done by invoking a Pulse script through the `ExecutePulseScript` action.

- Zoomify—Allows you to explore huge amounts (gigabytes) of graphical data that starts loading and displaying nearly instantly. It works by progressively and interactively loading more detail in the background as needed. It can work with media resembling images, panos, cubic VR, and object movies. All the view settings can be manipulated with wired actions.

- Axel—Another interactive 3D world similar to the Pulse component but more ideally suited for games and 3D user interfaces.

- Be Here—Streaming 360-degree video that allows you to change the camera angle on the fly as you watch the video. Great for sports broadcasts!

- iPIX—Similar to QTVR, but uses a different format. This was the only way to do cubic QTVR before QuickTime 6 came along.

In this chapter, we'll use some Zoomify media as an example of how to install and interact with third-party tracks. Zoomify is a great technology for science and education. Imagine looking at an aerial photograph of a city and having that image download quickly, as if it were a JPEG image. And then imagine being able to zoom in on one of the city parks and have just the image data associated with the park get downloaded and displayed. If you zoom in more, say, on a bench in the park, then just the bench data gets downloaded and displayed. You could then zoom in even more and read the headlines on the newspaper that the guy sitting on the bench is reading. Zoomify lets you get that much resolution in a seemingly effortless download process. It does it by progressively downloading only the detail that you want to see. Zoomify works not only with flat images but also with panoramic image data. For our example, we're going to take a virtual tour of an airplane cockpit (many thanks to David Urbanic at Zoomify Inc. for supplying this media).

Before we can start authoring the Zoomify media, we need to first install the custom component. To do this, go into the QuickTime Settings control panel. Choose Update Check from the selection menu. Oh, and make sure you're connected to the Internet. Then choose the option "Update and install additional QuickTime software" and click the Update... button. This will launch the QuickTime updater.

When the updater loads, it will probably tell you that you are fine and no updates are necessary, but since we want to install an optional custom component, click on the Custom button. This will display a list of all available QuickTime parts and pieces. Scroll down to the Zoomify checkbox, select it, and then click the Update Now button. Follow all of the standard installation dialogs as it downloads and installs Zoomify.

OK, now we're ready to zoom.

Launch LSPro and open Zoomify_start.lsd. Here we have a sprite track and a movie track (see Figure 29.1). We're going to load the Zoomify media inside of the movie track as there are several good reasons to do this. Many third-party track types have helper files associated with them, and these files don't always get embedded in the .mov file itself. Such is the case with Zoomify, and it makes a lot of sense since the zoom data can be huge, like gigabyte huge! Imagine telling a client to download a gigabyte movie file.

Zoomify gains all of its benefits by incrementally downloading image data from a separate data file called a .pff file (Pyramidal File Format). Usually the .pff file needs to be in the same directory as the Zoomify movie. But if we use movie tracks, we can load the Zoomify movie from anywhere, giving us a lot of flexibility in where we place our media files.

Figure 29.1   A zoom movie.

Movies:

1	Cockpit.mov

Figure 29.2   `Cockpit.mov` added to the URL list in the movie sample editor.

Another reason for using movie tracks is to be able to dynamically load different sets of data. For instance, Zoomify can function as panoramic QTVR, but it currently only supports a single node. However, with movie tracks, you can easily gain multinode functionality by simply loading the appropriate Zoomify movie when entering a new "node."

In the last chapter we saw how to add and load child movies from a script; this time, we're going to have the movie track load the movie for us. To do this, double-click the movie track sample to bring up the editor, and click the Add New URL... button. Type in the relative URL `Cockpit.mov`, then click Add and then Close. You should now have `Cockpit.mov` added to the URL list on the left (see Figure 29.2). This means it's going to load a movie called `Cockpit.mov` located in the same directory as the parent movie. Take a look in the project folder, and make sure `Cockpit.mov` is there. Let's set the movie track layout to Fill and leave all the other settings as they are.

If you preview the movie now, you'll see the default behavior of a Zoomify panorama. It works in basically the same way as QuickTime VR. See all of the dials, switches, and other controls on that Cockpit dashboard? Once we hook up our zoom-in and zoom-out sprite buttons, we'll be able to move up really close and see all of the small lettering on those knobs and display panels.

If you look in the QScript Reference window, you'll find that Zoomify is now listed under the "by track" category. LiveStage Pro is able to detect that the Zoomify custom component is installed and to show the wired actions associated with it. Zoomify has a couple dozen actions. For our project, we only need to use ZoomifyZoomIn and ZoomifyZoomOut.

Open the sprite sample editor and let's first script our zoom-in sprite. We're going to make it continually zoom in while the button is pressed. If you look at the Idle event script, it currently reads:

```
[Idle]
SpriteVar mouseIsDown

IF( mouseIsDown )
    //do something
ENDIF
```

Let's replace the //do something comment with a call to ZoomifyZoomIn. Since Zoomify tracks register themselves as the default target of Zoomify actions, we don't even need to target the Zoomify track in the child movie; all we need to do is replace the comment with ZoomifyZoomIn. This obviously wouldn't work if we had two Zoomify tracks (which we can do, unlike QTVR). The first track that gets loaded is the default target, so we would have to explicitly reference the second one. But in our case (as in most cases) we only have one Zoomify track, so it works nicely. Similarly, the zoom-out sprite's Idle event should look like:

```
[Idle]
SpriteVar mouseIsDown

IF( mouseIsDown )
    ZoomifyZoomOut
ENDIF
```

And that's all there is to it. Preview the movie and try zooming in on some of the controls. Notice that when you get close, it focuses in and reveals all of the intricate detail.

There are a couple things we should discuss about deploying such a movie. First of all, make sure the two associated files `Cockpit.mov` and `panorama.ppf` are always kept in the same directory as the movie. We can, of course, make the `Cockpit.mov` load from a different relative path, or even make it an absolute locator by changing the URL in the movie track sample editor.

If the person viewing the movie doesn't have the Zoomify component installed, currently QuickTime 6 will notify them that it needs to install it and will take them through the steps. Unfortunately, they then have to close the movie and reload to see the content. However, there is a way to make the experience more seamless. Instead of placing the URL into the movie track sample, we can load the movie from a script as we did in the last chapter. But before loading it, we can first check to see if the component is installed by checking for the Zoomify component version using the following action:

```
ComponentVersion( Type, Subtype, Manufacturer )
```

See Appendix J for a list of the type, subtype, and manufacturer data for most of the known QuickTime components. Also if you search in the QScript Reference, for `ComponentVersion`, there is an entry that has a similar list. The values for the Zoomify component are

```
ComponentVersion( "mhlr", "Zoom", "Zoom" )
```

Note In case you are wondering, "mhlr" stands for "media handler."

If the above call to the `ComponentVersion` action returns 0, that means Zoomify isn't installed yet; otherwise a number greater than zero will be returned. If it isn't installed, you can tell QuickTime to install through the `LoadComponent` action. This action takes the Subtype value. For Zoomify, you would use

```
LoadComponent("Zoom")
```

After calling this, QuickTime should either install the component itself or take the user through the installation process. While this is going on, you can continuously wait for Zoomify to get installed by checking the `ComponentVersion` on an `Idle` loop. Once you get a version that is greater than 0, you can continue to add and load the child movie. This is yet another good reason to use movie tracks for third-party components.

▶ Explorations

1. How would you modify the Zoomify project so that the cockpit loads already zoomed into one of the controls on the dashboard?

2. Explore some of the other third-party components. Pulse 3D is an interesting one.

3. Most of the available third-party components deal with 3D. What would be some other interesting track types to create?

Other Tracks

QuickTime has a *lot* of track types. We covered most of the major ones in the last several chapters, but I'd also like to touch on a few more so you at least know they exist.

▶ Video Tracks in Disguise

As you work with QuickTime, every once in a while you'll come across what appears to be a new track type, but it turns out to just be a video track in disguise. Examples of this include the picture track and the color track. These are just video tracks with a single frame displaying an image or a solid color. Video tracks are also used to store the image and hotspot information for QTVR. Video gets a lot of reuse in QuickTime, which is a strong testimonial to its modular and repurposable nature.

▶ Text Tracks in Disguise

There are also several specialized text tracks. For instance, an HREF track is just a text track that has URLs in each sample. As the movie plays, it will load the URLs (see Chapter 36 for information about how QuickTime loads URLs). Karaoke (imported from .kar files) and lyric tracks are simply text tracks that have been synchronized with a music audio track where words get highlighted as they are vocalized.

Chapter tracks are also just text tracks. They let you give names to different sections of a movie, and QuickTime will place a small pop-up menu on the standard controller to allow the user to jump directly to the defined sections (called *chapters*). QuickTime also provides movie-level wired actions for jumping to the beginning of chapters in a chapter track (only one chapter track allowed per movie). The action is GoToTimeByName(name). If you had a chapter called "Bob," you could skip to that time in the movie by calling

GoToTimeByName("Bob")

Note There are also wired actions for jumping to a chapter by index and skipping forward and backward a chapter at a time. Those actions are GoToChapterByIndex(index), GoToNextChapter, GoToPreviousChapter, GoToFirstChapter, and GoToLastChapter. There are also the following movie-level properties to determine how many chapters there are, which chapter the playhead is currently in, and the name of an indexed chapter: GetChapterCount, GetCurrentChapterIndex, GetCurrentChapterName, and GetChapterIndexNamed(name).

I remember back in the early QuickTime days getting excited about burnt text tracks. These are standard QuickTime text samples that also include pre-rendered bitmap information.

Note You can burn a text sample in LSP by selecting the burn text property in a text sample's Properties tab.

This is a good way to get text to look the same on all platforms even with custom fonts. It can also improve playback performance (at the cost of larger file size). All the original text is still in the sample so it can still be searched. One downside is burnt text can't be edited dynamically through scripts since it is being rendered by a static bitmap.

▶ Timecode Tracks

One track type that looks like it should be a text track in disguise is the timecode track (sometimes called a sync track). This track simply stores (and optionally displays) timing information for linear media. It's mainly useful for precise editing of audio and video. The timecode track supports the retrieval of timing information from an external source. It has flexible display options including the standard SMPTE (Society of Motion Picture and Television Engineers) formatting. It also supports frame dropping to represent NTSC timecodes with integer frame values (NTSC is 29.97 frames per second). There's an example movie with video with a timecode track on the CD (Projects/Chapter30/TimeCode/VideoWithTimecode.mov; see Figure 30.1).

03:41:04;03

Figure 30.1 A timecode example.

Being able to display timecodes while viewing linear media comes in very handy, especially when you want to add interactivity to the video. For instance, in designing the interactivity for the kangaroo video in Chapter 22, what I did was watch the video a couple of times while jotting down notes of when certain key events happened. Then when I went to script the sprite track, I knew what values to place in the GoToTime calls and the like. To display the timecode, however, I don't normally use timecode tracks since special software is required to create them (http:// developer.apple.com/samplecode/Sample_Code/QuickTime/TimeCodes/). What I did was make a sprite track that displays the current time (Projects/ Chapter30/TimeCode/currentTime.mov). Whenever I want to display timecodes, I simply add that sprite track scaled to the duration of the movie.

When working with timecodes, you will often want to do some calculations such as finding the duration between two time values, offsetting or scaling the timecode, or converting between timecode formats. Because of this, I made an interactive QuickTime movie that functions as a timecode calculator. Check it out. It's also located on the CD (Projects/Chapter30/ TimeCode/TCCalculator/; see Figure 30.2).

Modifier and Tween Tracks

And then there's a whole category of control tracks. These came about to give a way for the video guys to control things such as sprites and VR in a linear time-based fashion. LiveStage Pro lets you connect modifier and tween tracks to the properties of sprites. For example, you can add a "Path To Matrix Translation" tween track and specify a path that controls the location of a sprite over time. An example of such a tween track is

Figure 30.2 A timecode calculator.

included on the CD (Projects/Chapter30/XYPathTween). Tweens are also well suited to produce fades over time (for an example, see Projects/Chapter30/FlyInTitle). Tween tracks can be linked to sprites by choosing the appropriate tween from the source pop-up menu in the sprite's Property tab. You've probably noticed those source menus all over the place. For instance, there's one above the event names in the sprite Scripts tab. This lets you connect a modifier track that defines a sequence of events to be called as the movie plays. You can also hook modifier and tween tracks up to the graphics mode of video and to the pan and tilt angle of QTVR tracks.

Modifier and tween tracks allow you to create some interesting effects, but these tracks don't lend themselves well to interactivity. They also aren't that flexible. Modifier and tween tracks can't be changed or routed dynamically through scripts. That would allow for some interesting things to happen. Tricks such as placing the modifier or tween track in a movie track to modify a parent track don't work either.

One useful trick you can do with a modifier track is to use it to change the download resolution of certain single-sample media types such as QTVR nodes. At the beginning of Part V, we built a movie that had its own progress bar, indicating the amount of the movie that has downloaded so far. This works great for audio and video, but not so well with QTVR. As a single QTVR node is downloading across the network, QuickTime will indicate that 0% of the movie has downloaded all the way up until 100% of the node has been transferred. This means that a progress bar will show 0%, 0%, 0%, 0%, and then finally 100%. Sort of defeats the purpose of a progress bar. But, if you add a modifier track that repeats a sequence of values at a certain rate during the same duration as the VR node, it will cause MaxLoadedTimeInMovie to detect progress while downloading the VR track. (Thanks to Michael Shaff for discovering this useful trick.)

▶ QuickDraw 3D Track

QuickTime has had the ability to render 3D objects from the very early days of QuickTime. The 3D objects can even be interactive and can be manipulated through wired actions. The only problem is that they aren't cross-platform (they don't work on Mac OS X at all), and they aren't officially supported anymore. To get awesome cross-platform interactive 3D in QuickTime, have a look at the various third-party solutions such as Axel and Pulse 3D.

▶ Streaming Tracks

QuickTime supports streaming media over the network through RTP (Real-time Transport Protocol). This is different from fast start or progressive download. Streaming media data is transferred over the network, then presented in real time (more or less), and then the data is discarded. Data from progressively downloaded movies is saved to disk and QuickTime is able to play and replay any of it that has been downloaded so far.

QuickTime can stream video, audio, text, and MIDI data in the form of a streaming track. Streaming tracks contain information about the streaming media, such as the URL. These tracks can be incorporated into a QuickTime movie like any other track, but most developers choose to load them into a movie track. This way the movie can dynamically choose among multiple streaming sources.

Many streaming tracks have "infinite" durations, such as continuous radio broadcasts. When combining such streaming tracks with interactive sprite tracks, it's often necessary to create infinite sprite samples. To specify infinite duration in LSP, simply place an asterisk (*) in the sample's duration field.

Sprites can gain access to the status of streaming tracks by using the `GetMovieConnectionString` and `GetMovieConnectionFlags` actions.

▶ Hint Tracks

When you prepare a movie for streaming, this involves adding a hint track. This is an example of a server-side QuickTime track. Hint tracks have no purpose for client-side media. Hint tracks contain all the information necessary for the server to package up streamable media and stream it across the network. It would be cool if custom information could be stored in the hint track as well and somehow made accessible to sprites. This would allow a streaming video of a live talk to pass information about what slide number the presenter is currently on. A sprite track could then get this information and display a nice, high-resolution version of the slide image for the viewers watching remotely. Maybe the hint track wouldn't be the best for this, but some way to stream live data accessible to sprites would be very useful.

PDF Tracks

On Mac OS X, QuickTime 6 can actually load Adobe PDF files. They get loaded as a track with each page as a sample (see Figure 30.3). They can be dynamically loaded into a movie track to create custom documentation viewers. However, this currently only works on Mac OS X, but it has a lot of potential if Apple decides to make it cross-platform.

Fast Tracks (FT)

These are an invention of the Totally Hip LiveStage guys. They are a neat concept that streamlines the authoring process of several standard QuickTime constructs. They are basically combinations of standard track types with a nice authoring interface to make them easy to configure. For instance, there is a Status Bar fast track that allows you to easily add a progress bar to your movie. You can even point it at a child movie loading in a movie track. Totally Hip has several tutorials on their website about how to use fast tracks.

Cursor Tracks

Wired sprites can have custom cursors, but there aren't any tools available (yet) to add cursors to a sprite track. For this reason, I made some sprite tracks containing a variety of cursors (even animated ones) and called these specialized sprite tracks "cursor tracks." Developers can easily incorporate them into their movies and make calls to the sprites inside to show the cursors. I included an example cursor track on the CD (Projects/Chapter30/CursorTracks). It has the custom cursors shown in Figure 30.4.

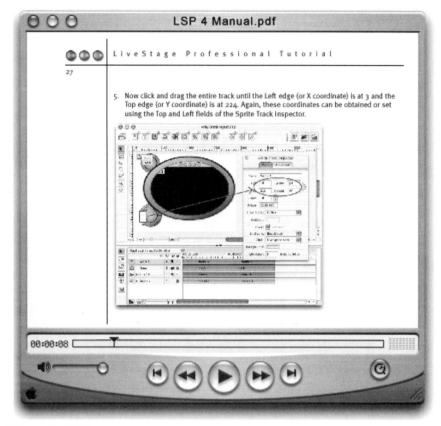

Figure 30.3 PDF on Mac OS X.

 1. quicktime	11. zoomout	21. menu	31. watch
2. speaker	12. bullseye	22. pencil	32. animatedwatch
3. cancel	13. dot	23. plus	33. fingers0
4. scissors	14. updown	24. minus	34. fingers1
5. x	15. leftright	25. crosshairs	35. fingers2
6. locked	16. updownleftright	26. recycle	36. fingers3
7. unlocked	17. backwardscursor	27. trash	37. fingers4
8. globe	18. maccursor	28. nsew	38. fingers5
9. hammer	19. question	29. drop	39. animatedfingers
10. zoomin	20. file	30. square	40. ball
			41. animatedball
			42. none

Figure 30.4 Custom cursors.

To show a certain cursor, simply execute event 1 on the sprite with the same name as the cursor. For example, to show the "animatedfingers" cursor use

```
TrackNamed("CursorTrack").SpriteNamed("animatedFingers") \
  .ExecuteEvent(1)
```

There's an example project on the CD.

WorldWideVariables Tracks

This is another of my inventions. QScript has local variables, sprite variables, global variables, and movie variables. Movie variables (as we'll learn more about in Chapter 38) are useful for transferring information across multiple movies playing on the same computer at the same time. But what about movies playing on different machines, or on the same computer but at different times? This is what WorldWideVariables tracks are for. They allow you to make movies with variables that get stored on the worldwidevariables.com server (see Figure 30.5). Look at Chapter 35 for more information, and visit the website worldwidevariables.com.

Base Tracks

When QuickTime comes across a track type that it doesn't understand, it considers it a base track. This is the generic track type. It doesn't "do" anything, but I thought I should mention it.

WorldWideVariables.com

Figure 30.5 The WorldWideVariables logo.

Explorations

1. For another example of using tween tracks, see `Projects/Contributors/MikeMatson.mov`. The stretching of each of the three-picture slideshows is accomplished through tweens. Mike Matson has donated the movie's project file (`Projects/Extras/MatsonTweenExample/`).

2. In the last chapter, we explored what new types of third-party tracks would be interesting to create. As we've seen here, it's often the case that old track types can be taught to play new tricks. Of the ideas you came up with in the last chapter for third-party tracks, how many of them can be implemented with tracks that already exist?

3. With the cursor track, try going back and enhancing some of the previous projects. For example, in the last chapter, we had zoom-in and zoom-out buttons. Why not use the "zoom-in" and "zoom-out" cursors, or even the "plus" and "minus" cursors? When would the "none" cursor come in handy?

Part

Communicating with the World

In some respects, we've saved the best aspects of QuickTime for last. So far we discussed how to build a wide range of self-contained interactive creations. In this last part of the book we'll explore the many ways QuickTime is able to communicate and connect to the outside world. We'll learn how to configure movies by dynamically loading XML (QTList) and media files from the local file system. We'll build movies that function as thin clients to back-end applications running on a remote server. We'll also see how to extend the control of QuickTime's rich user-interface capabilities to interactions with media players, Web browsers, and custom applications.

XML and QTLists

Until recently, the most common data structures in computer programming were arrays. Arrays let you store values that are accessed by index. These structures are useful for storing a set of values that you might want to have in a certain order. An example might be a list of names for students in a classroom:

Amy, Bart, Kobbi, Linda, Manuel, Omid, Ravi, Takumi, Wangfei

This works great if all you are interested in are the names, but often you are going to want to store more information about each student than just their name. This is where a table, such as the ones used in databases, becomes handy. A table has a list of entries, or rows, and each row has multiple named columns. Continuing with our classroom theme, you might want to have columns for things such as name, seat number, and grade (see Table 31.1).

Table 31.1 Student information.

Name	Seat number	Grade
Amy	1	A+
Bart	12	C−
Kobbi	4	A
Linda	3	A+
Manuel	5	A
Omid	9	A
Ravi	6	A
Takumi	8	A
Wangfei	7	A+

Tables have been used by teachers for ages, and they get the job done, but they aren't very expandable. For instance, say you wanted to store not just each student's final grade, but also their score on each test. Well, in the table, you could simply add another column for each test. OK, now what if you wanted to store not just the overall test scores, but the points for each question as well? If we add a column for each question, we're going to be adding fine details that look like they are just as important as the name of the student. This type of data is best stored in a tree structure.

Trees let you have multiple layers of detail, so you don't need to have the score on each question at the same level as the overall score in the class. Tree structures have become increasingly popular as a result of standardized markup language representations such as XML. The following is an example tree structure for the first two students using XML:

```
<ClassRoom teacher="Krouse" year="2002">
    <Student name="Amy" seatNumber="1" grade="A+">
        <TestScores>
            <Quiz date="October 2" score="100%">
                <question answer="c" rightAnswer="c"/>
                <question answer="a" rightAnswer="a"/>
                <question answer="d" rightAnswer="d"/>
            </Quiz>
            <Quiz date="October 9" score="100%">
                <question answer="b" rightAnswer="b"/>
                <question answer="c" rightAnswer="c"/>
                <question answer="a" rightAnswer="a"/>
            </Quiz>
        </TestScores>
    </Student>
    <Student name="Bart" seatNumber="12" grade="C-">
        <TestScores>
            <Quiz date="October 2" score="0%">
                <question answer="b" rightAnswer="c"/>
                <question answer="b" rightAnswer="a"/>
                <question answer="b" rightAnswer="d"/>
            </Quiz>
            <Quiz date="October 9" score="33%">
                <question answer="b" rightAnswer="b"/>
                <question answer="b" rightAnswer="c"/>
                <question answer="b" rightAnswer="a"/>
            </Quiz>
```

```
            </TestScores>
        </Student>
        . . .
        . . .
        . . .
</ClassRoom>
```

As you can see, the structure is very flexible and expandable. XML tree structures can be used to store arrays and tables and just about any data structure. And since it is hierarchical, you can store different levels of detail all in the same structure.

With the widespread adoption of XML as the data structure of choice, we are finally entering an era where different platforms are able to communicate with each other in a common language. Web browsers, Oracle databases, Microsoft Excel, Apple's WebObjects, and Macromedia Flash are just a few of a whole host of applications that know how to send and receive information in the XML language. Also, new standards are emerging, such as SOAP (Simple Object Access Protocol) and WSDL (Web Service Description Language), that employ XML to make it easy for diverse applications and platforms to communicate and share information.

QuickTime too is quickly adopting XML. QuickTime was an early supporter of SMIL, which is an XML way of describing multimedia presentations. QuickTime also has its own simplified version of XML data structures called QTLists. In this chapter we're going to learn how to use QTLists to store information and to communicate with other applications that know about XML.

▶ QTLists versus XML

If you are already familiar with XML, then we need to first discuss how QTLists are different from XML. Otherwise, you're going to run into trouble fast because QTLists are not going to act as you expect. For this discussion I'm going to assume that you are familiar with XML. If you aren't, don't worry; pretend you are and you'll pick it up as you read along. If you know HTML, then XML concepts will look very familiar to you.

QTLists are like a simplified version of XML. They support the main notion of named elements that can contain child elements, but QTLists differ from XML in several ways.

First, a QTList element can have a value or it can have child elements, but it can't have both at the same time. Having both values and children is called *mixed content,* and it's common in XML (very common in HTML), but QuickTime doesn't support it. When you turn an XML structure into a QTList, either the values or the children of mixed content will be lost. Take the following XML structure:

```
<Value>
    <Child>Hello <b>there</b></Child>
</Value>
```

The <Child> element has mixed content. It has a value, "Hello", and a child, <b>. When QuickTime turns this into a QTList, the "Hello" value will be lost, so you'll get

```
<Value>
    <Child>
        <b>there</b>
    </Child>
</Value>
```

Sometimes, however, the child will be lost, for instance, if you have value content on either side of an element, like

```
<Value>
    <Child>Hello <b>there</b> everyone</Child>
</Value>
```

Then you will lose the <b> child and the "everyone" part of the value to end up with

```
<Value>
    <Child>Hello </Child>
</Value>
```

The bottom line is that mixed content is not supported, so don't rely on QuickTime handling this in a consistent way. Mixed content will probably be supported eventually, but for now, you'll need to work around it.

Second, QTLists don't support XML comments. XML comments work like they do in HTML:

```
<Value>
    <Child>Hello there</Child>
<!-- this is a comment -->
</Value>
```

If you try to turn this into a QTList, you'll end up with nothing since QuickTime won't think it's valid. Since comments are used often, you need to be aware of this. If QuickTime isn't reading in your XML properly, check to see if it contains comments.

Third, QTLists don't fully support XML entities. XML entities are similar to QScript defines. They are named constants that are replaced when the XML parser reads in the document. For example, in XML you can define a new entity called mp that will be replaced with "Matthew Peterson" when the XML gets parsed. You define an entity as follows:

```
<!ENTITY mp "Matthew Peterson">
```

Once defined, you can refer to the entity anywhere in the document by placing "&" and ";" around the name of the entity. For example:

```
<Greetings>My name is &mp;</Greetings>
```

When this gets parsed, the <Greetings> element will have a value of "My name is Matthew Peterson".

Besides custom entities, XML has five predefined entities. These predefined entities are used to encode characters that have special meaning to XML, such as the "<" symbol. The five predefined entities are in Table 31.2.

In XML, you can also reference arbitrary Unicode characters using the form &#nnnn; where nnnn is the Unicode character's number in standard decimal notation. You can also use the form &#Xhhhh; where hhhh is the Unicode character's number in hexadecimal notation. For example, &#X91D1 is the Chinese character for gold.

In QTLists, however, custom entities are not supported. In fact, if you declare a custom entity in your XML document, you will make the entire document invalid as far as QuickTime is concerned. Unicode entities aren't supported either, but using them won't cause serious problems. QTLists, however, do support the first two out of the five predefined entities (the less than and greater than signs). Using one of the unsupported

Table 31.2 XML's predefined entities.

Entity name	Entity value
lt	< (less than)
gt	> (greater than)
amp	& (ampersand)
apos	' (apostrophe)
quot	" (double quote)

entities won't invalidate your QTList, but the entities won't be parsed as expected.

A fourth difference is that QTList elements can have names that aren't allowed in XML. XML doesn't let you use names that start with a number. For instance, the following isn't valid XML:

```
<9Lives>value</9Lives>
```

But for QTLists, this is perfectly acceptable. XML also only supports alphanumeric characters, hyphens, underscores, colons, or periods. Other symbols and punctuation are not allowed. And names can only start with letters, underscores, and colons. QTList names, on the other hand, can have just about any characters at any position. The only characters not supported by QTList names are spaces and the greater than sign. Yes, even the less than sign is acceptable as part of a name. Just because QTLists think these names are OK doesn't mean you should use them. First of all, other XML parsers won't accept them, and as QuickTime becomes more XML compliant, non-XML names might become invalid QTList names as well.

Note Since we're talking about names, I'd like to mention that the name "qtlist" is reserved in QuickTime, and it isn't advisable to use it as an element name. Doing so might make certain QTList functions behave strangely.

A fifth difference is that QTLists don't support namespaces. An XML namespace defines a vocabulary. SMIL and XHTML are examples of XML vocabularies. In XHTML, for instance, when I use an element called <body> it has a particular meaning. If I want to have an XML document that uses multiple vocabularies, I'll need to define multiple namespaces. If I define a namespace called matt, I can then qualify an element as coming from that namespace by using the following notation:

```
<matt:ElementName>Some value</matt:ElementName>
```

This is an element named ElementName coming from the matt namespace. Even though QTLists don't support namespaces, it will still parse XML documents with namespaces just fine. You'll just need to refer to the element as matt:ElementName.

A final difference is that QTLists don't fully support attributes. In XML, attributes are name-value pairs that can be placed on an element. In the following example, author and source are attributes:

```
<quote author="Shakespeare" source="Hamlet">
  Brevity is the soul of wit.</quote>
```

QTLists can import XML elements with attributes, but QScript provides us no way to access their names or values. That being said, it is still useful to at least be able to import the XML correctly because some applications we might want to talk to using XML will require the use of attributes.

Those are the main differences between QTLists and XML. It might sound like they are completely different, but there is enough overlap that many developers don't even know that they are different. For the rest of this chapter, we're going to learn how QTLists work, how to make them, how to manipulate them, and how to use them for data storage. In the next couple of chapters, we'll put QTLists to work to allow our QuickTime movies to communicate with the rest of the world.

Working with QTLists

The first task is to figure out where QTLists reside. QTLists sort of work like variables, but they can't be stored in variables. Each movie has a QTList associated with it, and each track has its own associated QTList. Any time you want to make a new tree data structure, you need to place it either into the movie's QTList or into a track's QTList. So, how do you make a QTList? Let's build a couple.

There are two ways to construct a QTList. You can make one from a string, or you can build one up using actions. We're going to try out both methods in the next example. In this example we dynamically build a price tag like you would see in a retail store. We want to be able to describe the way the price tag looks using a QTList because of the many advantages it provides. We'll delineate these advantages in a bit, but first, let's define the structure of our price tag description as follows:

```
<PriceTag>
    <OriginalPrice/>
    <SalePrice/>
    <TagColor/>
</PriceTag>
```

Note   If an XML tag ends in />, that means it is empty. In other words, <foo/> is the same as <foo></foo>.

As you can see, we have a parent element with three child elements. The three child elements will hold the pertinent values. For example, a price tag for an object that was originally $10.00 and is now on sale for $5.00 might have the following description:

```
<PriceTag>
    <OriginalPrice>$10.00</OriginalPrice>
    <SalePrice>$5.00</SalePrice>
    <TagColor>Yellow</TagColor>
</PriceTag>
```

What we want to do is create a movie that will load in a price tag description and build a tag accordingly. To see how this works, load the project SaleTag_demo.lsd. You'll notice that it has four tracks. The two text tracks are for displaying the original price and the sale price (see Figure 31.1). Have a look at the LoadXML custom event on the first sprite in the "Tag" track. This is an example of how to create a QTList from an XML string. The script looks like it has six script statements, but it's really just one statement. The "\" character at the end of the first line means that the statement continues on the next line. All of the rest of the line breaks happen inside of a string, which is allowed in QScript. Here's the script:

```
[1 LoadXML]

LoadListFromXML("", 1, \
"<PriceTag>
    <OriginalPrice>$10.00</OriginalPrice>
    <SalePrice>$5.00</SalePrice>
    <TagColor>Aqua</TagColor>
</PriceTag>")
```

The LoadListFromXML action takes the following three parameters:

```
LoadListFromXML( Path, Index, XMLString )
```

Figure 31.1 SaleTag project.

The Path and Index parameters tell the action where in the QTList we want to load the XML. The path needs to point to an existing element in the tree. This element will be the parent of the elements defined in the XML. If you want to load the XML elements as children of the very root of the tree, you can use "" for the path. The Index parameter lets you specify at what index you want to insert the new children. The Index has to be either the index of an existing child element, or one more than the total number of current children. The first child has an index of 1. I usually use a value of 1 for the Index parameter, which simply inserts the XML before any existing child elements. Finally, we have the XMLString itself.

Note QTList paths work similarly to paths to a file (a URL) but instead of a string of directory names separated by "/" characters, you have a string of element names separated by periods. For example, let's take the following list:

```
<GroceryCart>
    <FoodItems>
        <fruit>apple</fruit>
        <fruit>peach</fruit>
        <canned>tuna</canned>
        <fruit>banana</fruit>
    </FoodItems>
    <BathroomItems>
        <dental>toothpaste</dental>
        <hair>shampoo</hair>
        <hair>conditioner</hair>
    </BathroomItems>
</GroceryCart>
```

We can make a path to the first fruit element (the apple) as follows:

```
GroceryCart.FoodItems.fruit
```

And if we called GetListElementValue("GrocertyCart.FoodItems.fruit"), this would return "apple".

But, what if we want a path to the banana fruit element? It looks like it should have the same path as the one with the apple value. Fortunately, we can make a path to elements by index as well. Since "banana" is in the fourth child element, we can specify the following path:

```
GroceryCart.FoodItems.4
```

Unlike arrays, which start indexing from zero, the first element in a QTList has an index of 1. Since `FoodItems` has an index of 1, we could have also made a path like

```
GroceryCart.1.4
```

Both paths point to the banana fruit element. QTLists also give us another way of indexing child elements. The element with the banana value is the fourth child element, but it's really only the third fruit element. There's a canned element intermixed among the fruit. If we are only interested in fruit items, we can use the following notation:

```
GroceryCart.FoodItems.fruit[3]
```

This is a path to the third element named `"fruit"`. It's a nice notation, but proves to be confusing to developers familiar with JavaScript, where the above notation means something quite different.

At this point, let's run the movie and see how our price tag looks. Does it have the correct prices? $5.00 still seems a little steep for my pocketbook. Try changing the XML so that the sale price is only $2.50 and run the movie again. See how easy it is to change the settings when they are all in one nice data structure? Later we'll see how we can load QTLists from a local file or over the network.

We just saw how the data is loaded in, but how are the text tracks extracting the data? The text tracks are able to access the same QTList structure as our sprite track. This is because we are working with the movie's QTList. Each track also has a QTList associated with it, but if you don't specify the track, the movie's QTList is the default target. Open the first sample in the "OriginalPrice" text track and have a look at the Frame Loaded event. This is a good prototype for how to set the value of a text track from the value of a list element:

```
#define PATH = "PriceTag.OriginalPrice"
SetTextEditState(kScriptEditing)
ReplaceText( GetListElementValue($PATH), 0, -1 )
```

Here we replace the value of the text with the value of the element defined by the path `"PriceTag.OriginalPrice"`. You can get the value of an element by using the `GetListElementValue` action and passing in the path to the element.

Besides creating lists from XML, we can build up the elements through a series of actions. To make a new element, call the `AddListElement` action:

```
AddListElement( Path, Index, Name )
```

For example, if we started with the following QTList structure:

```
<Stooges>
    <Moe/>
    <Curly/>
</Stooges>
```

we can add a Larry element as the first child of the Stooges element by using the following script:

```
AddListElement("Stooges",1,"Larry")
```

This will produce the structure

```
<Stooges>
    <Larry/>
    <Moe/>
    <Curly/>
</Stooges>
```

We can set the value of an element by using the SetListElement(Path, Value) action. For example, the following script sets the Curly element to "Nyuk Nyuk Nyuk":

```
SetListElement("Stooges.Curly", "Nyuk Nyuk Nyuk")
```

Getting back to our price tag example, I'd like to discuss how QTLists are used to set the color of the price tag. Our price tag definition has an element named TagColor, and it currently has a value of "Aqua". I have the tag sprite track set up with four different tag images, each of a different color. I've mapped names to each of the images by using QTLists as a dictionary. A dictionary is something that lets you look up a value by supplying a name or a key, and the GetListElementValue(Path) function does exactly this. We supply the function with a path, and it returns a value. If you look at the MakeColorDictionary custom event on the tag sprite, you'll see that I've set up the color dictionary by adding four elements to the root of the movie's QTList:

```
AddListElement("", 1, "White")
SetListElement("White", $WhiteSaleTag)

AddListElement("", 1, "Yellow")
SetListElement("Yellow", $YellowSaleTag)

AddListElement("", 1, "Aqua")
SetListElement("Aqua", $AquaSaleTag)
```

```
AddListElement("", 1, "Green")
SetListElement("Green", $GreenSaleTag)
```

When the movie loads, it builds the dictionary, and then looks up the value according to the color name defined in the TagColor element. This is done in the SetColor custom event. Try changing the TagColor to "Yellow" in the LoadXML event, and see if the tag is colored correctly when you run the movie.

That concludes your QTList crash course. You've learned how to build tree structures and extract the data within. This is all you need to know to follow the rest of Part VI. But, to become a real list wrangler, you'll want to learn how to delete elements, rename them, turn them into XML, and determine how many children they have. But I'll let you learn all of that through the following explorations. In the next few chapters, we'll learn how to use QTLists to exchange information with the rest of the world.

Explorations

1. A set of related programming commands is often called an API (application programming interface). The QTList API takes a while to get used to, and for that reason, it's good to practice. When I practice working with a new API, I usually set up a test harness (as we did in Chapter 26). I've included a test harness for QTLists called QTListTest_demo.lsd. It contains input and output text tracks and a sprite Test button. Right now it's set up such that when you click the Test button, the input text gets turned into a QTList and then back to XML again and is displayed in the output text track. This simple tool allows you to test if a given XML string can be correctly turned into a QTList. For example, try typing in

   ```
   <Value>Hello <b>There</b></Value>
   ```

   Then click the Test button. The output should look like

   ```
   <Value>
       <b>there</b>
   </Value>
   ```

   This confirms what we discussed earlier about how QTLists don't accept mixed content. Try various different inputs and see how Quick-Time interprets them. Try adding an attribute:

   ```
   <Value test="works>hi</Value>
   ```

Is the attribute preserved?

What happens if you use an element with a blank name?

<>Hi</>

What do you think will happen when you enter the following?

<a/><a/>

2. Let's modify our QTList test harness to practice adding elements. Currently the Mouse Click event of the button sprite looks like

[Mouse Click]

ExecuteEvent($InputXML)

//transform QTList Here

ExecuteEvent($OutputXML)

Replace the *//transform QTList Here* line with the following:

AddListElement("Value",1,"New")

Preview the movie and click the button. Did an element named New get added to the Value element? It should have been added to the front. How would you change the code so the new element is added to the end? Try adding a line of script that sets the contents of the New element to the string "works".

3. The default input text has an element named A under the Value element. Try adding a line of script to the button's Mouse Click event that deletes the A element. The RemoveListElement action takes a path, a start index, and an end index.

4. Appendix D provides many useful functions for working with QTLists. Try a few of them out in this test harness. One interesting one to try is the Rename Element function. Try renaming the Value element to NewValue.

Loading Data

One of the powerful features of QTLists is that they can be loaded dynamically from a local or networked source. This enables us to build movies that can be customized and reconfigured on the fly without having to rebuild the movie. Take the price tag example from the last chapter. As it currently stands, every time we want to change the price or the color of the tag, we have to rebuild the movie. But since the tag's description is stored in a QTList, we can easily change it so that the data is loaded from an external file. This way we only have to change an XML file and we have a new price tag. And since most servers can dynamically generate XML files from databases and other information sources, our price tag can easily be autoupdated by a server without the server having to know anything about QuickTime or image generation.

Let's modify the price tag movie to load its definition from a file. Open the DynamicSaleTag_start.lsd project and edit the Frame Loaded script on the tag sprite. Currently, it reads:

```
[Frame Loaded]
SpriteOfID($ThisSpriteID).ExecuteEvent($LoadXML)
SpriteOfID($ThisSpriteID).ExecuteEvent($MakeColorDictionary)
SpriteOfID($ThisSpriteID).ExecuteEvent($SetColor)
```

Replace the first line with

```
SetListFromURL( "saletag.xml", "" )
```

This will load in the QTList data from a file named saletag.xml (located in the same directory as the movie itself) and place it into the root QTList path (as we've seen before, the root path is denoted by an empty string, "").

When you specify a URL with just a simple file name, it means it's a relative path, so QuickTime will look for the file within the same directory as the movie itself. When you preview a movie, LiveStage makes a temporary version of the movie in the same directory as the project, so that's where we want to place our XML file. If you look in that directory, you should see that I've already created a file called saletag.xml. Loading it into a text editor, you will discover that it has the familiar price tag structure:

```
<PriceTag>
    <OriginalPrice>$49.95</OriginalPrice>
    <SalePrice>$39.99</SalePrice>
    <TagColor>Yellow</TagColor>
</PriceTag>
```

Preview the movie and see if it works. It should work, as long as the pricetag.xml file is in the right place. This brings up an important case. What happens if the file is empty, or isn't there at all? To test this, let's try to load a different file. Change the first line of our Frame Loaded script to try to load from saletag2.xml:

SetListFromURL("saletag2.xml", "")

Run the movie and see what happens. It loads pretty much blank. All you see is a red X crossing out a price that isn't there. It's usually a good idea to catch the situations where a file doesn't load correctly. Since QuickTime doesn't report errors or throw exceptions, it can sometimes be difficult to determine if an action successfully executed or not. In this case, we know that the SetListFromURL action is supposed to create a new QTList element called PriceTag. What we can do is, after the SetListFrom-URL call, test to see if the PriceTag element exists. If it doesn't, then we know that either the file isn't there, or something is wrong with the file. This brings us to another quandary. How do we test the existence of a QTList element? It would have been nice if QuickTime provided us with a ListElementExists action, but such an action doesn't exist, so we need to be clever. The following script demonstrates the "unchanged variable" method for testing the existence of an element. Look it over first, and then let's discuss how it works:

```
[Frame Loaded]
LocalVars test

SetListFromURL( "saletag.xml", "" )
test = -1
```

```
test = GetListElementCount("PriceTag")
IF( test = -1 )
    //File didn't load correctly
    SpriteOfID($ThisSpriteID).ExecuteEvent($LoadXML)
ENDIF
SpriteOfID($ThisSpriteID).ExecuteEvent($MakeColorDictionary)
SpriteOfID($ThisSpriteID).ExecuteEvent($SetColor)
```

The "unchanged variable" method works because QuickTime properties don't return values if there's an error. So to detect an error, you first set a variable to a value that is outside of the range of a given property. You then set the variable to the property. If the variable's value didn't change, then you know something wrong happened while getting the property's value. In the above script, we use a variable named test. We first set it to –1 because an element can't have –1 children. We then set the test variable to the ElementCount property of the PriceTag element. If the PriceTag element doesn't exist, then an error will occur, and the test variable will remain –1. If the PriceTag element does exist, then the test variable will be set to a value greater than or equal to zero. The "unchanged variable" method is a general-purpose technique that every QuickTime developer should know about.

Now that we have a way of determining if the file was loaded correctly, we can do something graceful when an error happens. In this case, we call the LoadXML custom event as we did in the last chapter, but this time the event handler's script loads a QTList with "???" values for the Original-Price and the SalePrice elements (see Figure 32.1).

There is one more thing that I should mention about the SetListFromURL action. It loads data from a URL in a synchronous manner. What I mean by "synchronous" is that once you call SetListFromURL, QuickTime will wait and won't do anything else until the data has finished loading. Usually this isn't a problem, and it's often what you want to have happen. In the sale tag example, we need the data to load in before we know what values to place into the text tracks. However, if you are loading the file from across the network, and the network is really slow, your movie might

Figure 32.1   SaleTag project with unknown values.

pause for a while as it downloads. If the network is completely down, QuickTime will try to load the file for a moment and then will give up (with a network timeout). You can catch the network timeout error in the same way that we caught the "file doesn't exist" error. In the next chapter, we will learn how to load data asynchronously. This allows the movie to continue doing things while the data is loading. We'll also learn how to transfer information to and from a server.

▶ Explorations

1. For some good examples of dynamically configured movies, look in the XMLConfigured folder on the CD. Inside you'll find the following (see Figure 32.2):

   - BarGraph: Bar graph with configurable axis labels and bar properties.

   - BluePlayer: A sophisticated MP3 (and other audio) player with a song list menu. By Trevor DeVore.

   - QTCalendar: A media play-schedule calendar application. By Mario Piepenbrink.

   - PanoViewer: A QTVR multipano viewer with thumbnails and info display capabilities. By Eric Blanpied.

   All of these movies can be customized through an XML file, and they showcase some of the powerful things that can be done with this approach.

2. In Chapter 24, we experimented with a very simple speech synthesis technique. It was able to speak out a string of numbers. How would you make a movie that would speak out a number obtained from an XML file? Where would such a movie be useful? Along these lines, it would be fun to build a movie where you could dynamically change what a person says. You can do this by videotaping a person's face as they say a list of words. You then go through and determine the start and end times for each word. You could then create a simple XML format to make the person say different things. For example, the person could say, "I love you," when you supply the following XML file:

```
<Say>
    <Word>I</Word>
    <Word>LOVE</Word>
    <Word>YOU</Word>
</Say>
```

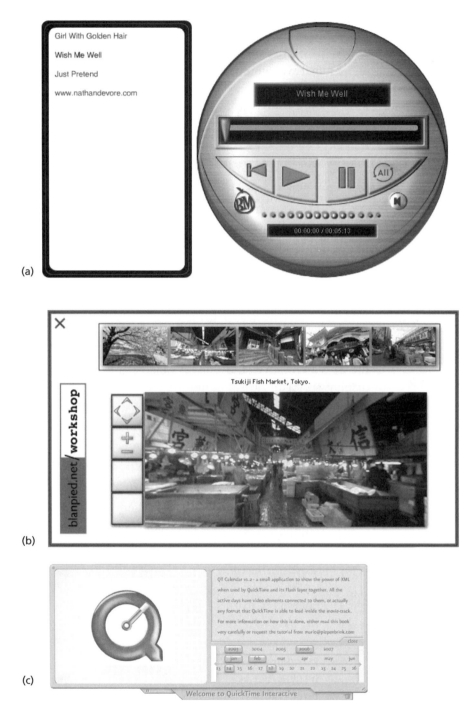

Figure 32.2 XML-configured movies: (a) Blue Player by Trevor DeVore; (b) Pano Viewer by Eric Blanpied; (c) QTCalendar by Mario Piepenbrink.

To turn the words into start and end times, you could use the same dictionary technique introduced in the last chapter for matching color names with image indices. How would you loop through all of the Word elements? How would you seamlessly (more or less) play the sequence of video sections?

3. In the DynamicSaleTag project, we read in an XML file on the Frame Loaded event. It's also possible to periodically load a file, allowing the movie to be reconfigured whenever the file changes. Under what situations would this be useful?

4. The following script sets a sprite named "display" to visible if a track named "control" is not enabled.

```
IF( TrackNamed("control").TrackEnabled == FALSE )
    SpriteNamed("display").SetVisible(TRUE)
ELSE
    SpriteNamed("display").SetVisible(FALSE)
ENDIF
```

It's very easy for a user to delete a track using QuickTime Pro. What would happen if the control track didn't exist? An error would occur while executing the above IF statement and the lines of script inside of the IF statement would not be executed. What if you also wanted the display sprite to be set visible if the control track doesn't exist? How would you modify the script to obtain this functionality?

5. In Chapter 28 we explored loading movies into movie tracks. Quick-Time has the ability to load a child movie and supply it with an XML fragment to be loaded in the movie-level QTList. The action is

```
LoadChildMovieWithQTList( ChildMovieID, XMLString )
```

What situations can you think of where this would be useful? How would you modify the SaleTag movie so the QTList is loaded in this way?

Setting Up a QTList Server

In the last chapter, we learned how to load QTLists from an external source using the SetListFromURL action. This loads a QTList either from a local file or from a remote server. In the next couple of chapters we'll learn how to use the ExchangeList and QueryListServer actions to transfer information to and from a server. The ExchangeList and QueryListServer actions only work with remote URLs, and they are asynchronous in nature. This means that, unlike the SetListFromURL action, they transfer data in a background process. This allows the movie to continue to function (receive events, execute scripts, and so on) while the information is being transferred to and from the server.

To test the examples in this chapter, you'll need to have a server installed that can dynamically create content. On the CD, I've included a demo version of a product called Tekadence Magik (Software/Tekadence), which is an application authoring tool with server capabilities. It is easy to install and runs on Linux, Windows, and Mac OS X. I've also included source code and compiled versions of some simple Java servlet classes that you can use if you have access to an application server (app server). The great thing about app servers is that the best ones are free (check out Tomcat: http://jakarta.apache.org/tomcat and Jetty: http://jetty.mortbay.org).

About Tekadence Magik

Tekadence Magik is a Java-based authoring tool developed by Sean Allen, Jared Kaplan, and myself. You should recall that Sean Allen is the one who created QuickTime's sprite tracks, and Jared Kaplan was one of the original developers at mFactory and has done a lot for QuickTime as well.

Tekadence Magik, however, isn't a QuickTime authoring tool; it's more of a general-purpose tool for creating applications. If you want to learn more about it, there are some nice demos and tutorials on the CD; you can also get a lot of information from the website: www.tekadence.com. In the next few chapters we'll use Tekadence Magik's ability to function as a server to demonstrate QuickTime's ExchangeList and QueryListServer functions.

▶ Setting Up the Test Server

Before we start getting into the meat of the matter, let's do a simple test to make sure that you have Tekadence Magik (TM) installed correctly and that QuickTime movies are able to talk to it. To do this, you first need to install TM on the platform of your choice and launch the application. Choose Open from the File menu, and open the testServer.tek file located in the Projects/Chapter33/TestServer/Server/ directory. After loading it, you should see the Object Browser window as shown in Figure 33.1. The Object Browser window shows a tree structure of all of the objects in the project. As you can see, there is an Application object at the root, and a WebServer with a WebPage object named test. TM lets you author live applications, so this is not just a description of our server application; it's an actual live application. The server should be running. To test that it's running, open a Web browser on the same machine, and go to the following URL: http://127.0.0.1:8080/test.

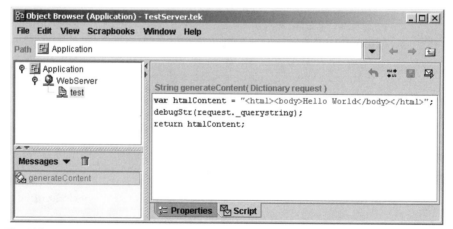

Figure 33.1 The Object Browser window.

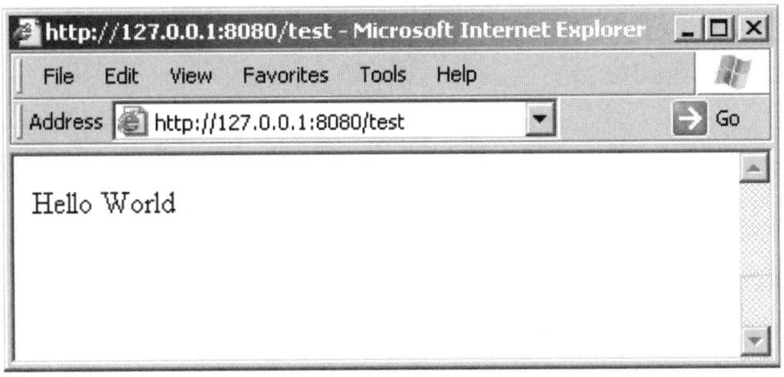

Figure 33.2 TestServer project.

This should bring up a simple Web page with the words "Hello World" (see Figure 33.2). If you are running Windows 98, then you might have to actually be connected to the network in order to access any server, even if the server is on the same machine. OS X and later versions of Windows don't have this limitation. If you can't get this page to display, then something isn't installed correctly.

Note The IP address 127.0.0.1 is reserved to refer to the local machine (also called local-host). You could have used your machine's actual IP address or domain name instead. The :8080 part means that the server is running on port 8080. Usually, Web servers run on port 80, but I set the test server to use port 8080 so that it wouldn't conflict with any Web servers you might already have running on your machine.

In the TM object browser, click on the WebServer object to view its properties. If you are running TM for the first time, you are probably in a novice user level that hides most of the more advanced properties from view. You should switch to the advanced user level by choosing Advanced from the User Level option of the Edit menu. At the advanced user level setting, you will see most of the WebServer properties, such as the port number, which is currently set to 8080, and the enabled property, which should currently be true. If you click the test object, you should see a generateContent message listed in the Messages pane (lower left). The generateContent message gets sent every time the WebPage object is accessed over the network. You can view its script by double-clicking the generateContent message. The scripting language used in TM is JavaScript, so if you are familiar with programming Web pages or using ActionScript in Flash, you should be very comfortable. But even with no JavaScript experience, this script should be easy to interpret:

```
var htmlContent = "<html><body>Hello World</body></html>";
debugStr(request._querystring);
return htmlContent;
```

Notice that the htmlContent variable holds an HTML string that also happens to be XML compliant (not all HTML is XML compliant). So we should be able to load this value into a QTList. To verify this, open the TestServer.mov movie in QuickTime Player. You should do this on the same machine on which you are running the server. Click the Load List button, and you should see the following content appear in the text track:

```
<html>
    <body>Hello World</body>
</html>
```

If you are going to be running your server on one machine and Live-Stage Pro on another machine, then you should test that you are able to access the QTList over the network by opening the TestServer_demo.lsd project. Change the 127.0.0.1 IP address defined in the Mouse Clicked event of the button sprite to the IP address (or domain name) of the machine running the Tekadence Magik server. Preview the movie and click the Load List button to verify that you have everything set up correctly.

Hopefully you have all the network stuff squared away, and now we can start experimenting with exchanging QTLists.

Explorations

1. For real-world server-side applications, I strongly suggest using servlets. There are many servlet-capable app servers out there such as Apple's WebObjects, Apache's Tomcat, Mortbay's Jetty, BEA WebLogic, IBM's WebSphere, and so on. If you don't have an app server running, I'd suggest either Jetty or Tomcat. They are both easy to set up, they have great performance, and they are free. There are just a couple things to be aware of when making QTList-aware servlets. The first thing is that QuickTime currently only supports GET requests. POST requests are not yet supported. This means that all of the data will be transferred through the query string of the URL. For this reason, it's good to keep the servlet URL on the short side. Long Akamai-like URLs are not good for working with QTLists. Second, as discussed in Chapter 31, QTLists

aren't completely XML compliant. If you refrain from sending back XML with mixed content, comments, and entities, then QuickTime should convert it into a QTList just fine.

In the `Servlet` directory on the CD, I've included a simple "hello world" servlet to test with the TestServer movie discussed in this chapter. It functions in the same way as the Tekadence Magik `TestServer` `.tek` project.

2. One thing that I didn't mention in the main text is Tekadence Magik's Console window. This is similar to the debugging console window in LiveStage Pro. You can open it by choosing Console from the View menu. Like in QuickTime, Tekadence applications can output messages to the console using the `debugStr` method (remember, JavaScript is case sensitive, so `DebugStr` is not equivalent to `debugStr`). In the TestServer application, the query string of each request is displayed in the console due to the `debugStr(request_querystring);` line in the `generateContent` script.

3. Have a look around the Tekadence Magik authoring platform. It's a powerful object-oriented tool for building applications.

Sending Data to a Server

In the last chapter you were hopefully able to successfully set up a server and access it from a QuickTime movie. Now, let's start doing something interesting. We'll start by building a small video quiz movie. The idea is that a teacher might distribute this movie to all the students in a classroom, either by email or by placing it on a Web page. Each student can then watch the movie and take the quiz. All of the responses will be transferred to the teacher's server to be graded at a later time. For this example, the movie sends data to the server, but the server doesn't need to send anything back. In the next chapter, we'll build a movie that performs two-way communication with a server.

▶ Launch the Server

To launch our video quiz server, open the VideoQuizServer.tek file into Tekadence Magik and double-click the Window object. This should bring up a Window editor as seen in Figure 34.1.

This server application has a spreadsheet interface to store the answers for each student. You can start running a Tekadence application by clicking the Instant Preview button (the small yellow projector 🎥). Once in run mode, start the server by clicking the Start Server button. The word "running" should appear in the status field at the bottom-left corner.

Now that we have our server running, let's open our video quiz movie project (in LiveStage Pro). The project is called VideoQuiz.lsd. Go to the Defines window (choose Document Defines... from the Edit window), and set the SERVER define to the correct URL. It is currently set to http://127.0.0.1:8080/SubmitQuiz, which is correct if the server is running on the

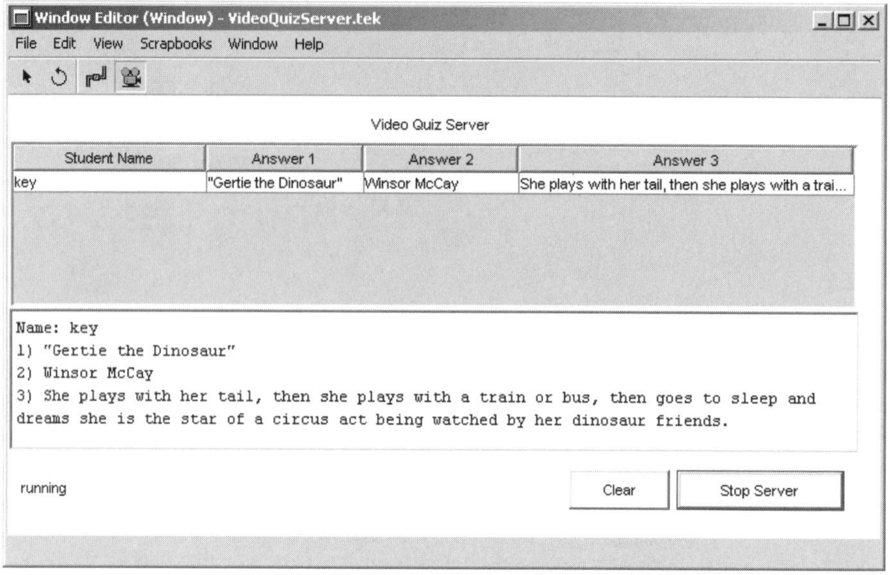

Figure 34.1 Tekadence Window editor.

same machine as the movie. If the server and the movie are running on two different machines, you'll need to change the address part of the URL to reflect the server's IP address (or domain name). If you were really going to use this movie with students, you would need to have a static IP address or a fixed domain name. But for testing, a local IP address will work fine.

The video quiz movie has a timeline that is comprised of three scenes: an instructions scene, a quiz questions scene, and a thank-you scene (Figure 34.2).

The first scene has instructions and a text field for the student to enter her name. The text field is set up so that hitting the Enter key has the same effect as clicking OK. Both result in the execution of the EnterName custom event on the button sprite. Let's have a look at what the EnterName script does:

```
[1010 EnterName]
LocalVars textLength
//Set up the list
AddListElement("",1,"name")
AddListElement("",2,"answer1")
AddListElement("",3,"answer2")
AddListElement("",4,"answer3")
```

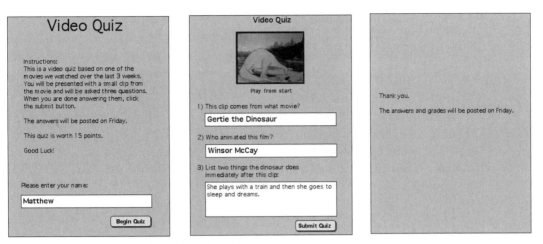

Figure 34.2 Timeline for the video quiz movie.

```
textLength = TrackNamed("Name").GetTextLength
SetListElement("name",TrackNamed("Name").GetText(0,textLength))
GoToTime(SampleNamed("Quiz").StartTime)
SetSelection(SampleNamed("Quiz").StartTime,SampleNamed("Quiz") \
  .EndTime-1)
SetPlaySelection(TRUE)
```

This script first sets up a QTList structure with the following list elements:

```
name
answer1
answer2
answer3
```

It then places the value of the Name text track into the name list element using the SetListElement action. When working with a fixed set of list elements, it's usually a good idea to build up the QTList structure early on in the movie so that the rest of the scripts can assume that the structure is in place.

After setting the name element, the script then calls GoToTime and passes in the start time of the quiz sample. This is the start of the second scene in the movie. The script also sets the selection to the quiz sample's duration and calls SetPlaySelection(TRUE). This is done so that QuickTime will limit the playback to the video track that has the same start and end time as the quiz sample. LiveStage doesn't currently support naming video samples, so you can't use the SampleNamed action with video tracks.

Note Notice that we are calling GoToTime and then executing some more lines of script. Even though this GoToTime call moves the playhead out of the sample, QuickTime will still finish executing the currently running script.

The quiz sprite sample is the main scene of the movie. This is where the student can play the video and answer questions about it. Inside there is a sprite called "play" that when clicked will play the video from the beginning. We also have a Submit button sprite called "submitQuiz." The Mouse Click event of this sprite contains the script that sends the student's quiz answers to the server. First have a look at the script and then let's walk through it:

```
[Mouse Click]
LocalVars textLength

textLength = TrackNamed("Answer 1").GetTextLength
SetListElement("answer1",TrackNamed("Answer 1").GetText(0,textLength))

textLength = TrackNamed("Answer 2").GetTextLength
SetListElement("answer2",TrackNamed("Answer 2").GetText(0,textLength))

textLength = TrackNamed("Answer 3").GetTextLength
SetListElement("answer3",TrackNamed("Answer 3").GetText(0,textLength))

QueryListServer($SERVER, "", kListQuerySendListAsKeyValuePairs, "")
StopPlaying
GoToTime(SampleNamed("thanks").StartTime)
```

The first several lines are straightforward. We are placing the values of the text tracks into the QTList elements. It's just like we did with the Name field in the instructions sample. It should be noted that the list elements for this project are stored in the QTList of the movie itself. This is because we've used implicit targeting that is directed to the movie's QTList. In the next chapter we'll work with track QTLists, which are necessary in order to get information back from a server. Here we are just sending data upstream to the server, so it's OK to work with movie-level lists.

The action that actually does the sending is called QueryListServer. It takes the following parameters:

```
QueryListServer( URL, KeyValuePairs, Flags, ListPath )
```

The URL is the locator for the server-side application. In this case we are using the $SERVER define we set up earlier. It points to the SubmitQuiz object in our video quiz server application.

The KeyValuePairs parameter is an optional string that will be appended to the query string of the URL. For example, calling

QueryListServer("http://localhost/SubmitQuiz", "version=32", ..., ...)

will append the "version=32" string to the URL like this:

http://localhost/SubmitQuiz?version=32

In our application, we don't have any extra key-value pairs to send along, so we can just pass in an empty string for the KeyValuePairs parameter.

The Flags parameter allows you to specify various options. The available flags include

kListQuerySendListAsKeyValuePairs
kListQuerySendListAsXML
kListQueryWantCallBack

Don't you like those long descriptive constant names? The first two flags define how you want the list data to be sent. kListQuerySendListAsKeyValuePairs specifies that you want the list to be turned into key-value pairs. This means if you point the ListPath parameter to the following structure:

<Parents>
    <Mom>Kathy</Mom>
    <Dad>Steve</Dad>
</Parents>

you will get "Mom=Kathy&Dad=Steve" appended to your URL. These will be appended to any key-value pairs that were created with the KeyValuePairs parameter. Continuing with our last example, the URL would look like

http://localhost/SubmitQuiz?version=32&Mom=Kathy&Dad=Steve

This is standard CGI querystring syntax. This only works if your QTList structure is only one layer deep. These are key-value pairs, not key-structure pairs. If you want to send deeper structures such as the following list:

<Family>
    <Parents>
        <Mom>Kathy</Mom>
        <Dad>Steve</Dad>

```
    </Parents>
    <Siblings>
        <Sister>Melissa</Sister>
    </Siblings>
</Family>
```

it would be better to use the kListQuerySendListAsXML flag. This sends the QTList as an XML string. It does so by passing the XML string as a value in a key-value pair keyed to the word "qtlist." For example, sending the following simple QTList:

```
<test>hello</test>
```

will cause the following key-value pair to be appended to the URL:

```
qtlist=<test>hello</test>
```

The "<" and ">" characters will be appropriately escaped with standard URL escape codes, so what actually will be sent is

```
qtlist=%3Ctest%3Ehello%3C%2Ftest%3E
```

This would produce a URL such as

```
http://localhost/SubmitQuiz?qtlist=%3Ctest%3Ehello%3C%2Ftest%3E
```

In our current case, we have a flat structure, so we'll send key-value pairs instead of an XML string. As you might have guessed, sending the data as XML requires a longer URL than key-value pairs. For instance, the URL with the Family QTList structure above would look like

```
http://localhost/SubmitQuiz?qtlist=%3CFamily%3E%3CParents%3E%3CMom
    %3EKathy%3C%2FMom%3E%3CDad%3ESteve%3C%2FDad%3E%3C%2FParents%3E
    %3CSiblings%3E%3CSister%3EMelissa%3C%2FSister%3E%3C%2FSiblings
    %3E%3C%2FFamily%3E
```

Note   If you are passing a lot of data that doesn't need to be structured, then I would suggest using key-value pairs. Many systems have a limit on how long a URL can be (often 512 characters). Unfortunately, QuickTime doesn't yet provide the ability to pass QTLists to the server in the POST data.

The final QueryListServer flag is kListQueryWantCallBack. You use this flag when you want to receive information back from the server. We'll discuss how this works in the next chapter.

The last parameter to the QueryListServer action is the QTListPath. This is the path to the QTList element to be sent. In our video quiz movie, we specified the root of our movie's QTList, which is simply the empty path, "".

Calling QueryListServer will send the list data to our server. Our server application then extracts the name and the answers to each question and adds these values to a new row in a spreadsheet. Meanwhile, the movie stops the video from playing and jumps to the "thank you" scene.

Try it out. Preview the movie and take the quiz (make sure the Teka-dence VideoQuizServer project is up and running first). After you enter your name and submit the answers to the quiz, you should see your submission show up as a new line on the server's spreadsheet.

In the next chapter we will explore how to exchange QTLists back and forth with a server in a two-way fashion.

▶ Explorations

1. In Chapter 32 we learned how to make reusable XML-configurable movies. If you were going to make lots of video quizzes, you would probably want to make one master movie that gets customized through an XML file. How would you change the video quiz movie in this chapter to do that?

2. To see how VideoQuizServer is implemented, have a look at the SubmitQuiz object (child of the WebServer object). Double-click its generate-Content message to view the script that gets executed every time a quiz is submitted.

Exchanging QTLists

QuickTime provides a way, called *exchanging* lists, to send a QTList to a server and then receive a QTList back in an asynchronous response. "Asynchronous" means that instead of having to pause and wait for the server to respond, the movie can continue with its activities until the server response has arrived. It's crucial that it works this way; otherwise your movie would hang up for a while, especially if you had a slow network connection or the server was down. Once the server response has arrived, a List Received event is triggered.

There are two ways to exchange list data with a server. You can use the QueryListServer action and specify the kListQueryWantCallBack flag, or you can use the ExchangeList action. I prefer the simplicity of the ExchangeList action. It just takes a URL and a path to the QTList:

```
ExchangeList( URL, QTListPath )
```

ExchangeList sends the QTList data as an XML string in the same way that QueryListServer does when using the kListQuerySendListAsXML flag. That is to say, it encodes the XML in the URL with a "qtlist" key. After sending the data, QuickTime will start a background process that constantly checks for a response to be returned from the server. When the server replies, QuickTime tries to parse the response as XML. If successful, it executes the List Received event (see Figure 35.1).

It's important to note that even though LiveStage places a List Received event on every sprite, it's really a track-level event. It's just like the Frame Loaded event in that it doesn't know what sprite it is associated with. For this reason, implicit sprite targeting cannot be used.

ExchangeList is ideally suited to asking a server a question and then getting back an answer. This sounds simple, but it's really quite powerful and

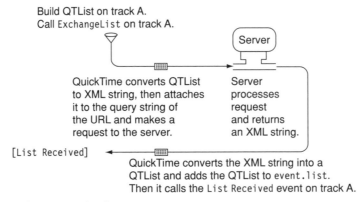

Build QTList on track A.
Call ExchangeList on track A.

QuickTime converts QTList
to XML string, then attaches
it to the query string of
the URL and makes a
request to the server.

Server
processes
request
and returns
an XML string.

[List Received]

QuickTime converts the XML string into a
QTList and adds the QTList to event.list.
Then it calls the List Received event on track A.

Figure 35.1 ExchangeList timeline.

forms the basis of most client-server applications. As an example, we're going to build a multimedia supply room server. The reason I chose this as an example is that I wish the multimedia supply room for my department had such a setup. My department's supply room holds a few basic pieces of equipment, such as a TV and a slide projector. The problem is that our department only has one of each piece, and often you'll walk all the way over to the supply room to find out that someone has already borrowed the thing you wanted to use. It would save people a walk over if they just had a little movie that you could use to check the status of a piece of equipment. That's what we're going to build here.

Let's first have a look at the server-side application. Open the MediaSupplyRoom.tek file in Tekadence Magik. As we did in the last chapter, double-click the Window object and go into instant preview mode. It should look like Figure 35.2.

As the person in charge of the multimedia supply room, you are supposed to keep the checkboxes up to date. When someone borrows an item, you uncheck the "Item is available" checkbox and fill in the information about who's using it and when it's due back (see Figure 35.3).

Before we start working on the client movie, first make sure that the server is running by clicking the Start Server button.

The LiveStage project is called MMediaSupplies_demo.lsd. It's a lot simpler than the video quiz from the last chapter. It just has a sprite track and a text track. The sprite track has pictures of each piece of equipment owned by the supply room. The way it's going to work is the user will click an item they are interested in, then the movie will ask the server the status of the item and display the result in the text track. To see how this

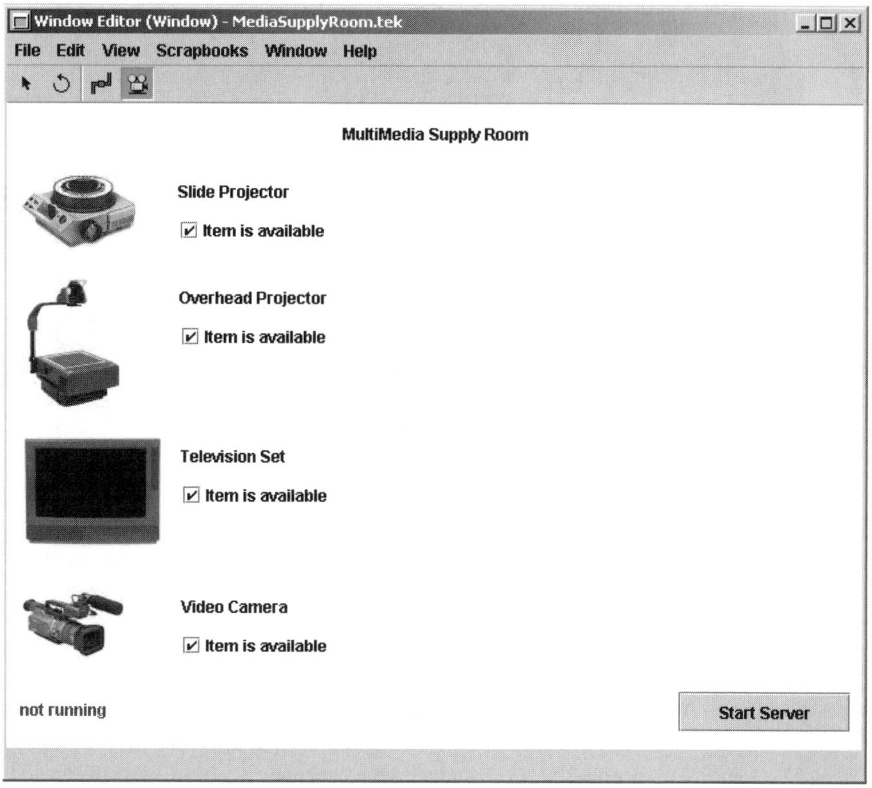

Figure 35.2 MediaSupplyRoom server.

works, let's examine one of the items. Let's look at the Mouse Click event of the SlideProjector sprite:

```
[Mouse Click]
GlobalVars ItemToCheck

ItemToCheck = ID
SpriteNamed("Status").ExecuteEvent($CheckItem)
```

Clicking the SlideProjector sprite calls a custom event on the Status sprite. The sprite uses its own sprite ID as the identifier of the item, which allows the script to be very modular. The OverheadProjector, TVSet, and VideoCamera sprites have the exact same script.

Note If you were going to build more than one of these movies or periodically add new items, it would be a good idea to make the Mouse Click, Mouse Down, and Mouse Up scripts into a behavior.

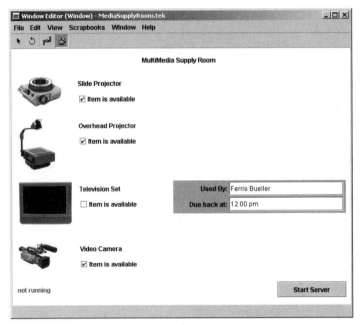

Figure 35.3 MediaSupplyRoom server with item checked out.

The Status sprite takes care of exchanging a list with the server and displaying the result to the user. This two-way transfer of information is carried out using the ExchangeList function.

Many developers get stumped the first time they try to use the Exchange-List action. The major reason for this is that they don't realize that it only works properly with track-level QTLists and not movie-level QTLists. If you call QTList actions without targeting a particular track, then you are using movie-level QTLists. For instance, calling

```
AddListElement("", 1, "fred")
```

will add a new element named fred to the movie's QTList.

Note For all the teachers reading this book, fred is a good variable name to use when teaching kids how to program. This is because it's easy to type on the keyboard and kids tend to find it easy to remember and amusing.

If we wanted to add fred to a track's QTList, you would have to target the track explicitly:

```
TrackNamed("Sprite 1").AddListElement("", 1, "fred")
```

Even when developers know this, they are often confused that the following doesn't work:

```
ThisTrack.AddListElement("", 1, "fred")
```

In theory, this *should* work, but current versions of LiveStage (up to at least 4.1) basically ignore the ThisTrack target. In fact it ignores the ThisSprite and ThisMovie targets as well. The only This target that LiveStage currently deals with correctly is the ThisEvent target, which we'll use in a moment. The above script actually adds fred to the movie's QTList. Are you starting to see why developers get stumped?

The reason why ExchangeList only works properly with track-level QTLists is that when the server replies with a chunk of XML, QuickTime calls the List Received event on the source of the outgoing QTList. If the source is a movie QTList, then QuickTime calls List Received on the movie. If the source is a track, then it calls List Received on the track. This is all fine and makes sense. The problem is that there is no way to place scripts on movie-level events. You can only place scripts on a track's List Received event. So, if you want to have access to the result of the Exchange-List call, you need to use track-level QTLists.

When I use ExchangeList, I usually build up my QTList structure right when the movie loads. That way it's ready for me to simply place values into the elements without having to worry if the elements exist yet or not. To see how this is done for our current movie, look at the Frame Loaded event of the Status sprite:

```
[Frame Loaded]
SpriteVars textTrackID

#define ThisTrackName = "Sprite"
textTrackID = TrackNamed("StatusText").GetID

TrackNamed($ThisTrackName).AddListElement("",0,"request")
TrackNamed($ThisTrackName).AddListElement("request",0,"itemName")
```

Since we need to target the sprite track explicitly to make the Exchange-List action work properly, I create a local define called ThisTrackName. This is a simple workaround for the ThisTrack target not working. I usually make these local defines in each script, and then later in the development stage I can switch over to a global define (choose Document Defines... from the Edit menu in LiveStage Pro) and then comment out all of the local statements. In the last two lines of the script, we add a few QTList elements into the track to define the following QTList structure:

```
<request>
   <itemName/>
</request>
```

It's a very simple structure since all we need to send to the server is the name of the item we want to do a status check on. We build up the list structure from the top down. We first add the request element to the root (denoted by an empty string, ""). Then we add itemName as a child of the request element.

With the structure in place, it's easy to set the value of the itemName element by simply calling SetListElement("request.itemName", value). For our current project this is done just before we call ExchangeList. Have a look at the CheckItem custom event:

```
[100 CheckItem]
GlobalVars ItemToCheck
SpriteVars spriteTrackID

#define URL = "http://127.0.0.1:8080/SupplyAvailable"
#define ThisTrackName = "Sprite"

TrackNamed($ThisTrackName).SetListElement("request.itemName", \
  SpriteOfID(ItemToCheck).GetName)
TrackNamed($ThisTrackName).ExchangeList($URL, "request")
```

Here we define the URL of our server-side application. As usual, you might have to modify this URL to match your particular setup. Before each sprite calls the CheckItem event, it first sets the ItemToCheck GlobalVar to the corresponding sprite ID. But the sprite ID is a number, and the server needs the name of the item, not the number. To get the name of the item, we simply get the name of the sprite with the ItemToCheck ID using

```
SpriteOfID(ItemToCheck).GetName
```

You might be wondering why I didn't just set ItemToCheck to the name of the sprite in the first place. Why bother with the ID? There are two reasons. The first is that setting a variable to a number is easier than setting it to a string. As we've seen before, strings need to be set using the SetString action. The second reason is that if we ever wanted to refer to the sprite that got clicked, we need to do so by ID instead of name. This is because QuickTime still doesn't support using variables in the SpriteNamed target. Now that we are on the subject of IDs versus names, I should point out that when calling ExchangeList, it's better to use TrackNamed instead of

TrackOfID as the target. The reason for this is that in QuickTime versions 5 and 6 there is a bug that causes ExchangeList to stall QuickTime on Mac OS 9 when using a TrackOfID target with a variable ID. The reason for the bug is complicated, but to avoid unwanted behavior, use TrackNamed with a static name reference (a define is OK) when calling the ExchangeList or QueryListServer actions.

The last line of our script contains the ExchangeList action. Here we specify that we want to send the request element of the track's QTList. QuickTime will send the QTList as an XML string appended to the end of the URL as a query string. For example, clicking the OverheadProjector sprite would pass the following query string:

```
?qtlist=<qtlist><itemName>OverheadProjector</itemName></qtlist>
```

Notice how it changed the name of the request element to qtlist. It's not clear why, but QuickTime always changes the root XML element to qtlist. The even stranger thing is that if you pass in an element already named qtlist, QuickTime will refuse to finish executing the ExchangeList action. It's generally a good idea not to use qtlist as the name of QTList elements.

Since certain characters always get escaped in URLs, the above query string will actually look like

```
?qtlist=%3Cqtlist%3E%3CitemName%3EOverheadProjector%3C%2FitemName%3E%3C
    %2Fqtlist%3E
```

But most server software will unescape the query string automatically for you. The Tekadence server certainly does. If you want to see the server-side code, you can check out the generateContent message of the Supply-Available object. Some knowledge of JavaScript will help, but it should be easy to follow without any JavaScript experience.

When the server responds to the ExchangeList call with a chunk of XML, QuickTime will call the List Received event on the track that originated the call. Another thing that stumps developers when they try to figure out how ExchangeList works is that they think the result will be placed into the track's QTList. What actually happens is that the QTList is placed into the event's QTList. Yes, events can have QTLists too. You can access an event's QTList through the following expression:

ThisEvent.GetListElementValue(elementPath)

Our current multimedia server application returns a simple structure, which looks like

```
<result>
    <isAvailable>0</isAvailable>
    <usedBy>Ferris Bueller</usedBy>
    <dueBack>12:00 pm</dueBack>
</result>
```

When QuickTime loads this XML into the event's QTList, it adds it to the event.list element. So the resulting QTList is a couple levels deep:

```
<event>
    <list>
        <result>
            <isAvailable>0</isAvailable>
            <usedBy>Ferris Bueller</usedBy>
            <dueBack>12:00 pm</dueBack>
        </result>
    </list>
</result>
```

To access the isAvailable element we would script:

ThisEvent.GetListElementValue("event.list.result.isAvailable")

The bulk of this project's List Received script involves turning the QTList returned from the server into an easy-to-read sentence for the user. In enterprise server terms, this is called the *presentation layer*. The cool thing about using QuickTime as the front end to a server-side application is that the presentation layer can be coded in the movie itself. It's up to the movie to determine how to display the information. Most server-side applications today stick the presentation layer on the server, which often involves generating HTML. This is a lot of extra work that the server has to do, and it isn't very modular. For instance, say you wanted to display it not only in HTML but also in some other format. This would require access points into the server with different presentation layers. But if the presentation code is on the client side, like it is with QuickTime, the server can concentrate on simply passing back data instead of having to process the data into a nice presentation. This is the future of Web applications. So let's see how our presentation layer is implemented.

First of all, notice that the Status sprite has the same ClearText and AppendText custom events that were used for the LCD clock project discussed in Chapter 25. These are general-purpose functions for dynamically creating textual displays. Here we're going to turn the server's XML response, as shown above, into the following human-readable sentence:

"The SlideProjector has been checked out by Ferris Bueller and is due back at 12:00 pm. Please check back with us then."

To do this, we employ the same clear-append technique we used to build up the time for the LCD clock project. Have a look at the List Received script.

Notice that we don't simply call

ExecuteEvent($AppendText)

In List Received events (as is the case with Frame Loaded events) we need to target the sprite explicitly:

SpriteOfID($ThisSpriteID).**ExecuteEvent**($AppendText)

If you run the movie and click an item, you should get a movie that looks like Figure 35.4.

With ExchangeList, we can use QuickTime movies to place interactive interfaces on server-side applications. Such an interface is often called a *thin client*. QuickTime enables a much richer user experience than what you can achieve with a Web browser alone. Since often you will want to deploy such thin client QuickTime movies embedded in a Web page, it's important to explore ways in which QuickTime can interact with the browser. This is the topic of the next chapter.

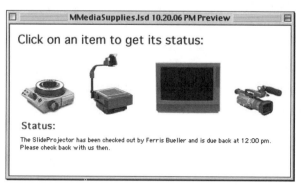

Figure 35.4   Multimedia supplies thin client movie.

⊙ Explorations

1. The `QueryListServer` action can be used to obtain the same functionality as `ExchangeList`. If you wanted it to work exactly like `ExchangeList`, what flags would you use in the `QueryListServer` call? (Remember, multiple flags can be used together by connecting them with the "+" operator.)

2. The event-level QTList exists on all events. In fact, the QTList on mouse and keyboard events has list elements containing the mouse location and the keystroke information. How would you go about determining what the event's QTList structure looks like?

3. The QTList on the `List Received` event has a useful element called `list-Name`. It contains the name of the list that was sent to the server. I use this value when the movie is conducting multiple server exchanges at the same time. It allows me to determine which result is coming back. A movie might ask one server for one piece of information and another server for another piece. If QTLists of different names are sent, then the `listName` element will have different values when the server reply comes back. To access the `listName` value, use

   `ThisEvent.GetListElementValue`("event.listName")

4. Most server-side applications are set up to deal with query strings more readily than XML. PHP, Pearl, Java servlets, and the like all know how to parse key-value pairs from a query string. Java 1.4 has built-in support for XML, but most other languages need an extra add-on to process XML. For this reason, QuickTime provided the `QueryListServer` action. To exchange a list as key-value pairs use the following template:

   ```
   TrackNamed("trackname").QueryListServer \
     ( "URL", "", kListQuerySendListAsKeyValuePairs + \
     kListQueryWantCallBack, "qtlistpath")
   ```

   The result from the server still needs to be in XML format, however.

5. In QuickTime, there are at least seven ways to exchange information with a server. How many can you think of? One way is to load a movie into a movie track. If the server returns text, QuickTime will turn that into a movie with a text track. Since the values of text tracks can be obtained through scripts, this is another way of asynchronously exchanging data with a server. In this case, the server doesn't need to return an XML string. Another way is to use a Flash track. Flash has a couple of different server communication options, but currently only the `LoadVariables` option works. In Flash, `LoadVariables` has the option

of sending a GET or a POST request. Unfortunately, only the GET request works in QuickTime. Furthermore, for some reason, Flash's LoadVariables action is synchronous when running in QuickTime (it's asynchronous when running in the Flash player).

6. In Chapter 28 we discussed dynamically loaded media (and we'll pick up this topic again in Chapter 37). What interesting applications can you thing of that utilize ExchangeList and dynamic media?

7. Being able to exchange data with a server opens many doors for the multimedia developer. The only problem is that it requires that you have a robust server, which can be expensive to maintain. One option is to subscribe to a server hosting service. There's one such service that I helped start called WorldWideVariables.com. It sports a very fast enterprise server and allows the developer to easily add data storage, usage logging, chat rooms, and a variety of other server-side functionality to their wired QuickTime projects. Have a look.

Communicating with the Browser

Since a large portion of QuickTime content is intended for the Web, it is important to know how to make your movies communicate with the browser. QuickTime provides standard ways to launch Web pages and call JavaScript functions. The browser can also pass information into a movie when it loads and has a limited ability to communicate with already loaded movies as well (see Figure 36.1).

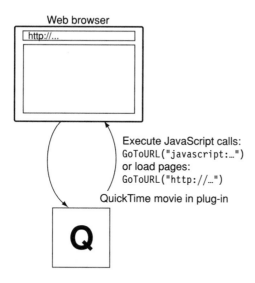

Figure 36.1 Browser communication gateway.

As we will see, a lot of QuickTime's browser communication functionality rests on a single action called GoToURL. It's a simple function that takes only one string parameter, but it packs a lot of features. The most straightforward usage is to simply pass in a URL, such as

GoToURL("http://www.apple.com")

If you call this from almost anywhere that QuickTime runs, this will launch a browser and load the specified Web page. Actually, I know a developer that was having a hard time loading browser pages from a Java 1.1 application. Since he was using QTJava, I told him to just use a Quick-Time movie to do the work of launching the browser. He was hesitant at first, but it worked so well, it became his standard solution for a while until he developed a pure Java cross-platform method of doing it. This is a good example of using QuickTime's modular characteristics to aid in application development. In Chapter 11, we explored using QuickTime movies as applications, but interactive movies can also become useful building blocks for applications where you might not expect them. We'll discuss this more in Chapter 39.

When a movie is already in a Web page, the default behavior of GoToURL is to replace the content of the browser window, or frame, with the new URL. If you want to explicitly spawn a new window, you can do so with the following construct (see Figure 36.2):

GoToURL("<http://www.apple.com>T<_blank>")

This is an old-school way of packing multiple parameters in a single-parameter function. The part before the "T" is the URL, and the part after the "T" is the target ("T" stands for target). Using a target of _blank means to load the URL into a new window.

We can load movies into QuickTime Player in a similar way. We just need to use a different target:

GoToURL("<http://www.somesite.com/someMovie.mov>T<QuickTimePlayer>")

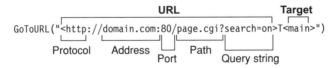

Figure 36.2 Anatomy of a URL.

If the movie is already playing in QuickTime Player, the default behavior is to load new movies into a new player window (although you can change this behavior in the QuickTime preferences). If you want to explicitly load the movie into the current player window, you can use the `myself` target:

```
GoToURL( "<http://www.somesite.com/someMovie.mov>T<myself>")
```

All of these are specialized targets. The original reason for the target notation is to provide a way of loading pages in a different frame. You simply pass in the name of the frame as the target. For example, the following loads a page in a frame named "Fred":

```
GoToURL( "<http://www.apple.com>T<Fred>")
```

Frame targeting only works for movies playing in the browser. You can't target frames from QuickTime Player.

As an example of loading pages, take a look at the project `WebLinks_ demo.lsp` (see Figure 36.3). This is an example of using a movie as a menu, where clicking sprites loads pages in a separate frame.

The default email client on the user's computer can also be launched and primed with a new message to a specified email address. Targeting the email client doesn't require the use of the `<>T<>` construct. Simply use a URL with the `mailTo:` protocol. For example:

```
GoToURL("mailTo:matthew@matthewpeterson.net")
```

Figure 36.3 `WebLinks_demo` project.

Other protocols should launch their respective helper applications as well. Theoretically, using GoToURL with an ftp:// URL should launch the default FTP client.

The types of URLs that are particularly interesting when communicating with the browser are JavaScript URLs. Such URLs provide a way of executing JavaScript from a QuickTime movie. You simply create a URL that starts with javascript: and then the rest will be executed by the browser's JavaScript engine. For example, to bring up an alert box displaying the string "cool!" (see Figure 36.4), you can use

```
GoToURL( "javascript:alert('cool!')" )
```

Remember to use single quotes within the URL string. If you need to use double quotes, you have to escape them with the \ character:

```
GoToURL( "javascript:alert(\"cool!\")" )
```

Otherwise LiveStage will get confused as to which quotes are in the string and which define the string.

The capability of executing JavaScript opens up many interesting possibilities. You can pack a lot of JavaScript into a single URL, but in my experience, I've found what works best is to place JavaScript functions in the HTML page, and then simply call the functions from the movie. For an example of this, open the project GraphTrace_demo.1sd. This movie lets the user move the mouse cursor over a line graph and see the *y* value at a given mouse *x* value. When the user clicks on the plot, it sends the *x* and *y* values to the Web page by calling a setXY JavaScript function. This separates the browser functionality from the movie functionality. All the movie does is announce that an *x,y* coordinate was clicked. The JavaScript in the Web page can then do whatever it wants with this information.

Figure 36.4 An alert box.

In this example, the setXY JavaScript function takes an X and a Y parameter. When calling the function, the movie builds up the JavaScript URL using StrConcat actions. Here's the CallJS script from the GraphTrace movie:

```
[103 CallJS]
SpriteVars angleValue sineValue
LocalVars x y url

#define URLSTART = "javascript:setXY("

x = angleValue * 180/PI
y = sineValue

SetString(url, StrConcat($URLSTART, x))
SetString(url, StrConcat(url, "," ))
SetString(url, StrConcat(url, y))
SetString(url, StrConcat(url, ")"))

GoToURL(url)
```

I've found this to be a good way to build up JavaScript URLs. Start off with the base, which always begins with "javascript:" followed by the name of the function and the "(" symbol. Then proceed to append the different parameters using the SetString-StrConcat construction.

To see how this movie works in the browser, launch the Graph-Track.html file. Clicking the plot will call the setXY JavaScript function, which places the values in the two HTML text fields at the bottom of the page (see Figure 36.5).

▶ Passing Data into a Movie

Invoking JavaScript functions with the GoToURL action is a good way to get information to flow from the movie to the browser. There are a few ways to pass data into a movie:

1. A string can be passed to the movie through the MovieName parameter of the embed and object tags. When the movie loads, it can pull out information from the MovieName (RootMovie.GetName). This method works in all major browsers with QuickTime versions 5 and higher. Since you can convert a string into a QTList using the ReplaceListFromXML action, this method is quite flexible.

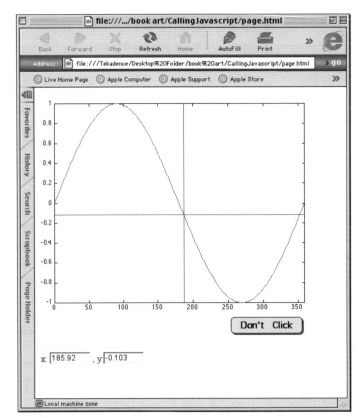

Figure 36.5 GraphTrack movie running in the browser.

2. Small numbers can be placed in the Volume and StartTime tags. The only time this would be advisable over the first method is if you needed it to work in QuickTime 3 and 4 for backwards compatibility reasons.

3. In Netscape browsers and QuickTime versions 4.1 and higher, there are special JavaScript functions for setting and getting QuickTime variables. In the movie, define MovieVars with variable IDs, such as

MovieVars fred:24, tony:87

Then in the embed tag, make sure you set the movieName and enable-JavaScript parameters as follows:

<embed movieName="CoolMovie" enableJavaScript="true"...>

You can then get and set the movie's MovieVars through the GetSprite-TrackVariable and SetSpriteTrackVariable JavaScript functions:

```
<javascript>
var theMovie = document.CoolMovie;
var numTracks = theMovie.GetTrackCount();
var fredVarID = 24;
var tonyVarID = 87;
theMovie.SetSpriteTrackVariable( numTracks, fredVarID, "fredValue");
var tonyValue = theMovie.GetSpriteTrackVariable(numTracks,
tonyVarID);
</javascript>
```

The reason for using `numTracks` as the track index is because LiveStage Pro always places the movie variables track as the last track of the movie. We will discuss movie variables in more depth in Chapter 38.

4. QuickTime 6 introduced a new embed and object tag parameter called `MovieQTList`. If you set this parameter to an XML string, it will automatically be converted to list elements and placed in the movie-level QTList. This method works in all browsers. For an example, see Brennan Young's `QTListEmbedded` demo.

As an example of using method number 1, have a look at the `MapCookie_demo.lsd` project. Cookies are a way that HTML pages can store temporary settings, preferences, and other information. Many Web pages that remember things about you do so through cookies. QuickTime doesn't have direct access to cookies (I wish it did), but it can gain access through JavaScript. The MapCookie project is an example of this. When a user loads the page for the first time, the movie presents a map and asks the user to click on the location that they call home. When the user leaves the Web page and then comes back, the movie will remember where on the map the user lives through the use of cookies (see Figure 36.6). Try it out.

▶ Explorations

1. At the beginning of this chapter, we saw how `GoToURL("<URL>T <_blank>")` launches the specified URL in a new window. What if you wanted to launch the URL in a new window with dimensions 200 × 200? How would this be done?

2. We discussed four ways that information can be transferred to a QuickTime movie in the browser. Can you think of any other methods? One technique that I left out involves intermovie communication, which is

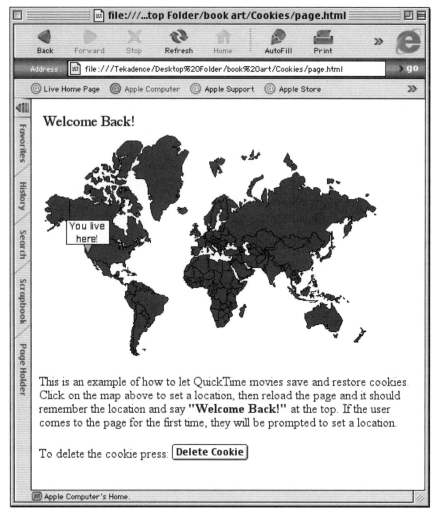

Figure 36.6 MapCookie movie running in the browser.

the topic of Chapter 38. Intermovie communication allows one movie to execute wired actions on another movie. How can this ability be employed to allow a Web page to pass information into a movie?

3. There's a hidden feature that allows the QuickTime browser plug-in to pop up a window when a DebugStr action is executed. This is useful for debugging wired movies in the browser. To activate this feature, open the QuickTime control panel and add a new media key. Name it QTPIShowDebugMessages and give it the value alert.

4. An underused wired action is SetStatusString:

SetStatusString(string, flags)

This allows a movie to display a string in the status bar of a Web browser (usually the bottom-left corner). I usually use this method instead of the DebugStr method described in the previous exploration. It's also a good way to provide feedback to a user. The following script will display "hello" in the browser's status bar (see Figure 36.7):

SetStatusString("hello", kStatusURL)

Figure 36.7 Netscape browser status bar.

Dynamic Media

In Chapter 32 we explored using movie tracks to dynamically add media to a running movie. As we've seen, movie tracks can be a rich gateway for information to flow both in and out of a QuickTime application (see Figure 37.1). I use the term "application" here instead of "movie" because once we start processing information and connecting to the outside world, wired movies start to meet the definition of thin client applications. This is the space that Macromedia is trying to fill with Flash, and QuickTime is suited to play this roll as well.

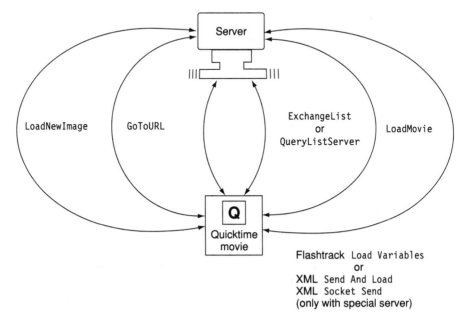

Figure 37.1 Server communication gateway.

"Information gateway"—what do I mean by that? We saw in the last couple of chapters that QuickTime can exchange information with the outside world using XML. The "X" in XML stands for extensible, and it is indeed an extensible data format, but it really isn't best suited (at least not yet) to transferring media. A QuickTime movie, on the other hand, is ideally suited to transferring a bundle of not only media, but all sorts of other data including XML. In fact, as we discussed in Chapter 3, the underlying building blocks of a QuickTime movie are these things called *atoms*. Atoms and atom containers are essentially binary XML elements. They are very similar. It's why QuickTime has such an extensible architecture, and why the MPEG-4 creators decided to use it as the basis for the MPEG file format.

If servers talked QuickTime, then information exchange would be very interesting. For example, say you were building a financial application and wanted to let a user enter the name of a company and receive stock information. You could query an XML server and get back textual information of the current stock price, headlines of any news, and so on. But imagine if the server returned a movie with all of that information, plus stock graph images and hooks to video and audio streams of relevant news reports. This is only the tip of the iceberg of what's possible using movies as information transport containers.

Since QuickTime understands such a rich range of media types, the previous scenario is already a reality. For instance, there are millions of servers out there that return textual information, and if you load text into a movie track, it simply turns it into a text track. The contents of text tracks, as we've seen, are perfectly accessible through wired actions. Images are another standard format that QuickTime understands, and there are many CGI ports out there that return images. For example, finance.yahoo.com has a URL where you can pass in a stock symbol and get back a graph of the stock prices over a day, month, or year interval. It's easy to incorporate such image sources into your movies. You simply load them into a movie track using the StrConcat function to append the query data to the end of the URL using standard CGI notation.

Flash is another great source of dynamic media. There are several server-side Flash generators out there functioning as the back end to chat rooms, mapping software, retail catalogs—you name it. You can funnel that Flash content directly into a movie track and maintain all of the interactivity. The parent movie can even access the Flash variables and perform Flash button clicks.

Given that we've already explored movie tracks in previous chapters, let's spend the rest of this chapter learning a powerful way to dynamically load image data into a sprite track. QuickTime has something called *URL images,* and there are two ways to make them. One way is to hard-code the URL in the sprite image definition. This can be done in LiveStage Pro by setting an image's source property to "Get from URL" and entering the URL in the provided field. When hard-coding the URL like this, you can also define a proxy image that will be displayed while image data downloads from the URL. These types of URL images start downloading as soon as the sprite sample is loaded (see Figure 37.2), and the URL can't be modified or accessed by scripts. The second method is more dynamic. New images can be added to a sprite sample by calling the `LoadNewImage` action. Images can also be disposed of using the `DisposeImage` action (which can be helpful in slimming down your movie's RAM usage).

Let's try out the hard-coded way first. This method is perfect when you want your movie to load an image from a fixed location every time it is played. Things such as images-of-the-day and banner ads fit this scenario. Yes, I know, everyone wants to watch movies for free and nobody wants to see banner ads. It's like the Chinese saying: "Those who get into the play for free boo the loudest." So for our example, we'll stay away from advertisements and build a cartoon-of-the-day movie. I scanned in a few cartoons from a panel series I drew a long time ago called Gridlock. The comic series was all about making fun of cars and traffic. So, start your engines.

Open the project `ComicOfTheDay_start.lsd`. Inside you'll find a sprite track with two sprites: one called "Title" and the other called "Panel." The panel sprite is the one that will display the comic of the day.

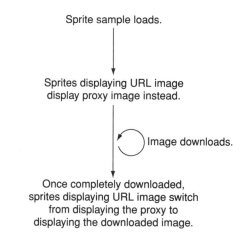

Sprite sample loads.

Sprites displaying URL image
display proxy image instead.

Image downloads.

Once completely downloaded,
sprites displaying URL image switch
from displaying the proxy to
displaying the downloaded image.

Figure 37.2   Timeline of a URL image.

Open the Images tab for the sprite sample. It should have three images. The first is the title picture, the second is a "Loading..." image, and the third is called "Comic." The panel sprite is set up to display the "Comic" image, but it's currently just a black square. What we want is for this image to load its data from an external file. Since external files can sometimes take a while to load, especially if they are loading across a slow Internet connection, we'll also want to employ a proxy image. Proxy images display in the place of a URL image while it downloads. Once the remote image data has completely loaded, any sprite displaying the image will automatically be updated with the new image data.

Let's set up our Comic URL image. In the Images tab, select the Comic image and set the source to "Get from URL." Then type today.jpg into the URL field. Set the Proxy setting to the "Loading..." image. That's all you have to do.

Note   We used a relative address that will work either from the local hard disk or when viewed on a Web page. Just make sure the files are in the same directory. Images can also be loaded from absolute URLs using the `file:`, `http:`, and `ftp:` protocols.

Since the cartoon picture can potentially have different dimensions than the Loading image, I've placed an `Idle` script on the panel sprite that continuously centers the sprite in the track so that once the new image is loaded, it will instantly center itself.

Preview the movie and enjoy a Gridlock comic (see Figure 37.3). If you want to change the today.jpg image, you can replace it with one of the other comic images that I've placed in the Gridlock folder. You then have to close the movie and load it again to see the new content. One method of reloading a hard-coded URL image without having to close the movie is to move the movie's playhead to a time outside of the sample, and then enter the sample again. Be aware that not only will this trigger all the URL images to reload, it will also reset all of the sprite properties (variables, however, will retain their values).

Another, more interactive way of loading URL images is through the LoadNewImage action:

```
LoadNewImage( URL, ID )
```

This action takes a string URL pointing to an image file, either remote or local, and an ID that will be given to the new image as a way of identifying it once it loads. You can determine the index of an image by its ID through the GetImageIndexByID action. In QuickTime 6, once an image is assigned an index, it remains constant throughout the lifetime of the movie. Even if

 GRIDLOCK
by Matthew Peterson

Ahhhh! Uncle Jim!... And I just washed my windshield too!

Figure 37.3 A Gridlock comic.

you call DisposeImage, all it does is ditch the image information, but the image's indexed spot remains filled with an empty image. Since you can't reuse an image ID more than once in a movie (if you do, the second image simply won't load), you have to make sure you pick unique IDs when calling the LoadNewImage action. For these reasons, I usually avoid using the image ID and just stick with the index. One neat trick is if you pass in zero for the ID when executing LoadNewImage, QuickTime will pick a unique ID for you. It will also instantly create a new image index holder at the end of the image pool. This means you never need to deal with IDs if you don't want to.

As an example of how to use LoadNewImage, let's build a URL image viewer that allows the user to type in the URL of an image, hit Enter, and then have that image loaded and displayed. Open the project ImageViewer _start.lsd. Inside we have a sprite track and a text track. The text track starts out in kDynamicEditing state. When the user types in a value and hits the Return key, the $LoadImage custom event on the display sprite is executed.

In the $LoadImage handler, we want the sprite to load a new image and display it. Here's the script:

```
[900 LoadImage]
LocalVars urlLength, urlString

urlLength= TrackNamed("Text").GetTextLength
SetString(urlString, TrackNamed("Text").GetText(0,URLLength))
LoadNewImage(urlString, 0)

SetImageIndexTo(NumImages)
```

Now, preview the movie and test it out. Type in the URL matthew.jpg. That should bring up a picture (see Figure 37.4) that the lovely Department of Motor Vehicles kindly took of me (after waiting in the line for four hours and having to fill out three forms because the woman accidentally

Figure 37.4   Another happy Department of Motor Vehicles customer.

gave me the service vehicle form by mistake, and of course the guy in front of me has to ask a million different questions to the one employee that isn't on a lunch break . . .). You can also try out `gulie.pct` or `bridge.png`, which are also the names of image files located in the project folder.

Try typing in a URL that doesn't exist, such as `efficientDMV.gif`. This will cause the sprite to continue to display the image from the last URL (see Figure 37.5). This happens because calling `LoadNewImage` with a bad URL does nothing (see Figure 37.6), and so `SetImageIndexTo(NumImages)`

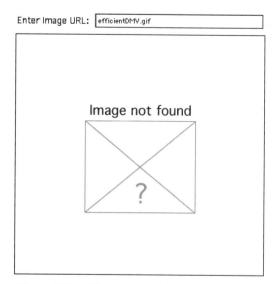

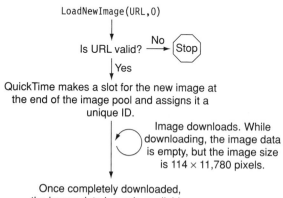

Enter Image URL: `efficientDMV.gif`

Image not found

Figure 37.5 `efficientDMV.gif` does not exist.

`LoadNewImage(URL,0)`

Is URL valid? ──No──▶ Stop

│Yes

QuickTime makes a slot for the new image at the end of the image pool and assigns it a unique ID.

Image downloads. While downloading, the image data is empty, but the image size is 114 × 11,780 pixels.

Once completely downloaded, the image data is made available.

Figure 37.6 Timeline of `LoadNewImage`.

simply sets the sprite image to the last image in the sprite sample, whatever that might be. Say you wanted to alert the user that they typed in a bad URL. How would you do that? By now, you should know all of the standard QuickTime tricks. You first determine how many images are in the sample (through the `imageCount` property), then call `LoadNewImage`, and then check to see if a new image was added. Here's the script:

```
[900 LoadImage]
LocalVars urlLength, imageCount, urlString

imageCount = NumImages
urlLength = TrackNamed("Text").GetTextLength
SetString(urlString, TrackNamed("Text").GetText(0,URLLength))
LoadNewImage(urlString, 0)

IF( NumImages > imageCount )
    SetImageIndexTo(NumImages)
ELSE
    SetImageIndexTo($NotFound)
ENDIF
```

Since the sprite sample contains a $NotFound image, this should work. Try it out.

Note The following are the known "issues" with the `LoadNewImage` action:

1. There is no official way to know if a new image has loaded. I use the fact that it's 11,780 pixels tall until it completely loads.

2. On Windows, if the window the movie is playing in is minimized and then restored, it's possible for remote images created with the `LoadNewImage` action to disappear. A similar thing happens on Mac OS 9, but after the image disappears for a brief moment, it comes back. This bug is in QuickTime 6.1 (current version as of writing this), but should hopefully be fixed in later versions.

3. Loading an image with an ID that already exists results in nothing happening. `LoadNewImage` doesn't even work with IDs that were supposedly removed through the `DisposeImage` action. For this reason, I always use `LoadNewImage(0)`, which forces QuickTime to pick a new ID for me.

4. After disposing of an image, the index it filled is not made available to new images. This means you can't loop through all images by index. Some indices could potentially be empty. This breaks the notion of an index.

5. Usually QuickTime (and applications in general) will ignore spaces at the beginning and end of a URL string. "file.jpg" should be the same as " file.jpg" or "file.jpg ", but the LoadNewImage action doesn't appear to trim whitespace from the ends of the URL string. If you are reading in a URL from an XML file, or allowing the user to type one into a text field, you will want to trim off any whitespace characters (see Appendix C for information on how to do this).

Since the LoadNewImage action is rather new (introduced in version 6), it still has a few kinks to work out. For instance, there isn't a good way to know when the image has completely loaded. As soon as you call Load-NewImage, it makes a blank image at the appropriate ID and index, but if it's a remote URL, it might take a while to actually download. During this time, a sprite showing the image will be invisible until the data transfer is complete. It would be nice to somehow display a loading image, especially if it's going to take a while.

Currently, there's no official way to know when the image actually arrives, but one thing you can do is look at the dimensions of a sprite showing the new image. When the image hasn't completely downloaded yet, the empty image has a width of 114 pixels and a height of 11,780. I don't know why it has these strange dimensions, but that's the way it is. At least, that's the way it is in QuickTime 6. It's likely to change. I'd suggest to the QuickTime engineering team that the dimensions should be 0×0 until the media has completely loaded. At any rate, you can take advantage of the fact that your image will probably be less than 11,780 pixels tall to detect if the image has loaded yet or not. While it loads, you can display a "Loading..." image and keep checking the height in an Idle script:

```
[Idle]
SpriteVars yOffset
LocalVars height, width, widthDiff, heightDiff, x, y

IF( ImageIndex != $NotFound )
    SetImageIndexTo(NumImages)
ENDIF

height = BoundsBottom - BoundsTop

IF( height = 11780 OR height = 0 )
    SetImageIndexTo( $Loading )
    height = BoundsBottom - BoundsTop
ENDIF
```

```
width = BoundsRight - BoundsLeft

widthDiff = TrackWidth - width
heightDiff = TrackHeight - yOffset - height

x = widthDiff/2
y = yOffset + heightDiff/2

MoveTo(x,y)
```

This script sets the sprite's image to the last image (NumImages), which should be the most recent image added with the LoadNewImage action. The script then calculates the height of the sprite (BoundsBottom - BoundsTop), and if it is equal to 11,780 (the magical height of the empty image during the download process), we display a $Loading image instead. This will at least work with QuickTime 6. If later Apple decides to "fix" the empty image height so it is 0 instead of 11,780 pixels tall, we've factored that into the script by checking for a height of 11,780 or a height of 0. It's always good to think ahead. The last few lines of the script are there to center the image in the display region.

Explorations

1. At the beginning of the chapter we talked about how Yahoo! Finance has a CGI script that returns an image for the stock chart of a given company. Reusing such Web resources in your own application is part of a broader range of techniques called *HTML screen scraping*. This is where an application grabs and uses bits and pieces of media and information that were intended to be displayed on a third-party's Web page. Search around and see if you can find any interesting dynamic media sources to scrape. As an exercise, try your hand at integrating that media into either a movie track or a dynamically loaded sprite image.

2. Memory management is an important consideration that is often overlooked by developers. In the URL image display movie we built, a new image gets created for each new URL that the user types in. All of those images are stored in RAM, and it's a waste of memory since we are only displaying the most recent URL. How would you go about making that movie less of a RAM hog? How would you test that your solution actually reduces the RAM usage? (Hint: There are programs out there that can log the RAM usage of any application, and QuickTime itself has a GetMemoryFree action.)

3. For the ComicOfTheDay project, we used a static URL image. We discussed briefly how to reload that image without having to close and reopen the movie. Try implementing such a feature. Maybe add a Reload button, or make it such that clicking the comic or the title will cause the image to reload.

4. The sprite in the URL image presenter gets centered in the display field, but it doesn't attempt to scale the image down if it is too big. How would you implement a shrink-to-fit feature?

Intermovie Communication

The wise John Donne told us that "no man is an island," and as we've seen in Part VI, QuickTime movies aren't islands either. Movies can communicate with the rest of the world in sophisticated ways. Movies can also communicate with other movies running in the same environment (see Figure 38.1). This is particularly useful for Web page design when you want different parts of an interface to reside in different parts of the HTML. For example, you might have a page with two frames, one with video and the other with a description and commentary on the video. Say you wanted to have a line of text that referred to a particular part of the movie. It would be useful to have a button embedded in the text that said "Click to play," and it would tell the video to go to the relevant section and start playing. This is not only possible with QuickTime, it's quite easy to do (for an example, see the `VideoPaper` folder).

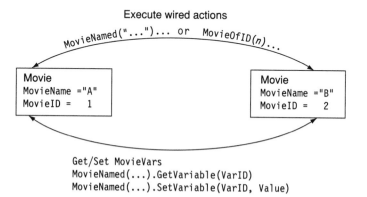

Figure 38.1   Intermovie communication gateway.

Movies can have names and IDs just like sprites. For some reason, Live-Stage Pro only lets you enter a movie name or an ID but not both (Quick-Time, however, allows a movie to have both). I usually just give my movies a name, which you can do in the Document Settings panel (see Figure 38.2) or in the movie inspector.

Once you give a movie a name or an ID, it then becomes accessible to other movies running in the same environment. You target the movie by using `MovieNamed()` or `MovieOfID()`. For instance, you make a movie named "video" start playing by calling

```
MovieNamed("video").StartPlaying
```

Once you target the movie, you can directly access all of the tracks, so if you had a track named "audio" you could mute it:

```
MovieNamed("video").TrackNamed("audio").SetVolume(0)
```

Let's build a simple example. Open the `Stick_demo.lsd` project and have a look at the Document Settings panel. You'll see that I've named the movie "Stick." This project has a sprite track, which I've also named "Stick," and in it there's a sprite, which, you guessed it, is also named "Stick." It's just one of those names that you can stick anywhere.

We're going to control this stick from another movie, so let's open a second project at the same time. The project is called `Controller_start.lsd`. It has a text track and a sprite track with two button sprites. The button on the top is named "Hide/Show," and we're going to hook it up to toggle the visible state of the stick sprite in the other movie. To do this, we simply place the following script into its `Mouse Click` event:

```
[Mouse Click]
LocalVars visibleState

visibleState = MovieNamed("Stick").TrackNamed("Stick") \
    .SpriteNamed("Stick").IsVisible

visibleState = NOT visibleState
```

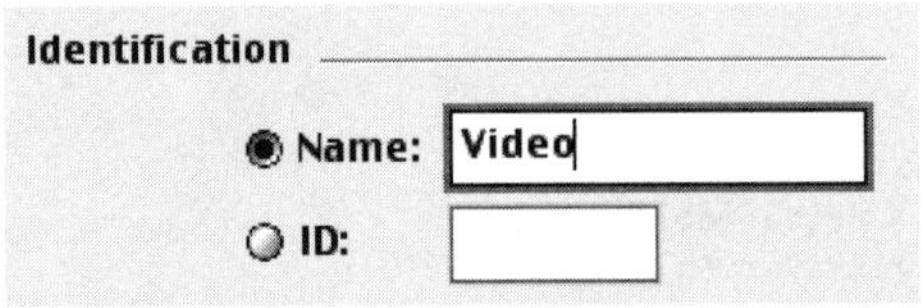

Figure 38.2 Document Settings panel with name and ID fields.

```
MovieNamed("Stick").TrackNamed("Stick").SpriteNamed("Stick") \
  .SetVisible(visibleState)
```

We get the visible state, toggle it with the NOT operator, and then apply the new visible state to the Stick sprite. Let's see if it works.

Note Before LiveStage version 4.1, you had to export and test intermovie communication in QuickTime Player due to a bug in the LiveStage preview code.

Launch both movies and click on the Hide/Show button. It should hide and show the little black stick in the other movie.

That's how you execute an event on sprites across movies. To obtain more interesting communication, you need to be able to access variables across movies as well. This is possible using movie variables. If you have a look at the Idle event of the Stick sprite, it reads:

```
[Idle]
MovieVars RotationSpeed:16

Rotate(RotationSpeed)
```

Here we've defined a movie variable named RotationSpeed with an ID of 16. When accessing variables across movies, you can currently do so only by ID. It's done through the SetVariable(ID, Value) and GetVariable(ID) actions. If we have our controller set variable 16 on the Stick movie, it can control how fast the stick rotates. Let's try it. Place the following script on the Set Speed button's Mouse Click event:

```
[Mouse Click]
LocalVars textLength speed

textLength = TrackNamed("Text").GetTextLength
speed = TrackNamed("Text").GetText(0,textLength)

MovieNamed("Stick").SetVariable(16,speedValue)
```

Preview the two movies again (make sure only one copy of each is running or else there will be a naming conflict). Type in 3 and click the Set Speed button. You should see the black stick start spinning at a moderate pace. Type in –3, then click the Set Speed button again and it should reverse directions.

Underneath the hood, all variables, even LocalVars, SpriteVars, and GlobalVars, have IDs. And that's all they have. The names are just a convenience that LiveStage provides to make it easier to write scripts. Once the movies are compiled, they lose any names assigned to them in LiveStage. Another important thing to know is that MovieVars reside in their own track. LocalVars, SpriteVars, and GlobalVars are part of the sprite track that they reside in. Since MovieVars are intended to be associated with any sprite track in a movie, the LiveStage developers decided that MovieVars should get their own, otherwise empty, sprite track to live in. They always call this sprite track "Movie Variables," and it's always the last track in the movie. I say it's important to know this because I know of other developers that accidentally delete the Movie Variables track while editing the movie in a different application and then wonder why certain functions don't work anymore.

As a second example, I'd like to share a trick of how to determine where two movies are relative to one another. This is useful when building multiwindowed experiences. Since QuickTime doesn't officially provide a way to determine where a movie resides on the screen, we have to figure it out in a somewhat sneaky way. QuickTime's evolution process has consisted of Apple releasing a certain set of functionality. Developers use it to its fullest and want more, so the developers hack around and figure out ways to push the envelope. The QuickTime engineers see the cool stuff that the developers are doing and then include an official solution in the next set of features. It's an ongoing process of inches and miles. Figuring where movies reside on the screen is currently in the edge-of-the-envelope stage. So let's see it in action first and then go over how it works.

Open and preview the two projects Compass_demo.1sd and North_demo.1sd. When you drag the North movie around the screen, the arrow in the Compass movie continues to point to it (see Figure 38.3).

Note Previous versions of LiveStage Pro don't accurately preview intermovie communication. You might have to export the movies and test the behavior in QuickTime Player.

The way this works is the Compass sprite asks the sprite track in the North movie where it thinks the mouse is located:

```
MovieNamed("North").TrackNamed("Sprite").MouseHorizontal
MovieNamed("North").TrackNamed("Sprite").MouseVertical
```

The sprite track will return where it thinks the mouse is relative to its own track location. The Compass sprite also knows where the mouse is relative to the compass sprite track. By taking the difference in the two perspectives of the mouse location, one obtains the distance between the

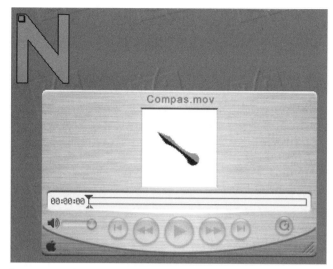

Figure 38.3 Compass movie pointing to the North movie.

two sprite tracks. Since both of these sprite tracks are located at 0,0 in their respective movies, the difference is also the distance between the movies. You can have a look at the Compass sprite's Idle event to see how all of this is calculated.

Another little trick that is used in the Compass sprite's Idle event is a technique for determining if another movie is open or not. It's just another version of the "unchanged variable" method described in Chapter 32. Here's the sniplet:

```
...
northMovieOpen = 0
northMovieOpen = MovieNamed("North").GetTrackCount

IF( northMovieOpen > 0 )
    //do something, the movie is open
ELSE
    //movie isn't open
ENDIF
```

This works because GetTrackCount always returns a value greater than zero for normal movies. If northMovieOpen remains 0 after the second line, then we know that an error happened and that the second line never succeeded, which we assume is because the North movie isn't open.

Note Reference movies will sometimes return zero for NumTracks.

▶ IsMovieActive

One final technique useful for multimovie projects is focus indication. Most modern desktop applications change their appearance when they are in the background. Buttons usually gray out and text often dims. This is to make it obvious which window is currently active. You might have noticed that the North movie fades when it isn't the frontmost movie. It knows when it is in front by checking the IsMovieActive property. You can have a look at the North sprite's Idle event to see how this is done:

```
[Idle]

IF( IsMovieActive )
    SetImageIndexTo($North)
ENDIF
    SetImageIndexTo($FadedNorth)
ENDIF
```

▶ Explorations

1. For an example of some interesting uses of intermovie communication in a Web page, launch the index.html file in your Web browser. This is an interactive video and transcript of a classroom session where students discuss a particular math problem (in Creole and English). Throughout the "segmented" transcript, you'll find play buttons, and even some slow-motion play buttons. If you choose Room Layout from the Documents menu, you'll be presented with a map of the classroom (see Figure 38.4). If you then play the video, you'll see that the map indicates who's currently talking. You can also mouse over each student to see what they look like. This "video paper" was built using the VideoPaperBuilder 2.0 application available from http://vpb.concord.org.

2. Launch both of the movies inside of the FishBowl folder (see Figure 38.5). Drag the Fish movie on top of the bowl movie and let go. How do you think this was accomplished?

3. For the most part, intermovie communication works as expected, but sometimes funny things happen. For instance, what would you expect the following script to do?

   ```
   MovieNamed("presenter").GoToURL("<NewMovie.mov>T<myself>")
   ```

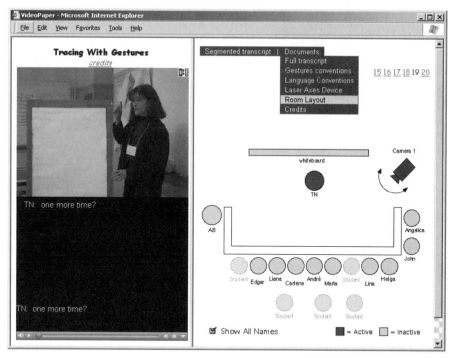

Figure 38.4 A video paper.

Figure 38.5 Fish and Bowl movies.

You might expect it to load NewMovie.mov into the window playing the presenter movie. But what actually happens is NewMovie.mov loads into the window from which the script is being executed. In other words, Go-ToURL ignores the MovieNamed target. LoadChildMovie, EnterFullScreen, CloseThisWindow, and SendAppMessage are some other actions that can be problematic during intermovie communication. The workaround for these problems is to set a flag in the remote movie's MovieVars to indicate to the movie that it should perform a specified action. As you experiment with intermovie communication, be aware of potential targeting issues.

Communicating with Applications

Apple has put a lot of effort into making it easy for developers to build applications that utilize all the resources that QuickTime provides. And QuickTime provides a lot more than just playing movies. QuickTime provides a rich graphics engine to enable applications to build customized sprite worlds beyond what the sprite track enables. The QuickTime libraries have the ability to record audio, to capture video, to convert data between all kinds of different formats, and much, much more. We won't be able to cover all of the cool ways that QuickTime can ease the building of applications, but we can talk a little about communicating with interactive movies (see Figure 39.1).

These days, Web presence is a big deal. Developers spend a lot of time and energy building rich interactive interfaces for their Web pages. If they

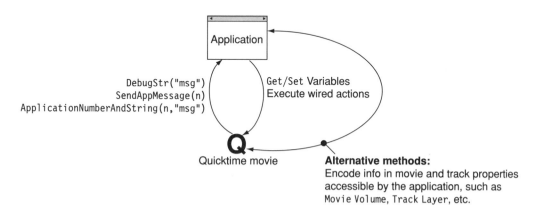

Figure 39.1 Application communication gateway.

then come to the point that they need to build a custom application, they often have to re-create the same interactive interfaces with the same look and feel. However, if they do their interfaces with QuickTime they are in luck. They can most likely integrate those movies into their custom application with little work.

Movies can send commands to their host application in a few different ways. One way is through the SendAppMessage action. This is the action that you use to tell QuickTime Player to go full screen and to close the movie:

SendAppMessage(kAppMsgEnterFullScreen)

and

SendAppMessage(kAppMsgWindowClose)

LiveStage has wrapped these calls into simpler abbreviations:

EnterFullScreen

and

CloseThisWindow

But they compile down to the same SendAppMessage call. The parameter that gets passed in is an integer. kAppMsgWindowClose has a value of 3, for instance. Your movie can send coded messages to your custom application this way as well. For instance when a certain button is clicked, you might call

SendAppMessage(77)

In your application, you know that 77 means the button was clicked. Listening for such messages is easy in C/C++ and Java. You simply need to install an ActionFilter on the movie controller. If you've worked with QuickTime at this level, you'll know what I mean. Certain authoring environments, such as Tekadence Magik, give you easy scripting access to this action as well.

Since numbers aren't always the most friendly way of encoding information, QuickTime also provides a way of sending strings to the host application. We've used this action before; it's called DebugStr(). It's so named because it's useful for debugging purposes, but it's also a way to control an application. DebugStr is much more widely supported in authoring environments including Metacard, Runtime Revolution, the AX Quick-Time plug-in for mTropolis (www.axlogic.com), Tekadence Magik, and iShell (Macromedia Director doesn't support DebugStr for some reason).

Let me tell you a little hypothetical story to illustrate the potential power and modularity of using QuickTime inside of custom applications. Say you are a sought-after developer without a lot of time (as you probably are). A wealthy fiction publisher wants you to build an interactive website to feature some samples from their nighttime reading category. The publisher wants it to be special. So you spend a lot of time making an interactive bookshelf interface with realistic candlelight effects and the works. As a typical developer, you spent more time on it than you invoiced, but the site came out great, and the feeling of accomplishment paid for the difference. The rich interactivity attracts lots of customers and becomes so successful that the publisher comes back to you and asks how much it would cost to build a kiosk application for their new literature museum. You tell them that HTML isn't robust enough to work as a kiosk and that you would have to build a custom application and basically redo the project. They say, "No problem, whatever it takes, we'll pay you double, no, triple what we paid last time." You agree, and this time come out ahead because all the interactivity was encapsulated into QuickTime movies that are easily repurposed as application modules.

Since this book is built around examples, not stories, let's actually build that kiosk application. The bookshelf interface movie is called bookshelf.mov. (Many thanks to Mike Matson for supplying this movie.) You can open it in QuickTime Player to see how it works. Drag the candle around to highlight the different books (see Figure 39.2). Whenever the candle is released, it sends a DebugStr() message to the host application with an abbreviated title of the book being highlighted. Also in the Bookshelf folder are HTML files with a sample selection from each book.

We can use lots of different authoring tools to build this kiosk application. Metacard and iShell are good choices, but I'm going to use Tekadence Magik since it literally only takes one line of code to hook up the candle to the HTML file that gets displayed in a text field. It's that easy. You can look at the project, BookshelfApp.tek. Once it's loaded in Tekadence Magik, simply run it (from the File menu). If you wanted, you could make it a kiosk-style application so it fills the entire screen by changing the Window style to Full Screen, but it's easier to test the functionality in a normal window. Since Tekadence apps only work with Java 1.2, it won't work on OS 9. If you're on OS 9, I built a special version in the OS9App folder so you can test it out.

The bookshelf app is an example of QuickTime sending commands and "controlling" the host app. Sometimes it's necessary to go the other way too. For instance, in Chapter 24 we started to build a speech synthesis movie module with my voice. If we put a lot of time into it, we shouldn't

Figure 39.2 Application using the bookshelf.mov as a UI element.

have to redo the work in order to integrate it into an application. Unfortunately, most authoring tools don't have ways to talk to sprites directly. Some people use hacks, such as setting the volume and having an internal sprite constantly checking the movie volume. I've seen people use various other similar tricks. In Java and C++ you can get and set sprite variables and execute actions on sprites. The next version of Tekadence Magik will also give you access to sprite variables and events.

Explorations

1. Director is a very popular authoring tool, but it doesn't provide very good support for interactive movies. Brennan Young is the expert in integrating wired QuickTime into Director applications. He's provided an example of how to use XML and QTLists as a line of communication between Director and wired movies. Take a look. It's in the folder DirectorXMLAndQT.

2. In Metacard, you can receive DebugStr messages. It's sort of a hidden feature. On a player object, add the following message handler:

```
on QTDebugStr debugMessage
    #Script goes here
end QTDebugStr
```

3. The `DebugStr` call is limited to 255 characters. It truncates strings longer than that. QuickTime, however, is capable of holding much longer strings inside of a variable. How can you get around the `DebugStr` limitation and pass longer strings of text to the parent application?

4. At the beginning of this chapter, we discussed ways in which a wired movie can communicate with QuickTime Player. If the movie is running in the pro version of the player, there are some other neat tricks available. For one thing, it's possible to persist small amounts of data. When the user chooses Save from QuickTime Pro's File menu, certain aspects of the movie will be saved to disk. Variables and sprite properties won't be saved, but track properties will. By adding some dummy tracks to your movie, you can encode a small amount of information in the track position, layer, enabled, volume, and other properties. For an example of this, see the BuildAFace movie. It allows you to assemble eyes, noses, and other pieces into a face. If you save the movie, close it, and then load it again, it'll remember your face. The `MovieChanged` and `SoftwareWasChanged` messages are supposed to notify QuickTime Player that something has changed in the movie and cause QuickTime Pro to pop up a save dialog when the movie closes. As of QuickTime 6.1, however, this feature doesn't appear to work.

5. Another way of interacting with QuickTime Player is through the Favorites menu. A movie can add an item to QuickTime's Favorites menu through the following call:

```
AddSubscription( name, URL, IconURL )
```

IconURL should be an absolute path to a 33 × 28 GIF image (other image formats don't seem to work). For example, a movie can add itself using the following:

```
AddSubscription( "CoolMovie", GetMovieURL,
"http://www.mydomain.com/coolIcon.gif")
```

Subscriptions can be removed using

```
RemoveSubscription( URL )
```

Appendices

Appendix A
Useful Numbers

Euler number, _e_ This number comes up all over the place in mathematics. _e_ is approximately 2.718281828. . . . The QScript formula is

```
e = Exp(1)
```

golden mean Since the early Greeks, it's been claimed that a certain aspect ratio is particularly pleasing to the eye. This "ratio" is actually an irrational number called the Golden Mean (see Figure A.1), and it's found in the artwork of many great artists (such as Leonardo da Vinci) and pops up in natural geometry. The Golden Mean approximately equals 1.618 (1.618033987 . . .). The QScript formula for this number is

```
goldenMean = 1 + ( Sqr(5) - 1 ) / 2
```

Note that this is a different aspect ratio than the standard TV and computer screen aspect ratio of 1.3333 . . . (640/480).

pi, π This is the ratio of the circumference of any circle to its diameter. It's approximately equal to 3.14159265358979. . . . But in QScript, you can simply use the constant PI.

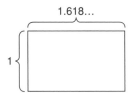

Figure A.1 The Golden Mean.

NaN NaN stands for Not a Number. It pops up sometimes in scripts that perform undefined calculations such as Log(-1). See IsNaN in Appendix B.

prime numbers Relatively large prime numbers play an essential role in many programming recipes and algorithms, such as encryption and random number generation (see the section on random numbers in Appendix E). Here are some prime numbers that come in handy:

Largest prime less than 255	251
Largest prime less than MAX_SHORT	32749
Largest prime less than 65535	65521
Largest prime less than MAX_LONG	2147483629 (note, MAX_LONG is also a prime)

Here are 11 of the largest primes less than the square root of MAX_LONG (so that two can be multiplied and still be less than MAX_LONG):

46229, 46237, 46261, 46271, 46273, 46279, 46301, 46307, 46309, 46327, 46337

biggest number What's the biggest number in QScript? The answer depends on what the number is being used for. There are several types of numbers. When working with integer values, the biggest number is called MAX_LONG, which is about 2 billion (2147483647). When working with floating-point numbers, the max is MAX_FLOAT, or $3.4028e+38$. But many parameters have their own max values. See "Parameter ranges."

smallest number What's the smallest positive number in QScript? This is sometimes called epsilon, or in QScript, it's called MIN_FLOAT, and is approximately equal to $1.175e-35$. Some algorithms require such a number for roundoff error correction, but in QScript, MIN_FLOAT isn't the right number to use. See "Numerical Correction" in Appendix E.

degrees^2 per sphere There are 360 degrees per circle, but how many square degrees per sphere? This number comes in handy when working with cubic VR. There are 41,253 degrees^2 in a sphere.

minimums and maximums

```
MIN_SHORT = -32768
MAX_SHORT = 32768
MIN_LONG = -2147483647
MAX_LONG = 2147483647
MIN_FLOAT = 1.17549435e - 35
MAX_FLOAT = 3.402823466e + 38
```

infinity QScript doesn't have a way to encode infinity. Strangely enough, 1/0 in QuickTime is equal to 0. 1/MIN_FLOAT equals 8507059173023461 587000000000000000000, which is less than MAX_FLOAT. Infinity does crop up in some calculations, however. For instance Log(0) is negative infinity, or "-INF".

To specify an infinite duration for a track sample, use the * symbol.

parameter ranges Below are the value ranges for some commonly used properties and parameters.

> Layer: -32767 to 32767 (MIN_SHORT to MAX_SHORT)
> Volume: 0 to 255
> Color values: 0 to 65535
> Idle delay: -1 (meaning don't idle), 0 (as fast as possible), 1 to MAX_LONG
> ID: 1 to MAX_LONG (numbers less than 1 will work, but it isn't advisable)

string lengths Strings in QuickTime can have up to 32,768 characters (32 kilobytes).

first index In QuickTime, usually the first item in a sequence of items has an index of 1. This is true for images, sprites, tracks, text hotspots (text links), instruments in an instrument track, QTList elements, and chapters. There are other situations, however, where 0 is used as the first index, such as items in an array and text selection positions (including character offsets in a string).

16384 Use this number in place of the standard 1 value for the last parameter of SetMatrix action calls. See the "Matrix Transformations" section of Appendix F.

11780 This is the height of a URL-loaded image (loaded through the Load-Image action; see Chapter 37) while it's in the download process. This might change in a future version of QuickTime (current version while writing this is 6.1).

file size How large is the file size for a sprite track? The answer obviously depends on the sprite track. Most of the file size will be due to images. The basic file size of a movie with no tracks is about 500 bytes. Each empty sprite track will add about 200 bytes. Each sprite will add a tiny 8 bytes. An average line of QScript will also take up about 8 bytes. All the rest of the file's bytes will be due to images. For the wired sprite projects that I'm usually involved in, small images take up between 300 bytes to 1K each. Larger simple graphics can be between 1K and 5K. Small photographic images are often around 12K. A relatively large (640 × 480) photograph might take up to 90K of storage space. All of these numbers are conservative and assume the movie is compressed and the images are using reasonable codecs. Wired QuickTime movies generated from LiveStage Pro are usually zlib compressed (the zip compression scheme). Uncompressed wired sprite movies can often be eight times larger.

QScript execution speed How fast do wired scripts get executed? There's a large spectrum of computers out there that crunch through wired actions at different rates. For me, I've found it useful to consider two groups of machines, which roughly represent both sides of the range of computing power that I typically target. One group consists of machines that were considered reasonably good in 1999. You can often find such machines in K–12 classrooms in the urban United States. I usually count on them executing an average line of QScript in about 200 nanoseconds. An average line consists of an action, a variable reference, and a simple math operation. A second group of machines are ones that a family would buy in the year 2003, like a G4 iMac, or a 1.x GHz Pentium. I usually give around 30 nanoseconds per average line of QScript for this second group. In this estimate, I've taken into account the processing overhead of executing an event.

The Idle event is one place you don't want the movie to spend too much time processing scripts. For smooth idle rates, you will want to take up less than 75% of the idle delay. For example, if you wanted a movie to work smoothly for the first group of machines with an idle delay of 1 (60 events per second, or 16.7 milliseconds each), then you need to limit the number of lines to under 25. That's 25 average lines of QScript for all Idle event scripts for all sprites in the movie combined. For new computers (the second group), you can have over 150 lines for the Idle scripts.

download speeds How long will it take viewers to download a movie? This obviously depends on the type of Internet connection they are on. Here is the approximate time (under optimal conditions) it will take QuickTime to download a 1 MB movie on various Internet connections:

56K modem:	2 min, 19 sec
64K ISDN:	2 min, 2 sec
128 ISDN:	1 min, 1 sec
640K DSL:	0 min, 12 sec
T1:	0 min, 5 sec

Cable modems vary in their downstream bandwidth. In practice, the 1 MB download time for a cable modem usually falls between 20 and 90 seconds, but it can sometimes take over 2 minutes.

A good way to simulate the downloading process of QuickTime movies is through an application called DeliVRator (www.vrtools.com).

number of variables In QScript, you can have a total of 2000 LocalVars, 2000 SpriteVars, and over 10,000 GlobalVars. You can manually declare 10,000 MovieVar addresses, and many more thousand are available for automatic addressing. Since each item in an array will use up one variable, be careful not to overflow a variable space.

musical note rates QuickTime audio tracks can be played at different rates to emulate different notes on a musical scale. Assuming the normal rate of 1 is middle C, here are the rates for the other notes on the scale:

C	1
C#	1.0595
D	1.1225
D#	1.1892
E	1.2599
F	1.3348
F#	1.4142
G	1.4983
G#	1.5874
A	1.6818
A#	1.7818
B	1.8877
C	2

Here's a QScript formula for turning standard MIDI note values (where 60 is middle C) into play rates:

playRate = **Exp**((note-60)***Log**(2)/12)

This formula can be optimized by evaluating Log(2)/12 ahead of time:

playRate = **Exp**((note-60)*0.0578)

colors QuickTime usually represents colors as three integers between 0 and 65535, representing red, green, and blue (RGB). Other authoring tools, however, usually use values between 0 and 255. To convert a 0–255 value to a 0–65535 value, simply multiply by 257. To go the other way, divide by 257. See the HEX2Dec conversion function in Appendix C for a way to convert to HTML-style colors. See the Rgb2Hsv function in Appendix B for how to convert to HSV color encoding. Here are RGB values for some standard colors:

Color name	Red	Green	Blue
Black	0	0	0
White	65535	65535	65535
Gray	32896	32896	32896
Beige	62965	62965	56540
Red	65535	0	0
Pink	65536	49344	52171
Magenta	65536	0	65535
Orange	65535	42405	0
Dark orange	65535	35980	0
Gold	65535	55255	0
Yellow	65535	65536	0
Green	0	65535	0
Aqua/cyan	0	65535	65535
Blue	0	0	65535
Navy	0	0	32896
Purple	32896	0	32896
Violet	61166	33410	61166

Green is the brightest color on the computer monitor (about twice as bright as red and six times as bright as blue), and at full saturation it looks a little yellowish. For this reason, it often looks better to tone down the green a little bit.

Since about 8% of males and 1% of females are color-blind, a movie with moderate distribution is bound to be seen by users with some difficulty distinguishing colors. The most common type is red-green color blindness. When designing a wired movie where objects are somehow color-coded, try to limit the number of red-green distinctions. If you do use red-green distinctions, try to make one brighter than the other so they'll be distinguishable based on luminance as well as hue.

pixels per inch For certain projects, I've wanted a sprite to appear a certain physical size on the screen. It's easy to specify a sprite's width and height in pixels, but what if you wanted to work in inches or centimeters? The number of pixels per inch obviously depends on the monitor. A pretty common display setting is 15 inches with 1024 × 786 pixel resolution, which corresponds to 85.3 pixels/inch (33.6 pixels/cm). Here are some other common values:

12-inch display, 1024 x 786:	106.7 pixels/inch (42.0 pixels/cm)
12-inch display, 640 x 480:	66.7 pixels/inch (27.2 pixels/cm)
14-inch display, 1024 x 786:	91.4 pixels/inch (36.0 pixels/cm)
17-inch display, 1024 x 786:	75.3 pixels/inch (29.6 pixels/cm)
17-inch display, 1600 x 1200:	117.6 pixels/inch (46.3 pixels/cm)

font sizes Font sizes are different for Macintosh and Windows platforms. On the Macintosh, fonts are 72 dots per inch (dpi), but on Windows, they're 96 dpi. If you don't correct for this, fonts will look about 1/3 larger on Windows than on the Mac. To convert from Mac to Windows font sizes, multiply by 0.75. To go the other way, divide by 0.75 (dividing by 0.75 is computationally more precise than multiplying by 1.3333).

computer intensity Over the years, I've built many QuickTime-based applications for research projects. Often these projects have strict requirements about how much noise comes out of the speakers or how much light comes out of the monitors. Sometimes the researchers are worried that it'll be too loud, or maybe not loud enough. It's useful to know that most computer systems can attain a speaker output of up to 80 dB. Most monitors have a mean luminance of around 40 cd/m^2.

degrees and radians Since π radians is the same as 180 degrees, you can convert an angle from degrees to radians by multiplying by $\pi/180$. This is approximately the same as dividing by 57.3 (57.2958 . . .). To go from radians to degrees, you multiply by 57.3. QuickTime also has `DegreesToRadians` and `RadiansToDegrees` actions, but when optimizing and simplifying an equation, it's often beneficial to use the 57.3 scale factor instead of the functions.

timescale Movies created with LiveStage have a timescale of 600 per second. This has nothing to do with the movie's frame rate, it simply means that to convert a time value to seconds, you divide by 600.

binary numbers Since they pop up all over the place, it's useful to have a quick reference to the decimal equivalents of place values in a binary number. The following is a list of 2^n, where n ranges from 1 to 32:

n	2^n	n	2^n
1	2	17	131072
2	4	18	262144
3	8	19	524288
4	16	20	1048576
5	32	21	2097152
6	64	22	4194304
7	128	23	8388608
8	256	24	16777216
9	512	25	33554432
10	1024	26	67108864
11	2048	27	134217728
12	4096	28	268435456
13	8192	29	536870912
14	16384	30	1073741824
15	32768	31	2147483648
16	65536	32	4294967296

trig table Some actions, such as `SetMatrixBy` and `SetMatrixTo`, can only take constant parameters. Often these constant parameters are the result of a trig calculation. Furthermore, when optimizing a script, it can be beneficial to replace trig calculations with static values when possible. Here's a table of common trig values (rounded to four decimal places):

Degrees	Radians	Sin	Cos	Tan
0	0	0	1	0
15	0.2618	0.2588	0.9659	0.2679
30	0.5236	0.5	0.8660	0.5774
45	0.7854	0.7071	0.7071	1
60	1.0472	0.8660	0.5	1.7321
75	1.3090	0.9659	0.2588	3.7321
90	1.5708	1	0	Infinity
105	1.8326	0.9659	−0.2588	−3.7321
120	2.0944	0.8660	−0.5	−1.7321
135	2.3562	0.7071	−0.7071	−1
150	2.6180	0.5	−0.8660	−0.5774
165	2.8798	0.2588	−0.9659	−0.2679
180	3.1416	0	−1	0

02BF25D5-8C17-4B23-BC80-D3488ABDDC6B I thought I'd end the topic on useful numbers with a really big number. This is the ActiveX class ID for the QuickTime plug-in. See Appendix L for more information.

Appendix B
Math Functions

This appendix provides QScript recipes for common math functions. For simplicity, I've made each recipe look like an actual function that takes parameters, but it's important to note that LiveStage Pro currently doesn't support directly passing parameters to a custom event. See Chapter 9 for a discussion of how to create custom functions in QScript.

The convention used here is that the input variables are designated by the letters a, b, c, d, and so on. The output variable is given the name of the function. I've tried to make all the functions a single expression, but for various reasons, it might be appropriate to break the calculation into multiple parts. When necessary, I've defined intermediate values as LocalVars.

Functions that start with the words "Is," "Does," or "Has" indicate that the result of the function is a Boolean value. All the other functions return numbers or strings as indicated. Sometimes multiple versions of a function are provided.

ToNumber(a) To convert a variable to a number, simply add zero:

```
ToNumber = a + 0
```

ToString(a) To convert a variable to a string value:

```
SetString(ToString, a)
```

ToBoolean(a) To convert a variable to a Boolean value:

```
ToBoolean = (a = TRUE)
```

IsNumber(a) There are a couple of ways to test if a variable is a number or a string. A simple way is to perform a string comparison with the variable + 0. If they are equal, then it's a number, if not, then it's a string:

```
IsNumber = StrCompare( a, a + 0, FALSE, FALSE )
```

IsString(a) See IsNumber.

> IsNumber = (**StrCompare**(a, a + 0, **FALSE, FALSE**) = **FALSE**)

AbsoluteValue(a) The absolute value function is built into QScript:

> AbsoluteValue = **ABS**(a)

ATan(a) The inverse tangent is a built-in function. It takes a slope value and returns an angle in radians.

> ATan = **ArcTan**(a)

ATan2(y,x) This is a built-in function. It takes a point (y and x) and returns the angle to that point in radians:

> ATan2 = **ArcTan2**(y,x)

Sign(a) This function returns 1 for positive values, –1 for negative values, and 0 for zero:

> Sign = a/**ABS**(a)

Ceil(a) The ceiling function converts a floating-point value to an integer by rounding up. The following function works for both positive and negative values:

> Ceil = a **DIV** 1 + (a - a **DIV** 1 > 0)

It's possible to cache the (a DIV 1) calculation, but setting and getting a variable takes the same amount of time as calculating a DIV 1, so it wouldn't help.

Floor(a) The floor function converts a floating-point value to an integer by rounding down. The following works for both positive and negative values:

> Floor = a **DIV** 1 - (a - a **DIV** 1 < 0)

If you're only dealing with positive numbers, then you can use a simpler function:

> Floor = a **DIV** 1

Round(a) This function rounds a floating-point value to the nearest integer. The following works with positive and negative numbers:

> Round = a*(1 + 0.5/**ABS**(a)) **DIV** 1

If you're only dealing with positive numbers, then you can use a simpler function:

```
Round = (a + 0.5) DIV 1
```

IntegerDivide(a,b) Integer division is a built-in function called DIV, which returns a/b minus the remainder. For example, 5 DIV 2 = 2.

Remainder(a,b) This is a built-in function called REM, which returns the remainder of a/b.

```
Remainder = a REM b
```

For example, 5 REM 2 = 1. For negative values, this is different from the Modulus function (see Modulus).

Note The REM function returns only integer remainders.

Modulus(a,b) This function brings the value a into the range of the modulus base b. A common use of this function is to bring an integer angle into the range of 0 to 360. For positive values, this is the same as the Remainder function, Modulus(361, 360) = 1. But for negative values, the two differ. Modulus(−1, 360) = 359, but −1 REM 360 = −1. Here's the Modulus function that works for positive and negative numbers:

```
Modulus(a,b) = ( a REM b + b) REM b
```

Trunc(a) This function truncates the decimal portion off of floating-point values to create an integer:

```
Trunc = a DIV 1
```

Maximum(a,b) This function returns the larger of the two values a and b:

```
Maximum = (a + b + ABS(a - b))/2
```

Minimum(a,b) This function returns the smaller of the two values a and b:

```
Minimum = (a + b - ABS(a - b))/2
```

Exponential(a) This returns e^a. It's a built-in function:

```
Exponential = Exp(a)
```

NaturalLog(a) This returns the logarithm base e, where e is the Euler number (see Appendix A). This is a built-in function called Log:

```
NaturalLog = Log(a)
```

Log10(a) This returns the logarithm base 10:

> Log10 = **Log**(a)/**Log**(10)

LogN(n,a) This is the logarithm base n of a, $\log_n$ (a):

> LogN = **Log**(a)/**Log**(n)

Note Logarithm functions are only valid for positive values.

IsNaN(a) NaN means Not a Number. Certain calculations that are undefined can produce a NaN value, for instance, Log(–1). NaN has the property that using it in any math operation results in NaN. Use this function to test if a value is NaN or not (see IsInf for why this works):

> IsNaN = **NOT**(1/a - 1/a = 0)

Note When QuickTime converts a NaN value into a string, it becomes "NAN(036)" for undefined numbers and "NAN(001)" for complex numbers. This is useful to know when attempting to debug an algorithm.

IsInf(a) Returns true if a is infinite. Infinite values can arise from certain calculations. x/0 doesn't produce infinity as you might expect. Dividing by zero results in zero. Log(0), on the other hand, does return an infinite value. In QuickTime, we can use the fact that 1/infinity equals zero to determine if a value is infinite or not.

> IsInf = (1/a = 0 **AND NOT**(a + 1 > a))

(See the "Numerical Correction" section of Appendix E.)

You wouldn't use the above function to test if a track has an infinite duration. Tracks of infinite duration have a value of MAX_LONG (see Appendix A). So you would use

> IsTrackInfinite = (GetDuration = **MAX_LONG**)

SquareRoot(a) The square root function, called Sqr, is built in:

> SquareRoot = **Sqr**(a)

Note The square root of a negative number is an imaginary number that gets treated as NaN. See IsNaN.

NthRoot(n,a) To calculate the nth root of a value use

> **Exp**(1/n * **Log**(a))

Power(n,a) To calculate the nth power of a value use

> **Exp**(n * **Log**(a))

ASin(a) The inverse sine function returns an angle in radians:

ASin = **ArcTan**(x/**sqr**(1-x*x))

ACos(a) The inverse cosine function returns an angle in radians:

ACos = **PI**/2 - **ArcTan**(x/**sqr**(1-x*x))

Tangent(a) The tangent function is built in, Tan. It takes an angle in radians and returns the ratio of the lengths of opposite/adjacent sides of a right triangle.

Tangent = **Tan**(a)

Cosine(a) The cosine function is built in, Cos. It takes an angle in radians and returns the ratio of the lengths of the adjacent/hypotenuse sides of a right triangle.

Cosine = **Cos**(a)

Sine(a) The sine function is built in, Sin. It takes an angle in radians and returns the ratio of the lengths of the opposite/hypotenuse sides of a right triangle.

Sine = **Sin**(a)

Cotangent(a) The cotangent function is the reciprocal of the tangent function:

Cotangent = 1/**Tan**(a)

Sinh(a) The hyperbolic sine function:

Sinh = (**Exp**(a) - **Exp**(-a))/2

Cosh(a) The hyperbolic cosine function:

Cosh = (**Exp**(a) + **Exp**(-a))/2

tanh(a) The hyperbolic tangent function:

Tanh = (**Exp**(a) - **Exp**(-a))/(**Exp**(a) + **Exp**(-a))

Factorial(a) The factorial function, often symbolized as an exclamation mark (a!), is the sum of the integers from 1 to a. This function is commonly used in probability (such as combinatorial calculations), statistics, and physics equations. The function can obviously be calculated using a loop, but that's slow. Most uses of the function can make do with a faster approximation to the function using Stirling's formula, which also works with noninteger numbers:

```
Factorial = Exp(a*Log(a)-a)*Sqr(2*PI*a)*(1+1/12/a))
```

Simply rounding the above approximation will correct for the small deviations for integer input values.

Note With a slight modification, the above is also an approximation to the Gamma function, where Gamma(a) = Factorial(a − 1).

Gamma See Factorial.

Random See "Random Number Generation" in Appendix E.

Deg2Rad(a) To convert degrees to radians, use the simple scale factor of π/180, or approximately 0.0175 (or divide by 57.3). QuickTime also has a built-in function for this conversion:

```
Deg2Rad = DegreesToRadians(a)
```

Rad2Deg(a) To convert radians to degrees, use the simple scale factor of 180/π, or approximately 57.3 (57.2958 . . .). QuickTime also has a built-in function for this conversion:

```
Rad2Deg = RadiansToDegrees(a)
```

WeekDay(y,m,d) This function returns a number from 0 to 6 representing the weekday for a given calendar day: 0 represents Sunday, 1 Monday, . . . , and 6 Saturday. The input parameters are all indexed from 1, so January 2, 2003, would correspond to y = 2003, m = 1, and d = 2. This day corresponds to a Thursday, which should result in a WeekDay value of 4.

```
LocalVars y2, isLeapYear

y2 = y - 2001
y4 = y2 DIV 4

WeekDay = (y2 + y4 + (y4 = 0 AND m > 2) + SubString \
  ("0033614625035",m,1) + d ) REM 7
```

Notice the SubString function. Here we use string manipulation to serve as a lookup table. See Appendix C for string functions.

Note The above formula is intended for the years 2001 and on. The formula would need to be corrected slightly to work with older dates.

Rgb2Hsv(r,g,b) This converts a color in RGB format to HSV format. HSV stands for Hue, Saturation, and Value. The input values (r, g, and b) are assumed to be in the 0–255 range. To convert from QuickTime's standard 0–65535 range, simply divide each input by 257. The output parameters in this function are h, s, and v. h (hue) is an angle on the color wheel with values between 0 and 360. s (saturation) and v (value) each range between 0 and 100.

```
LocalVars maxGB, maxRGB, minRGB

maxGB = (g + b + ABS(g - b))/2

IF( r >= maxGB )
    maxRGB = r
    minRGB = (g + b - ABS(g - b))/2
    h = 60 * (g-b)/(maxRGB - minRGB)
ELSEIF( g >= maxGB )
    maxRGB = g
    minRGB = (r + b - ABS(r - b))/2
    h = 180 * (b-r)/(maxRGB - minRGB)
ELSE
    maxRGB = b
    minRGB = (r + g - ABS(r - g))/2
    h = 300 * (r-g)/(maxRGB - minRGB)
ENDIF

s = (maxRGB-minRGB)/maxRGB*100
v = maxRGB/2.55
```

Rgb2Luminance It's sometimes useful to know how bright a color will look to a normal observer. The following function converts an RGB color into a luminance value. The luminance value will be in the same range as the input values (for example, if the RGB range is 0–255, the luminance value will be between 0 and 255 as well):

```
Luminance = 0.3*r + 0.59*g + 0.11*b
```

Cart2Polar Use the following script to convert Cartesian coordinates (x, y) into polar coordinates (radius, angle):

```
radius = Sqr( x*x + y*y)
angle = ArcTan2( y, x )
```

Note The angle is measured in radians.

Polar2Cart Use the following script to convert polar coordinates (radius, angle) into Cartesian coordinates (x, y):

```
px = radius * Cos(angle)
y = radius * Sin(angle)
```

Note The angle is measured in radians.

Appendix C
String Functions

The following is a list of handy routines for manipulating strings in QScript. Input strings have variable names s1, s2, and so on. Other numeric input parameters are given letter names: a, b, c. . . . Output variables have the same name as the function unless otherwise specified. Functions that start with "Is," "Does," or "Has" return a Boolean value (TRUE/FALSE). Otherwise, functions return a number if the = operator is used and a string if the SetString action is used.

In QScript, string constants are created by placing characters inside of double quotes:

```
"this is a string"
```

The following special characters can be escaped when used inside of a string:

```
return      \r
tab         \t
quotes      \"
backslash   \\
```

For example, to specify a string with double quotes in it, use

```
"And the pig said \"Not by the hair on my chinny chin chin!\"."
```

Neither the tab character nor the return character need to be escaped. A \ followed by a return character, whether in a string or otherwise, means to ignore the return character. This is a way of breaking a long line of script into multiple lines.

Very long (< 32K) strings can be loaded from a file in the Library folder using

#StringFromFile("nameOfFile.txt")

To set a variable to a string, you must use the SetString action. For example:

LocalVars aString

SetString(aString, "hello")

To set variables to strings across movies, use the SetStringVariable(ID, value) action. Attempting to set a string using the = operator will treat the string as a number.

Local variables may be defined to hold intermediate values.

Concatenate(s1,s2) To concatenate two strings, use the built-in function StrConcat:

    SetString(Concatenate, **StrConcat**(s1, s2))

Extract(s1, start, length) To extract a section from a longer string, use the built-in function SubString. The start parameter indicates the first character to be extracted. In this case characters are indexed starting with zero. The length parameter defines how many characters to extract:

    SetString(Extract, **SubStr**(s1, start, length))

Note Using a length longer than the remaining characters in the string is the same as using a length equal to the number of remaining characters. Using a start value greater than the length of the string will cause this function to return an empty string.

IsEqual(s1, s2) To see if two strings are exactly equal, use the built-in StrCompare function:

    IsEqual = **StrCompare**(s1, s2, **TRUE, TRUE**)

To see if two strings are equal ignoring case and diacritical marks, use

    IsEqual = **StrCompare**(s1, s2, **FALSE, FALSE**)

The StrCompare takes the following four parameters:

    StrCompare(s1, s2, isCaseSensitive, isDiactriticalSensitive)

NumCharacters(s1) To determine how many characters a sting contains, use the built-in function StrLength:

    NumCharacters = **StrLength**(s1)

StartsWith(s1, s2) To test if s1 starts with the string s2, use

> **LocalVars** length2, preString
>
> length2 = **StrLength**(s2)
> **SetString**(preString, **SubString**(s2,0,length2))
> StartsWith = **StrCompare**(preString, s2)

Note This returns a Boolean value.

EndsWith(s1, s2) To test if s1 ends with the string s2, use

> **LocalVars** start, postString
>
> start = **StrLength**(s1) - **StrLength**(s2)
> **IF**(start < 0)
>   EndsWidth = **FALSE**
> **ELSE**
>   **SetString**(postString, **SubString**(s2,start,**MAX_LONG**))
>   StartsWith = **StrCompare**(postString, s2)
> **ENDIF**

Note This returns a Boolean value.

Insert(s1, s2, n) To insert s2 into s1 before the nth character (indexing from zero), use

> **LocalVars** preString, postString
>
> length2 = **StrLength**(s2)
> **SetString**(preString, **SubString**(s1,0,n))
> **SetString**(postString, **SubString**(s1,n, **MAX_LONG**))
> **SetString**(Insert, **StrConcat**(preString, **StrConcat**(s2, postString)))

For example: Input: s1, "12567"; s2, "34"; n, 2
              Output: "1234567"

Remove(s1, start, end) This function removes characters from the string s1 starting with index start to index end (both indexed from zero).

> **LocalVars** preString, postString
>
> **SetString**(preString, **SubString**(s1,0,start))
> **SetString**(postString, **SubString**(s2,end, **MAX_LONG**))
> **SetString**(Remove, **StrConcat**(preString, postString))

For example: Input: s1, "1234567"; start, 2; end, 3
              Output: "12567"

Trim(s1) This function removes spaces from the beginning and end of the string.

```
LocalVars length, start, end, isSpace, i
#define SPACE = " "

//find the first nonspace character:
length = StrLength(s1)
IF( length > 0 )
    end = length - 1
    FOR i = 0 TO (end)
        isSpace = StrCompare( $SPACE, SubString(s1,i,1), TRUE, TRUE)
        IF( NOT isSpace )
            start = i
            i = MAX_LONG //break
        ENDIF
    NEXT

//now find the last nonspace character
    FOR i = end DOWNTO start
        isSpace = StrCompare( $SPACE, SubString(s1,i,1), TRUE, TRUE)
        IF( NOT isSpace )
            end = i
            i = -1 //break
        ENDIF
    NEXT

    SetString(Trim, SubString(s1, start, end - start + 1))
ELSE
    SetString(Trim, "")
ENDIF
```

Find(s1, s2) This function checks to see if the string s1 exists within the larger string s2. If it does, this function returns the character offset (indexed from 0) for the substring. If s1 is not found in s2, –1 is returned. Find(s1,s2) > –1 can be used to return true if the string is found.

```
LocalVars length1, length2, part, i

#define CS = TRUE //case sensitive
#define DS = TRUE //diacritic sensitive
length1 = StrLength(s1)
length2 = StrLength(s2)
```

```
    IF( length1 = 0 )
        Find = -1 //can't look for an empty string
    ELSEIF( length1 < length2 )
        Find = -1
    ELSEIF( length1 = length2 )
        Find = StrCompare( s1, s2, $CS, $DS ) - 1
    ELSE
        Find = -1 //assume it won't be found
        FOR i = 0 TO (length2 - length1)
            SetString(part,SubString(s2,i,length1))
            IF( StrCompare(s1, part, $CS, $DS ) )
                Find = i
                i = MAX_LONG //break
            ENDIF
        NEXT
    ENDIF
```

Hex2Dec(s1) This converts a hexadecimal string into a decimal number.

```
    LocalVars length, char, isNum, place, i, j
    #define HEX = "abcdef"

    length = StrLength(s1)
    Hex2Dec = 0
    IF( length > 0 )
        place = 1
        FOR i = (length - 1) DOWNTO 0
            SetString(char, SubString(s1, i, 1))
            isNum = StrCompare( char, char + 0, FALSE, FALSE )
            IF( isNum = FALSE )
                FOR j = 0 TO 5
                    IF( StrCompare( char, SubStr($HEX, j, 1), FALSE, \
                        FALSE ))
                        char = 10 + j
                        j = MAX_LONG
                    ENDIF
                NEXT
            ENDIF
            Hex2Dec = Hex2Dec + place*char
            place = place * 16
        NEXT
    ENDIF
```

Example: "F5" --> 20

Appendix D
QTList Functions

This appendix presents some useful routines for working with QTLists. See Chapter 31 for an overview of QTLists and XML. The routines presented below target the movie's QTList by default (see the last entry for a method of making QTList routines generic in their target). Many of the routines take input parameters in the form of paths. These input parameters are named p1, p2, p3, and so on. Some routines take an XML input. Such input parameters are named xml.

GetNumChildren(p1) This function returns the number of child elements at the specified path. This uses the built-in function GetListElementCount.

    GetNumChildren = **GetListElementCount**(p1)

PathExists(p1) This function returns TRUE if an element exists at the specified path. FALSE is returned otherwise.

    LocalVars numChildren

    numChildren = -1
    numChildren = **GetListElementCount**(p1)

    PathExists = (numChildren >= 0)

InsertElement(p1, n, xml) This function makes a new element from the xml parameter and inserts it into the QTList at path p1 as index n. Elements are indexed from 1. This uses the built-in function LoadListFromXML. This assumes that the path p already exists. For a routine that creates a QTList structure from a path, see CreatePath.

    LoadListFromXML(p1, n, XML)

Note I like using this method better than `AddListElement` because it allows you to specify a value in the same action. For example:

```
LoadListFromXML("A.B",1,"<name>value</name>")
```

Otherwise you would have to call `SetListElement` to set the value. `LoadListFromXML` also allows you to specify attributes. There's no other way to add attributes to a list element than to load it from XML.

AddNewChild(p1, xml) This function adds a new child element at the specified path. The child element is added as the last index. The child element is specified by an XML string. This routine requires that the specified path exists. See `CreatePath` for a routine that makes sure all the elements in a path exist.

```
LocalVars numChildren

numChildren = -1
numChildren = GetListElementCount(p1)
IF( numChildren >= 0 )
    LoadListFromXML(p1,numChildren+1,xml)
ENDIF
```

CreatePath(p1) This function creates or makes sure that the specified path exists. It iterates through the path elements. If it doesn't find an element, it creates it. This script is on the long side because it needs to perform string parsing on the path.

```
LocalVars numChildren, length, i, nameStart, nameLength
LocalVars path, pathStart, lastPath, char, name

numChildren = -1
numChildren = GetListElementCount(p1)
IF( numChildren = -1 )
    //path doesn't already exist
    //append a "." to the end of the path
    SetString(path, StrConcat(p1,"."))
    length = StrLength(path) - 2
    nameStart = 0
    SetString(lastPath, "")
    FOR i = 0 TO length
        SetString(char, SubString(path,i,1))
        IF(StrCompare(char, ".", TRUE, TRUE))
            //It's a path separator
            SetString(partPath, SubString(path,0,i))
```

```
                      numChildren = -1
                      numChildren = GetListElementCount(partPath)
                      IF( numChildren = -1 )
                          //element doesn't exist
                          nameLength = i - nameStart
                          SetString(name, SubString(path,nameStart,nameLength))
                          numChildren = GetListElementCount(lastPath)
                          AddListElement(lastPath, numChildren+1, name)
                      ENDIF
                      SetString(lastPath, partPath)
                      nameStart = i + 1
               ENDIF
        NEXT
  ENDIF
```

Note This routine assumes a path in the `name.name` format. Paths that specify elements by index using the `name.index` format or the `name[index]` format are not guaranteed to work properly.

DeleteChildElement(p1, n) This function removes the child element at index n of the element at path p1. It uses the built-in `RemoveListElement` action, which takes a range of children. This routine modifies that slightly to simply remove a single child.

```
LocalVars numChildren

numChildren = -1
numChildren = GetListElementCount(p1)

IF( numChildren >= n )
    RemoveListElement(p1,n,n)
ENDIF
```

DeleteAllChildren(p1) This routine removes all the children of the element at the specified path.

```
LocalVars numChildren

numChildren = -1
numChildren = GetListElementCount(p1)

IF( numChildren > 0 )
    RemoveListElement(p1,1,numChildren)
ENDIF
```

CopyChildren(p1, p2) This routine copies all the children of the element at path p1, then adds them to the element at path p2. This assumes that the element at p2 exists. To make sure it exists, you can use the CreatePath routine. To copy the children, this routine converts the child elements to an XML string using the GetListAsXML(path, startIndex, endIndex) action.

```
LocalVars xmlCopy, numChildren

numChildren = -1
numChildren = GetListElementCount(p1)
IF( numChildren > 0 )
    SetString(xmlCopy, GetListAsXML(p1, 1, numChildren)
    numChildren = -1
    numChildren = GetListElementCount(p2)
    IF( numChildren >= 0 )
        LoadListFromXML(p2, numChildren + 1, xmlCopy)
    ENDIF
ENDIF
```

RenameChild(p1, n, newName) This routine renames the child at index n of the element at the path p1. To do this, it converts the child to XML, then uses string manipulation to change the name. It then converts the XML back into a QTList. The name of the root element in an XML string always appears twice when created from a QTList. For example:

```
<name></name>
```

The first name string starts with the second character and ends before either a space or a " > " character. The last name ends with the second-to-last character and starts after a "/" character. Using similar methods, you can determine the names of children (for some reason, there isn't a QTList function for that).

By doing a little more parsing, you can gain access to attributes and perform other advanced XML functions not currently made available by QTList functions.

```
LocalVars xmlCopy, numChildren, i, length
LocalVars nameStart, nameLength, char
LocalVars isSpace, xmlOffset, xmlLength

numChildren = -1
numChildren = GetListElementCount(p1)
IF( numChildren >= n )
    SetString(xmlCopy, GetListAsXML(p1,n,n))
    RemoveListElement(p1,n,n)
```

```
            length = StrLength(xmlCopy) - 1
            nameStart = 1
            FOR i = 2 TO length
                SetString(char, SubString(xmlCopy,i,1))
                isSpace = StrCompare(char," ",TRUE,TRUE)
                IF( isSpace OR StrCompare(char,">",TRUE,TRUE))
                    nameLength = i - nameStart
                    xmlOffset = i
                    i = MAX_LONG //break
                ENDIF
            NEXT
            xmlLength = length - xmlOffset - nameLength - 1
            //rebuild the xml string
            SetString(xmlCopy,SubString(xmlCopy,xmlOffset,xmlLength)
            SetString(xmlCopy,StrConcat(newName,xmlCopy))
            SetString(xmlCopy,StrConcat("<",xmlCopy))
            SetString(xmlCopy,StrConcat(xmlCopy, newName))
            SetString(xmlCopy,StrConcat(xmlCopy, ">"))
            //reinsert the child
            LoadListFromXML(p1,n,xmlCopy)
        ENDIF
```

Note Since this is a rather long script, I've included an example of its use in the Projects/Extras/RenameChild/ directory. The project is based on the QTListPractice project from Chapter 31.

GenericGetValue(target, path) This is an example of how to make a QTList routine able to dynamically target the different QTLists in a movie. The routine returns the value of the element at the given path. It specifies the target using a number. When the number is greater than 0, it targets the TrackOfIndex(targetIndex) QTList. A target of –1 specifies the movie's QTList. A value of –2 specifies the ThisEvent QTList.

```
#define MOVIE_LIST = -1
#define THISEVENT_LIST = -2

IF( target >= 0 )
    SetString(GenericGetValue, TrackOfIndex(target). \
      GetListElementValue(path))
ELSEIF( target = $MOVIE_LIST )
    SetString(GenericGetValue, GetListElementValue(path))
ELSEIF( target = $THISEVENT_LIST )
    SetString(GenericGetValue, ThisEvent.GetListElementValue(path))
ENDIF
```

Note that SetString is being used. This is because QTList elements hold string values. Setting the variable with the = operator would turn the value into a number.

This simple method can be applied to all of the routines in this appendix to make them more modular.

Appendix E
Programming Techniques

This appendix discusses several ways to apply standard programming techniques to QuickTime. Also discussed are techniques unique to wired sprites.

▶ Spatial Programming

When computer programmers set out to build a wired movie, they usually approach the problem like they do any other programming language such as C or Java. I've found that artists, on the other hand, tend to build the movie as if they were constructing a physical machine. This is obviously a generalization, but my point is that there are two approaches to programming wired sprites: the analytical and the spatial. Here I'd like to illustrate some ways to approach programming in a spatial way.

Sprites have many of the characteristics of physical objects. You can move them around, rotate them, stretch them, and touch them (through mouse events and SpriteAtPoint calls). When you rotate a sprite, you aren't just updating a numerical property, you are changing the way the sprite appears on the screen; and other properties, such as the bounds and the corners, will instantly reflect the changes caused by the rotation. We can take advantage of this aspect of sprites when programming. For example, before version 5, QuickTime didn't support trig functions. Many programmers resorted to storing trig tables, or using Taylor expansions to approximate the sine, cosine, and tangent functions, but that was neither efficient nor accurate. The most accurate and efficient way to perform these calculations at the time was to use a sprite like a protractor and spatially perform the trig calculation (see Figure E.1).

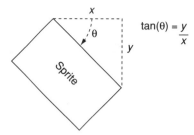

Figure E.1 A sprite as a protractor.

If you rotate a sprite by a specified angle, the ratio of the vertical and horizontal distances between the first and second corners is the definition of the tangent function for that angle. Similarly, the sine, cosine, and other functions can be calculated using this kind of spatial approach.

The techniques for cel-based animation discussed in Chapter 11 are good examples of spatial approaches to programming. In that chapter we learned ways to capture information inside of images. These techniques were also used in later chapters, such as the construction of sliders in Chapter 18.

Many examples of spatial programming can be seen in the Solitaire movie presented in Chapter 10. In that game, each card is represented by a sprite. Shuffling amounts to randomizing the layers of the card sprites. When you click on the deck, three cards turn over. The way the movie determines which cards to turn over is by utilizing SpriteAtPoint to find which (if any) sprite is currently positioned over the card well. If a sprite is there, it's moved over using the MoveBy action and flipped to show the face side using SetImageIndex. This is repeated three times. The movie doesn't have to maintain separate data structures describing the state of the deck like programmers usually do when building a card game. All the information is already contained in the spatial properties of each card sprite. Using sprites in this way is not only efficient but also intuitive because that's how a real physical game of solitaire works.

▶ Breaking a Loop

QScript doesn't have a break statement, but, using some simple tricks, you can effectively break out of FOR and WHILE loops. When working with FOR loops, simply set the iterator to a value outside the range of the loop. For example:

```
LocalVars i

FOR i = 1 TO 100
    IF( shouldBreak )
        i = 101
    ELSE
        ...
    ENDIF
NEXT
```

Just be sure you set the iterator outside of the range in the correct direction. The above break wouldn't work if the FOR loop was iterating from 100 down to 1 (using the DOWNTO or NEXT −1 construct).

With WHILE loops, you want to make the conditional evaluate to false. There are usually ways to do it in an efficient way, but the following will work in general:

```
LocalVars breakWhile

breakWhile = FALSE

WHILE( (condition_statement) AND NOT breakWhile )
    IF( shouldBreak )
        breakWhile = TRUE
    ELSE
        ....
    ENDIF
ENDWHILE
```

Exception Handling and Error Detection

A very nice addition to the QuickTime wired architecture would be a robust way to catch and handle errors and exceptions. Currently, the best way I've found to detect errors is the "unchanging variable" technique introduced in Chapter 32. This technique utilizes the fact that when an error occurs while executing a line of QScript, QuickTime simply ignores that line and moves on. If a variable is set during that line, then the error will result in the variable being unchanged. Taking advantage of this behavior can be tricky at times, but it's quite effective when used correctly. Let's look at an example.

Say you wanted to determine if the first track in a movie is a sprite track or not. QuickTime doesn't provide a track property that indicates its type. However, using the unchanging variable technique, it's possible to get around this limitation. What we can do is set a variable to –1, then set that same variable to the NumSprites property of the first track. Getting the Num-Sprites property on anything but a sprite track will result in an error, causing the variable to remain –1. Otherwise, NumSprites would return at least 0 for a valid sprite track. So by checking if the variable has changed, we can determine if the track is a sprite track or not. Here's a script that does this:

```
LocalVars testVariable

testVariable = -1
testVariable = TrackOfIndex(1).NumSprites
IF( testVariable = -1 )
    //not a sprite track
ELSE
    //It is a sprite track
ENDIF
```

▶ Functions, Methods, and Subroutines

Reusable functions, methods, and subroutines are a staple of modern programming. Subroutines are implemented in QuickTime through the use of custom events. Functions and methods, which take input parameters and return a result, are built on top of custom events as well. Object-oriented programmers will gasp, but the current way to "pass" parameters into and out of a custom event is through some sort of global variable. This was discussed at length in Chapter 9, but I'd like to add a few points.

Calling Functions across Tracks and Movies

When calling functions within a sprite track, I've found it best to use GlobalVars as a way to provide input parameters and receive output parameters. However, it's often useful to be able to call functions across tracks and even across movies. For that, MovieVars are an obvious alternative to GlobalVars. This works fine for the most part, but there are three main limitations to using MovieVars. The first is the task of keeping the variable IDs in synch. When you define a MovieVar that will be called across tracks or movies, you need to give it an ID. MovieVars with the same name can refer to completely different variables if they don't have the same ID. A second but related limitation is that setting variables across movies is done by ID and not by name. This can make scripts hard to read. The third limitation is that MovieVars, the way LiveStage has implemented them, require a separate track (called "Movie Variables"). It's sometimes the case that you will want to create a reusable sprite track and somehow provide functions that can be called from outside of the track. In this case requiring a separate track to hold MovieVars is not feasible.

A possible solution is to go back to the spatial approach to programming wired movies discussed earlier. Say you wanted to provide a reusable sprite track that functioned as a volume knob. You might want to allow the knob to be able to control the volume of any track, in a dynamically configurable way. The object-oriented approach might be to have a method called SetTargetTrack that would take the target track's index as a parameter. One way to supply such a parameter to a sprite track is through a "parameter sprite." Don't laugh. This is a completely valid and useful approach. Just as you might provide a slider as a user interface element, an invisible slider can also be used behind the scenes to provide a way for sprite tracks to communicate with each other. In this case, our volume knob track might have an invisible and nonclickable sprite named TargetTrack. In order to configure the knob to control the volume of track 7, you could simply set the x position of the TargetTrack sprite to 7:

```
TrackNamed("VolumeKnob").SpriteNamed("TargetTrack").MoveTo(7,0)
```

This solves all the limitations of using MovieVars discussed earlier. Since the parameter sprite can be referenced by name, there aren't any ID synchronization issues. The parameter sprite also allows the sprite track to be self-contained without the need for a Movie Variables track.

▶ Recursion

Recursion is a common programming construct. In essence, recursion is where a function calls itself. QuickTime handles recursion of events just fine. The only problem is that recursion algorithms usually require "true" local variables that are scoped to each function invocation. LiveStage's LocalVars are not truly local. A LocalVar can only be targeted from within the local script, but the same variable is used every time the script is executed. This means that LocalVars are the same as global variables when recursion is used. So, how do you do recursion with wired actions? Use QTLists.

Each execution of an event has its own local (truly local) QTList. This QTList is accessed through the ThisEvent target. The ThisEvent QTList can be used as a local variables space and is appropriate for recursive algorithms.

To illustrate how to use ThisEvent QTLists as local variables, here are two script sniplets that perform the same simple calculation. The first uses LocalVars, and the second uses ThisEvent QTLists:

```
LocalVars a, b
a = 10
b = a + 42

ThisEvent.AddListElement("",1,"a")
ThisEvent.AddListElement("",1,"b")
ThisEvent.SetListElement("a", 10)
ThisEvent.SetListElement("b", ThisEvent.GetListElementValue("a") + 42)
```

▶ Numerical Correction

Computers don't represent all numbers perfectly precisely. For this reason, errors can crop up when doing even simple arithmetic. It's important to know that such errors exist. The good news is that they can often be corrected. Since this is an extensive topic, we can't cover all the types of errors and how to correct everything, but we can discuss a few examples.

Floating-Point Precision

One common source of error is often called roundoff error. It results from the fact that floating-point numbers represented in decimal aren't always precisely represented in binary. Take, for example, the following script:

```
LocalVars x, i

x = 0.1 + 0.1 + 0.1 + 0.1 + 0.1 + 0.1 + 0.1

IF( x = 0.7 )
    DebugStr("Equal")
ELSE
    DebugStr("Not Equal")
ENDIF
```

Here the variable x is set to the number 0.1 added seven times. That should equal 0.7, so you might think that the above script would output "Equal" to the debug console. What actually happens is that "Not Equal" is sent to the console. That's because in the binary representation, the sum of seven 0.1's is not exactly equal to 0.7, but rather 0.700000062. This can be dangerous. For instance, looping until a variable equals an expected value can turn into an infinite loop if you aren't careful.

How to correct roundoff errors? The short answer is that there isn't a simple solution that will fix all roundoff errors. However, for a particular situation, there is often a solution. One solution is to realize that the errors exist and put up with them by not checking for equality but checking if a number is within a certain range. For instance, the above IF statement might work better as follows:

```
IF( ABS( x - 0.7 ) < 0.01 )
    DebugStr("Equal")
...
```

Here x is considered equal to 0.7 if the difference between x and 0.7 is less than 0.01. The range of equality used obviously depends on the particular application, but using ranges instead of checking for exact equality is usually an acceptable solution.

Another solution is to change the calculations to employ mostly integer arithmetic. In the case of the above example, instead of adding 0.1 seven times, you can add 1 seven times and then at the end divide by 10. For example:

```
x = 1 + 1 + 1 + 1 + 1 + 1 + 1

x = x / 10

IF( x = 0.7 )
    DebugStr("Equals")
ENDIF
```

This is obviously not a real-world example, but the point is that integer arithmetic is more precise than calculations with floating-point numbers. The above script will output "Equals" to the console.

Dividing by Zero (Epsilon Correction)

A positive number divided by zero equals infinity. Infinity, needless to say, is often best represented by a very large number. However, in QuickTime, dividing a number by zero equals zero. Another issue with dividing by zero is evaluating equations that have nice limits at zero. Take the following script:

LocalVars x, r

```
x = 0
r =  Sin(x) / x
```

What would you expect the r variable to equal? Since sin(0) is 0, the above calculation amounts to 0/0. Zero divided by zero is an undefined number and can be different values for different equations. The way to find out is to have x approach 0 and extrapolate what sin(x)/x is as x gets very close to 0 (called the limit). At the limit, sin(0)/0 is equal to 1. Therefore, you would probably want the above calculation of r to equal 1, but QuickTime evaluates it as zero.

These issues with dividing by zero can easily be corrected through what is sometimes termed *epsilon correction.* Epsilon is the smallest representable number. Adding epsilon to another number effectively leaves that number unchanged, but when added to zero, it changes it just enough to fix the division problems discussed above. There are ways to determine the correct epsilon to use on different platforms, but since QuickTime seems to cast numbers to different precisions under different situations, I've ended up just using 0.000001 as a crude approximation to epsilon. For me, this number usually works well. Here's how it works:

When there's a possibility of dividing by 0, simply offset the denominator by epsilon:

LocalVars a, b, c, epsilon

```
epsilon = 0.000001

a = 10
b = 0

c = a / (b + epsilon)
```

Here c will equal 10 million, which is a large number. Obviously nowhere close to infinity, but depending on the application, 10 million might be as close to infinity as you need (but don't tell that to Buzz Lightyear).

For calculations that approach a stable value as a parameter approaches zero, adding epsilon will help. Modifying the Sin(x)/x example discussed earlier, we get

```
LocalVars x, epsilon, r

x = 0
epsilon = 0.000001
x = x + epsilon
r = Sin(x) / x
```

Here r will be 1 as expected by the limit.

Random Number Generation

QuickTime provides a function to generate a random number (technically pseudorandom because it's generated through a predictive algorithm). The function takes two numbers that define the range from which a random integer is generated:

```
n = Random( start, end)
```

Calling Random(0,100) will generate a random integer in the inclusive range of 0 to 100. To generate a floating-point number, simply use something like

```
f = Random(0,10000)/10000
```

This will produce a random number between 0 and 1.

Randomized Boolean (TRUE/FALSE) values can be generated using Random(FALSE,TRUE). On average, this will generate TRUE 50% of the time and FALSE the rest of the time. Sometimes you might want to skew the distribution such that TRUE is generated with a different probability. The following script generates TRUE 20% of the time:

```
LocalVars probability, boolean

#define RESOLUTION = 10000

probability = 20/100

boolean = Random(0,$RESOLUTION) > probability * $RESOLUTION
```

Before QuickTime 6, the Random function would produce the same sequence of numbers each time the movie played. This wasn't very good for movies that were supposed to do something different each time they ran. For that reason, I created my own random number generator that works within the constraints of QScript. In QuickTime 6, however, a new action was created to change the seed of QuickTime's internal random number generator.

A random number generator usually just produces one very long sequence of numbers that are nicely distributed and where the next number generated is not easily predicted by the previous numbers. Starting from the beginning of the sequence will produce one series of numbers. To get a different series of numbers, you simply start at different locations in the larger sequence. Where you start is called the *seed*. QuickTime has a SetRandomSeed(number) function that allows you to specify a particular seed. This is good for resetting the random number generator, but it isn't good for producing a reproducible sequence of numbers. Calling SetRandomSeed(982) will cause the generator to produce one sequence of numbers, but later if you call SetRandomSeed(982) again, you won't get the same sequence you obtained before (as you would expect from normal random number generators). This is acceptable behavior for most applications, but if you want more control over the generation process, it isn't that difficult to make your own random number generator.

Custom Random Generator

The standard random number algorithm looks like

n = (A*n + B) **REM** C

Every time you call the function, n is passed in and a new "random" n is generated between 0 and C. To produce a "nice" distribution of numbers, it's important to choose good values for A, B, and C. See the RandomManager behavior in the Projects/Extras/RandomManager/ folder for a discussion of how to choose good parameters for QuickTime. For an example use of this behavior, have a look at the Solitaire project (Projects/Chapter10/Solitaire/).

▶ Dictionaries and Lists

Dictionaries and lists are two commonly used data structures. Dictionaries hold key-value pairs. You can place a value into a dictionary with a certain key and later retrieve it with the key. Lists, also known as vectors, store an ordered sequence of values. Lists, unlike fixed-sized arrays, are expandable. New items can be added and removed from the list dynamically.

In QuickTime, dictionaries and lists can be implemented using QTLists (see Appendix D for more information). A Flash track can also serve as a dictionary. SetFlashVariable can add a key-value pair to the Flash track:

```
SetFlashVariable("", key, value, FALSE)
```

Later the value can be retrieved using

```
GetFlashVariable( "", key )
```

Debugging

When computer programming is involved, debugging always seems to follow. This is true for beginners and veterans alike. I'd like to point out a few ways to aid in debugging a wired movie.

DebugStr

The DebugStr action is a simple way to get a glimpse at what is happening while a movie is running. The DebugStr action outputs a string to the debugging console. You can use it to show the value of a certain variable, or to display simple messages, such as errors or success indicators. DebugStr is a straightforward action, but if you don't know how it works, you can get yourself in trouble. Here are a couple oddities you should know about.

First, numbers get truncated. When a variable with a number value is passed into the DebugStr action, it will be truncated to three decimal places. For example:

```
LocalVars n
```

```
n = 1.0001
DebugStr(n)
```

Executing the above script results in the following output to the console:

```
1.000
```

Problems could arise as a result of n not being exactly 1, but when debugging, you might not notice that problem because the output gets truncated. To fix this problem, I usually multiply by 1 followed by as many zeros as I want to see. For example:

```
LocalVars n

n = 1.0001
DebugStr(n * 10000)
```

Then just remember to move the decimal places over when looking at the number in the console. You can also do some string manipulation to make the output look pretty, but for debugging purposes, it isn't worth it.

Second, strings are also truncated. The DebugStr will only output the first 255 characters of a string. To fix this, use the SubString action to output the string in multiple chunks.

Third, you need a debugging console. One drawback to the DebugStr action is that a debugging console isn't always available everywhere QuickTime movies can run. Sometimes a problem might be limited to a particular playback environment. When this happens, I usually add a text track to the movie and then output debugging messages there.

Finally, LiveStage Pro doesn't provide a way of tracing through scripts, but it does have a feature that can get you close to this functionality. At any point in a script, you can add a #debug on statement to instruct LiveStage to start outputting each executed line of QScript to the console. Take the following script, for example:

```
MoveBy(-10,10)
IF( BoundsLeft > 10 )
    #debug on
    SetVisible(FALSE)
    #debug off
ELSE
    SetVisible(TRUE)
ENDIF
```

Here SetVisible(FALSE) will be sent to the console when the IF statement evaluates to TRUE. This is one way to see the flow execution.

▶ Profiling

If it takes 2 seconds to walk out of your house, and 20 minutes to walk to the store, doubling the speed at which you leave your house isn't going to noticeably improve the amount of time it takes to get to the store. This is an obvious point, but I often have to remind myself of this when trying to optimize the performance of a movie.

The best way to improve the performance of a movie is to find which aspect is decreasing performance the most. This is called profiling. Since we don't have the source code to QuickTime, this can be difficult to do at times. One technique that I use is to simply measure how much time is spent in each script. The following script has some profiling code in it to store how many times it gets executed and how much time is spent executing it:

```
[EventA]
GlobalVars EventATicks, EventAHits
LocalVars startTicks

startTicks = TickCount
EventAHits = EventAHits + 1

//the normal script here
..
..

EventATicks = EventATicks + TickCount - startTicks
```

If you add this code to the largest scripts in a movie, at some point you can then output how many times each script was executed (hits) and how many total ticks were spent executing the script. Unfortunately, TickCount is the best time measurement available to wired movies. It only has a resolution of 1/60th of a second. Most scripts won't take many (if any) ticks to execute, so the execution time measurement won't be very accurate. I have this old 100 MHz machine that I keep around. On a slow machine you can get a much better measurement of execution time.

▶ Lazy Constructors

One underused optimization technique is the lazy constructor. It doesn't sound very "optimized," but it's a way to decrease the amount of things a movie has to do when it first starts up. The first impression someone will have of your movie is how quickly it starts up. Movies that do lots of calculations on Frame Loaded scripts tend to be sluggish starters. When a movie first starts, it is already taking up lots of processor resources to load the media, allocate RAM, and get everything "situated." At that time, script execution performance is at its worst.

Wired movies usually have setup code that needs to be executed before other scripts can execute properly. For example, consider a movie that uses a QTList structure. Before list values can be set and retrieved, the list elements need to first be added and initialized (using AddListElement). Instead of rushing and setting up the list structure right away, let the scripts be a little lazier and only set up the QTList when it's needed. Create a custom event called SetUpQTList and define a variable called IsQTListReady. Then right before the QTList structure needs to be used in a script, simply check if it's ready. If it's not, call the SetUpQTList event. Then continue with the script.

Parallel Processing

Wired movies are single-threaded processes. Only one script can be executed at a time. Because of this, scripts that take a long time can cause the movie to pause and act sluggish and unresponsive. One way to get around this is to simulate a multithreaded process by breaking a long script into multiple parts executed on an Idle event. As we saw in Chapter 15, sprites can be deleted and restored as an efficient way to turn specific Idle event scripts on and off. Let's look at an example.

Say you want to find out how many times a space appears in a long string. This can be accomplished through the following script:

```
SpriteVars theString, spaceCount
LocalVars i, numChars, char

#define SPACE = " "
numChars = StrLength( theString )

spaceCount = 0
FOR i = 1 TO numChars
    char = SubString( theString, i-1, 1)
    IF( StrCompare(char, $SPACE, TRUE, TRUE) )
        spaceCount = spaceCount + 1
    ENDIF
NEXT
```

This will work fine, but if the string is very long, this script will take a while to finish. While the script is executing, no mouse events or any other event can take place in any QuickTime movie running within the same playback application. Let's see how this can be accomplished across multiple Idle events:

```
[StartProcessing]
SpriteVars theString, processingString, spaceCount, charIndex
SpriteVars numChars

IF( processingString != TRUE )
    processingString = TRUE
    charIndex = 0
    spaceCount = 0
    ExecuteEvent($NextChar)
ENDIF

[FinishedProcessing]
SpriteVars processingString

processingString = FALSE

[NextChar]
SpriteVars theString, processingString, spaceCount, charIndex
SpriteVars numChars
LocalVars char

#define SPACE = " "
char = SubString(theString, charIndex, 1)
IF( StrCompare( char, $SPACE, TRUE, TRUE ))
    spaceCount = spaceCount + 1
ENDIF
charIndex = charIndex + 1
IF( charIndex >= numChars )
    ExecuteEvent($FinishedProcessing)
ENDIF

[Idle]
SpriteVars theString, processingString, spaceCount, charIndex
SpriteVars numChars

IF( ProcessingString )
    ExecuteEvent( $NextChar )
ENDIF
```

The "parallel" process of looking through the string is triggered by calling the $StartProcessing event. This initializes some variables and sets the processingString flag to TRUE. While TRUE, the Idle event calls $NextChar, which checks a new character. Once the full length of the string has been checked, the $FinishProcessing event is called and the processingString flag is set to FALSE.

This is a good template for implementing a parallel process. Multiple sprites can have the same code and essentially process multiple strings at the same time. Other events can also determine if the process is in progress by checking the processingString flag.

Sustainable Hacking

A computer hack is where you get something to work in a way that it wasn't meant to work. When pushing the envelope of an environment, some amount of hacking is inevitable, and it's acceptable as long as it's sustainable. By "sustainable," I mean it doesn't completely rely on some bug or quirk that is bound to be fixed and thus break the functionality of the hack.

If you are gaining functionality out of a possible bug, it's a good idea to anticipate what will change when that bug is fixed. A good example is the method used to test if a URL-loaded image has completed its download or not. This was discussed in Chapter 37. We used the fact that in the current versions of QuickTime, when a URL-loaded image is in the process of downloading, its height is 11,780 pixels. The QuickTime engineers probably didn't design it to explicitly be 11,780 pixels tall; it's likely just a side effect of the way it's implemented. The more intuitive height of an image that hasn't downloaded yet is zero, and so a reasonable guess is that in some future version of QuickTime, downloading-in-progress movies will have a height of 0 and not 11,780. For this reason, our image downloading algorithm checked for a height of 0 or 11,780.

Dynamic Script Evaluation

Many scripting languages have a way of dynamically parsing a string and evaluating it as a script. Hypercard was one of the earliest languages to do this through the doScript function. JavaScript has an eval function. There is no equivalent for QScript, but it's possible to build a QScript parser in QScript. For an example of this, see the QTParser project (Projects/Extras/QTParser/).

▶ Collaboration

Here are three tips to make it easier for multiple developers to work on the same QuickTime project:

1. Use a code server: It's relatively easy to set up a code server. The most common type is a CVS (concurrent versions system) server. There are free versions out there and free easy-to-use clients for Mac and Windows (www.wincvs.org). A CVS server not only stores a project directory on the server, but also keeps tracks of every version that gets checked in (the history of the project). It also knows how to merge certain types of files, including XML files, and integrate changes from multiple developers. The trick to using CVS with LiveStage projects is to save the project as XML (choose File > Export > XML).

2. Use behaviors: Along with using a CVS server, it's helpful to break scripts (especially long scripts) into behaviors. LiveStage behaviors are simply text files that can contain multiple scripts for a single sprite. This is also good for modularity and reusability since multiple sprites can use the same behavior. Behavior files are easier to manage and merge changes if multiple developers are modifying the same scripts at the same time.

3. Use movie tracks: In Chapter 28 we discussed how movie tracks work. Even without a CVS server, large projects can often be broken into multiple parts (movies). One developer can work on one movie while another developer works on a different movie. The movies can then be integrated either through the use of movie tracks or by simply dragging the movies into LiveStage Pro. LiveStage Pro can integrate tracks from external movies (just make sure you close and reopen the project when the source movie changes).

Appendix F
Sprite and Track Geometry

This appendix covers basic geometry principles useful when authoring wired QuickTime. The emphasis here is on the 2D geometry of sprites and visual tracks, but general geometric concepts are also discussed.

▶ Coordinate System

distance units QuickTime uses a standard computer graphics 2D Cartesian coordinate system with distances measured in pixels. Even though it is pixel-based, QuickTime can render fractions of a pixel just fine. For example, calling MoveBy(0.1,0) ten times will move the sprite to the same position as calling MoveBy(1,0) one time.

Note In theory it's OK to scale a sprite or a track to dimensions less than a pixel, but be careful. Scaling a track or a sprite too small (smaller than 1 x 1) can cause a QuickTime movie to suddenly close on Windows platforms.

nested spaces Spatial operations on objects always take place in the local coordinate system, which could be different from the parent system. For instance, calling MoveBy(10.5,0) on a sprite will always move the sprite to the right 10.5 pixels in the sprite track's local space. But if the sprite track is rotated by 90 degrees and scaled to double its normal size, then MoveBy (10.5,0) will result in the sprite moving downwards by 21 pixels in the movie's coordinate system. If the movie itself is also scaled to double in size, then on the screen the sprite will move downwards by 42 pixels.

origin definition The origin defines the (0,0) point in a given coordinate space. The origin of a sprite is defined by the registration point of the image displayed by the sprite at that time. The origin of tracks and movies always corresponds to the top-left corner.

direction of rotation In QuickTime, positive angles rotate objects in a clockwise direction.

Spatial Properties

As you can see from Figure F.1, sprites have many more spatial properties than tracks. Nevertheless, sprites are still missing some important properties, namely, the rotation angle and the scale factor. A sprite's rotation and scale can be estimated as follows:

rotation angle The rotation angle be estimated by finding the angle between the second corner and the first corner. If the sprite is simply rotated and not stretched in some strange way, this will, in fact, be the rotation angle. Otherwise it'll serve as a reasonable estimate of the rotation state. Here's a script:

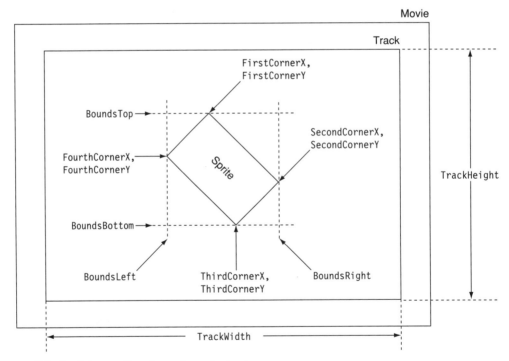

Figure F.1   Spatial properties of a sprite and a track.

```
SpriteVars rotationAngle
LocalVars deltaX, deltaY

deltaX = SecondCornerX - FirstCornerX
deltaY = SecondCornerY - FirstCornerY
rotationAngle = ArcTan2(deltaY, deltaX)
```

This can be simplified into one line:

```
SpriteVars rotationAngle

rotationAngle = ArcTan2(SecondCornerY - FirstCornerY, \
  SecondCornerX - FirstCornerX)
```

scale Calculating the scale (magnification) of a sprite is a little more complicated. To calculate the horizontal scale of a sprite, you start by finding the distance between the first and second corners of the sprite. You then need to reset the sprite's matrix and compare that distance with the width of the sprite under normal untransformed conditions. The following script caches the positions of a sprite's four corners, calculates the length of the edges of the sprite, then resets the sprite, calculates the width and height, then restores the sprite to its original cached state:

```
SpriteVars horizontalScale, verticalScale
LocalVars x1, x2, x3, x4, y1, y2, y3, y4
localVars deltaX, deltaY, width, height
LocalVars topEdgeLength, leftEdgeLength

x1 = FirstCornerX
y1 = FirstCornerY
x2 = SecondCornerX
y2 = SecondCornerY
x3 = ThirdCornerX
y3 = ThirdCornerY
x4 = FourthCornerX
y4 = FourthCornerY

deltaX = x2 - x1
deltaY = y2 - y1
topEdgeLength = Sqr( deltaX * deltaX + deltaY * deltaY )

deltaX = x4 - x1
deltaY = y4 - y1
leftEdgeLength = Sqr( deltaX * deltaX + deltaY * deltaY )
```

```
ResetMatrix
```

```
width = (BoundsRight - BoundsLeft)
height = (BoundsBottom - BoundsTop)
horizontalScale = topEdgeLength / width
verticalScale = leftEdgeLength / height
```

```
Stretch(x1, y1, x2, y2, x3, y3, x4, y4)
```

▶ Distance between Two Tracks

It's often necessary to calculate the distance between two spatial tracks. This is theoretically easy, but the problem is that QuickTime doesn't provide properties to determine the location of a track. Since the mouse location, obtained by using the MouseHorizontal and MouseVertical properties, is relative to the track's origin, these properties can be used to calculate the distance between two tracks (as long as they aren't scaled, rotated, or stretched in some way):

```
HorizontalDistance = TrackOfIndex(B).MouseHorizontal - \
   TrackOfIndex(A).MouseHorizontal
VerticalDistance = TrackOfIndex(B).MouseVertical - \
   TrackOfIndex(A).MouseVertical
```

This will even work with tracks from two different movies. In this way, the above method can also be used to estimate the distance between two movies. See Chapter 38 for an example.

▶ 2.5 Dimensions

QuickTime spatial objects (sprites and tracks) are, for the most part, two-dimensional. But they have some inkling of a third dimension through the Layer property. Spatial objects can be moved behind other spatial objects in the same container (tracks in the same movie, or sprites in the same track) by increasing their Layer property. Decreasing the Layer property brings objects farther in front. Changing the layer doesn't change the size or the perspective of an object like a real third dimension would. It simply determines the order that spatial objects draw to the screen. Some have designated this as half of a dimension, thus making QuickTime movies and sprite tracks 2.5-dimensional systems.

Screen Updates

After a QuickTime object undergoes a spatial transformation, the effects of the transformation aren't visible until the screen is updated. It's important to note that QuickTime updates the screen differently for different types of objects. For tracks and movies, the screen is updated immediately after each spatial transformation. On the other hand, spatial transformations applied to sprites aren't drawn to the screen until all currently running scripts have finished executing. For this reason, moving a sprite to the right and then down in two steps during the same script looks like it has simply moved diagonally in one step. However, moving a track to the right and then down will force a screen update after each step so that you'll actually see the track move to the right and then down.

Matrix Transformations

The standard 2D transforms found in most graphical systems can be represented by a 3 x 3 grid of numbers called a transformation matrix:

$$\begin{bmatrix} a & b & u \\ c & d & v \\ e & f & w \end{bmatrix}$$

The matrix transformation is applied to points through matrix multiplication. I should note that QuickTime uses postmultiplication as opposed to the premultiplication found in most textbooks:

$$[x_2\ y_2\ w_2] = [x_1\ y_1\ w_1] \times \begin{bmatrix} a & b & u \\ c & d & v \\ e & f & w \end{bmatrix}$$

This matrix multiplication is simply shorthand for the following calculations:

x2 = x1 * a + y1 * c + w1 * e
y2 = x1 * b + y1 * d + w1 * f
w2 = x1 * u + y1 * v + w1 * w

The w values are usually set to 1.

Technically, this transform is called a *projective transform*. It can arbitrarily stretch an object (sprite or track) into a variety of convex four-sided polygon shapes (quadrilaterals). When transforming into odd-shaped quadrilaterals, it's usually easier to work with the Stretch action, which allows the four corners to be positioned independently (see Chapter 14). However, there is a subset of projective transformations that are commonly used and nicely represented in their matrix form. Transforms in that subset are called *affine transforms* and are obtained by simply setting u and v to zero and the w weighting values to 1:

$$[x'\ y'\ 1] = [x\ y\ 1] \times \begin{bmatrix} a & b & 0 \\ c & d & 0 \\ e & f & 1 \end{bmatrix}$$

This affine matrix multiplication is shorthand for the following calculations:

$x2 = x1 * a + y1 * c + e$
$y2 = x1 * b + y1 * d + f$

The special thing about affine transforms is that they limit the group of quadrilateral stretches to parallelograms. This means that after an affine transform, the left side of an object will remain parallel to the right side. The top will remain parallel to the bottom. Examples of affine transforms include rotating, scaling, translating, and shearing.

In QScript arbitrary matrix transformations can be applied to sprites and tracks through the action

SetMatrixTo(a,b,u,c,d,v,e,f,w)

For affine transformations, this becomes

SetMatrixTo(a,b,0,c,d,0,e,f,16384)

Notice that the third and sixth parameters (u and v) are zero and the last parameter is the number 16384. Because of a quirk in the way this wired action was implemented, 16384 in the last parameter will actually be interpreted as a 1 when the matrix transformation is applied.

Note Be aware that the 16384 "quirk" might be fixed in a future version of LiveStage, so be ready to replace 16384 with 1 if needed.

The SetMatrixTo action will replace a sprite or track's current matrix with the supplied transform. A second action, SetMatrixBy, will apply the new transform on top of any transforms the sprite might have already undergone. SetMatrixBy takes the same set of parameters:

SetMatrixBy(a,b,0,c,d,0,e,f,16384)

Note An important point to make is that both the `SetMatrixBy` and `SetMatrixTo` actions only take constant values. Nevertheless, even a constant matrix transform comes in handy. Hopefully the matrix calls will become more dynamic in a future release of QuickTime.

Let's take a look at some common matrix transformations:

identity matrix The identity matrix transform leaves a spatial state unchanged. It's just like how multiplying a number by 1 doesn't change the number. Here's what the identity matrix looks like:

$$\begin{bmatrix} 1 & 0 & 0 \\ 0 & 1 & 0 \\ 0 & 0 & 1 \end{bmatrix}$$

If you apply this transform to an object using `SetMatrixTo`, that object will revert to its natural size and position and lose any other spatial transformations. This is done by calling

SetMatrixTo(1,0,0,0,1,0,0,0,16384)

For instance, if a sprite was rotated, setting its transform to the identity matrix would unrotate it. On the other hand, calling `SetMatrixBy` with the identity matrix would have no effect on the sprite's spatial state. In QScript the above call has been wrapped into a more convenient action called `ResetMatrix`.

translation matrix The `MoveTo` and `MoveBy` actions used all the time for moving sprites around can also be expressed as `SetMatrixTo` and `SetMatrixBy` actions. The following matrix translates a sprite by (or "to" depending on the action used) `OffsetX` in the *x* direction and `OffsetY` in the *y* direction:

$$\begin{bmatrix} 1 & 0 & 0 \\ 0 & 1 & 0 \\ OffsetX & OffsetY & 1 \end{bmatrix}$$

So, to move a track to the right 10 pixels and down 20 pixels, you can use

SetMatrixBy(1, 0, 0, 0, 1, 0, 10, 20, 16384)

QScript has simplified this call by creating `MoveMatrixBy(x,y)` and `MoveMatrixTo(x,y)` actions.

rotation matrix Another common spatial transformation is rotation. The following matrix rotates an object by the angle theta:

$$\begin{bmatrix} \cos\theta & \sin\theta & 0 \\ -\sin\theta & \cos\theta & 0 \\ 0 & 0 & 1 \end{bmatrix}$$

For instance, to rotate a track 15 degrees, you would first need to calculate the sine and cosine of 45 degrees (for a table of trig values, see Appendix A), which happen to be approximately 0.2588 and 0.9659, respectively. We need to calculate ahead of time because the matrix actions only take constant parameters. So to set a track's rotation "to" 15 degrees, call

SetMatrixTo(0.9659, 0.2588, 0, -0.2588, 0.9659, 0, 0, 16384)

and to rotate a track "by" 15 degrees, call

SetMatrixBy(0.9659, 0.2588, 0, -0.2588, 0.9659, 0, 0, 16384)

You get the picture.

The rotation transform comes in useful in all sorts of situations, and you can use it outside of the context of a matrix action. To rotate a point (x,y) by the angle alpha (in radians) about the origin, you can use the following QScript calculations:

```
newX = x * Cos(alpha) - y * Sin(alpha)
newY = x * Sin(alpha) + y * Cos(alpha)
```

scale matrix The following matrix scales an object to ScaleX times its width and ScaleY times its height:

$$\begin{bmatrix} ScaleX & 0 & 0 \\ 0 & ScaleY & 0 \\ 0 & 0 & 1 \end{bmatrix}$$

SetMatrixTo(ScaleX, 0, 0, 0, ScaleY, 0, 0, 0, 16384)

In QScript, the SetMatrixBy version of this transform has been wrapped into a more convenient ScaleMatrixBy(x,y) action.

shear matrix Shearing is an interesting transformation. The following matrix applies a horizontal shear to an object:

$$\begin{bmatrix} 1 & 0 & 0 \\ \text{ShearH} & 1 & 0 \\ 0 & 0 & 1 \end{bmatrix}$$

SetMatrixBy(1,0,0,ShearH,1,0,0,0,16384)

A ShearH of 0.5 means the bottom edge of the object shifts to the right by 0.5 times the height of the object (see Figure F.2).

Here's the equivalent for a vertical shear:

$$\begin{bmatrix} 1 & \text{ShearV} & 0 \\ 0 & 1 & 0 \\ 0 & 0 & 1 \end{bmatrix}$$

SetMatrixBy(1,ShearV,0,0,1,0,0,0,16384)

A vertical shear factor (ShearV) of 0.5 means the right edge of an object gets shifted downwards by 0.5 times the width of the object.

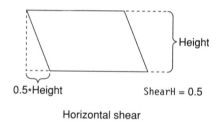

Height

0.5*Height   ShearH = 0.5

Horizontal shear

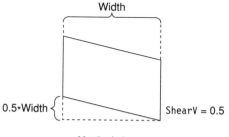

Width

0.5*Width   ShearV = 0.5

Vertical shear

Figure F.2   ShearH and ShearV.

combining matrix transformations One of the great aspects of matrix transformations is that they can be applied on top of each other. Quick-Time takes advantage of this aspect in order to allow sprites in a track to operate in their own local coordinate system but still allow it to draw correctly to the screen even when the track and the movie have been spatially transformed in different ways. This works because QuickTime can apply the movie's transform to the track's transform and apply that combined transform to the sprite's transform to determine how the sprite is mapped into screen coordinates.

A transformation matrix is applied to another transformation matrix in the same way that it's applied to a series of points—through matrix multiplication.

Consider the following matrix multiplication:

$$
\begin{bmatrix} a\ b\ 0 \\ c\ d\ 0 \\ e\ f\ 1 \end{bmatrix}
=
\begin{bmatrix} a_1\ b_1\ 0 \\ c_1\ d_1\ 0 \\ e_1\ f_1\ 1 \end{bmatrix}
\times
\begin{bmatrix} a_2\ b_2\ 0 \\ c_2\ d_2\ 0 \\ e_2\ f_2\ 1 \end{bmatrix}
$$

This is shorthand for the following calculations:

$a = a1 * a2 + b1 * c2$
$b = a1 * b2 + b1 * d2$
$c = c1 * a2 + d1 * c2$
$d = c1 * b2 + d1 * d2$
$e = e1 * a2 + f1 * c2 + e2$
$f = e1 * b2 + f1 * d2 + f2$

One useful simplification is to realize that if you multiply a rotation, scale, or shear by a translation transformation, the resulting matrix takes the *a, b, c,* and *d* values from the rotation, scale, or shear matrix, and the *e* and *f* values from the translation matrix. For example, here's a scale and translation transformation:

$$
\begin{bmatrix} \texttt{ScaleX} & \texttt{0} & \texttt{0} \\ \texttt{0} & \texttt{ScaleY} & \texttt{0} \\ \texttt{OffsetX} & \texttt{OffsetY} & \texttt{1} \end{bmatrix}
$$

One important point to note is that matrix multiplication is not commutative. This means that multiplying transform A times transform B is not the same as multiplying transform B times transform A. In other words, the order in which the transforms are applied matters. This makes sense when you think about it in spatial terms. If you scale an object vertically and then rotate it by 45 degrees, that's different than if you first rotate it and then scale (see Figure F.3).

Let's discuss a real-world example to see how combining matrices works. Say you had the movie layout shown in Figure F.4. It consists of a background sprite track with a button labeled "Flip Horizontal." In the center of the sprite track is a video track. Say you wanted to wire this movie such that the video gets flipped horizontally (mirror image) every time the button gets clicked. Since an object can be flipped by scaling it by −1, you might be tempted to use the following script:

```
[Mouse Click]
```

```
TrackNamed("video").ScaleMatrixBy(-1,1)
```

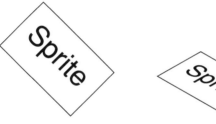 

Scale then rotate   Rotate then scale

Figure F.3   Scale then rotate versus rotate then scale.

Video

Flip Horizontal

Figure F.4   A movie layout.

Figure F.5 The video track flipped off to the left.

The problem with this is that the scale transformation is relative to the origin of the container. Since we're working with a track, the container is the movie, and the above script results in a flip about the left edge of the movie. This has the side effect of translating the video way off to the left of the sprite track (see Figure F.5).

What we want is for the video track to flip about its center so that its bounds don't change. To do this, we need to perform a combination of transformations. We first need to translate the video track so its center is aligned with the left edge of the movie. We then flip it horizontally by scaling, and then translate it back to its original position. This amounts to the following sequence of matrix multiplications:

$$
\begin{bmatrix} 1 & 0 & 0 \\ 0 & 1 & 0 \\ -C_x & 0 & 1 \end{bmatrix} \times \begin{bmatrix} -1 & 0 & 0 \\ 0 & 1 & 0 \\ 0 & 0 & 1 \end{bmatrix} \times \begin{bmatrix} 1 & 0 & 0 \\ 0 & 1 & 0 \\ C_x & 0 & 1 \end{bmatrix}
$$

Translate left · · · · · Flip horizontal · · · · · Translate right

Here C_x is the location of the video's horizontal center. We could apply each of these transformations individually using the `SetMatrixBy` action. The only problem is that with tracks each spatial transformation will result in a screen update, and this would cause the movie to expand and contract visually as the track undergoes these manipulations. It's better to do all of these transformations in one action. This amounts to doing the matrix multiplication ourselves. Using the matrix multiplication equations introduced earlier, the above transformation can be expressed as a single matrix:

$$
\begin{bmatrix} -1 & 0 & 0 \\ 0 & 1 & 0 \\ 2*C_x & 0 & 1 \end{bmatrix}
$$

Thus if the left edge of the video was located at 50 pixels, and the movie was 200 pixels wide, C_x would equal 50 + 200/2, or 150; $2*C_x$ would therefore equal 300. So our horizontal flip transformation is achieved through the following script:

```
[Mouse Click]

SetMatrixBy(-1, 0, 0, 0, 1, 0, 300, 0, 16384)
```

In essence, we've developed a FlipAboutPoint function. We could easily do a similar thing to make a RotateAboutPoint transform; in fact, QScript has already wrapped up such a transform into a function called Rotate-MatrixBy:

```
RotateMatrixBy(Angle, XPos, YPos)
```

That just about covers all the basics of matrix transformations. Practice a bit, and try designing some of your own transforms. It's a fun and useful skill even outside of the realm of QuickTime.

▶ Area of Sprites

Situations arise that require you to determine the area of a sprite. In its natural state, the area is simply the area of a rectangle—width * height. But what about when the sprite is stretched into a nonrectangular shape? To determine the area of a sprite no matter how it's stretched, you can use the following formula:

$$area = 0.5 * p * q * \sin(\theta)$$

The variables p and q are the lengths of the diagonal lines connecting the pairs of opposing corners (see Figure F.6), and θ is the angle between the two diagonal lines (see the "Two Lines" section later in this appendix for how to find that angle).

Here's a QScript routine to find the area of a sprite (using the default sprite target):

```
SpriteVars area
LocalVars p, q, dx1, dx2, dy1, dy2, m1, m2, theta

dx1 = ThirdCornerX - FirstCornerX
dy1 = ThirdCornerY - FirstCornerY
dx2 = SecondCornerX - FourthCornerX
dy2 = SecondCornerY - FourthCornerY
```

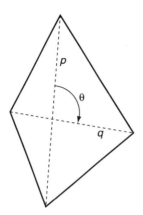

Figure F.6 Area of a sprite.

```
m1 = dy1 / dx1
m2 = dy2 / dx2
theta = ArcTan( (m2 - m1)/(1 + m2 * m1) )
p = Sqr( dx1 * dx1 + dy1 * dy1 )
q = Sqr( dx2 * dx2 + dy2 * dy2 )

area = 0.5 * p * q * Sin(theta)
```

▶ Sprite Center

To find the center of a sprite, it's useful to think of the center as the average position. The horizontal center of the bounds of a sprite is simply the average of the left and right edges of the sprite:

```
centerX = (BoundsLeft + BoundsRight) / 2
```

Likewise, the vertical center is

```
centerY = (BoundsTop + BoundsBottom) / 2
```

If you want to find the center of mass of a sprite that has been stretched in an arbitrary way, average all four corners:

```
centerX = (FirstCornerX + SecondCornerX + ThirdCornerX + \
  FourthCornerX)
centerY = (FirstCornerY + SecondCornerY + ThirdCornerY + \
  FourthCornerY)
```

▶ Two Points

Here are several useful geometrical properties of two points (x1,y1) and (x2,y2). The position halfway between the two points (the midpoint) is

```
midpointX = (x1 + x2) / 2
midpointY = (y1 + y2) / 2
```

The distance between the two points is

```
deltaX = x2 - x1
deltaY = y2 - y1
distance = Sqr( deltaX * deltaX + deltaY * deltaY )
```

The angle between the two points is

```
deltaX = x2 - x1
deltaY = y2 - y1
angleRadians = ArcTan2( deltaY, deltaX )
angleDegrees = RadiansToDegrees( angleRadians )
```

The slope, m, between the two points is

```
m = (y2 - y1)/(x2 - x1)
```

The equation of the line going through the two points is

```
y = m * x + b
```

where m (slope) = (y2 − y1)/(x2 − x1)
and b (y-intercept) = y1 − (m * x1)

▶ A Point and a Line

Here's how to calculate the distance between a point (x1,y1) and a line (y = m * x + b):

```
distance = ( m * x1 - y1 + b ) / Sqr( m * m + 1 )
```

See the previous section ("Two Points") for how to turn two points into an equation of a line.

Two Lines

The angle between two lines y = m1 * x + b1 and y = m2 * x + b2 is solely determined by the following relationship between the slopes:

```
angleBetween = ArcTan( (m2 - m1) / ( 1 + m1 * m2 ) )
```

If two lines are parallel, the two slopes will be equal, m1 = m2. If two lines are perpendicular, then m1 * m2 = −1.

Regular Polygons

Consider a regular polygon with n sides. The angle (in degrees) between each adjacent side is

```
angle = 180 * (n - 2)/n
```

r, the "apothem" (sometimes called the inner radius), is the distance from the center to the middle of one of the sides. The length of each side is

```
sideLength = 2 * r * tan(PI/n)
```

Triangles

Figure F.7 shows some common properties of triangles.

Circles

Consider a circle with radius r. The circumference is

```
2 * PI * r
```

or approximately

```
6.2832 * r
```

The area is

```
PI * r * r
```

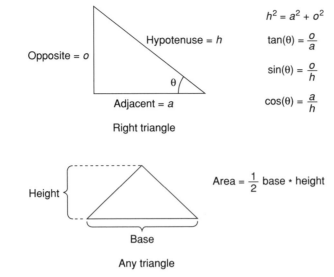

Any triangle

Figure F.7 Triangle properties.

The point on the circle at a given angle (in radians) is located at

```
x = r * Cos( angle )
y = r * Sin( angle )
```

▶ Spheres

Consider a sphere with radius r. The surface area is

```
4 * PI * r * r
```

The volume of the sphere is

```
4/3 * PI * r * r * r
```

or approximately

```
4.1888 * r * r * r
```

Appendix G
Graphics Modes

When sprites and visual tracks get drawn to the screen, they can be composited with the rest of the movie in different ways. The different compositing methods are called *graphics modes*. An example is the Transparent graphics mode, which makes a specified color transparent. Some graphics modes take a color as a parameter, called an opColor. The initial graphics mode for a sprite can be set in the Rendering section of the sprite's Properties tab. The graphics mode can also be changed dynamically through a script by using either of the following two actions:

SetGraphicsModeTo(mode, opColorRed, opColorGreen, opColorBlue)

SetGraphicsModeBy(mode, opColorRed, opColorGreen, opColorBlue)

The opColor channel parameters take values in the range of 0 to 65535.

For the "mode" parameter, use one of the following 25 constants:

Constant	Full name	Takes OpColor
ditherCopy	Dither	
transparent	Transparent	x
blend	Blend	x
graphicsModeStraightAlpha	Alpha Channel	
srcCopy	Copy	
notSrcCopy	Inverse Copy	
srcOr	Or	
notSrcOr	Inverse Or	
srcXor	Exclusive Or	
notSrcXor	Inverse Exclusive Or	
srcBic	Bit Clear	
notSrcBic	Inverse Bit Clear	
addMax	Add Max	
addMin	Add Min	
addOver	Add Over	
addPin	Add Pin	x
subOver	Sub Over	
subPin	Sub Pin	x
grayishTextOr	Grayish Text Or	
hilite	Hilite	x
graphicsModePreWhiteAlpha	Pre-White Alpha	
graphicsModePreBlackAlpha	Pre-Black Alpha	
graphicsModeComposition	Composition	
graphicsModeStraightAlphaBlend	Alpha Blend	x
graphicsModePreMulColorAlpha	Pre-Multiply Alpha	x

For a description of what these graphics modes do, refer to the Live-Stage Pro manual.

Appendix H
Codecs

Codec stands for compressor-decompressor. Codecs are methods of compressing and decompressing data. QuickTime supports a wide variety of codecs for encoding media such as images, video, and audio. Here I'd like to cover the standard codecs that can be used to compress sprite images. Each codec has its own "personality" and situations where it is best suited. There's usually a trade-off between high compression ratios (small file size) and fast decompression performance (fast load speed). Since larger file sizes can start to hamper load speeds, you're usually going to want some compression. Other considerations include the type of image information being compressed. Is it a photograph? Does it have large patches of solid color? Are you willing to lose image quality? All of these factors need to be taken into account when choosing the optimal codec.

That being said, I usually stick with the Animation codec for computer-generated graphics, especially for ones with transparent regions. For images with an alpha channel, I use the PNG codec, or Animation + Alpha if I want click-through transparency. For photographs, I usually just use the JPEG codec.

Note For a good book on codecs and their different characteristics, check out the book *Compression for Great Digital Video: Power Tips, Techniques, & Common Sense* by Ben Waggoner. Also visit `www.codeccentral.com`.

The following is a list of the standard 13 codecs with a brief description of their personalities:

animation This is one of my favorite codecs. It works well with computer-generated graphics with areas of solid color. It works at any bit depth. The compressed file sizes are reasonable, but the decompression performance is great. The best part is that this codec can take a transparent color parameter that turns all pixels of that color transparent, both visually as well as transparent to mouse clicks. It isn't very good for photographic images.

Animation+Alpha This is similar to the Animation codec, but can work with an alpha channel to produce a nice blended transparency. Make sure to use the Alpha graphics mode. This codec also supports the transparent color parameter.

Cinepak For many years this was the standard video codec. It has good compression ratios and fast decompression for high-quality video. It does an OK job for images.

Don't Recompress Use this noncodec for images that have already been compressed outside of LiveStage. Note that this isn't the same as the None codec.

Graphics This codec works well with medium to large 8-bit (256-color) graphics. It has a better compression ratio than the Animation codec (small file sizes), but it takes longer to decompress and thus can affect performance.

H261 High compression rate for medium- to low-resolution video. It places a high computational demand on the processor.

H263 Codec intended for videoconferencing. Good compression ratios and fast encoding.

JPEG Also called the Photo codec. This is a good codec for photographic images without much high-frequency information. If you can live with slightly reduced image quality, you can get very good compression ratios.

Motion JPEG A See JPEG.

Motion JPEG B See JPEG.

PNG Good codec for images with alpha channels. Doesn't support click-through transparency like the Animation + Alpha codec. Uses similar compression to zlib.

Sorenson Like JPEG, this is also used for photographic images, but is processor demanding and can present drawing problems with stretched sprites.

Video The Apple video codec. The main benefit is fast compression, but that's not an issue with sprite images. This codec isn't commonly used in today's production environment.

Appendix I
General MIDI

MIDI stands for Music Instrument Digital Interface. For an overview of how to control MIDI instruments and controllers using wired actions, see Chapter 24. This appendix provides a list of the instruments, controllers, and drum kits defined by the General MIDI standard.

▶ Instruments

General MIDI defines 128 instruments in a synthesizer. There are 16 groups of 8 instruments each. The names of the groups are (in order) Piano, Chromatic Percussion, Organ, Guitar, Bass, Strings & Orchestra, Ensemble, Brass, Reed, Pipe, Synth Lead, Synth Pad, Synth Effect, Ethnic, Percussive, and Sound Effects.

Here are the names of the instruments:

1.	Acoustic Grand Piano	15.	Tubular Bells
2.	Bright Acoustic Piano	16.	Dulcimer
3.	Electric Grand Piano	17.	Drawbar Organ
4.	Honky-tonk Piano	18.	Percussive Organ
5.	Electric Piano 1	19.	Rock Organ
6.	Electric Piano 2	20.	Church Organ
7.	Harpsichord	21.	Reed Organ
8.	Clavi	22.	Accordion
9.	Celesta	23.	Harmonica
10.	Glockenspiel	24.	Tango Accordion
11.	Music Box	25.	Acoustic Guitar (nylon)
12.	Vibraphone	26.	Acoustic Guitar (steel)
13.	Marimba	27.	Electric Guitar (jazz)
14.	Xylophone	28.	Electric Guitar (clean)

29.	Electric Guitar (muted)	70.	English Horn
30.	Overdriven Guitar	71.	Bassoon
31.	Distortion Guitar	72.	Clarinet
32.	Guitar Harmonics	73.	Piccolo
33.	Acoustic Bass	74.	Flute
34.	Electric Bass (finger)	75.	Recorder
35.	Electric Bass (pick)	76.	Pan Flute
36.	Fretless Bass	77.	Blown Bottle
37.	Slap Bass 1	78.	Shakuhachi
38.	Slap Bass 2	79.	Whistle
39.	Synth Bass 1	80.	Ocarina
40.	Synth Bass 2	81.	Lead 1 (square)
41.	Violin	82.	Lead 2 (sawtooth)
42.	Viola	83.	Lead 3 (calliope)
43.	Cello	84.	Lead 4 (chiff)
44.	Contrabass	85.	Lead 5 (charang)
45.	Tremolo Strings	86.	Lead 6 (voice)
46.	Pizzicato Strings	87.	Lead 7 (fifths)
47.	Orchestral Harp	88.	Lead 8 (bass + lead)
48.	Timpani	89.	Pad 1 (new age)
49.	String Ensemble 1	90.	Pad 2 (warm)
50.	String Ensemble 2	91.	Pad 3 (polysynth)
51.	SynthStrings 1	92.	Pad 4 (choir)
52.	SynthStrings 2	93.	Pad 5 (bowed)
53.	Choir Aahs	94.	Pad 6 (metallic)
54.	Voice Oohs	95.	Pad 7 (halo)
55.	Synth Voice	96.	Pad 8 (sweep)
56.	Orchestra Hit	97.	FX 1 (rain)
57.	Trumpet	98.	FX 2 (soundtrack)
58.	Trombone	99.	FX 3 (crystal)
59.	Tuba	100.	FX 4 (atmosphere)
60.	Muted Trumpet	101.	FX 5 (brightness)
61.	French Horn	102.	FX 6 (goblins)
62.	Brass Section	103.	FX 7 (echoes)
63.	SynthBrass 1	104.	FX 8 (sci-fi)
64.	SynthBrass 2	105.	Sitar
65.	Soprano Sax	106.	Banjo
66.	Alto Sax	107.	Shamisen
67.	Tenor Sax	108.	Koto
68.	Baritone Sax	109.	Kalimba
69.	Oboe	110.	Bagpipe

111.	Fiddle	120.	Reverse Cymbal
112.	Shanai	121.	Guitar Fret Noise
113.	Tinkle Bell	122.	Breath Noise
114.	Agogo	123.	Seashore
115.	Steel Drums	124.	Bird Tweet
116.	Woodblock	125.	Telephone Ring
117.	Taiko Drum	126.	Helicopter
118.	Melodic Tom	127.	Applause
119.	Synth Drum	128.	Gunshot

Note When using low-level MIDI calls outside of wired QuickTime, the instruments are indexed from 0 to 127, so you would subtract one from the above indices.

Drum Kits

A MIDI drum kit is a single instrument that plays different drum sounds for the different notes. A drum kit is an efficient way to add multiple sound effects to a movie since it only involves a single instrument. The standard drum kits conform to the same layout, meaning that a particular note will always play the same type of sound but it might vary from kit to kit. For example, note 56 is always a cowbell, but the exact sound and timbre of the cowbell might vary across different drum kits.

Here are the names of the drum kit sounds for notes 35 thru 81 (the rest of the notes are not part of the specification):

35.	Acoustic Bass Drum	50.	High Tom
36.	Bass Drum 1	51.	Ride Cymbal 1
37.	Side Stick	52.	Chinese Cymbal
38.	Acoustic Snare	53.	Ride Bell
39.	Hand Clap	54.	Tambourine
40.	Electric Snare	55.	Splash Cymbal
41.	Low Floor Tom	56.	Cowbell
42.	Closed Hi-hat	57.	Crash Cymbal 2
43.	High Floor Tom	58.	Vibraslap
44.	Pedal Hi-hat	59.	Ride Cymbal 2
45.	Low Tom	60.	Hi Bongo
46.	Open Hi-hat	61.	Low Bongo
47.	Low-mid Tom	62.	Mute Hi Conga
48.	Hi-mid Tom	63.	Open Hi Conga
49.	Crash Cymbal 1	64.	Low Conga

65.	High Timbale	73.	Short Guiro
66.	Low Timbale	74.	Long Guiro
67.	High Agogo	75.	Claves
68.	Low Agogo	76.	Hi Wood Block
69.	Cabasa	77.	Low Wood Block
70.	Maracas	78.	Mute Cuica
71.	Short Whistle	79.	Open Cuica
72.	Long Whistle	80.	Mute Triangle
		81.	Open Triangle

▶ Controllers

In addition to 128 instruments, General MIDI also defines 128 controllers that modify the properties of instruments. Here is a list of the available controllers (the ones left out of the list are either special purpose or left open in the General MIDI specification). The names are the constant names assigned to them by LiveStage Pro:

kControllerModulationWheel	kControllerTuneTranspose
kControllerBreath	kControllerPartVolume
kControllerFoot	kControllerTuneVolume
kControllerPortamentoTime	kControllerSustain
kControllerVolume	kControllerPortamento
kControllerBalance	kControllerSostenuto
kControllerPan	kControllerSoftPedal
kControllerExpression	kControllerReverb
kControllerLever1	kControllerTremolo
kControllerLever2	kControllerChorus
kControllerLever3	kControllerCeleste
kControllerLever4	kControllerPhaser
kControllerLever5	kControllerEditPart
kControllerLever6	kControllerMasterTune
kControllerLever7	kControllerMasterTranspose
kControllerLever8	kControllerMasterVolume
kControllerPitchBend	kControllerMasterCPULoad
kControllerAfterTouch	kControllerMasterPolyphony
kControllerPartTranspose	kControllerMasterFeatures

Appendix J
Components

The QuickTime platform has a very modular architecture. New features such as tracks and codecs can be added in the form of a component. Most of the components are supplied by Apple, but many are created by third parties. Chapter 29 discusses how to install and use third-party track types. The example used is the Zoomify media type.

From QScript, you can check if a component is installed using the following action:

```
ComponentVersion( Type, Subtype, Manufacturer )
```

Type: A four-character string designating the type of component. This is the type defined by Apple. A track is a media handler type that is designated by the "mhlr" string.

SubType: The four-character string of the subtype. The subtype is defined by the party that created the component. There is often a one-to-one correspondence between the subtype and the particular component.

Manufacturer: The four-character string of the party that created the component. For Apple, this is "appl". For Zoomify, it's "Zoom".

All of the parameters are case-sensitive four-character strings. If you see a type, subtype, or manufacturer code that is less than three characters, this usually means there are space characters at the end. For example, the movie importer type is "eat " (movie exporters are of type "spit". . . cute, eh?).

You can also tell QuickTime to attempt to load a component by calling

```
LoadComponent(SubType)
```

If the component isn't already installed, QuickTime directs the user to install the component.

Here's a list of component types:

Type	Name
mhlr	Media Handler
wire	Wired Action Handler
dhlr	Data Handler
devc	Device Conrol
imdc	Image Decompressor
imco	Image Compressor
grip	Graphics Importer
grex	Graphics Exporter
sdec	Sound Decompressor
scom	Sound Compressor
ddec	Data Decompressor
eat	Movie Importer
spit	Movie Exporter
pars	Parser
play	Movie Controller
nets	Network Status
rtpr	Real-Time Protocol Handler
clok	Clock Component
blit	Graphics Blitter
pnot	File Preview Component
pmak	Preview Image Maker
vout	Video Out
musi	Music Component (MIDI)
cons	Constructor
hint	Hinter Component (for streaming media)
url	URL Data Handler

The following is a list of Types, SubTypes, and Manufacturers for some components that might not be installed on a user's machine:

Type	SubType	Manufacturer	Name
imdc	qdrw	appl	Apple QuickDraw
imdc	path	appl	Apple Curve Codec (decoder part)
imdc	ACTL	SBXC	Streambox ACT-L2 Component
eat	.axs	Axel	MindAvenue AXEL Movie Importer
mhlr	.axs	Axel	MindAvenue AXEL Media Handler
play	bhiv	appl	Be Here iVideo
imdc	bhiv	behr	Be Here iVideo
eat	IPIX	iPmh	iPIX Movie Import Component
mhlr	iPmh	iPXC	iPIX Movie Import Component
imco	VP31	?On2	VP32 Video Player
imdc	VP31	?On2	VP32 Video Player
imdc	glas	appl	Glass
pnot	3DMF	appl	3D Preview Viewer
grip	qdgx	appl	QuickDraw GX
musi	gm	appl	General MIDI Music Player
eat	Midi	musi	Standard MIDI
musi	gene	appl	Generic MIDI Music Player
spit	Midi	musi	Standard MIDI
musi	midi	appl	MIDI Note Player
eat	3DMF	qd3d	3DMF
mhlr	qd3d	appl	QuickDraw 3D Media Handler
mhlr	Zoom	Zoom	Zoomify Media Handler Component
imco	ZyGo	ZyGo	ZyGoVideo
imdc	ZyGo	ZyGo	ZyGoVideo
mhlr	PULM	PULM	Pulse Media
eat	PW3	PULM	Pulse Media
eat	PWC	PULM	Pulse Media
wire	PULM	PULM	Pulse Media

Appendix K
QTText Tags

QuickTime can import time-based styled text tracks from a text format called QTText. Since text processing is a very common feature of server-side applications, it's easy to dynamically generate styled text tracks for an HTTP request. Wired QuickTime movies can then load such dynamic text into a movie track to perform the same sorts of functions that HTML servers do when generating dynamic Web pages. The QTChat movie introduced a few years ago used dynamic text tracks to create a chat client inside of an interactive movie.

The QTText format is similar to HTML in that it uses tags with attributes, but the specification of the tags is different. QTText has two types of tags:

1. Timestamp tag: Uses square brackets to define when along the track's timeline the text should appear.

   Example: [00:00:01.00]

2. Text descriptor tag: Uses curly braces to define the style and other properties of the text.

   Example: {bold}

   Some text descriptor tags take options. An option comes after the name separated by a : character.

   Example: {font: Courier}

Here's an example 4-second, 200 × 200 pixel text track that says "Hi" in a red italic Times font at the very start, and then 2 seconds into the movie it says "Bye" in a large (48-point) bold.

```
{QTtext}
{font:Times}{size:10}{italic}{textColor: 65536,0,0}
{language:0}
{timeScale:30}{timeStamps:absolute}
{width:200}{height:200}
[00:00:00.00]
Hi
[00:00:01.00]{size:48}{bold}
Bye
[00:00:04.00]
```

Here's a list of text descriptor tags:

{QTText}—A required tag that comes at the very beginning of the file.

{width:pixels}—The width of the track.

{height:pixels}—The height of the track.

{timeStamps:relative}—This means that timestamp tags represent time offsets from the last timestamp tag.

{timeStamps:absolute}—This specifies that timestamps represent absolute times from the beginning of the track.

{timeScale:ticksPerSecond}—This specifies the timescale of the timestamps.

{textBox: top, left, bottom, right}—This sets the location of the text box relative to the track. For information on text boxes, see Chapter 25.

{clipToTextBox:on}—Clips the track to the text box.

{clipToTextBox:off}

{shrinkTextBox:on}—Resizes the text box so that it just fits the text inside.

{shrinkTextBox:off}

{font: fontname}

{plain}

{bold}

{italic}

{underline}

{outline}

{shadow}

{condense}

{extend}

{justify:left}

{justify:right}

{justify:center}

{justify:default}

{size: point-size}—Uses a platform-specific specification of font size. (See "Font sizes" in Appendix A.)

{dropShadow:on}

{dropShadow:off}

{dropShadowOffset:x,y}—How far to offset drop-shadowed text in pixels.

{dropShadowTransparency:level}—Sets the level of transparency for the drop shadow (0–255).

{textColor: red, green, blue}—Specifies the text color. The red, green, and blue channels take numeric values between 0 and 65535.

{hilite:startChar, endChar}—Highlights the characters from startChar to endChar. Characters are indexed from 1 in this case.

{hiliteColor:red,green,blue}

{inverseHilite:on}

{inverseHilite:off}

{anti-alias:on}—Makes the text anti-aliased.

{anti-alias:off}

{backColor: red, green, blue}

{useMovieBackColor:on}—Use the movie's background color instead of the track's background color.

{useMovieBackColor:off}

{keyedText:on}—Makes the background of the text transparent such that the text draws on whatever tracks are behind the text track.

{keyedText:off}

{doNotDisplay:on}—Sets the text track to invisible.

{doNotDisplay:off}

{scrolling:on}—Turns text scrolling on.

{scrollDelay:ticks}—Sets the scroll delay in the track's timescale.

{scrollIn:on}—Sets the scrollIn flag.

{scrollIn:off}

{scrollOut:on}—Sets the scrollOut flag.

{scrollOut:off}

{horizontalScroll:on}—Sets the horizontalScroll flag.

{horizontalScroll:off}

{reverseScroll:on}

{reverseScroll:off}

{continuousScroll:on}

{continuousScroll:off}

{flowHorizontal:on}

{flowHorizontal:off}

Appendix L
HTML Embed Parameters

When embedding a QuickTime movie in HTML, there are many parameters that can be specified. Here's a template HTML structure for embedding an interactive movie in a Web page with maximum compatibility across the various browsers:

```
<OBJECT CLASSID="clsid:02BF25D5-8C17-4B23-BC80-D3488ABDDC6B"
        CODEBASE="http://www.apple.com/qtactivex/qtplugin.cab"
        WIDTH="320"
        HEIGHT="240" >
    <PARAM NAME="src" VALUE="MyMovie.mov" >
    <PARAM NAME="autoplay" VALUE="false" >
    <PARAM NAME="controller" VALUE="false" >

<EMBED SRC="QTMimeType.pntg"
        TYPE="image/x-macpaint"
        PLUGINSPAGE="http://www.apple.com/quicktime/download"
        QTSRC="myMovie.mov"
        WIDTH="320"
        HEIGHT="240"
        AUTOPLAY="false"
        CONTROLLER="false" >
    </EMBED>
</OBJECT>
```

There are a few things to notice:

First, what's that long number? That's the ActiveX classID for the QuickTime plug-in. This is needed for newer versions of Internet Explorer.

Second, each parameter is specified twice. For compatibility, both the object tag and the embed tag should be used. Older browsers don't understand the object tag and will use the embed tag to load the movie. Browsers that do understand the object tag know to ignore embed tags that occur within the object tag. And yes, this means that each parameter needs to be entered twice.

Third, what's with the QTMimeType.pntg src attribute? That's to prevent plug-ins in older browsers from hijacking the QuickTime movie MIME type. This points to a MacPaint file. The file doesn't have to exist; it's just to throw off other plug-ins that claim to understand QuickTime. Since the QTSRC attribute is there, QuickTime will ignore the SRC file and load the movie defined by the QTSRC attribute. You don't need to do this for the object tag because the classID uniquely identifies the QuickTime plug-in.

The QuickTime plug-in understands a whole host of attributes (sometimes called parameters). The above embedding only uses the AUTOPLAY and CONTROLLER attributes to turn autoplay and the controller off (for interactive movies, I usually don't use a movie controller). One attribute particularly useful for wired movies is the MovieQTList attribute. This attribute takes an XML string that will be added to the movie's QTList when loaded. This is a good way to pass parameters into a movie (see Chapter 36 for more information).

Embed Attributes

The following is a list of the QuickTime embed attributes. I'm listing them mainly because it's useful to have a list to look at when trying to remember the name of a certain tag. Descriptions are not given. For an in-depth description of how each attribute works, see Apple's Web reference on the subject: http://www.apple.com/quicktime/authoring/embed.html.

Each attribute is listed as a NAME=value pair. The value is given a name. If the name is true/false, that means the value can take the values "true" or "false." If the value takes a number, the value will be named number. You get the idea. The names are all capitalized by convention, but HTML isn't case sensitive, so this isn't necessary. Some names have a lowercase "n" character after them, such as HOTSPOTn. This means that the "n" should be replaced with an integer. The standard embed attributes used by all plug-ins, such as SRC, WIDTH, HEIGHT, are not listed.

```
AUTOHREF=true/false
AUTOPLAY=true/false
BGCOLOR=hex_color
BGCOLOR=name
CACHE=true/false
CONTROLLER=true/false
CORRECTION=none/full
DONTFLATTENWHENSAVING=true
ENABLEJAVASCRIPT=true/false
ENDTIME=timecode
FOV=angle
GOTOn=url
HIDDEN=true
HOTSPOTn=url
HREF=url
KIOSKMODE=true/false
LOOP=true/false/palindrome
MOVIEID=integer
MOVIENAME=string
NODE=integer
PAN=angle
PLAYEVERFRAME=true/false
PLUGINSPAGE=url
QTNEXTn=url
QTSRC=url
QTSRCCHOKESPEED=datarate_number
QTRSCDONTUSEBROWSER=true/false
SCALE=number/TOFIT/
STARTTIME=timecode
TARGET=quicktimeplayer/myself/framename
TARGETn=quicktimemplayer/myself/framename
TARGETCACHE=true/false
TILT=angle
TYPE=mimeType
URLSUBSTITUTEn="<string>:<newString>"
VOLUME=integer
```

Appendix M
Wired Actions

This appendix is simply a list of all the wired actions, properties, and targets available for use in LiveStage Pro. Calls that take parameters are shown with parentheses and parameter names. For example:

```
SetLayerTo(layer)
```

The main difference between "actions" and "properties" is that properties return values and aren't supposed to change the state of the movie. Actions don't return values and usually do change the state of the movie (some change the state outside of a movie). Properties are sometimes called "operands." Be aware that there are some actions that act like properties except that instead of returning a value, they place a value in a variable specified by the `variableID` parameter. See Chapter 9 for a more in-depth discussion.

I added this appendix because I often forget the exact spelling of certain actions, or the order of the parameters. Descriptions of each action are not provided here. See the QScript Reference window built into LSPro. You can also refer to the QScript section of the LiveStage Pro Manual, which is online at `http://www.totallyhip.com/lsdn/resources/qscript/qscript_index.html`.

Note The following names are the names designated by Totally Hip. They often differ from the low-level names Apple uses when working with wired actions using C/C++ or Java. In fact, some of them are just simplifications or combinations of low-level actions, and thus there isn't a one-to-one correspondence. See Appendix P for more information.

Targets

ThisEvent
ChildMovieNamed(name)
ChildMovieOfID(id)
ChildMovieTrackNamed(name)
ChildMovieTrackOfID(id)
ChildMovieTrackOfIndex(index)
ParentMovie
RootMovie
MovieNamed(name)
MovieOfID(id)
ObjectNamed(name)
ObjectOfID(id)
ObjectOfIndex(index)
TrackNamed(name)
TrackOfID(id)
TrackOfIndex(index)
TrackOfType(MediaTypeConstant, index)
SpriteNamed(name)
SpriteOfID(id)
SpriteOfIndex(index)
SampleNamed(name)
QD3DObjectNamed(name)

General Actions

GotoURL(URLString)
DebugStr(string)
ApplicationNumberAndString(number, \
    string)
CloseThisWindow
DisplayChannels
EnterFullScreen
ExitFullScreen
SendAppMessage(number)
SetStatusString(string, flag)
SoftwareWasChanged
ExecuteAppleScript(string)
ExecuteGenericScript(string)
ExecuteJavaScript(string)
ExecuteLingoScript(string)

ExecuteProjectorScript(string)
ExecuteVBScript(string)
SetCursor(cursorID)
AddSubscription(name, URL, iconURL)
RemoveSubscription(URL)
LoadComponent(componentID)

General Properties

GetEventKey
GetEventModifiers
GetEventMouseX
GetEventMouseY
GetEventScanCode
KeyIsDown(modifiers,key)
MouseButtonDown
ConnectionSpeed
GetNetworkStatus
ComponentVersion(type, subtype, \
    manufacturer)
GetMemoryFree
GetSystemVersion
IsRegistered
Platform
Registered
Subscription
Version
GMTDay
GMTMonth
GMTYear
GMTHours
GMTMinutes
GMTSeconds
LocalDay
LocalMonth
LocalYear
LocalHours
LocalMinutes
LocalSeconds
TickCount
CustomHandlerID
IsCustomHandlerOpen(handlerID)

Movie Actions

```
GoToBeginning
GoToEnd
GoToTime(time)
GoToTimeByName(string)
StepBackward
StepForward
SetRateBy(number)
SetRateTo(number)
StartPlaying
StopPlaying
SetPlaySelection(boolean)
SetSelection(startTime,endTime)
SetSelectionByName(string)
TogglePlaySelection
SetLanguage(language)
SetMovieScale(scaleX,scaleY)
SetLoopingFlags(loopFlags)
SetVolumeBy(number)
SetVolumeTo(number)
PopAndGoToLabeledTime(string)
PopAndGoToTopTime(time)
PushCurrentTime
PushCurrentTimeWithLabel(string)
MovieChanged
SetStringVariable (variableID,Value)
SetVariable(variableID, numberValue)
```

Movie Properties

```
GetMovieURL
GetParentMovieURL
GetRootMovieURL
GetMovieAnnotation
   (annotationName,flag)
GetMovieDuration
GetWidth
GetHeight
GetLoadState
GetID
```

```
GetName
GetTimeScale
GetTrackCount
GetVariable(variableID)
IsMovieActive
MaxLoadedTimeInMovie
MovieIsLooping
MovieLoopIsPalindrome
MovieRate
MovieTime
MovieVolume
```

General Track Actions

```
SetEnabled
ToggleEnabled
```

General Track Properties

```
GetDuration
GetID
GetName
TrackEnabled
MarkerNamed(Name).StartTime
```

Sample Actions

```
StartTime
EndTime
```

Visual Track Actions

```
EatKeyEvent
SetClipRegionTo(#RegionFromRect \
   (x,y,width,height))
SetClipRegionTo(#RegionFromImageFile \
   (fileName))
SetFocus
SetGraphicsModeBy(mode, red, green, \
   blue)
```

```
SetGraphicsModeTo(mode, \
    red, green, blue)
SetLayerBy(number)
SetLayerTo(layer)
MoveMatrixBy(x,y)
MoveMatrixTo(x,y)
ResetMatrix
RotateMatrixBy(angle,x,y)
ScaleMatrixBy(x,y)
SetMatrixBy(a,b,u,c,d,v,e,f,w)
SetMatrixTo(a,b,u,c,d,v,e,f,w)
```

Visual Track Properties

```
CanBeFocus
IsFocus
GetWidth
GetHeight
MouseHorizontal
MouseVertical
TrackHeight
TrackLayer
TrackWidth
```

Sprite Track Actions

```
MakeNewSprite(ID,handlerID, \
    imageIndex,isVisible,layer)
DisposeSprite(ID)
SetIdleDelay(delay)
SetHitTestingMode(mode)
```

Sprite Track Properties

```
GetIdleDelay
GetHitTestingMode
NumSprites
NumImages
SpriteAtPoint(x,y)
HandlerRef
```

Sprite Actions

```
ClickOnCodec(x,y)
DisposeImage(imageIndex)
ExecuteEvent(eventID)
LoadNewImage(URL,ID)
PassMouseToCodec
SetSpriteHitTestFlag(flag)
MoveBy(x,y)
MoveTo(x,y)
ResetMatrix
Rotate(angle)
Scale(x,y)
Stretch(x1,y1,x2,y2,x3,y3,x4,y4)
SetGraphicsModeBy(mode, red, \
    green, blue)
SetGraphicsModeTo(mode, red, \
    green, blue)
SetImageIndexBy(number)
SetImageIndexTo(index)
SetLayerBy(number)
SetLayerTo(index)
SetVisible(boolean)
ToggleVisible
```

Sprite Properties

```
GetName
ID
Index
IsVisible
Layer
BoundsBottom
BoundsLeft
BoundsRight
BoundsTop
FirstCornerX
FirstCornerY
SecondCornerX
SecondCornerY
ThirdCornerX
```

```
ThirdCornerY
FourthCornerX
FourthCornerY
GetImageIDByIndex(imageIndex)
GetImageIndexByID(imageID)
ImageIndex
ImageRegistrationPointX
ImageRegistrationPointY
```

Text Track Actions

```
FindText(string,red,green,blue,flags)
HandleMouseClick
ScrollText(deltaX,deltaY)
SetIdleDelay(delay)
SetSelection(startChar,endChar)
SetTextEditState(stateFlags)
SetTextHilite(startChar,endChar, \
    red,green,blue)
SetTextLinkColor(linkIndex,red, \
    green,blue)
SetTextLinkStyle(linkIndex,style)
EnterText(asciiNumber)
ReplaceText(string,startChar,endChar)
SetTextColor(red,green,blue)
SetTextFont(fontID)
SetTextSize(number)
SetTextStyle(style)
SetBackgroundColor(red,green,blue)
SetTextAlignment(alignment)
SetTextBox(x,y,width,height)
SetTextDisplayFlags(flags)
SetTextDropShadow(offsetX, offsetY, \
    transparency)
SetTextScrollDelay(delay)
```

Text Track Properties

```
GetEditState
GetIdleDelay
```

```
GetSelectionStart
GetSelectionEnd
GetText
GetTextBoxBottom
GetTextBoxLeft
GetTextBoxRight
GetTextBoxTop
GetTextLength
```

Chapter Track Actions

```
GoToNextChapter
GoToPreviousChapter
GoToFirstChapter
GoToLastChapter
GoToChapterByIndex(index)
```

Chapter Track Properties

```
GetChapterCount
GetCurrentChapterIndex
GetCurrentChapterName
GetChapterNameAtIndex(index)
GetChapterIndexNamed(name)
```

Movie Track Actions

```
RestartAtTime(time,rate)
AddChildMovie(ID,URL)
LoadChildMovie(ID)
LoadChildMovieWithQTList(ID,XML)
```

Audible Track Actions

```
SetBalanceBy(number)
SetBalanceTo(number)
SetBassTrebleBy(number)
SetBassTrebleTo(number)
SetVolumeBy(number)
SetVolumeTo(number)
```

Audible Track Properties

GetBass
GetTreble
TrackBalance
TrackVolume

Instrument Track Actions

PlayNote(instrumentID,delay,pitch,
    volume,duration)
SetController(sampleIndex,instrument- \
    ID,delay,controllerID,value)

Flash Track Actions

GoToFrameNamed(name)
GoToFrameNumber(index)
PerformFlashClick
    (path,buttonID,eventName)
SetFlashVariable(path,variableName, \
    value,isFocus)
SetPan(percentX,percentY)
SetZoom(zoomFactor)

Flash Track Properties

GetFlashVariable(path,variableName)

QTVR Track Actions

GoToNodeID(ID)
EnableHotSpot(hotspotID)
DisableHotSpot(hotspotID)
HideHotSpots
ShowHotSpots
SetPanAngleBy(angle)
SetPanAngleTo(angle)
SetTiltAngleBy(angle)
SetTiltAngleTo(angle)
SetFieldOfViewBy(angle)
SetFieldOfViewTo(angle)

SetViewState(type,state)
SetIdleDelay(delay)
ShowDefaultView

QTVR Track Properties

GetIdleDelay
ViewHorizCenter
ViewVertCenter
AreHotSpotsVisible
GetCurrentViewState
GetViewStateCount
PanAngle
TiltAngle
FieldOfView
NodeID

Zoomify Track Actions

ZoomifyZoomIn
ZoomifyZoomOut
ZoomifyPanRight
ZoomifyPanLeft
ZoomifyTiltUp
ZoomifyTiltDown
ZoomifyRollRight
ZoomifyRollLeft
ZoomifyMoveRight
ZoomifyMoveLeft
ZoomifyMoveUp
ZoomifyMoveDown
ZoomifyMoveForward
ZoomifyMoveBack
ZoomifyResetView
ZoomifyToggleTextures
ZoomifyToggleOpenGL
ZoomifyToggleSpin
ZoomifyGetZoom(variableID)
ZoomifyGetOrientationPitch \
    (variableID)
ZoomifyGetOrientationYaw(variableID)

```
ZoomifyGetOrientationRoll(variableID)
ZoomifySetLocationXTo(number)
ZoomifySetLocationYTo(number)
ZoomifySetLocationZTo(number)
ZoomifySetOrientationPitchTo(number)
ZoomifySetOrientationYawTo(number)
ZoomifySetOrientationRollTo(number)
ZoomifySetZoomTo(number)
```

Pulse3D Track Actions

```
ExecutePulseScript(scriptString)
```

QD3D Object Actions

```
RotateTo(angleX,angleY,angleZ)
ScaleTo(scaleX,scaleY,scaleZ)
TranslateTo(x,y,z)
```

QTList Actions

```
AddListElement(path,index,name)
RemoveListElement(path, \
    startIndex,endIndex)
SetListElement(path,value)
ExchangeList(URL,QTListpath)
QueryListServer(URL,keyValuePairs, \
    flags,QTListpath)
LoadListFromXML(path,index,XML)
ReplaceListFromXML(path,XML)
SetListFromURL(URL,path)
```

QTList Properties

```
GetListAsXML(path)
GetListElementCount(path)
GetListElementPath(path,index)
GetListElementValue(path)
```

Appendix N
Wired Constants

This appendix lists the names of constants used in conjunction with wired actions. As with Appendix M, descriptions are not given. This reference is intended as a cheat sheet of sorts. Most constant names are long and hard to remember, so it's useful to have a place to look them up. For descriptions of what they mean, see the QScript Reference window in LiveStage Pro, or look in the LiveStage manual.

These constant names are the names designated by Totally Hip for use in LiveStage Pro (QScript). The names are usually the same as or similar to, but can differ from, the low-level names defined in Apple's Movies.h header file. To get the actual value that these constant names stand for, do a search in the Movies.h file using the constant name.

Constant names usually start with a 'k' character, but there are exceptions.

When working with flags and modes, multiple constants can usually be used in combination. Use the + operator to combine them. For example:

`SetTextEditState(kScriptEditing + kDirectEditing)`

There are some exceptions to the above rule. For example, when using the KeyIsDown property, multiple modifiers are combined using the | operator, for example:

`KeyIsDown(kOptionKey|kShiftKey,"s")`

The above returns true if Option-Shift-S is being pressed.

Track Type Constants

kBaseMediaType
kFlashMediaType
kMPEGMediaType
kMusicMediaType
kSoundMediaType
kSpriteMediaType
kStreamingMediaType
kTextMediaType
kTimeCodeMediaType
kTweenMediaType
kThreeDeeMediaType
kQTVRQTVRType
kQTVRPanoramaType
kQTVRObjectType
kQTVROldPanoType
kQTVROldObjectType
kVideoMediaType

SendAppMessage Constants

kAppMsgDisplayChannels
kAppMsgRequestEnterFullScreen
kAppMsgRequestExitFullScreen
kAppMsgSoftwareChanged
kAppMsgWindowClose

Status String Constants

kStatusCode
kStatusError
kStatusStreaming
kStatusURL

Cursor ID Constants

kQTCursorArrow
kQTCursorOpenHand
kQTCursorClosedHand
kQTCursorPointingHand
kQTCursorRightArrow

kQTCursorLeftArrow
kQTCursorDownArrow
kQTCursorUpArrow

Key Codes

kReturnKeyCode
kEnterKeyCode
kTabKeyCode
kBackSpaceKeyCode
kDeleteKeyCode
kInsertKeyCode
kUpArrowKeyCode
kDownArrowKeyCode
kLeftArrowKeyCode
kRightArrowKeyCode
kEscapeKeyCode
kPageUpKeyCode
kPageDownKeyCode
kHomeKeyCode
kEndKeyCode

Key String Constants

kReturnKey
kTabKey
kDeleteKey
kUpArrowKey
kDownArrowKey
kLeftArrowKey
kRightArrowKey

Constants Returned by
GetEventModifiers

kModifierActiveFlag
kModifierButtonState
kModifierCommandKey
kModifierShiftKey
kModifierAlphaLock
kModifierOptionKey

```
kModifierControlKey
kModifierRightShiftKey
kModifierRightOptionKey
kModifierRightControlKey
```

Modifier Constants for `KeyIsDown`

```
kNone
kOptionKey
kShiftKey
kCommandKey
kControlKey
kCapsLockKey
```

Character Constants

```
kReturnKey
kTabKey
kDeleteKey
kUpArrowKey
kDownArrowKey
kLeftArrowKey
kRightArrowKey
kDoubleQuoteCharacter
kLineFeedCharacter
kCRCharacter
kLFCharacters
kCRLFCharacters
```

Network Status Constants

```
kConnected
kNoNetwork
kNotConnected
kUncertain
```

Platform Constants

```
kMacintosh
kWindows
```

Looping Constants

```
kNoLoop
kLoop
kLoopPalindrome
```

Annotation Strings

```
Author: "qt-userdata-aut"
Comment: "qt-userdata-cmt"
Copyright: "qt-userdata-cpy"
CreationDate: "qt-userdata-day"
Description: "qt-userdata-des"
Director: "qt-userdata-dir"
Disclaimer: "qt-userdata-dis"
FullName: "qt-userdata-nam"
HostComputer: "qt-userdata-hst"
Information: "qt-userdata-inf"
Keywords: "qt-userdata-key"
Make: "qt-userdata-mak"
Model: "qt-userdata-mod"
OriginalFormat: "qt-userdata-fmt"
OriginalSource: "qt-userdata-src"
Performers: "qt-userdata-prf"
Producer: "qt-userdata-prd"
Product: "qt-userdata-PRD"
Software: "qt-userdata-swf"
SpecialPlaybackRequirements:
    "qt-userdata-req"
Warning: "qt-userdata-wrn"
Writer: "qt-userdata-wrt"
EditDate1: "qt-userdata-ed1"
Chapter: "qt-userdata-chp"
```

Annotation Constants

```
kAnnotationAsString
kAnnotationAsXML
```

Graphics Modes

srcCopy
srcOr
srcXor
srcBic
notSrcCopy
notSrcOr
notSrcXor
notSrcBic
blend
addPin
addOver
subPin
transparent
addMax
subOver
addMin
grayishTextOr
hilite
ditherCopy
graphicsModeStraightAlpha
graphicsModePreWhiteAlpha
graphicsModePreBlackAlpha
graphicsModeComposition
graphicsModeStraightAlphaBlend
graphicsModePreMulColorAlpha

Movie Load States

kComplete
kLoading
kLoadStateError
kPlayable
kPlaythroughOK

Idle Delay Constants

kIdleOff

Layer Constants

KSpriteBackgroundLayer

Hit-Testing Mode Constants

kUseSpriteHitTestSetting
kAllSpritesAreHitTestable
kNoSpritesAreHitTestable

FindText Flags

kSearchAgain
kSearchCaseSensitive
kSearchCurrentSample
kSearchReverse
kSearchWraparound

Text Alignment Constants

kCenterJustify
kLeftJustify
kRightJustify

Text Display Flags

kAntiAlias
kClipToTextBox
kContinuousScroll
kDontAutoScale
kDontDisplay
kDropShadow
kHorizScroll
kInverseHilite
kKeyedText
kReverseScroll
kScrollIn
kScrollOut
kShinkTextBoxToFit
kTextColorHilite
kUseMovieBGColor

Text Font ID Constants

kAthensFont
kCairoFont
kCourierFont

kGenevaFont
kHelveticaFont
kLondonFont
kLosAngelesFont
kMobileFont
kMonacoFont
kNewYorkFont
kSanFranciscoFont
kSymbolFont
kTimesFont
kTorontoFont
kVeniceFont

Text Edit States

kDirectEditing
kNoEditing
kScriptEditing

Text Styles

kBoldFace
kCondenseFace
kExtendedFace
kItalicFace
kNormalFace
kOutlineFace
kShadowFace
kUnderlineFace

Instrument (MIDI) Controller Constants

kControllerModulationWheel
kControllerBreath
kControllerFoot
kControllerPortamentoTime
kControllerVolume
kControllerBalance
kControllerPan
kControllerExpression
kControllerLever1

kControllerLever2
kControllerLever3
kControllerLever4
kControllerLever5
kControllerLever6
kControllerLever7
kControllerLever8
kControllerPitchBend
kControllerAfterTouch
kControllerPartTranspose
kControllerTuneTranspose
kControllerPartVolume
kControllerTuneVolume
kControllerSustain
kControllerPortamento
kControllerSostenuto
kControllerSoftPedal
kControllerReverb
kControllerTremolo
kControllerChorus
kControllerCeleste
kControllerPhaser
kControllerEditPart
kControllerMasterTune
kControllerMasterTranspose
kControllerMasterVolume
kControllerMasterCPULoad
kControllerMasterPolyphony
kControllerMasterFeatures

Flash Mouse Events (Transitions)

kIdleToOverUp
kOverUpToIdle
kOverUpToOverDown
kOverDownToOverUp
kOverDownToOutDown
kOutDownToOverDown
kOutDownToIdle
kIdleToOverDown
kOverDownToIdle

QTVR Node Constants

kCurrentNode
kDefaultNode
kPreviousNode

QTVR ViewStateType Constants

kDefaultViewState
kCurrentViewState
kMouseDownViewState

QueryListServer Constants

kListQueryDebugTrace
kListQuerySendListAsKeyValuePairs
kListQuerySendListAsXML
kListQueryWantCallBack

Math Constants

EPSILON_FLOAT
MIN_SHORT
MAX_SHORT
MIN_LONG
MAX_LONG
MIN_FLOAT
MAX_FLOAT
PI
TRUE
FALSE

QuickTime Event IDs

kQTEventFrameLoaded
kQTEventIdle
kQTEventKey
kQTEventListReceived
kQTEventMouseClick
kQTEventMouseClickEnd
kQTEventMouseClickEndTriggerButton
kQTEventMouseEnter
kQTEventMouseExit
kQTEventMouseMoved
kQTEventMovieLoaded
kQTEventRequestToModifyMovie

Appendix O
ASCII Table

The following is a table of standard ASCII values with their character equivalents.

Number	Character	Name
0	NUL	Null
1	SOH	Start of heading
2	STX	Start of text
3	ETX	End of text
4	EOT	End of transmission
5	ENQ	Enquiry
6	ACK	Acknowledge
7	BEL	Bell
8	BS	Backspace
9	HT	Horizontal tab
10	LF	Linefeed
11	VT	Vertical tab
12	FF	Form feed
13	CR	Carriage return
14	SO	Shift out
15	SI	Shift in
16	DLE	Data link escape
17	DC1	Device control, X-ON
18	DC2	Device control
19	DC3	Device control, X-OFF
20	DC4	Device control
21	NAK	Negative acknowledge
22	SYN	Synchronous idle
23	ETB	End transmission blocks
24	CAN	Cancel

Number	Character	Name
25	EM	End of medium
26	SUB	Substitute
27	ESC	Escape
28	FS	File separator
29	GS	Group separator
30	RS	Record separator
31	US	Unit separator
32		Space
33	!	Exclamation mark
34	"	Double quote
35	#	Hash
36	$	Dollar
37	%	Percent
38	&	Ampersand
39	'	Apostrophe
40	(	Open parenthesis
41	)	Close parenthesis
42	*	Asterisk
43	+	Plus
44	,	Comma
45	–	Minus (hyphen)
46	.	Dot (period)
47	/	Slash (forward slash)
48	0	Digit
49	1	Digit
50	2	Digit
51	3	Digit
52	4	Digit
53	5	Digit
54	6	Digit
55	7	Digit
56	8	Digit
57	9	Digit
58	:	Colon
59	;	Semicolon
60	<	Less than
61	=	Equals
62	>	Greater than
63	?	Question mark

Number	Character	Name
64	@	At
65	A	Uppercase letter
66	B	Uppercase letter
67	C	Uppercase letter
68	D	Uppercase letter
69	E	Uppercase letter
70	F	Uppercase letter
71	G	Uppercase letter
72	H	Uppercase letter
73	I	Uppercase letter
74	J	Uppercase letter
75	K	Uppercase letter
76	L	Uppercase letter
77	M	Uppercase letter
78	N	Uppercase letter
79	O	Uppercase letter
80	P	Uppercase letter
81	Q	Uppercase letter
82	R	Uppercase letter
83	S	Uppercase letter
84	T	Uppercase letter
85	U	Uppercase letter
86	V	Uppercase letter
87	W	Uppercase letter
88	X	Uppercase letter
89	Y	Uppercase letter
90	Z	Uppercase letter
91	[	Open square bracket
92	\	Backslash
93	]	Close square bracket
94	^	Caret
95	_	Underscore
96	`	Back quote
97	a	Lowercase letter
98	b	Lowercase letter
99	c	Lowercase letter
100	d	Lowercase letter
101	e	Lowercase letter
102	f	Lowercase letter

Number	Character	Name
103	g	Lowercase letter
104	h	Lowercase letter
105	i	Lowercase letter
106	j	Lowercase letter
107	k	Lowercase letter
108	l	Lowercase letter
109	m	Lowercase letter
110	n	Lowercase letter
111	o	Lowercase letter
112	p	Lowercase letter
113	q	Lowercase letter
114	r	Lowercase letter
115	s	Lowercase letter
116	t	Lowercase letter
117	u	Lowercase letter
118	v	Lowercase letter
119	w	Lowercase letter
120	x	Lowercase letter
121	y	Lowercase letter
122	z	Lowercase letter
123	{	Open brace
124	l	Vertical bar
125	}	Close brace
126	~	Tilde
127	DEL	Delete

Appendix P
Wired Sprites with Java

All the wired QuickTime movies built in this book are created using the application LiveStage Pro. But that certainly isn't the only way to build wired movies. Apple provides low-level APIs (application programming interfaces) for building QuickTime movies using C/C++ or Java. Most of the knowledge learned about building wired movies using LiveStage Pro can be applied when working at the lower level.

I've provided a sample Java project on the CD (Projects/Extras/Build-WiredMovie/). It builds a movie with a single sprite track. In the sprite track is a sprite that rotates 10 degrees each time it's clicked. The entire project is a single Java class called BuildWiredMovie.java. It's about the minimum amount of code required to build such a movie.

The project on the CD is a JBuilder project. JBuilder is a cross-platform Java development environment from Borland. You can download a trial version from Borland.com. However, any Java compiler will work. Just make sure you set the class path to point to the QTJava.zip library (if you don't have this library installed, run the QuickTime installer and choose to install the Java QTJava.zip library).

As you look through the code, you'll see how atoms and atom containers are constructed to build structures for samples, sprites, image data, and scripts.

One thing that might look strange is the frequent use of flipNativeTo-BigEndian() methods. These methods make sure that binary representations of data are in the correct format. Different platforms can store binary data in different byte orders. "Little-endian" means that the lowest-order byte of data is stored at the lowest address. "Big-endian" means the highest-order byte is stored at the lowest address. QuickTime movies require that data be stored in big-endian order. On some platforms, this requires that the order be flipped from the native order. Calling flipNativeToBigEndian() will do the necessary flipping.

Appendix Q
Web Links

The following is a list of the Web links mentioned in the text:

ADInstruments (page 8)
http://www.adinstruments.com

Spritz application (page 26)
http://home.earthlink.net/~dmcgavrin/spritz/

Crossover for Linux (page 11)
http://www.codeweavers.com/products/crossover/

Apple QuickTime (page 11)
http://www.apple.com/quicktime/products/qt/

Judy and Robert's Little QuickTime Page (page 16)
http://www.judyandrobert.com/quicktime

Totally Hip (page 27)
http://www.totallyhip.com/
http://www.totallyhip.com/lsdn/
http://blueabuse.totallyhip.com

Apple Developer's Site (page 27)
http://developer.apple.com/quicktime/

Developer Tools (page 28)
http://developer.apple.com/quicktime/quicktimeintro/tools/

Copyright Law Information (page 52)
http://www.loc.gov/copyright/

Applescript and LSP (page 57)
http://www.totallyhip.com/lsdn/resources/applescripts/as_index.html

DMCA (page 57)
http://www.eff.org/IP/DMCA/

Calculating Triangle Intersections (page 102)
http://www.acm.org/jgt/papers/Moller97/

Carl Adler's Interactive Physics (page 214)
http://carladler.org/QTimePhysics.html

QuickTime Movie Trailers (page 257)
http://www.apple.com/trailers/

BMW Films (page 257)
http://bmwfilms.com/

Video hotspots tool (page 269)
http://www.elinetech.com/

Sound Fonts (page 289)
http://www.thesoundsite.net
http://www.hammersound.net
http://www.dashsynthesis.com

Creative Labs (page 293)
http://www.creative.com

VRHotwires application (page 332)
http://vrhotwires.com/

VRScript (page 341)
http://developer.apple.com/samplecode/Sample_Code/QuickTime/
QuickTime_VR/vrscript.htm

VRScript unofficial support (page 332)
http://www.vrhotwires.com/VRSUPPORT.HTM

Zoomify (Chapter 29)
http://www.zoomify.com

Timecode track sample application (page 361)
http://developer.apple.com/samplecode/Sample_Code/QuickTime/TimeCodes/

World Wide Variables (page 366)
http://www.worldwidevariables.com

Tomcat and Jetty Java servers (page 391)
http://jakarta.apache.org/tomcat/
http://jetty.mortbay.org

Tekadence (page 392)
`http://www.tekadence.com`

Your machine (page 392)
`http://127.0.0.1`

Videopaper Builder (page 444)
`http://vpb.concord.org`

AXLogic (page 448)
`http://www.axlogic.com`

Michael Shaff's Site (page 59)
`http://www.smallhands.com`

Yahoo! Finance (page 428)
`http://finance.yahoo.com`

DeliVRator (page 459)
`http://www.vrtools.com`

Codeccentral (page 521)
`http://www.codeccentral.com`

QuickTime plug-in embed tags (page 536)
`http://www.apple.com/quicktime/authoring/embed.html`

QScript online manual (page 539)
`http://www.totallyhip.com/lsdn/resources/qscript/qscript_index.html`

QuickTime ActiveX codebase (page 535)
`http://www.apple.com/qtactivex/qtplugin.cab`

Borland JBuilder (page 557)
`http://borland.com`

Backstage (page 561)
`http://brennan.young.net/Comp/LiveStage/backstage.html`

QTBridge (page 561)
`http://www.qtbridge.com`

QuickTiming (page 561)
`http://www.quicktiming.org`

Navicast (page 561)
`http://www.navicast.net`

CVS (page 561)
`http://www.wincvs.org`

Appendix R
Contributing Developers

The following developers have contributed in some way to this book. Some have supplied example movies or software for the CD. Others have supplied helpful feedback on the text. They're a great bunch of people, and I thank them for their contributions. I'd like to introduce them to you. On the CD (Projects/Extras/Contributors/) you'll find interactive movies along with short bios of many of the people in this list.

Many thanks for their wonderful contributions:

Carl Adler	Ken Loge
Sean Allen	Frank Lowney
Sam Balooch	Ian Mantripp
Ralph Bitter	Mike Matson
Eric Blanpied	Bill Meikle
Todd Blume	Ricardo Nemirovsky
David Connolly	Elsa Peterson
Dion Crannitch	Mario Piepenbrink
Trevor DeVore	Hans Rijnen
Cara DiMattia	Thorsten Schmiedel
David Egbert	Michael Shaff
Erik Fohlin	Luke Sheridan
Ryan Francesconi	John Sklavos
Francis Gorge	Brad Smith
Guillaume Iacino	David Urbanic
Steve Israelson	Clifford VanMeter
Anders Jirås	Michael Vogt
Jared Kaplan	Selwyn Wan
	Brennan Young

Appendix S
CD Contents

This is a listing of the directory structure on the CD. If you are looking for a particular project but can't remember what chapter it was in, look here.

Glossary

annotations Text string values associated with standard movie information fields, such as the movie's producer, the copyright info, the version, and so on.

anticipation An animation technique that draws the user's attention to the beginning of a motion sequence.

atom The building block of QuickTime's hierarchical and extensible file format.

behavior In LiveStage Pro, a text file that contains a collection of scripts and parameters that allow one to easily add functionality to a sprite.

C/C++ A popular programming language that gets compiled into platform-specific software. C++ is an object-oriented version of C.

caching A programming technique where the result of a calculation is stored so it doesn't need to be calculated again the next time it is needed.

cel An element in an animated character's image sequence. This is a derivative of the word *celluloid* (a transparent material). The advantage of using cels in animation is that multiple characters can be animated and positioned independently instead of having to draw each character together in each frame.

CGI Common Gateway Interface. This is a standard way to pass a query string to a server-side application.

child An element in a hierarchical structure that is contained by another element (the parent). Child movies are often called "movie tracks." *See also* movie track, parent, root.

CODEC Stands for "code-decode." A software component that allows the importation and exportation of a particular format or compression scheme. Sometimes the word *CODEC* is also used to refer to the particular format or compression scheme. For example, "This image uses the jpeg CODEC."

decompile In QuickTime, the process of turning the wired actions of a built movie into a human-readable scripting language. LiveStage Pro, for security reasons, doesn't provide a decompiling feature for movies, but does allow decompiling of certain groups of tracks called "FastTracks."

define In LiveStage Pro, a named constant that the user can create either globally for a project, or locally within a script. Also called "definition."

DHTML Dynamic HTML.

DRM Digital rights management.

Easter egg A hidden feature (usually a useless feature) added to software or media meant to reward curious users that like to hunt for such things. This book has several Easter eggs. For example, see the glossary entry for recursion.

epsilon correction A technique for correcting roundoff errors and division by zero through addition of a very small number.

escape To encode a character in a string so it doesn't get interpreted as part of the text formatting syntax. For example, in XML, the " < " character has a special meaning, so one has to use the "<" escape code to represent the less-than symbol.

event In QuickTime, simply something that can trigger the execution of wired actions. A mouse click on a sprite is an example of an event.

fail fast An optimization technique where an algorithm tries to detect errors early before executing a sequence of costly or time-consuming statements. For example, take an algorithm that reads a sound file, converts it to MP3 format, and saves it to a file in a target directory. A possible fail fast optimization would be to first check if the target directory exists before going through all the work of reading and converting the sound file.

Fast Start *See* progressive download.

FastTrack A template for a collection of tracks in LiveStage Pro (versions 4.0 and higher) that allow a user to quickly add canned functionality to a movie. An example is the movie controller FastTrack, which allows one to configure the position and appearance of play/pause, stop, fast-forward, reverse, and other standard controller buttons.

GUI   Graphical user interface.

hotspot   A spatial region that can respond to mouse events. A hyperlink in a text track is an example of a hotspot.

HREF   Hypertext Reference. Essentially a reference to a URL. QuickTime supports HREF tracks, which are text tracks that contain references to URLs. As an HREF track plays, each URL can either load in a browser, be executed as JavaScript, or be loaded as a movie in QuickTime Player.

idle delay   The amount of time to wait between idle events, usually measured in 1/60ths of a second. A synonym for "idle period," "idle frequency," and "idle rate."

idle event   A periodic event that is sent to interactive elements (such as sprites and hotspots) to indicate that time in the real world (as opposed to on the movie's timeline) has passed.

iTV   Interactive television.

Java   A popular programming language created by SUN Microsystems that allows the creation of platform-independent software as long as the target platform has a Java virtual machine (JVM). Most platforms, even cell phones and PDAs, can run some version of a JVM.

layer   The order in which sprites draw to the screen depends on their index and their layer property. Sprites with a higher layer draw first. If two sprites have the same layer, then the one with the smaller index draws first. Tracks use this same ordering scheme.

linear media   A temporal lookup table of media data. This means that what gets presented is completely determined by the temporal offset into the media. Nonlinear media have other factors besides the temporal offset that influence what gets presented.

listener   An object that has requested to be notified when something happens on a second object.

localhost   When a machine is both a client and a server, localhost, or the IP address 127.0.0.1, is a way for the machine to reference itself.

LSB   LiveStage behavior document.

LSD   LiveStage project document.

manager   An object that maintains state variables and handles events for another object or set of objects.

matrix   An *n*-dimensional array of numbers. In QuickTime, this usually refers to a 4 x 4 array of numbers that defines how a sprite's image data is spatially mapped onto the screen. For example, a matrix can define how the sprite's image is positioned, scaled, and rotated.

media sample   A piece of media data. Media samples come in different types, such as images, audio segments, sprite world, formatted text, and so on. QuickTime movie tracks contain a temporal sequence of media samples.

MIAM   Movie In A Movie. *See* movie track.

MIDI   Music Instrument Digital Interface.

movie   In QuickTime, a collection of tracks. Since many track types contain nonlinear media (*see* linear media), QuickTime movies are often more like software applications than a piece of film that you would watch at a movie theater.

MovieClip   The analog of a sprite in Macromedia's Flash environment.

movie track   A QuickTime track whose media type is a QuickTime movie.

nonlinear media   *See* linear media.

nudge   A small shift in position to correct for errors inherent in discrete animation.

onionskinning   A frame-based animation technique where a sequence of images are made semitransparent to aid in their alignment.

OpColor   The color parameter supplied when specifying a graphics mode. For example, the OpColor specifies which color to make transparent for the transparent graphics mode.

overshoot   An animation technique where the user's attention is drawn to the end of a motion sequence by having the object move past its target, then snap back into place.

parallax   The phenomenon where objects farther away from a moving observer seem to move more slowly than nearby objects.

parent   An element in a hierarchical structure that contains other elements.

point testing Determining if a sprite is located at a particular point. This can be a convenient way of implementing collision detection routines.

progressive download QuickTime movie files can be saved in such a way that a user can view the movie as it downloads instead of having to first wait for the entire file to finish transferring.

proxy image Image data that is temporarily used in place of an image that can't be found or that is in the process of downloading.

QScript The scripting language used in LiveStage Pro. QScript provides convenient names and syntax for the underlying wired actions defined by QuickTime.

QTList A data structure in QuickTime that maps well to and from XML.

QTVR QuickTime Virtual Reality. A set of media types that let you examine photorealistic 3D objects and environments.

rasterize To turn visual media into a pixel-based format.

recursion A programming technique where an algorithm references itself as a subroutine. *See* Easter egg.

root The element at the top of a hierarchical structure.

roundoff error Calculation errors that result from the limited precision of fixed-digit numbers.

scope The level in a hierarchical system of objects in which a reference is understood by name. For example, in script on an object in a text sample, referencing GetTextLength will return the number of characters in that text sample. However, referencing GetTextLength in a sprite's script will be undefined since the sprite is out of the scope of the text track. The sprite's script would need to reference the path to the text track, such as TrackNamed ("text track").GetTextLength. Some references can't be made across scopes; for example, local variables can only be accessed from within the script in which they are defined.

SDK Software development kit.

short circuiting An optimization technique where an algorithm finishes calculating if it's determined that the rest of the calculation won't change the result.

skin In QuickTime terminology, a track that defines a movie's window shape.

SMIL   Synchronized Multimedia Integration Language.

SMPTE   Society for Motion Picture and Television Engineers. Often refers to a particular type of timecode format. *See also* timecode.

spline   A type of smooth path interpolation where subsections of the path are fit by overlapping polynomial functions.

sprite   A virtual two-dimensional object that can present images and respond to events, such as mouse clicks and keyboard strokes. Sprites respond by executing wired actions.

state machine   A representation of an algorithm as a set of states and rules that determine when to transition from one state to another. Any computer program can be represented as a state machine. Also called a "finite state machine."

SWF   Macromedia's Shockwave Flash file format.

thin client   A graphical user interface that communicates with an application running on a remote server.

timecode   A format for representing a temporal offset. The most common timecode format is SMPTE, which separates hours, minutes, seconds, and frames by colons. For example: 00:18:12:01.

track   A sequence of media samples. QuickTime movies are made up of one or more tracks.

URL   Universal Resource Locator.

wired actions   Code, interpreted by the QuickTime engine, that allows sprites and other interactive objects to perform calculations and dynamically manipulate the state of a movie.

XML   Extensible Markup Language. A generalized text-based method of storing structured information. It uses a hierarchical tag system similar to HTML. *See also* QTList.

Index

P

paddle
  activation, 78
  ball position and, 79
  center, 80
  horizontal distance, 80
  idle event, 79
  origin, 79
  positioning, 79, 81
  registration point, 79
  See also simple PONG world
Palladium, 57
Pano Viewer, 388, 389
parabolas
  in a box, 171
  for describing motion, 169
  with different parameters, 170
  equation, 171
  generic, function, 170
parallax, 183
parallel processing, 496–498
parameter ranges, 457
PassMouseToCodec action, 274, 275, 276
password fields, 244–247
  building, 244–245
  project illustration, 247
  See also text input
Password.lsb behavior, 244
PathExists function, 477
paths, 176–179
  continuous closed, 180
  sprites moving along, 176
PDF
  files, 14
  tracks, 364
pendulums, 212–213
  acceleration, 213, 214
  demonstration, 213
  friction, 213
  motion, 212
pendulum_start.lsd project, 213
PerformFlashClick action, 322–323
  ButtonID, 323
  ButtonPath, 322
  MouseEvent, 323
  signature, 322
  triggering buttons with, 324
  using, 323
period, 182
perspective, 191–193
  3D, 194
  defined, 191
  script, 191
.pff file, 354
physics
  collisions, 210–212
  explorations, 212–214
  forces, 205–208
  friction, 208–210

knowledge of, 205
  modeling, 205–214
  simplification from, 212
Physics for Game Developers, 205
pianos, MINI numbered-keys, 286
Picasso_demo.lsd project, 118–120
pie charts, 194–195
pixel-level detection
  defined, 99–100
  illustrated, 100
  See also collision detection
pixels per inch, 460–461
platform constants, 549
PlayButton.mov, 46
PlayNote action, 217, 285–286
  Delay, 286, 288, 294
  Duration, 286, 287
  InstrumentIndex, 286, 288
  parameters, 285
  Pitch, 286
  Velocity, 286
PNG codec, 119, 522
point and a line, 515
point testing, 109–114
  with arrow image, 110
  with crosshairs image, 111
  defined, 100–101, 109
  illustrated, 101
  locations for Tetris shapes, 114
  locations near ground and ceiling, 114
  for moving sprites, 114
  with single SpriteAtPoint call, 112
  uses, 112, 114
  See also collision detection
points, two, 515
PointTesting_demo.lsd project, 109
PointTesting2_demo.lsd project, 111
Polar2Cart function, 469
polygons, regular, 516
PONG, 69
pop quiz, 140–141
PopupMenu_demo.lsd project, 163
Power function, 466
PowerPoint, 27
presentation layer, 412
prime numbers, 456
product simulation, 228
profiling, 494–495
programming techniques, 483–499
  breaking a loop, 484–485
  collaboration, 499
  debugging, 493–494
  dictionaries, 492–493
  dividing by zero, 489–491
  dynamic script evaluation, 498
  error detection, 485–486
  exception handling, 485–486
  functions, 486–487
  lazy constructors, 495–496
  lists, 492–493

About the Author

Matthew Peterson is a neuroscientist at the University of California, Berkeley; co-founder of the M.I.N.D. Institute, in Irvine; and chief science officer and co-founder of Tekadence, Inc., in San Francisco. Matthew has made many contributions to the QuickTime community in the form of open-source projects, libraries, and applications. He is a familiar speaker at QuickTime Live!, MacWorld, and Apple's World Wide Developer Conferences.

QuickTime Developer Series

Apple's QuickTime is a way to deliver multimedia—video, sound, styled text, MIDI, Flash, virtual reality, 3D models, sprites, and more—wrapped in a package that will play on Windows or Macintosh computers, on CD-ROM, over the Internet, in a browser window, a PDF document, a Power-Point presentation, a Word document, or all by itself. The **QuickTime Developer Series**, developed in close cooperation with Apple, is devoted to exploring all of the capabilities of this powerful industry standard. Books in the series are written by experienced developers, including engineers from within the development team at Apple. All of the books feature a practical, hands-on approach and are prepared according to the latest developments in QuickTime technology. Morgan Kaufmann and Apple work together to represent the series to the growing ranks of digital media developers.

Interactive QuickTime: Authoring Wired Media
  Matthew Peterson

QuickTime for the Web: For Windows and Macintosh, Third Edition
  Steven Gulie

Forthcoming

QuickTime Components
  Gary Woodcock

QuickTime for Java: A Programmer's Guide to Building Multimedia Applications with Java, Second Edition
  Tom Maremaa and William Stewart

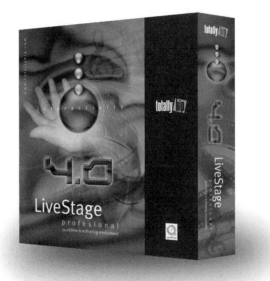